Gilded Age
and Progressive Era

Almanac

Gilded Age
and Progressive Era

Almanac

Rebecca Valentine

Lawrence W. Baker, Project Editor

U·X·L
An imprint of Thomson Gale,
a part of The Thomson Corporation

THOMSON
GALE

Detroit • New York • San Francisco • New Haven, Conn. • Waterville, Maine • London

Gilded Age and Progressive Era: Almanac

Rebecca Valentine

Project Editor
Lawrence W. Baker

Rights and Acquisitions
Margaret Abendroth, Emma Hull,
Andrew Specht

Imaging and Multimedia
Dean Dauphinais, Lezlie Light,
Michael Logusz, Christine O'Bryan

Product Design
Pamela Galbreath, Jennifer Wahi

Composition
Evi Seoud

Manufacturing
Rita Wimberley

LIBRARY OF CONGRESS CATALOGING-IN-PUBLICATION DATA

Valentine, Rebecca.
  Gilded Age and Progressive Era reference library / Rebecca Valentine; Lawrence W. Baker,
project editor.
     v. cm.
  Includes bibliographical references and index.
  Contents: [1] Almanac -- [2] Biographies -- [3] Primary sources.
  ISBN-13: 978-1-4144-0193-5 (set : alk. paper) --
  ISBN-10: 1-4144-0193-0 (set : alk. paper) --
  ISBN-13: 978-1-4144-0194-2 (Almanac : alk. paper) --
  ISBN-10: 1-4144-0194-9 (Almanac : alk. paper) --
  [etc.]
  1. United States -- History -- 1865-1921 -- Juvenile literature. 2. United States -- History --
1865-1921 -- Biography -- Juvenile literature. 3. United States -- History -- 1865-1921 --
Sources -- Juvenile literature. 4. Almanacs, American -- Juvenile literature. I. Baker,
Lawrence W. II. Title.
  E661.V35 2006
  973.8 -- dc22
                                                                                  2006022839

ISBN-13:

978-1-4144-0193-5 (set)
978-1-4144-0194-2 (Almanac)
978-1-4144-0195-9
  (Biographies)

978-1-4144-0196-6
  (Primary Sources)
978-1-4144-0197-3
  (Cumulative Index)

ISBN-10:

1-4144-0193-0 (set)
1-4144-0194-9 (Almanac)
1-4144-0195-7
  (Biographies)

1-4144-0196-5
  (Primary Sources)
1-4144-0197-3
  (Cumulative Index)

This title is also available as an e-book.
ISBN-13: 978-1-4144-1046-3, ISBN-10: 1-4144-1046-8
Contact your Thomson Gale sales representative for ordering information.
Printed in the United States of America

10 9 8 7 6 5 4 3 2 1

Contents

Reader's Guide

The Gilded Age and Progressive Era in American history blended so seamlessly into one another that they can hardly be thought of separately. The Gilded Age was a major turning point in the nation, as it marked the rise of industrialism (an economy based on business and industry rather than agriculture) and the decline of an economy based on agriculture. Roughly 1877 to 1900, the Industrial Revolution made celebrities of robber barons such as oil magnate John D. Rockefeller and railroad tycoon Cornelius Vanderbilt. It encouraged the growth of a middle class as more and more Americans became members of the working class. It fostered competition in business even as it grew through the questionable practices of forming trusts and monopolies, and it made unimaginable wealth for a handful while sending millions of others into unrelenting poverty.

The Gilded Age was a time of great discontent as angry workers gave birth to the labor movement and muckraking journalists such as Ida M. Tarbell exposed big business for what it really was. The 1890s was a decade of economic depression for the entire nation; American farmers and laborers were so desperate that they took the radical measure of forming their own political party, the Populist Party. In no other era in history has America been led by so many presidents that time seems to have forgotten, and yet the Gilded Age led directly to the Progressive Era, which was ushered in by one of the most passionate, deliberate, incorrigible presidents: Theodore Roosevelt.

The Progressive Era, approximately 1900 to 1913, was a time of great reform in a nation that was just beginning to understand who it was, who it no longer could be, and who it just might become, given the right circumstances. The temperance movement eventually led to Prohibition (when the Eighteenth Amendment banned the manufacture and sale of alcohol). Labor laws gave rights to workers, and concerned citizens such as child labor photographer Lewis Hine and photojournalist Jacob Riis used their talents to secure improved living and working conditions for the urban poor and their children.

America in the Progressive Era was a melting pot that included millions of immigrants from around the world. As cities became overpopulated with people living in poverty, those who could moved to the outskirts of town, and suburban America was born. Those who could not escape the city led lives of intense hardship and heartache, but their underpaid and underappreciated labor kept America's economy going, even through the Panic of 1907. Reformers such as Jane Addams and Hannah Solomon dedicated their lives to helping where help was most needed: in urban slums.

Coverage and features

Gilded Age and Progressive Era: Almanac gives comprehensive coverage of these decades by examining them from political, social, and cultural perspectives. Unlike other periods in history, these were not so directly informed by major wars or other political events (though war was certainly a contributor to the times), but by other more socially centered influences. The *Almanac* paints the Gilded Age and Progressive Era as they were: times of great sorrow and grand luxury. The eleven chapters begin with a brief review of Reconstruction, when the United States rebuilt itself following the Civil War (1861–65). In doing so, readers understand just how tumultuous a time in history the Gilded Age was. From there, students are given a tour of the business of doing business, including the struggles within the new labor movement. Immigration and its impact on the nation are detailed as it occurred, from sea to sea. The *Almanac* gives readers an understanding of the myth of the Wild West versus its reality as it concerned Native Americans. Students may also analyze the plight not only of the late nineteenth century farmer, but also of the African American in the South who was emancipated but not truly freed. Populism leads to Progressivism as readers see how a change in one aspect of life— whether business, social, cultural, or political—affects every other. The *Almanac*'s chapters are filled with the greats such as the Wright Brothers, Theodore Roosevelt, Jane Addams, and Andrew Carnegie.

But they do not forget the lesser-known figures whose contributions led to reform and true progress: Eugene Debs, Terence V. Powderly, Mother Jones, and Helen Hunt Jackson.

Gilded Age and Progressive Era: Almanac includes informative sidebars, some containing brief biographies of influential people during the Gilded Age and Progressive Era. Approximately ninety black-and-white photographs enliven the work. *Gilded Age and Progressive Era: Almanac* also includes a timeline of important dates and events, a section defining important Words to Know, and a list of research and activity ideas with suggestions for study questions, group projects, and oral and dramatic presentations. *Gilded Age and Progressive Era: Almanac* concludes with a bibliography of sources for further reading and a subject index.

U•X•L Gilded Age and Progressive Era Reference Library

Gilded Age and Progressive Era: Almanac is just one component of a three-volume U•X•L Gilded Age and Progressive Era Reference Library. The other titles in this set are:

Gilded Age and Progressive Era: Biographies presents profiles of twenty-five people important to the development of the Gilded Age and Progressive Era. The volume covers such key figures as politicians Grover Cleveland and Theodore Roosevelt; writers Mark Twain and Upton Sinclair; activists Ida B. Wells-Barnett and Booker T. Washington; and sports great Ty Cobb and musician Scott Joplin.

Gilded Age and Progressive Era: Primary Sources informs not through narrative, but by presenting actual documents, photographs, and other primary sources of the time. Eighteen entries show just how transitional this time period was to the United States. Included are texts of important legislation, such as the Dawes Severalty Act and the ruling from *Plessy vs. Ferguson.* Students will read a portion of the groundbreaking novel *The Jungle,* which led directly to the passage of several important laws concerning the food and drug industries. Readers will become acquainted with the famous Gibson Girl illustrations, and have the opportunity to peruse original images from the Sears Modern Homes catalog of the early twentieth century.

A cumulative index of all three titles in this set is also available.

Acknowledgments

My deep gratitude goes to copyeditor Theresa Murray; proofreader Amy Marcaccio Keyzer; the indexers from Factiva, a Dow Jones & Reuters Company; and typesetter ITC/International Typesetting & Composition. I would be remiss if I failed to thank Larry Baker, project editor extraordinaire, and my family, who made do with less of my attention for longer than they would have liked.

Special thanks are due for the invaluable comments and suggestions provided by U•X•L's Gilded Age and Progressive Era Reference Library advisors and consultants:

- Sally Collins, Library Media Specialist, Highland Park Middle School, Dallas, Texas
- Nina Levine, Library Media Specialist, Blue Mountain Middle School, Cortlandt Manor, New York
- Bernadette Monette, Library Media Specialist, Sacopee Valley High School, Hiram, Maine

Comments and suggestions

We welcome your comments on *Gilded Age and Progressive Era: Almanac* and suggestions for other topics in history to consider. Please write: Editors, *Gilded Age and Progressive Era: Almanac,* U•X•L, 27500 Drake Road, Farmington Hills, MI 48331-3535; call toll-free 800-877-4253; fax to 248-699-8097; or send e-mail via http://www.gale.com.

Timeline of Events

1873 Mark Twain publishes his novel titled *The Gilded Age;* this term is used as the name of the era characterized by robber barons and their ostentatious displays of wealth.

1877 The Industrial Revolution begins, shifting America's economic focus from one of agriculture to industry.

January 4, 1877 The original robber baron, Cornelius Vanderbilt, dies with an estate worth $100 million.

July–August 1877 The Great Railroad Strike takes place across the nation, after the Baltimore & Ohio Railroad had cut wages for a second time in one year. The strike soon spread throughout the nation, and federal troops were called in. It is the first major strike of a newly industrialized nation. Forty-five days later, the strikes were put down.

1878 Thomas Edison founds the Edison Electric Light Company. It puts rival companies out of business and becomes General Electric.

January 10, 1878 The "Anthony Amendment," named after women's rights pioneer Susan B. Anthony, is introduced to Congress. It requests giving women the right to vote.

April 12, 1878 Politician William "Boss" Tweed, the corrupt leader of New York's Tammany Hall, dies in prison. Political cartoonist Thomas Nast was largely credited with Tweed's arrest.

1879 California passes a law forbidding the employment of Chinese laborers.

September 1879 Terence V. Powderly becomes grand master workman and leader of the Knights of Labor, a powerful labor union.

1880 The National Farmers' Alliance is formed. Farmers find themselves in tragic circumstances due to drought and flood, high interest rates on loans, and unfair railroad rates.

1880 The U.S. population reaches 50.1 million. More than 6 million are foreign born.

1880 The Arts & Crafts movement begins, hailing a return to furniture and interior decoration based on simplicity.

1880 The Alaska gold rush begins.

1880 Andrew Carnegie monopolizes the steel industry.

1881 President Rutherford B. Hayes forbids the sale of alcoholic beverages at military posts. His wife had already acquired the nickname "Lemonade Lucy" for her refusal to serve alcohol in the White House.

1881 Native American rights activist Helen Hunt Jackson publishes *A Century of Dishonor*.

1881 Booker T. Washington founds the Tuskegee Normal and Industrial Institute.

March 4, 1881 U.S. representative James A. Garfield of Ohio becomes president; New York politician Chester A. Arthur is vice president.

May 1881 Kansas becomes the first state to outlaw the sale of liquor.

July 2, 1881 President James Garfield is shot in a Washington, D.C., train station. He dies in September; Vice President Chester A. Arthur becomes president.

July 14, 1881 Famous criminal Billy the Kid is shot and killed.

1882 John D. Rockefeller organizes the Standard Oil Trust. The trust gets him around the laws of each state and becomes the model for future corporations.

1882 The first parade is held in New York City in observance of Labor Day, as ten thousand workers take the day off to march.

1882 The first commercial electric light system is installed on Pearl Street in New York City.

1882 Congress sets restrictions on immigration standards. Exceedingly poor people, convicts, and those declared insane are no longer welcome at Ellis Island.

May 6, 1882 The Chinese Exclusion Act passes. Chinese immigrants are no longer welcome in the United States. The law would be repealed ten years later.

1883 The Brooklyn Bridge is completed. After taking fourteen years to build, New Yorkers consider it the eighth wonder of the world.

1883 Frances Willard founds the World Woman's Christian Temperance Union.

1883 Jewish poet Emma Lazarus writes the poem "The New Colossus," which is engraved on a plaque and hung at the base of the Statue of Liberty.

January 16, 1883 The Pendleton Act is passed, transforming the Civil Service to an agency of qualified employees who must pass tests in order to be hired.

1884 The Home Life Insurance building in Chicago, Illinois, is constructed. It is the world's first skyscraper. It is also the first building to have a steel frame upon which floors and walls are hung.

November 1884 New York governor Grover Cleveland is elected president.

1886 Riots against the Chinese occur in Washington. At least four hundred Chinese are forced from their homes. Federal troops intervene to restore order.

1886 Samuel Gompers organizes the American Federation of Labor.

May 4, 1886 The Haymarket Square Riot takes place in Chicago, Illinois. About fourteen hundred people gather to protest police brutality against workers on strike. Nearly two hundred police arrive to break up the crowd. A bomb is thrown into the midst of the police. The nation begins to equate workers on strike with violent anarchists.

October 28, 1886 President Grover Cleveland accepts the Statue of Liberty from France and delivers his dedication address.

February 4, 1887 The Interstate Commerce Act becomes law. A commission is created to ensure fair and reasonable rates for freight carriers.

February 8, 1887 Congress passes the Dawes Severalty Act. Every Native American family is to be given 100 acres of land to farm.

1888 Congress establishes a Department of Labor.

1888 Susan B. Anthony founds the National Council of Woman of the United States.

January 12, 1888 The Schoolchildren's Blizzard claims the lives of between 250 and 500 immigrants on the Dakota-Nebraska prairie; most of them are children.

November 1888 Former U.S. senator Benjamin Harrison of Indiana is elected president.

1889 North Dakota, South Dakota, Montana, and Washington become states.

1889 Jane Addams opens Hull-House in Chicago, Illinois, the first social services system.

1889 Land in Oklahoma that was given to the Native Americans is opened to white settlers, furthering antagonizing the relationship between Native Americans and whites.

May 31, 1889 The Johnstown flood claims the lives of more than two thousand Pennsylvanians.

June 1889 Andrew Carnegie publishes his famous philosophy, the "Gospel of Wealth."

1890 The American Women's Suffrage Association merges with the National Women's Suffrage Association, bringing solidarity to the suffrage movement.

1890 The McKinley Tariff Act is passed, establishing record-high tariffs on many imported goods.

1890 Photojournalist Jacob Riis publishes *How the Other Half Lives,* a book that provides a glimpse into the lives and hardships of America's urban poor and reveals the squalor of New York City's tenement homes. At the time, Theodore Roosevelt was the police commissioner of New York. He was moved by Riis's exposé and joined in the efforts to clean up the city.

January 25, 1890 Journalist Nellie Bly completes her trip around the world, which took her seventy-two days, six hours, and eleven minutes.

July 2, 1890 The Sherman Anti-Trust Act is passed, making it unlawful for businesses to form trusts that prohibit competition.

July 10, 1890 Wyoming becomes a state; later, it becomes the first state to give women the right to vote.

July 14, 1890 The Sherman Silver Purchase Act is signed by President Benjamin Harrison. The law increased the amount of money in circulation in the economy, but it also put a serious strain on the federal gold reserve.

October 1, 1890 Yosemite Park is created. Congress set aside 1,500 square miles of reserved forest lands.

December 15, 1890 Chief Sitting Bull is fatally wounded by one of his own men.

December 29, 1890 The Massacre at Wounded Knee officially closes the American frontier.

1891 Thomas Edison receives a patent for the first motion picture camera.

1892 Conservationist John Muir helps establish the Sierra Club. He remains its president until his death in 1914.

1892 Nearly 2 million acres of Crow Indian reservation in Montana are given to white settlers.

1892 Lizzie Borden is accused of murdering her father and stepmother with an axe. Though later found not guilty, her alleged crime remains one of the country's great unsolved mysteries.

January 1, 1892 Ellis Island opens to become the port of entry for all immigrants entering America via the Atlantic Ocean.

June 29, 1892 Carnegie Steel workers are locked out, an event that began the Homestead Steel Strike, one of the bloodiest work strikes in industrial history.

July 1892 The Populist Party is formed.

1893 Hannah Solomon establishes the National Council of Jewish Women.

1893 Frederick Jackson Turner delivers his lecture called "The Significance of the Frontier in American History."

1893 Ida B. Wells publishes a pamphlet on racism for distribution at the Chicago World's Fair. "The Reason Why the Colored American Is Not in the World's Columbian Exposition" was written by Wells, reformer Frederick Douglass, and other activists, and includes information on lynching, unfair legislation, and the convict lease system as well.

March 1893 Grover Cleveland is inaugurated to serve his second term as president of the United States. He is the first president to serve non-consecutive terms.

May 1, 1893 The World's Columbian Exposition, also known as the Chicago World's Fair, opens.

May 4, 1893 The New York Stock Exchange crashes, beginning the worst economic depression in American history to that point. The economy would not begin to recover until 1896.

May 24, 1893 The Anti-Saloon League is founded in Oberlin, Ohio.

June 1893 President Grover Cleveland successfully calls upon Congress to repeal the Sherman Silver Purchase Act.

June 20, 1893 Eugene V. Debs establishes the American Railway Union, the first industrial union in the United States.

1894 Congress officially declares the first Monday of every September to be Labor Day. This declaration is a sign of the growing importance of and concern given to American labor.

1894 Charles Dana Gibson's first illustration of the All-American Girl appears in print. His "Gibson Girl" was the symbol of America's modern woman through World War I (1914–18).

March 25, 1894 Jacob Coxey leads one hundred men from Ohio to Washington, D.C., in protest of the economic depression and with a demand that the government aid its citizens by creating jobs. "Coxey's Army" grew to include more than five hundred men by the time they reached Washington on April 30. Some of the men were arrested for trespassing on the lawn of the Capitol.

May 11, 1894 Fifty thousand Pullman Palace Car Company employees strike in Chicago, Illinois. The strike eventually included railroad workers across the nation, and President Grover Cleveland called upon federal troops to break up the event. Violence erupted and many strikers were killed and wounded.

1895 Lillian Wald opens Henry Street Settlement House on New York's East Side.

1895 George Eastman introduces the first pocket Kodak camera.

1895 Suffragist Elizabeth Cady Stanton publishes the controversial book *Woman's Bible.*

May 18, 1896 In *Plessy v. Ferguson,* the U.S. Supreme Court approves racial segregation by upholding the "separate but equal" doctrine.

July 9, 1896 William Jennings Bryan delivers his rousing "Cross of Gold" speech.

November 1896 Ohio governor William Mckinley defeats former U.S. representative William Jennings Bryan of Nebraska in the presidential election.

1897 The Dingley Tariff is passed, raising tariffs to a new high of an average of 50 percent.

November 1, 1897 The Library of Congress is housed in its own building for the first time.

February 15, 1898 The *U.S.S. Maine* explodes and sinks, killing 266 crew members. This event triggers the Spanish-American War, which lasts for one hundred days.

July 7, 1898 America annexes Hawaii.

1899 President William McKinley advocates an "Open Door" policy with China.

1899 Southern regionalist writer Kate Chopin publishes her scandalous novel, *The Awakening.*

February 4, 1899 The Philippine-American War breaks out. America had purchased the Philippine Islands after defeating the Spanish in Cuba. But the Philippines did not want to go from being ruled by one country to being ruled by another, so they rebelled. The bloody war lasted until July 4, 1902, when America won and did its best to modernize the Philippines. The islands gained their independence in 1946.

1900 The average American family has three or four children, compared to 1800, when it included seven or eight.

1900 Ragtime becomes the most popular genre of music in America. It has its roots in African American music and features fast tempos with syncopated rhythms.

May 25, 1900 Congress passes the Lacey Act, which protects particular animals and their habitats and outlaws the interstate shipment of wildlife that has been hunted illegally.

June 1900 The Boxer Rebellion takes place in China and lasts until August.

1901 Steel magnate Andrew Carnegie sells his steel mill to U.S. Steel and becomes the world's wealthiest man.

1901 J. P. Morgan incorporates the United States Steel Company, giving America its first billion-dollar company.

1901 The Tenement House Act is passed, improving the construction and safety of New York City's housing for the poor.

September 5, 1901 President William McKinley is shot by immigrant Leon Czolgosz. Nine days later, McKinley dies from his wounds and Vice President Theodore Roosevelt is sworn in as president.

1902 President Theodore Roosevelt dissolves the Beef trust and the Northern Securities Company (a railroad monopoly).

1902 Suffragist Carrie Chapman Catt organizes the National American Woman Suffrage Association.

1902 Muckraker Ida Tarbell publishes the first chapter of her exposé on the Standard Oil Company.

May 12, 1902 Anthracite coal miners walk off their jobs in Pennsylvania. The strike lasted 164 days and ended when President Theodore Roosevelt intervened and appointed J. P. Morgan to arbitrate the dispute.

1903 The Women's Trade Union League is formed.

1903 Reformer and activist W. E. B. Du Bois publishes his famous treatise, *The Souls of Black Folk,* in which he challenges the philosophy of Booker T. Washington and proposes his own "Talented Tenth" philosophy.

December 17, 1903 Wilbur and Orville Wright make history by becoming the first humans to ever fly. Their first flight lasted 12 seconds and went a distance of 120 feet (3.7 meters).

1904 The National Child Labor Committee forms and works tirelessly to campaign for child labor laws.

1904 President Theodore Roosevelt initiates the building of the Panama Canal. The project would take ten years and thirty thousand workers to be completed; the canal opened for business on August 15, 1914.

1904 Breaker boys (boys aged 7 to 13 who worked in the coal mining industry) earn 45 to 50 cents for a day's work. Each work day lasted ten to twelve hours.

February 8, 1904 Japan attacks Port Arthur and conducts a quick series of victorious attacks on Russian naval fleets, marking the start of the Russo-Japanese War. The war ended in defeat for Russia in 1905.

October 27, 1904 The New York subway opens.

1905 The Victrola disc player is first sold on the market; by 1911, this early version of the record player could be found in millions of homes across America.

March 3, 1905 President Theodore Roosevelt gives the Bureau of Forestry a new name: the Forest Service; he appoints conservationist Gifford Pinchot as its director. Under Pinchot's leadership, the country's forests grew from 56 million acres to 172 million acres.

1906 Upton Sinclair publishes his muckraking novel *The Jungle.* It is an immediate best-seller and leads to federal reform in the food industry.

1906 The Meat Inspection Act is passed, providing hygiene standards in the meatpacking industry.

1906 The Pure Food and Drug Act is passed, requiring manufacturers to label their products with a list of ingredients.

April 18, 1906 San Francisco experiences one of the most significant earthquakes of all time. Resulting fires burned for more than three days. Hundreds of thousands of the city's residents were left homeless, and the death toll ranged between five hundred and three thousand.

December 10, 1906 President Theodore Roosevelt accepts the Nobel Peace Prize for his peacekeeping efforts in negotiating an agreement between Russia and Japan.

1907 Several large businesses and banking institutions file bankruptcy, causing an economic crisis known as the Panic of 1907. The crisis lasted just a few weeks because President Theodore Roosevelt worked with financier J. P. Morgan to provide assistance to needy firms so they could avoid bankruptcy.

1908 Henry Ford introduces the Model T automobile.

1908 Sears, Roebuck & Co. begins selling home-building kits through the mail.

June 8, 1908 The American Antiquities Act is passed, giving the president of the United States the authority to designate specific lands as historic monuments, thereby giving them federal protection for the purposes of preservation.

July 26, 1908 The Federal Bureau of Investigation (FBI) is established.

November 1908 Former U.S. secretary of war William Howard Taft is elected president of the United States.

December 26, 1908 Jack Johnson becomes the first African American boxer to win the heavyweight championship.

1909 The National Association for the Advancement of Colored People (NAACP) is established.

April 6, 1909 Explorer Robert Peary becomes the first human to reach the North Pole.

1910 Hannah Solomon founds the Chicago Women's City Club.

1911 Baseball is known as "America's favorite pastime."

March 25, 1911 The Triangle Shirtwaist Factory fire claims the lives of 146 immigrant workers, most of them young girls. It is the largest industrial accident to date in the country.

1912 The Progressive, or "Bull Moose," Party is established. Former president Theodore Roosevelt becomes that party's presidential candidate in the 1912 election after losing the Republican Party nomination to incumbent president William Howard Taft.

April 9, 1912 President William Howard Taft creates the Federal Children's Bureau, which provided much-needed money to help maintain the health and well-being of children throughout the nation.

April 15, 1912 The ocean liner *Titanic* sinks into the Atlantic Ocean, killing 705 passengers.

November 1912 New Jersey governor Woodrow Wilson is elected the twenty-eighth president of the United States by defeating incumbent president William Howard Taft and former president Theodore Roosevelt.

1913 The Armory Show is presented in New York and attended by five thousand people. The exhibit featured art by the Ashcan School artists as well as Pablo Picasso and Marcel Duchamp. America was appalled by the new style of painting, but within a few years, the Modernist style would be all the rage.

1913 Miners in Ludlow, Colorado, go on strike. Events lead to the murder of the miners and their families at the hands of federal troops on April 20, 1914.

December 23, 1913 President Woodrow Wilson passes the Federal Reserve Act, which calls for banking and currency reform.

July 28, 1914 World War I, also known as the Great War, begins. America remains neutral until April 2, 1917, when President Woodrow Wilson declares war on Germany. The war ends on November 11, 1918.

Words to Know

abolitionists: People who worked to end slavery.

aeronautics: The study of flight and aircraft.

Ancient Order of Hibernians (AOH): A Catholic organization formed in America in 1836. Some of its members came from various organizations created centuries earlier in Ireland. The purpose of the AOH was to help Irish Catholic immigrants settle in America and to defend them from persecution. One way the AOH defended its members was to keep its meetings and actions secret.

anti-Semitism: Prejudice against Jewish people.

antitrust: Against the formation of monopolies or trusts.

bimetallism: A movement of the late nineteenth century aimed at expanding the amount of money in circulation by backing it with silver as well as gold. Also sometimes referred to as free silver.

boomtowns: Towns that were built quickly by gold-seekers.

capitalism: An economic system in which property and goods are privately owned, produced, and distributed.

civil service: The system in which civilians work for various government agencies and departments. Before civil service reform, people were appointed to positions depending on whom they knew in politics and business. After reform, people had to apply for a job and pass examinations in order to qualify.

conspicuous consumption: The buying of expensive and unnecessary items as a way of displaying one's wealth.

coolies: Unskilled Asian workers.

deflation: A decline in the prices of goods and services.

Democratic Party: One of the oldest political parties in the United States. Originally linked with the South and slavery, it transformed into one associated with urban voters and liberal policies.

depression: A long-term economic state characterized by high unemployment, minimal investment and spending, and low prices.

electoral votes: The votes a presidential candidate receives for having won a majority of a state's popular vote (citizens' votes). The candidate who receives the most popular votes in a particular state wins all of that state's electoral votes. Each state receives two electoral votes for its two U.S. senators and a figure for the number of U.S. representatives it has (which is determined by a state's population). A candidate must win a majority of electoral votes (over 50 percent) in order to win the presidency.

farm tenancy: An arrangement whereby farmers who no longer owned their own farm farmed someone else's land and were paid a share of the harvest.

Gilded Age: The period in history following the Civil War and Reconstruction (roughly the final twenty-three years of the nineteenth century), characterized by a ruthless pursuit of profit, an exterior of showiness and grandeur, and immeasurable political corruption.

grubstake: To advance money or supplies to miners in exchange for a percentage of profits from any discoveries.

horizontal integration: A business strategy in which one company buys out the competition; commonly known as a merger.

immigration: Leaving one's country to live in another.

imperialism: The practice of one country extending its control over the territory, political system, or economic system of another country.

Indian agents: Representatives of the U.S. government who worked with Native Americans. Their responsibility was to resolve conflicts and take the Native Americans' concerns to the government.

industrialism: An economy based on business and industry rather than agriculture.

inflation: A rise in the prices of goods and services.

Interstate Commerce Act: Passed in 1887, this law created the Interstate Commerce Commission (ICC), the first federal regulatory agency. It was designed to address railroad abuse and discrimination issues.

Ku Klux Klan: An organization of whites who believed in white superiority and who terrorized African Americans and their supporters in the South after the Civil War.

labor strike: A refusal of workers to work until management agrees to improvements in working conditions, wages, and/or benefits.

labor union: A formally organized association of workers that advances its members' views on wages, work hours, and labor conditions.

Molly Maguires: A secret society of workers established in Ireland in the 1840s whose mission was to fight discrimination. Some of its members immigrated to America later in the century. The Mollies were blamed for violence in the coal regions, though evidence against them was nonexistent.

monopoly: A condition created when one company dominates a sector of business, leaving the consumer no choices and other businesses no possibility of success.

mortgage: A loan of money to purchase property, such as a farm. The property is used as security for repayment of the loan; that is, if the borrower fails to pay, the property is seized.

muckrakers: Journalists who exposed scandal in Gilded Age society. These scandals usually involved public figures and established institutions and businesses, and focused on social issues such as child labor, political corruption, and corporate crime. The term "muckraking" was coined by President Theodore Roosevelt in 1906.

Mugwumps: A breakaway group of the Republican Party whose goal was to return Ulysses S. Grant to the White House.

naturalization: The process by which a person becomes a citizen of a country other than the one in which he or she was born.

patent: A grant by the government of the ownership of all rights of an invention to its creator.

patronage system: Also known as the spoils system. In patronage, someone donates large sums of money to help ensure the election of a candidate. That candidate repays the favor by making job appointments or by passing and proposing legislation that safeguards the interests of the business or person who donated the money.

philanthropy: Community service, financial donations, and volunteerism to promote human well-being.

political boss: A politically powerful—and often corrupt—person who can direct a group of voters to support a particular candidate.

popular vote: The result of the total number of individual votes in an election.

port: For an immigrant, the point of entry into a country.

poverty line: The least amount of income needed to secure the necessities of life. If someone lives below the poverty line, he or she cannot afford to purchase the basics needed to live, such as food, shelter, or medical care.

Progressive Era: A period in American history (approximately the first twenty years of the twentieth century) marked by reform and the development of a national cultural identity.

prospector: An explorer looking for minerals, such as gold.

reform: Change intended to improve a situation.

Republican Party: One of the oldest political parties in the United States. Founded as an antislavery party in the mid-1800s, it transformed into one associated with conservative fiscal and social policies.

reservations: Specific land allotted to the Native Americans by the U.S. government, as part of the solution to the "Indian Problem." The tribes did not own the land, but they managed it. These areas were the only places the Native Americans were allowed to live in the nineteenth century.

robber barons: The negative label given to powerful industrialists who amassed personal fortunes during the late nineteenth century, generally through corrupt and unethical business practices.

rustlers: Cattle thieves.

"Separate but Equal" doctrine: A policy enacted throughout the South that theoretically promoted the same treatment and services for African Americans as for whites, but which required the two races to use separate facilities.

settlement house: A center that provides community services to the poor and underprivileged in urban areas.

severalty: Individual ownership of land, as opposed to tribal ownership.

sluice: A wooden trough for washing gold. Soil is shoveled into a steady stream of water. Gold and other larger particles get caught in the bottom. Smaller sluices called rockers were often used during the gold rush. These sluices could be rocked back and forth to hasten the process of separating the gold from the soil.

Smithsonian Institution: A government institution with most of its grounds located in Washington, D.C. It includes 16 museums, 7 research centers, and 142 million items in its collections.

socialism: An economic system in which the government owns and operates business and production as well as controls the distribution of wealth.

sojourners: Immigrants who planned to stay in the United States temporarily; they usually stayed for a particular season or for a predetermined number of years before returning to their homeland.

Spanish-American War: A war fought in 1898 in Cuba. Cuba wanted independence from Spanish rule. The United States fought on the side of Cuba and beat Spain within three months.

stampeders: Gold-seekers.

stock: A share of ownership in a business.

strike: A work stoppage by employees in protest of unfair treatment.

strikebreakers: Companies or individual employees who provide work during a strike; sometimes called scabs.

suffrage: The right to vote.

tariffs: Taxes imposed on goods imported from other countries.

temperance: A movement that campaigned for the public to refrain from drinking alcohol.

transcontinental railroad: The railroad system that traveled across the entire United States; this included five routes through the West. The last stake was driven into the railroad on May 10, 1869.

trust: The concept of several companies banding together to form an organization that limits competition by controlling the production and distribution of a product or service.

vertical integration: A business strategy in which one person or company is involved in more than one phase of production of a product or service, making the production process more efficient and, thereby, increasing the amount of production and level of profit.

wages system: An economic system in which people rely on other people to earn a living. Employees are paid money for their services.

Yukon: One of Canada's extreme northwest territories. It was the site of a gold rush in the 1880s. Sixty percent of the territory's population lives in its capital city, Whitehorse.

Research and Activity Ideas

The following research and activity ideas are intended to offer suggestions for complementing social studies and history curricula, to trigger additional ideas for enhancing learning, and to provide cross-disciplinary projects for library and classroom use.

Tell it like it is: Imagine you are a muckraker at the beginning of the twentieth century. Using a fictitious company and people, make up a scandal and write a newspaper story.

Dear diary: Imagine you are a teenage boy or girl who just stepped off your immigrant ship and through the doors of the main building on Ellis Island. Write a journal entry describing your first impressions and how you feel about your experience.

Who made America great: List as many people you can think of and their contributions to America's Gilded Age or Progressive Era.

You're so funny: Draw a political cartoon about any newsworthy event of the Gilded Age or Progressive Era.

Pick an artist, any artist: Choose any artist (including writers, musicians, painters, illustrators, etc.) and develop a list of interview questions you would ask him or her. Then imagine the answers you would get and write a feature magazine article on that person.

What's that you say: Write a paragraph or two defending or refuting the theory of Social Darwinism.

On strike: With a group of three or four other students, stage a mock labor strike. One of you should be a newspaper reporter interviewing the strikers. Be sure to make clear who you are, who you work for, and why you are striking.

Then and now: Make a list of society's attitudes toward the rich during the Gilded Age. Make another list of society's attitudes toward the poor during that same era. Now make the same lists concerning society's attitudes today. Compare the lists, noting the similarities and differences.

Newsies: Watch the film *Newsies,* then write a summary and a review.

Baseball greats: Research a famous baseball player who played between the 1880s and the 1930s. Compare his statistics to your favorite modern (1980s and beyond) player.

All in a day's work: Choose a company in society. Imagine its workers going on strike. Write a few paragraphs summarizing what is going on and why.

Wrights on radio: Stage a radio call-in show featuring Wilbur and Orville Wright. Be sure to cover their roles not only in the history of flight, but as bicycle builders as well.

Write your own test: Imagine you are in charge of writing the test given to immigrants upon entry to the United States. You can include twenty questions. What would those questions be?

Compare the lives: Research the lifestyles of the Gilded Age robber barons and those of the poor immigrants who lived in tenement housing. Draw the interior of one room as you imagine it from a robber baron's mansion. Draw the same for a tenement. Be sure to include details such as furniture, wall coverings, and any art or sculpture that may be included. Compare the two.

Life of a child: Using various resources, note the average life of a child laborer. Develop a list of a typical day's activities. Now make a list of a typical day for yourself. Compare the lists.

Map it: Find a map of your town from the late 1890s or early 1900s. Compare it to a map of your town as it is today. List the differences you find.

Life on the frontier: Imagine you are a young mother (twenty-five years old) on the frontier in the 1890s or 1900s. You have four children. Since you cannot write, draw a series of pictures depicting a typical day for you.

Life made easier: Make a list of all the ways in which the various inventions of the Gilded Age and Progressive Era made life easier.

Play it again: If you play a musical instrument, learn a song written between 1880 and 1913. Play it for the class.

What would you say: Imagine you have been commissioned to write a poem for placement at the base of the Statue of Liberty. Write that poem.

North and South: Research and find accounts of the lives of two African Americans (famous or not famous) between 1880 and 1915. One person should live in the South, one in the North. Find the similarities as well as the differences in the lives of these individuals, including society's attitude toward each.

A matter of philosophy: Stage a debate between Booker T. Washington and W. E. B. Du Bois. Be sure questions allow each participant to clearly state and explain his philosophy on the role of African Americans in the late nineteenth and early twentieth centuries. What are the advantages and disadvantages of each philosophy?

Compare the presidents: Make a list of the political beliefs and actions taken by your favorite president from the Gilded Age or Progressive Era. Compare those beliefs and actions to the current president of the United States. How are they different? Similar?

Captured by the Native Americans: Imagine you are a ten-year-old child who has been captured by a Native American tribe during the Plains Indian Wars. Write a paper on your experience with your captors. Questions to keep in mind: Are you treated well? What are you experiencing emotionally? How is the life of the tribe similar to and different from your own? Are you set free?

Going to the Fair: Research the 1893 Columbian Exposition. Draw a scene from the fair.

What should they learn: With a small group of students, develop a curriculum that will be used to educate the Native American children who have been forced to live on reservations. Choose one of the following subjects, and develop the curriculum for a one-month time period: history; English; life skills; sociology. Choose any grade level between sixth and twelfth.

Change your school: Imagine you are your century's John Dewey. Either on your own or within a small group, design an experimental school. Be sure your plan includes your mission, educational philosophy, and academic goals.

Gilded Age
and Progressive Era

Almanac

1

A Country at Odds with Itself

America in 1878 was just coming out of the Reconstruction Era (1865–77). The Reconstruction years were a time of rebuilding and renewal in the South, which had suffered bitter defeat in the American Civil War (1861–65). The Civil War was a conflict that took place from 1861 to 1865 between the Northern states (Union) and the Southern states (Confederacy) that had seceded, or formally withdrawn, from the Union. Union troops had destroyed cities and countryside throughout the Confederacy during the war, and Reconstruction was a time for rebuilding those areas from the ground up. But more than physical buildings and land had been ruined; Southern society was in disarray as well. After four years of bloodshed and conflict, the Southern way of life no longer existed. The plantation economy, which relied so heavily on the work of slaves, could no longer be sustained now that slavery was illegal. White Southerners had to relearn how to live from day to day without the use of slaves.

If whites had difficulty making the transition to a slave-free lifestyle, African Americans found the change even more challenging. For many, slavery was the only life they had ever known. Now they were expected to find jobs and a place in society in a culture that still considered African Americans inferior. For a while, rights were extended to freedmen and free-born African Americans. By the end of Reconstruction, however, there was more animosity between the two races than ever before. By law, African Americans had the same rights as whites. In practice, however, these laws were not always upheld, and the hatred in the hearts of many Southern whites had not been erased.

False hopes and broken promises

The eleven Southern states that had participated in the Civil War were charged with forming new governments. For the first time, African Americans served in politics. These citizens were guaranteed the same

1

WORDS TO KNOW

abolitionists: People who worked to end slavery.

deflation: A decline in the prices of goods and services.

electoral votes: The votes a presidential candidate receives for having won a majority of a state's popular vote (citizens' votes). The candidate who receives the most popular votes in a particular state wins all of that state's electoral votes. Each state receives two electoral votes for its two U.S. senators and a figure for the number of U.S. representatives it has (which is determined by a state's population). A candidate must win a majority of electoral votes (over 50 percent) in order to win the presidency.

Gilded Age: The period in history following the Civil War and Reconstruction (roughly the final twenty-three years of the nineteenth century), characterized by a ruthless pursuit of profit, an exterior of showiness and grandeur, and immeasurable political corruption.

inflation: A rise in the prices of goods and services.

Ku Klux Klan: An organization of whites who believed in white superiority and who terrorized African Americans and their supporters in the South after the Civil War.

Mugwumps: A breakaway group of the Republican Party whose goal was to return Ulysses S. Grant to the White House.

patronage system: Also known as the spoils system. In patronage, someone donates large sums of money to help ensure the election of a candidate. That candidate repays the favor by making job appointments or by passing and proposing legislation that safeguards the interests of the business or person who donated the money.

political boss: A politically powerful—and often corrupt—person who can direct a group of voters to support a particular candidate.

popular vote: The result of the total number of individual votes in an election.

---

rights—political and civil—as whites. African Americans were given hope that they would enjoy equal status with their white peers.

This ideal never happened. Northern abolitionists (people who worked to end slavery) who had shown concern for slaves in the South during the war now focused their energies and efforts elsewhere. Freed slaves found life outside the master's house nearly impossible; they had never had the chance to develop the skills needed to live life independently. Mostly, the failure to achieve equality was due to the refusal of many white Southerners to tolerate African

Americans as their equals. Not only did these whites not accept the idea, many aggressively fought against it with terrorism in the form of an organization called the Ku Klux Klan. The Klan implemented a campaign of violence that included random torture, lynchings (executions without a legal trial), rape, and murder of African Americans and the whites who supported them. While African Americans theoretically had rights, they were too afraid to exercise them.

By the end of Reconstruction, the Republican Party all but disappeared from the South. Republicans had been the loyal supporters of black equality, but at a time when African Americans needed them most, they gave in to the pressures of powerful Southern whites. The white supremacists (whites who believed that African Americans were inferior to them in every way) kept Republicans and African Americans from the polls. Those African Americans who once held political office were subsequently voted out. Little by little, the South was returning to the power structure it had known before, despite the law.

By 1878, the rights afforded to African Americans had all but disappeared. Without a vote or representation in government, and without the ability to obtain an education or necessary life skills, most African Americans were forced to take jobs as sharecroppers. In the sharecropping system, whites continued to own the land that African Americans worked and lived on. The workers were responsible for buying all supplies and equipment needed to harvest crops, an obligation that kept them in debt most of the time. Workers also had to pay rent on the land. The only difference between sharecropping and slavery was that African Americans had more control over their time and work conditions as sharecroppers. They also were given a portion of the crops they harvested. But they would never gain independence or wealth; most of the time, they were barely getting by.

Dawn of the Gilded Age

As the Gilded Age (the period in history following the Civil War and Reconstruction, characterized by a ruthless pursuit of profit, an exterior of showiness and grandeur, and immeasurable political corruption) was ushered in, the South was returned to Democratic power. According to Nell Irvin Painter, author of *Standing at Armageddon,* these Democrats called themselves the "wealth and intelligence of the South." In their eyes, they had "redeemed" their states by recapturing political power and saving society from corruption and incompetence. They managed to overlook the hypocrisy of their methods, which involved violence and corruption.

Democrats and even some Republicans blamed Reconstruction for the economic difficulties facing Southern states. They accused the carpetbaggers (Northerners who had moved to the South) and scalawags (Southern whites of limited income) of weak leadership, and claimed that only men of wealth should enter politics. Traditionally, wealthy men were educated men. They felt this qualified them—and disqualified everyone else—from the world of politics. These wealthy men believed the new politicians were using politics for personal gain rather than to serve society. But too often, "society" in their minds meant the wealthy.

The dawn of the Gilded Age saw the struggle for political power reach an intensity like no other time in American history. Voters turned out for political elections in numbers not equaled since. According to historian Richard Jensen in *The Gilded Age: Essays on the Origins of Modern America,* U.S. senator Henry Blair (1834–1920) of New Hampshire summed it up best: "We love our parties as we love our churches and our families."

Republicans versus Democrats

Party identification The Republicans identified themselves by who they were and what they did. Sometimes called the Grand Old Party (GOP) after 1880, Republicans entered the Gilded Age with campaigns that appealed to Americans' sense of patriotism (love of country), morality (goodness), and prosperity (wealth).

Boss Tweed and Tammany Hall

Harper's Weekly *magazine political cartoon of William Marcy "Boss" Tweed, who ruled Tammany Hall, the Democratic political machine, in the 1860s and 1870s.* ILLUSTRATION BY THOMAS NAST. © BETTMANN/CORBIS.

Corruption in late nineteenth-century politics was not rare. But one name rises above the others: William Marcy Tweed. Born in 1823 in New York City, he held a number of jobs before

entering politics, including firefighting, chair-making, and bookkeeping.

Tweed became a New York City alderman (representative) in 1851. He quickly rose through the ranks of city government. He earned the nickname "Boss," and his friends were known as the "Tweed Ring." Tweed had appointed so many of his friends to political positions in New York City that in 1870, he was able to pass a charter allowing him and his friends to control the city treasury.

Tweed's headquarters were located in a building known as Tammany Hall. Tweed's power was such that he controlled the mayor, and he rewarded his political supporters with money he received in bribes and kickbacks from friends to whom he awarded city contracts. This process was known as the patronage system, and Tweed's was a prime example of machine politics.

Tweed's crimes were many. He and his ring of friends faked leases on city-owned buildings, padded bills with charges for repairs that never happened, and bought overpriced goods and services from suppliers controlled by the ring. All in all, they managed to steal between $30 million and $200 million from the city between 1865 and 1871.

Tweed's most notorious deed was the construction of the New York County Courthouse,

Republicans took full credit for saving the Union in the Civil War, and used that power to demand that they alone were worthy of serving the Union in peace. Many veterans from the war joined the Republican Party. A poll taken in Indiana in 1880 showed that 69 percent of veterans voted Republican. So close were the ties between the party and the war that in eight of nine presidential elections between 1868 and 1900, the Republican candidate was a Union veteran.

The party depended on people to vote according to their moral beliefs. They never missed an opportunity during election years to begun in 1861. For instance, he paid a carpenter $360,751 (equal to $4.9 million in modern value) for one month's worth of work. But the courthouse had very little woodwork throughout its rooms. Three tables and forty chairs cost $179,729 (equal to $2.5 million). A plasterer received $133,187 (equal to $1.82 million) for two days' work. These laborers were friends of Tweed. Tweed himself profited from a financial interest in the quarry that provided the marble for the courthouse. When a committee investigated why the building of the courthouse took so long (ten years, and it still was not done), Tweed spent $7,718 (about $105,000) to print the report. In reality, it did not cost him a thing, since he owned the printing company.

Tweed controlled the Democratic Party of New York City. By 1870, he was appointed commissioner of public works. This position gave him even greater opportunity to steal the city's money. One example of his illegal activity was when he bought three hundred benches for $5 each and resold them to the city for $600 apiece. Tweed also organized the development of City Hall Park. His original estimate for the project was $350,000. By the time he had completed the job, spending had escalated to $13 million.

In 1871, someone, most likely a disgruntled city official, leaked word of Tweed's embezzling activities (fraudulent use of funds). Thomas Nast (1840–1902), a political cartoonist working for the magazine *Harper's Weekly*, learned of the corruption and began a campaign to expose Tweed and his ring. Tweed tried to bribe Nast with a half million dollars. This was a hundred times the yearly salary Nast earned at the magazine, but he refused to be bought. When that did not work, Tweed pressured Harper Brothers, the company that owned the magazine. They refused to fire Nast, and the company lost its profitable contract to supply New York schools with books, a contract controlled by Tweed.

On July 21, 1871, the *New York Times* published some of the contents of New York County's financial records. When the public realized that Tweed was paying his friends $41,190 for a broom and $7,500 for a thermometer, chaos erupted. A committee was established to investigate Tweed and his ring. In 1873, Tweed was arrested, found guilty of corruption, and sentenced to twelve years behind bars. He served only two years but was rearrested almost upon release. New York sued him for $6 million.

Tweed did not have the money, so he was held in debtor's prison. He was allowed daily trips to visit his family, and on one of these trips, he escaped to Spain. There he worked as a seaman on a Spanish ship. But one of Nast's cartoons caused someone to recognize him and he was captured in 1876. Tweed died in a New York prison on April 12, 1878.

remind Americans that Democrats were the former slave owners who also ran saloons and joined the Ku Klux Klan. To dramatize their point, they often mentioned William "Boss" Tweed (1823–1878; see box). Tweed was arguably the most corrupt politician of the Gilded Age. Republicans were painted as religious, devoted, hard-working members of society who resisted the temptations of alcohol in favor of attending church functions.

Prosperity, or economic growth, was on the minds of everyone during the Gilded Age. Republicans took the credit for creating the policies that allowed for postwar prosperity. This much was true: The Republican reforms did empower the federal government to become more involved and have a greater role in the economy, thus improving economic conditions.

Whereas the Republican Party defined itself by who it was and what it did, the Democratic Party built itself on a platform of what it opposed. In large part, it was informed by the principles of an attorney named Samuel Tilden (1814–1886). Tilden led the revival of the Democratic Party in New York through the early 1870s. His program did not include federal government involvement to any great extent but instead promoted individual states' rights. Throughout the Gilded Age, Democrats were against most taxes and against land grants that gave public lands to corporations. Democrats felt the land should be set aside to provide farms for private citizens.

Party beliefs In modern society, a set of political and moral beliefs can indicate whether a person is more likely to be affiliated with a particular political party. For example, conservatives, who tend to include people in favor of the death penalty and against abortion, are more apt to vote Republican. Liberals, who generally support women's reproductive rights and gun control, are more likely to vote Democrat. These labels are not always accurate, but they tell a lot about how a person votes.

In the Gilded Age, religious affiliation often determined how a citizen would vote. Methodists, Baptists, Congregationals, Presbyterians, and some Lutherans usually voted Republican if they lived outside the South. Most African Americans, regardless of region, were Republican, as were the majority of abolitionists.

Democratic candidates could usually count on the votes of Episcopalians, Catholics, and German Lutherans—religions that defined sin more narrowly. In addition to religious affiliation, race played an important role as well. The majority of Southern whites voted Democrat. Democrats defended white supremacy and considered other races inferior. They were more tolerant of religious differences but more race intolerant than Republicans, generally speaking.

The issues If simplified, the major difference between the Republicans and Democrats of the Gilded Age was their stance on the role of government. Republicans believed the government should use its authority to expand the nation's economy through funded programs and legislation. Democrats wanted the government to stay out of economic and business affairs. They considered unrestricted competition as the most direct route to prosperity.

Taxes: Republicans wanted the government to implement a protective tariff (tax). They felt high taxes on foreign-made products would ensure that American agriculture and industry were not left behind. American workers would enjoy job security and receive higher wages than their foreign peers. Republicans played on the emotionalism of patriotism to advance their cause, claiming that the tariff would preserve the quality of life of the American workman.

Most Democrats looked at a protective tariff as nothing but a burden on consumers. They believed taxes should be used only if necessary to fund government services. Democrats did not embrace the concept of free trade (trade and business arrangements without tariffs or regulations), however. They saw taxes as a way to finance a government. Not all Democrats wanted lower tariffs; those who supported tariffs did so out of a fear of foreign competition. The tariff issue served to unify the Republicans, whereas it divided the Democrats.

Religion: Religion was another area that pitted Republican against Democrat. Republicans promoted moralistic policies based on Protestant values. (Protestantism is a branch of Christianity that accepts the Bible as the only source of revelation or truth.) They embraced restrictions on the sale and use of alcohol as well as limitations on the rights of businesses to open on Sunday.

Democrats believed in the separation of church and state. They felt religion was a personal issue and should not be regulated by government. Democrats were against any laws that promoted a particular faith. Because of this, Democrats found supporters in Roman Catholics and other Christians who were not so active in evangelism (preaching the gospel).

Money: Throughout the Gilded Age, America's economy was unstable. Much of the era was spent in deflation (a decline in the prices of goods and services). The government's monetary policy held that every dollar in circulation had to be backed with an equal amount of gold. The world's supply of gold was unchanging. But the population of the world was growing, so the value of every dollar rose. People in debt had trouble meeting their financial responsibilities. One solution was to increase the amount of money in circulation.

There was no definitive line between Democrats and Republicans on this issue. Members of each party fell into two camps: those who advocated the use of gold, and those who wanted to use silver. The world's supply of silver was growing, which made the actual value of the metal on currency markets low. Consumers with debt did not like the idea of paying off their obligations with dollars of increasing value. They preferred the inflation (decline in the purchasing power of money) that would arise from an increase in the amount of currency in circulation. Creditors, however, did not want to be paid in dollars of shrinking value. Clearly, no one, regardless of party affiliation, was going to be happy with either gold or silver.

Civil service: Compared with modern times, nineteenth- and early-twentieth-century government was small. Politicians enjoyed a patronage system that is still in place today, though to less obvious extent. Also known as machine politics, or the spoils system, the patronage system awards contracts, favors, and appointments to people in return for their political support. This system does not operate on justice or fair play; it is unfair and costly to American citizens. But in the years of Reconstruction and the Gilded Age, politics was ruled by corruption.

By the 1870s, the patronage system was being loudly criticized. Those against patronage claimed that its highest priority was maintaining party loyalty rather than appointing officials with true ability. The people wanted a separate group of workers to perform government business. Politicians were against a civil service, as they recognized it as a reform that would reduce their power. They liked having friends in official positions. Others were against the reform because it would be based on academic achievement rather than ability. As with the religion issue, Democrats and Republicans were not clearly divided on the idea of a civil service. By 1876, though, the spoils system had reached a level of corruption that made both parties call for reform.

The "other" parties

Although politics were dominated by the Democratic and Republican parties, there were other, smaller political parties active throughout various periods of the Gilded Age.

Mugwumps One smaller political party formed as an offshoot of the Republican Party. The men of this group reached higher degrees of education and enjoyed an elevated social status. Labeled Mugwumps by their critics, these reform-minded men were based in Boston and New York City. No one is certain of the origin of the word Mugwump. One version is that it derives from a Native American word for a young male who believes he knows more than his elders. Another claims a mugwump is a bird sitting on a fence: Its "mug" is on one side, its "wump" on the other. Being called a fence-sitter is an insult hurled at people who cannot make up their minds. The Mugwumps seemed to fit the description, as they sometimes were unable to decide whether or not to support the Republican candidate. They chose to redefine the word Mugwump as one who acts on principle rather than blind loyalty.

Mugwumps supported the idea of minimal government involvement in business and the economy. The patronage system so prevalent in Gilded Age society infuriated them, and they promoted a civil service program based on testing and ability.

Most Mugwumps were Republican, though they were criticized for breaking with party loyalty. In 1884, they voted for Democrat Grover Cleveland (1837–1908; served 1885–89 and 1893–97) in the presidential election. Their obvious disloyalty to Republicans made them the target for contempt of most politicians, who considered them annoying, though relatively

President Grover Cleveland is shown dressed as a woman. The Mugwumps, a group of reformers from the east coast, tended to vote Republican, but switched their allegiance to Cleveland, a Democrat, in the 1884 presidential election. Critics compared the Mugwumps to women (implying that they were not manly enough to stick to one party), hence Cleveland's attire in the cartoon. © BETTMANN/CORBIS.

harmless. Political peers began comparing the Mugwumps to women, an insult insinuating they were not manly enough to adhere to party loyalty. Gilded Age women had no vote; their role was limited to the home. To be called a woman in politics was a major slur. When all was said and done, the Mugwumps never achieved great status or had a major impact on Gilded Age politics.

Farmer and labor parties Some of the smaller political parties developed out of a need perceived by laborers and farmers, who felt underrepresented by Democrats and Republicans. These coalitions formed at local levels, but never gained enough momentum or strength to become national forces.

These parties, though separate, were known collectively by various names, including Reform, Independent, Greenback, Grangers, and Labor. They worked closely and identified with the major labor and farm organizations of the Gilded Age.

The farm and labor parties identified themselves as the producing classes in the economy. According to their labor theory, one is either a producer (whose labor produces value) or a parasite (who gets rich on the value produced by others). The use of the word "parasite" stems from its biological definition: an organism that relies on another organism for its life and contributes nothing to its survival. Parasites included bankers, wholesalers, gamblers, lawyers, and others who made their profits off the laborers and farmers. Supporters of the labor theory thought that producers should form cooperatives that would eliminate the need for parasites.

The first official group to embrace the labor theory was the Grange, also known as the Patrons of Husbandry. Oliver H. Kelley (1826–1913) founded the Grange in 1867 in an effort to improve the efficiency of farming methods. It quickly grew throughout the Midwest and the central South. By 1874, Grangers formed political parties in eleven states; each state party had its own name, including Reform, Anti-Monopoly, or simply Granger Party. Because farms were dependent upon railroads, much of the focus of the Granger movement was on railroad legislation. Mostly, Grangers wanted a limit on shipping rates.

The Grange hit its peak in the mid-1870s before it began experiencing financial difficulties.

Members began fighting among themselves, and by the end of the decade, the Grange no longer existed.

The Greenback Party was founded in 1875, much for the same agricultural reasons as those that motivated the Grange. Some of the Granger parties actually joined forces with the Greenbackers, who took their name from the paper money printed during the Civil War. The Greenbackers promoted the quantity theory of money. This theory states that if the money in circulation grows more quickly than the economy, inflation (rising prices) occurs. If the opposite happens, deflation (falling prices) results. They also supported the concept of fiat money, which says money has value because the government says it does, not because it can be redeemed for gold or anything else. Bankers and other money experts criticized both theories as illogical.

As deflation took over the economy, Greenbackers demanded the government issue more paper money. Farmers agreed with this request, as throughout the nation, they were experiencing serious amounts of debt.

The party focused its attentions not only on economy, but on labor. Through the mid-1880s, Greenbackers called for more rights for laborers as well as safer working conditions. (See more about these topics in Chapter 3.) Although they managed to nominate one of their own in the 1880 presidential election—U.S. representative James Baird Weaver (1833–1912) of Iowa—he got just over 3 percent of the popular vote. They fared even worse in 1884, when their nominee, Massachusetts politician and former Civil War general Benjamin Butler (1818–1893), got less than 2 percent of the vote.

The Greenback Party aligned itself with local and state labor parties throughout the

1880s. In 1886, an Independent Labor mayoral candidate in New York City finished second in the race, behind the Democratic candidate but ahead of the Republican. The United Labor Party did even better that same year when its candidate won the mayoral race in Milwaukee, Wisconsin.

In 1887, spurred on by the success of the labor parties, the Greenbackers joined with the farm and labor organizations to form the Union Labor Party. Despite its efforts and hopes, the Union Labor Party presidential candidate—state senator Alson J. Streeter (1823–1901) of Illinois—drew less than 1 percent of the votes in the 1888 election. The farm and labor parties, though successful on local levels, never realized their goals on a national level.

Presidents of the Gilded Age

Rutherford B. Hayes (1822–1893; served 1877–81) was the president in office as America entered the Gilded Age. He had won the 1876 presidential election, which turned out to be one of the most controversial in American history.

To understand the importance of the 1876 election, it is essential to understand the political climate of the time. America was reeling from the corruption of the administration of the previous president, Ulysses S. Grant (1822–1885; served 1869–77). Though Grant himself was considered an honest man, he did not run his administration wisely. He had been elected nearly four years after the end of the Civil War, after having served as general of the Union army. It was a time of strife—the assassination of President Abraham Lincoln (1809–1865; served 1861–65) was still a recent memory and his successor, Andrew Johnson (1808–1875; served 1865–69), was unpopular. The war-torn country

was depending on Grant to unify the North and South and put America back in business.

Instead, Grant depended on Congress to lead the way. He seemed bewildered to be in office, unable to make decisions that would move America forward. At a time when the country needed strong leadership, Grant failed to take control. As a result, his two-term presidency was one of the most corrupt and ineffective administrations in history. By 1876, America wanted little more than honesty in the White House.

Who won the 1876 election? To this day, there are people who insist Hayes, then-governor of Ohio, did not win the 1876 election. He had run against Samuel Tilden, a Democrat from New York. Tilden was a district attorney there before he had been elected governor.

By the final days of the campaign, Tilden was favored to win. Even Hayes was convinced he had lost. A record 81.8 percent of eligible voters had participated in the election; clearly, America wanted a say in choosing its new leader.

After all the votes had been counted, it was clear Tilden had won the popular vote (total number of votes by individuals). However, electoral votes (which are assigned to states based on population) from four states—Florida, Louisiana, South Carolina, and Oregon—were in dispute. A congressional committee was appointed to investigate the situation. The committee comprised five Supreme Court justices, five members from the House of Representatives, and five senators. The plan was to have seven Democrats, seven Republicans, and one independent. However, the sole independent, Supreme Court associate justice David Davis (1815–1886), was elected a U.S. senator from Illinois and did not serve on the committee. His committee replacement was Republican. As a result, every vote the committee took after reviewing the evidence resulted in an 8–7 split in favor of the Republican Hayes. He was awarded all the electoral votes that had been in question, and scored a victory at 185–184.

Hayes in office Though Tilden was not happy with the results, he did not dispute the final count and let America move on. In order to do that, the Democrats and Republicans needed to resolve their conflicts. They did this by developing the Compromise of 1877. Under this agreement, the Democrats accepted the Republican president if certain conditions were met. One condition required the president to appoint a Democrat to his Cabinet, a requirement he met but that angered his fellow Republicans nonetheless. He also had to withdraw federal troops from the South, a move that worked against African Americans there and the rights they had recently been granted. Without the protection of federal soldiers, there was no one to enforce racial equality. The new president brought an end to Reconstruction soon after taking oath. After just four months in office, he was faced with the first nationwide labor strike. Railroad workers had been forced to take pay cuts beginning in 1873. By July 1877, they went on strike in hopes of putting an end to the unfair treatment (see Chapter 3).

Hayes dispatched federal troops to control the strikes that were erupting throughout the states. In doing so, he ushered in an era when state and federal forces sided with companies against aggravated laborers.

Hayes's years in office were uneventful compared to the conflict under which he entered.

Rutherford B. Hayes was inaugurated president in March 1877 following a highly disputed election in November 1876. THE LIBRARY OF CONGRESS.

Although he had promised civil service reform, the House of Representatives and Senate made it impossible for him to overturn the patronage system. He refused to participate in the system himself, however. This simple act only served to turn his fellow Republicans against him.

While Hayes was president, the Treasury put into action two currency policies. The Resumption Act was passed in 1875. This act specified that greenbacks—the money issued during the Civil War—could be redeemed in gold after 1879. Until the passage of the Resumption Act, there were, in addition to greenbacks, gold coins and gold certificates in circulation. Then, after the war, a gold dollar was issued. All these monies had different values and

Election 2000: Another Mystery

Vice President Al Gore (left), the Democratic presidential nominee, shakes the hand of his Republican opponent, Texas governor George W. Bush, at the presidential debate in Boston, Massachusetts, on October 3, 2000. © REUTERS/CORBIS.

The presidential election of 2000 was even more controversial than the election of 1876. Democratic vice president Al Gore (1948–) ran against the Republican governor of Texas, George W.

Bush (1946–), in a race that became a national obsession.

Polls showed the two candidates running in a dead heat: the election was considered too close to call. November 7, 2000, was Election Day. That evening, many media outlets announced their belief that Gore had won the state of Florida, a key state in any election because of its high number of electoral votes. As the night progressed, however, television networks retracted their statement. It was clear that the race was so close that whichever candidate took Florida would be the next U.S. president.

Early the next morning, the networks announced Florida and the presidency belonged to Bush. Gore heard the news that he lost by fifty thousand votes and called to congratulate Bush on his victory. Shortly afterward, Gore was told that the governor's lead in Florida had shrunk to a couple thousand votes at best.

As media focus shifted to Florida—a state whose governor was Jeb Bush (1953—), brother of the Republican presidential candidate—it became clear that the voting process in that state was questionable. Palm Beach County, for example, used butterfly ballots. These ballots put the names of the candidates on the left and right margins and a column of punch holes running

made the system confusing. The Resumption Act linked the greenbacks to the gold supply.

The other currency policy was called the Bland bill, named after Democrat Richard Bland (1835–1899), the U.S. representative from Missouri who introduced it. This bill called for the introduction of silver coinage. Because of

favorable silver market conditions of the time, introducing silver coinage would make the value of circulating currency rise. The bill was passed in the House and was sponsored by U.S. senator William Allison (1829–1908) of Iowa. Although Hayes opposed the bill, it was passed as the Bland-Allison Act in 1878.

down the center. It was difficult to tell which hole went with which candidate, especially for older or visually impaired voters. In other counties throughout the state, authorities found disqualified ballots and ballots in which no presidential vote was registered.

The confusion surrounding the election led to a recount of the ballots. Soon, controversy erupted over chads. On punch card ballots, voters must push out a small piece of the ballot to indicate the vote. This piece of the ballot is called a chad. Ideally, chads are completely removed by voters. However, many ballots had "hanging" chads, "pregnant" chads (pushed to the point where they were sticking out, but not removed), and "dimpled" chads (clearly tampered with, probably in an effort to remove them). These controversial ballots had been disqualified and ignored in the original round of vote counts.

After several recounts of the ballots and as many lawsuits and emergency motions filed by both sides of the controversy, certified results gave Bush the victory in Florida with 537 votes over Gore. Gore appeared on national television and informed the public that the final count failed to include thousands of votes. He contested the election results at a U.S. Supreme Court hearing on December 2. The U.S. Supreme Court challenged the Florida Supreme Court to explain why it extended deadlines for the hand recounts. While Gore told the court that they were wrong to uphold the certification of the recount, Bush's legal team was telling them to let the final numbers stand.

On December 8, the Florida Supreme Court voted 4–3 for another manual recount. Bush appealed that decision, and it was overturned by the U.S. Supreme Court, 5–4. On December 12, the U.S. Supreme Court announced that no further recounts would be allowed. The following day, Gore conceded defeat to his opponent, and George W. Bush, son of former president George H. W. Bush (1924–; served 1989–93), was declared the victor.

Final counts showed Gore having won 48.38 percent of the popular vote, compared to Bush's 47.87 percent. Independent candidate Ralph Nader (1934–) earned 2.74 percent of the vote. Bush officially took 271 electoral votes, leaving 266 to Gore. Of all the registered voters in America, 51.3 percent voted in that election.

Many Americans felt Bush had not been elected to the White House, that he had won the election through questionable tactics in his brother's state. Regardless, Bush was inaugurated as the nation's forty-third U.S. president in January 2001, and was reelected in 2004.

Hayes kept good his promise to serve only one term. He was succeeded by James A. Garfield (1831–1881), who lived to serve just over six months of his presidential term.

Garfield: assassination of a president By the time of the 1880 election, the Republican Party was divided. Led by political boss (politician in control of a party's votes) Roscoe Conkling (1829–1888; see box), a faction, or group, broke away from the majority of Republicans and called themselves the Stalwarts. These men favored electing former president Ulysses S. Grant to a third term in the White House. (Though there was no law that limited the number of presidential terms a person may serve, it

Roscoe Conkling: Radical Republican

Longtime New York politician and Republican Party boss Roscoe Conkling. THE LIBRARY OF CONGRESS.

Born in Albany, New York, on October 30, 1829, Roscoe Conkling practiced law before entering politics in 1858. His initial political loyalty lay with the Whig Party, which was primarily concerned with promoting internal transportation improvements such as canals, railroads, and river routes. He joined many of his fellow Whigs and switched to the Republican Party at its beginnings. In 1858, Conkling was elected to serve in the U.S. House of Representatives. It was the beginning of a long political career that included terms as congressman (1865–67) and senator (1867–81).

Conkling was an outspoken member of the Radical Republicans. This group favored the abolition of slavery and embraced the unpopular idea that freed slaves should enjoy the same rights and quality of life as whites.

When Rutherford B. Hayes became president in 1877, Conkling was Hayes's main obstacle to reforming the civil service. Having enjoyed great power as a result of the patronage system, Conkling was not eager to give it up. He took full advantage of the policy that gave senators a great breadth of personal control over all federal appointments in their states.

Conkling headed the Stalwarts in 1880. The Stalwarts wanted to send former president Ulysses S. Grant back to the White House for a third term. That dream was dashed when U.S. representative James A. Garfield of Ohio was elected president. When it became clear Garfield would not bow to the patronage system or Conkling's demands for appointments, Conkling resigned from the Senate. He returned to practicing law in New York City and turned down President Chester A. Arthur's nomination of him for the Supreme Court in 1882. Conkling died in 1888.

was standard for presidents to serve only two terms. It was not until 1951 that the Twenty-second Amendment was ratified, limiting presidents to two terms in office; this came about as a result of Franklin D. Roosevelt [1882–1945; served 1933–45] being elected to four terms.) The other Republican candidate was U.S. representative James A. Garfield of Ohio. Garfield had served in the Civil War as the Union's youngest major general. New York lawyer Chester A. Arthur (1829–1886) was the Republican nominee for vice president.

Campaign poster from 1880 showing Republican presidential nominee James Garfield (left) and his running mate, Chester A. Arthur. © CORBIS.

The Democrats nominated Winfield Hancock (1824–1886), another Civil War general. Unlike Garfield, Hancock had minimal political experience. The Greenback candidate was U.S. representative James Baird Weaver (1833–1912) of Iowa. He, too, had served as a general in the Civil War, but as a presidential candidate, he inspired few votes. Garfield narrowly won the popular vote by half a percentage point. He managed to win the electoral vote without the support of one Southern state. This was a major victory for the Republicans, as it proved they could win even without the Southern African American vote.

Garfield, like Hayes, wanted to appoint a Cabinet that would maintain the unity of the Republican Party. Conkling, still a powerful political boss, demanded the president adhere to the patronage system. When Garfield refused, a power struggle ensued. Being a senior senator, Conkling felt Garfield was obligated to take his advice when it came to making important appointments in the Cabinet. Garfield, however, felt some appointments were too important to surrender to patronage, that they should be given to those men who were truly qualified.

The situation intensified when it came time for Garfield to appoint a head to the New York Customhouse. New York was Conkling's state; he wanted to name the official himself. Garfield ignored him, an act that let all senators know he would not play the patronage game.

On July 2, 1881, Garfield was assassinated by Charles Guiteau (c. 1840–1882), a religious fanatic who called himself a Stalwart. His defense was that he was saving the Republican Party. Garfield had served just four months of his term before being shot. He lived another two-and-a-half months before dying, at which time Vice President Arthur was sworn in as president.

As tragic as the assassination was, it was the event that led directly to the much-needed civil service reform.

Arthur: an unlikely president Vice presidents in the late nineteenth century were not chosen for their ability to lead so much as for their ability to maintain party unity. Arthur was no exception to the rule. No one viewed Arthur as presidential material, but his commitment to running an honest administration surprised everyone, especially Roscoe Conkling.

Arthur had been a longtime political ally of Conkling's, and a loyal Stalwart. Years before his vice presidency, Arthur served as collector of New York's Customhouse, a key position at the building where most of the taxes on imported goods were collected. He had never considered himself above taking advantage of the patronage system. Even during his brief stint as vice president, Arthur fought Garfield on his attempts to destroy patronage. In that way, Arthur and Conkling were united.

But when Arthur got to the White House, he had a change of heart. He was determined to prove to the American people that he was too ethical to participate in machine politics (the political system that relied on patronage and behind-the-scenes control). This sudden shift on Arthur's part incensed Conkling, who viewed it as a betrayal; the two parted company when Conkling refused to work with the president.

A direct result of Arthur's commitment to ethics was the passing of the Pendleton Act in 1883. The Act called for an unbiased commission to oversee the Civil Service. Appointment to government service and promotion from within the service would finally be based on ability as demonstrated in written examination. In the past, civil service employees were forced to give a portion of their salary to the political party that had appointed them; that rule was outlawed with the Act. In addition, employees could no longer be fired for political reasons.

That same year, Arthur signed the Tariff Act. This law put a limit on taxes so that the government would not have a surplus at the end of each year.

Arthur was the first president to limit immigration when he signed a law in 1882 that excluded criminals, lunatics, and beggars from coming to the shores of America. He also suspended Chinese immigration for ten years (see Chapter 4).

For all his dedication to honesty, the president kept one secret from the country. He was dying of Bright's disease, a kidney disorder. He ran for the Republican nomination in 1884, but was defeated by former U.S. senator James Blaine (1874–1934) of Maine. Arthur died two years later.

Cleveland: in, out, back in The presidential campaign of 1884 was waged between the more experienced Republican nominee, James Blaine, and Democrat Grover Cleveland, the governor of New York. In a surprising upset, Cleveland defeated Blaine, with the support not only of Democrats but of the Mugwumps as well. The victory made Cleveland the first Democrat in the White House since before the Civil War. Another first involving Cleveland is when he became the first president to be married in the White House. The forty-nine-year-old president married twenty-one-year-old Frances Folsom in June 1886; their age difference caused something of a stir among social circles.

In his inaugural address, Cleveland promised equal justice to all. He kept his word when he vetoed a bill that would fund the distribution of seed grain to drought-stricken farmers. True to the traditional Democratic view that federal government should have a limited role in the economy, Cleveland held the belief that federal aid encouraged the expectation of charity and weakened the strength of the nation's character. His beliefs led him to veto pension bills to Civil War veterans when their claims were fraudulent. When Congress passed a bill that would award pensions for disabilities not caused by military service, he vetoed it, as well. Cleveland saw such acts as favoritism, and he refused to support them. Moving into the twenty-first century, no president in American history had used the power to veto as often as Grover Cleveland.

No president before him had ever taken a stand against the railroads. But Cleveland ordered an investigation into railroad land holdings and ordered them to return eighty-one million acres to the government, which then returned the land to the public domain (meaning it belonged to no one person or company). This land had been given to them via government grant. Further, the president signed the Interstate Commerce Act in 1887 (see Chapter 2). This law imposed federal regulations on the railroads, which reduced their power as well as their opportunity for corruption in the form of rate discrimination. Prior to the Act, railroads charged higher rates to shippers sending freight short distances than they did to those needing long-distance service. Sometimes the discrimination originated with the shipper. Standard Oil was notorious for demanding "rebates" from railroads as a reward for choosing one railroad over another (see Chapter 2). The Act was the first attempt to put an end to discrimination involving railroads, regardless of who instigated it.

The other major reform passed in 1887 was the Dawes Severalty Act (see Chapter 5). This law dismantled the reservation system and gave separate parcels of land to individual Native Americans and their families. The results of the Dawes Severalty Act would require Native Americans to adapt to a lifestyle they were unaccustomed to living. Throughout history, they had lived in tribes. Now they would be forced to live apart. Despite Native American protests, the Act was signed into law. In the end, the Act only served to cause the Native Americans to lose their most valuable land. It did not put an end to reservation life, nor did it reduce their dependence on federal assistance.

Cleveland's last attempt at reform was to reduce the protective tariff. Although both Republicans and Democrats drafted bills that slightly reduced the tariff, they were, for the most part, unable to compromise on this important issue.

Cleveland's assault on institutions such as the railroad and private pensions coupled with his attack on the tariff cemented his fate. He was defeated in the 1888 election by the Republican candidate, former U.S. senator Benjamin Harrison (1833–1901; served 1889–93) of Indiana.

Cleveland would be reelected as president after Harrison's term in office. He would deal with severe economic depression (a period marked by low production and sales and high unemployment; businesses often fail in a depression) and its fallout: unemployment, business failure, and farm closures.

President Cleveland intensified his popularity with the way he handled a railroad strike in Chicago. Cleveland sent federal troops to control the situation and force the strikers to adhere to an injunction (order). As noted on Whitehouse. gov, the president assured the American public: "If it takes an entire army and navy of the United States to deliver a post card in Chicago, that card will be delivered."

Cleveland retired from politics and moved to New Jersey. He died in 1908.

Harrison: unable to escape the tariff Harrison received one hundred thousand fewer popular votes than did Cleveland, but he took the majority of electoral votes, 233–168. Even more important, Harrison's election put a Republican in the White House and helped put a majority of Republican seats in both the House of Representatives and the Senate. Prior to his election, Democrats ruled in both the Senate and the House. For the first time in thirteen years, the Republican Party had a solid chance of changing public policy.

From his first day in the White House, Harrison left no doubt that he was there to do business. The Democrats in Congress were used to getting their way, however, and used every strategy they had to block or disable bills and

legislation they did not like. New rules for voting were established to counteract the Democrats' tactics, and with them, the Republicans were able to implement reform.

Harrison's four years in office saw progress in foreign relations. The president also approved funding for internal improvements and naval expansion. He signed the Sherman Anti-Trust Act (see Chapter 2), which prohibited the forming of monopolies (companies that control and retain economic power over an entire service or industry).

But the priority issues were the protective tariff and the surplus (extra) federal budget. The Republicans wanted to reduce the surplus without reducing the tariff. A bill sponsored by Ohio governor William McKinley (1843–1901) and influenced by James Blaine (who was in his second stint as secretary of state, having served for just over nine months for Presidents Garfield and Arthur in 1881) added farm goods to the list of products that would be protected from taxation. By allowing more items to enter the country free, the federal budget would be reduced.

The second part of the bill involved the reciprocal tariff reduction clause. Any country that reduced tariffs on American exports would receive lower tariffs on the goods they exported to America. The McKinley Tariff passed into law on October 1, 1890.

Harrison ran for reelection in 1892 but was defeated by former president Grover Cleveland. Harrison died in 1901.

McKinley: focus on foreign policy Republican William McKinley took over the White House in 1897, making him the last of the Gilded Age presidents. The depression that plagued Cleveland's final term had almost disappeared

WHERE IS HARRISON ?

E. H. ULLMAN, 79 Dearborn Street,
......CHICAGO.

Illustration shows a three-headed presidential bust depicting (from left) President Grover Cleveland, President Benjamin Harrison (who defeated the incumbent Cleveland in 1888), and Cleveland again (who defeated Harrison in 1892 to win back the White House). THE LIBRARY OF CONGRESS.

by 1897, so McKinley was able to turn the focus of America's leadership to foreign policy.

While in office, Spanish military in Cuba was fighting a bloody war against revolutionaries (citizens who organized to fight the government). A quarter of the Cuban population had been wiped out, and those left living were suffering. McKinley announced in April 1898 that America

would intervene in the struggle and fight to help Cuba gain its independence from Spain.

The Spanish-American War lasted one hundred days (see Chapter 11). The United States destroyed the Spanish fleet in Cuba, took the city of Manila, and moved forces into Puerto Rico. McKinley realized that if America was to expand its commercial power into the Far East (and thereby become a superpower throughout the world), it would need to acquire possession of islands in the Pacific. With that in mind, America added the Philippines, Puerto Rico, and Guam to its territory. Never before had America gained control of land and people such a long distance from the United States.

America was pleased with McKinley's leadership and elected him to serve a second term in 1900. Tragedy changed the course of events when the president was shot by Leon Czolgosz (1873–1901), a mentally disturbed anarchist (one who is against rules of any kind), on September 6, 1901. The president died eight days later.

Enter the Progressive Era

McKinley's assassination marked the end of the Gilded Age. He was also the last of what historians call the Log Cabin Presidents, those men who were born into simple, sometimes poverty-stricken, circumstances, yet worked their way up the political ladder to the ultimate seat of leadership.

Republican Theodore Roosevelt (1858–1919; served 1901–9) became the first president of the Progressive Era, a period in history that is remembered for its diligent commitment to change.

For More Information

BOOKS

Ashby, Ruth. *Boss Tweed and Tammany Hall.* San Diego: Blackbirch Press, 2002.

Calhoun, Charles W., ed. *The Gilded Age: Essays on the Origins of Modern America.* Wilmington, DE: Scholarly Resources, 1996.

Cherny, Robert W. *American Politics in the Gilded Age, 1868–1900.* Wheeling, IL: Harlan Davidson, 1997.

Lynch, Denis Tilden. *"Boss" Tweed: The Story of a Grim Generation.* New York: Boni and Liveright, 1927. Reprint, New Brunswick, NJ: Transaction Publishers, 2002.

Painter, Nell Irvin. *Standing at Armageddon.* New York: W. W. Norton & Co., 1987.

WEB SITES

"Big Apple History: Tammany Corruption." *PBSKids.org.* http://pbskids.org/bigapplehistory/business/topic21.html?print (accessed on March 16, 2006).

"Compromise of 1877." *U-S-History.com.* http://www.u-s-history.com/pages/h396.html (accessed on June 16, 2006).

"Election 2000: How We Got Here: A Timeline of the Florida Recount." *CNN.com.* http://archives.cnn.com/2000/ALLPOLITICS/stories/12/13/got.here/index.html (accessed on March 16, 2006).

Library of Congress. "America's Story: Boss Tweed Escaped From Prison December 4, 1875." *America's Library.* http://www.americaslibrary.gov/cgi-bin/page.cgi/jb/recon/boss_1 (accessed on March 16, 2006).

Lincoln Institute. "Roscoe Conkling (1829–1888)." *Mr. Lincoln and New York.* http://www.mrlincolnandnewyork.org/inside.asp?ID=53&subjectID=3 (accessed on March 16, 2006).

The President Benjamin Harrison Home. http://www.presidentbenjaminharrison.org/ (accessed on March 16, 2006).

"Presidential Elections: 1876." *HistoryCentral.com.* http://www.multied.com/elections/1876.html (accessed on March 16, 2006).

"The Presidents of the United States." *The White House.* http://www.whitehouse.gov/history/presidents/ (accessed on March 16, 2006).

"The Rise of the City." *Digital History.* http://www.digitalhistory.uh.edu/database/article_display.cfm?HHID=211 (accessed on March 16, 2006).

"Roscoe Conkling." *Spartacus Educational.* http://www.spartacus.schoolnet.co.uk/USAconkling.htm (accessed on March 16, 2006).

Rutherford B. Hayes Presidential Center. http://www.rbhayes.org/hayes/ (accessed on March 16, 2006).

"Tammany Society." *Spartacus Educational.* http://www.spartacus.schoolnet.co.uk/USAtammany.htm (accessed on March 16, 2006).

2

The Industrialization of America

During and prior to the American Civil War (1861–65), men's roles in society were limited to statesman, farmer, slave, and soldier. But the society that survived the Reconstruction (1865–77) and development of the New South became more diverse. The focus of economic development shifted to business, and the promise of America's future was to be found in industrialism (an economy based on business and industry rather than agriculture). This time period in American history is known as the Industrial Revolution, and it roughly spans from 1877 to 1900.

Industrialism in the Gilded Age was a period of transition. The Gilded Age was the period in history following the Civil War and Reconstruction (roughly the final twenty-three years of the nineteenth century), characterized by a ruthless pursuit of profit, an exterior of showiness and grandeur, and immeasurable political corruption. The country found itself having to adapt to a way of life that no longer centered on agriculture. In 1800, three-quarters of the workforce was in agriculture. By 1900, only four of every ten workers labored in the agrarian (agricultural) sector. The most intense changes took place in the New South, which once depended on a plantation economy (an economy dependent upon agricultural mass production; plantations were huge farms centered around one specific crop, such as tobacco or cotton). Traditionally, Southerners grew crops that were picked by slaves and then shipped to the North and across the oceans to other countries. With the dawn of industrialism, the South could now be directly involved in manufacturing goods. Improved modes of transportation (such as the railroad) and means of communication (such as the telegraph) increased the South's chances for success.

Progress, but at what cost?

Industrial development was not new to the American way of life. Factories already dotted the landscape of New England and the mid-Atlantic

WORDS TO KNOW

antitrust: Against the formation of monopolies or trusts.

Gilded Age: The period in history following the Civil War and Reconstruction (roughly the final twenty-three years of the nineteenth century), characterized by a ruthless pursuit of profit, an exterior of showiness and grandeur, and immeasurable political corruption.

horizontal integration: A business strategy in which one company buys out the competition; commonly known as a merger.

Interstate Commerce Act: Passed in 1887, this law created the Interstate Commerce Commission (ICC), the first federal regulatory agency. It was designed to address railroad abuse and discrimination issues.

monopoly: A condition created when one company dominates a sector of business, leaving the consumer no choices and other businesses no possibility of success.

muckrakers: Journalists who exposed scandal in Gilded Age society. These scandals usually involved public figures and established institutions and businesses, and focused on social issues such as child labor, political corruption, and corporate crime. The term was coined by President Theodore Roosevelt in 1906.

robber barons: The negative label given to powerful industrialists who amassed personal fortunes during the late nineteenth century, generally through corrupt and unethical business practices.

trust: The concept of several companies banding together to form an organization that limits competition by controlling the production and distribution of a product or service.

vertical integration: A business strategy in which one person or company is involved in more than one phase of production of a product or service, making the production process more efficient and, thereby, increasing the amount of production and level of profit.

---

states. What made the industrialization of the Gilded Age different from the manufacturing that was already in place at the time was the influence of new technological innovations. The transcontinental railroad, which was completed in 1869, now allowed goods to be shipped all over the country. The telegraph, which preceded the invention of the telephone, opened communication lines and instantly increased the size of the American marketplace. Now it no longer mattered if the manufacturer's plant was located in the East. Within days, the product could be transported across the country to buyers on the West coast. Although trade with Britain continued, the industrialization of America secured its national independence: With or without Britain's business, the country would thrive.

Other factors contributed to the birth of industrialism in the late nineteenth century. Machinery was made to be more durable. Some of the sturdy, long-lasting machines being built were specialized, that is, made to do just one thing. These new machines allowed manufacturers to produce goods in larger quantities than once was possible. This method of manufacturing became known as the "American System." This system introduced into the economy goods such as sewing machines, bicycles, and cars.

In addition to changes in manufacturing, new ideas about how to market products helped increase consumers' interest in the products. For the first time ever, advertising was a business all its own. Companies used advertising to build brand-name recognition in society and alert consumers to new products on the market.

Metalwork as an industry flourished. Advances in metal production and improvements in cutting and shaping techniques helped usher in the age of industry. The invention of electricity presented Americans with the promise of unlimited power. Ways of working changed inside the factories, too. Engineers reorganized work processes and applied the concept of scientific management. This concept relies on the idea of minimum input or effort for maximum output. Scientific management requires specially designed tools and machinery that work together to develop a product.

Each of these factors added together was responsible for the greatest expansion of industry in American history up to that time. Most people considered this expansion progress, but it did not come without a price. Agrarian workers found their way of life threatened by the newfound technology and industry. The economy no longer depended upon them for survival. These men found themselves out of work, with no hope of finding factory work because they lacked the skills required to run the machinery or manage the factories.

Nevertheless, cities became overcrowded as families moved away from the country to be closer to work. Cities soon became infested by disease and poor living conditions, as Americans and immigrants settled into tenement housing. (See Chapter 8.) Tenement housing was similar in appearance to modern-day apartment buildings, except that the units were incredibly small and had little to no ventilation (fresh air). It was not uncommon for a large family to live in one two-room apartment. Disease developed and spread rapidly through these housing units.

In addition to the dirt and disease found in tenement housing, many Americans thought cities in general were full of sin and corruption. European and Chinese immigrants had settled alongside Americans in these cities. Alcohol consumption, gambling, dancing, and fighting were popular pastimes for city dwellers who worked ten- to twelve-hour days and needed some relaxation in their lives. Although such activities were accepted as a part of the city lifestyle, Americans who enjoyed a higher quality of life or a higher standard of living neither approved of nor understood such behavior.

As evidenced by the necessity of tenement housing, not everyone enjoyed the wealth brought on by industrialism. The distribution of wealth was uneven; most of it went to the already well-to-do white men of the nation. Groups that were already marginalized (part of a lower social standard)—women, African Americans, Native Americans—remained so.

For the most part, Americans came to accept industrialization and all its evils because they enjoyed the benefits it brought them. They had a wider variety of choices as consumers. Products were manufactured more quickly. Household appliances made domestic chores easier and gave women a leisure time they never had before. Jobs were created on a regular basis. Even if life was still not perfect, it was better for many than it had ever been before.

Who really led the Industrial Age?

Although companies such as Standard Oil and Carnegie Steel are largely credited with the

Immigrants rest in their New York City tenement in 1888. Photograph by Jacob Riis. © BETTMANN/CORBIS.

industrial expansion of the Gilded Age, their role in the Industrial Revolution is overemphasized. Their place in history is extraordinary mostly for the business strategies used by their owners, John D. Rockefeller (1839–1937) and Andrew Carnegie (1835–1919). The fact is, most industrial firms of the Gilded Age were not large businesses, but smaller organizations. These smaller firms did not attract as much attention because there was nothing outstanding or unusual about them. Their owners were not

multimillionaires; the companies were not corrupt on any grand scale.

The smaller firms relied on a manufacturing strategy known as custom and batch production. This type of production is the concept of specialty goods made in small lots; this was different from the giant corporations, who manufactured their products in bulk (large quantities). Sometimes these goods were products with short lives that had to be replaced on a regular basis. Other goods were at the

Women in Industry

Industrialization gave birth to consumerism (the idea that the more goods and products a society buys, the better off its economy will be), and women were the primary consumers. The Gilded Age population was 48 percent women. Unlike women in the twenty-first century, there was such a thing as a "typical" woman of the Gilded Age. She was white, middle class, and American born. She was Protestant (Christian, but not Catholic), married, and lived in a small town.

Women were assumed to be morally superior to men and closer to God. This assumption led to double standards in terms of societal values. For example, it was socially acceptable for men to smoke. Women who smoked were looked upon as morally deficient. Men could frequent saloons without being judged; women had no business setting foot inside a bar. Women of the Gilded Age stayed home except to be involved in church functions. They were not allowed to be seen in public alone or together, but rather, only with their husbands.

This difference in the lives of men and women is called the "separate sphere," because women's lives were led separately from men. Women belonged in the home; men had their place in business. Industrialization began to change the concept of the separate sphere by changing domestic work. This occurred for two reasons: Household appliances such as the washing machine and vacuum cleaner made housework easier than it had ever been, and chores that once took hours to complete now could be finished in minutes. This gave women some new-found free time.

Industrialization also created jobs outside the home. By 1900, one in seven women worked outside the home, a statistic that was never even measured before the twentieth century. Most of these jobs were in social reform such as women's and children's rights, education, and housing. (See Chapter 8 for more on the women's movement.)

mercy of fashion and the latest trends. Examples of these products include jewelry, clothing, furniture, and fabrics.

Because of the ever-changing societal attitudes toward fashion and design, these smaller firms had to be flexible. They were not able to produce their goods ahead of demand but had to be able to keep up with trends. For these companies, there was little room for error. If they made a product that did not match what was popular or selling at the moment, they were stuck with it and had to suffer a monetary loss.

These custom and batch production firms did not enjoy the remarkable power of the big business firms like Standard Oil and Carnegie Steel, but they had something those giants lacked: the trust of the American people. The smaller companies still fit within the framework of traditional American values. They seemed, on the surface, at least, to be more concerned with providing a desired product than with making huge profits. They were often run by several generations of the same family. These companies did not dictate the kind of product or the quality of the product to consumers; consumers made the demands and these firms responded.

America's Robber Barons

The term "robber barons" dates back to the twelfth and thirteenth centuries. It described the feudal lords of land who used corruption to increase their wealth and power. Feudalism was a class system of medieval Europe. Only those in the upper class could own land. Citizens of the lower classes could live on and work the land as long as they pledged their loyalty and services to the feudal landlords. The term was revived in the late nineteenth century and used to describe a handful of industrialists who used questionable means to build up personal fortunes. Today, these men would be called billionaires; they had seemingly unlimited amounts of money and were not afraid to let people know it. These business owners used modern strategies like vertical integration (the involvement of a business in all aspects of the production of a product) to increase their wealth and put competitors out of business.

Cornelius Vanderbilt (1794–1877) was considered to be the first robber baron. He quit school at age eleven to help his father make money to support the family. At sixteen, the native New Yorker bought a sailing ship for $100 and began a ferry service from Staten Island to New York City. Vanderbilt eventually established a line of steamboats and became a millionaire before the age of fifty. His net worth increased to $11 million before his sixtieth birthday. In 1857, Vanderbilt invested in the New York & Harlem Railroad. Within six years, he was the company's president. By 1875, the railroad king merged several lines so that his empire served all of the country. Vanderbilt was known to be loud, hardheaded, and somewhat crude. He rarely gave away his money, and when he died in 1877, his $100 million estate was left to William Vanderbilt (1821–1885), one of his thirteen children.

Another robber baron was Andrew Carnegie (1835–1919), a Scottish immigrant who created unimaginable wealth in the American steel industry. Another believer in vertical integration, Carnegie overworked and underpaid his employees, a practice that kept his operating costs to a minimum. He was able to supply his product at a cost less than that of his competitors. As a result, he became one of the world's wealthiest men when he sold his company to U.S. Steel in 1901 for $250 million. Unlike some of his infamous colleagues, Carnegie gave away much of his money to build thousands of library buildings as well as the well-known Carnegie Hall in New York. He also donated to colleges and universities to set up scholarships. When Carnegie died at the age of eighty-three, he had given away most of his wealth.

Among the robber barons was John D. Rockefeller (1839–1937), the man responsible for the establishment of the Standard Oil Company and the American petroleum industry. Rockefeller built his first oil refinery in 1863. By 1877, he controlled 90 percent of the American oil

How big business did business

Big business represented the harshest side of the Industrial Revolution in America. Americans felt pride at the progress their nation was making, but there was also an underlying fear of the power behind these huge corporations. For many people, the concept of big business was equal to greed and corruption. The very men who built their reputations on and made their industry. His business became so large that he found it difficult to manage. Rockefeller's response was to form the first "trust." A trust is an organization of several businesses in the same industry. By banding together, the trust can control the production and distribution of a product or service, thereby limiting competition.

Many considered Jay Gould (1836–1892) to be the prototype (original example) of the robber baron. Viewed in some circles as more corrupt than Carnegie, Rockefeller, and Vanderbilt

combined, Gould became a railroad financier who engaged in a battle with Cornelius Vanderbilt over the Erie Railroad. As soon as Vanderbilt bought stock in the railroad, Gould issued more, illegally. When he was arrested for this act, Gould bribed the New York state legislature to change the laws. By 1872, he was the director of seventeen major railroads and the president of five others. Most of Gould's success was the result of dishonest behavior and corruption. When he died at fifty-seven, his fortune was worth $77 million.

An editorial cartoon shows lowly laborers "supporting" the industries of such wealthy businessmen as Cyrus Field, Jay Gould, Cornelius Vanderbilt, and Russell Sage, whose money is shown weighing down the workers. © HULTON ARCHIVE/GETTY IMAGES.

livelihood in big business were eventually nicknamed the "robber barons" (see box).

Several strategies made big business what it was: big. The first and most obvious difference

between big business and batch and custom firms was size. Big business companies involved such large quantities of money that the concepts of stock markets and investment banking were created to help manage and control the financing of and for these companies.

Whereas the smaller firms were run by one person or a few people, big business was structured using a hierarchy (chain of command) of salaried executives, each of whom had his own special responsibilities and a corresponding salary. Traditional businesses operated in one geographical location, usually a city. These businesses generally had one product to offer, although there could be many styles of that product, as was the case for jewelers, textile manufacturers, and furniture makers. Big businesses may have had one location known to be its central headquarters, but they also had smaller offices or factories elsewhere.

The railroad: leading the way

The best example of big business was the railroad, which was considered the pioneer of big business and became an almost immediate symbol of industrialization in America. Every American, regardless of income level or social class, could identify with the railroad. Since around 1860, the railroad was the center of the national market. It transported not just goods but also people and information. Restrictions on transportation that existed prior to the Civil War, such as weather conditions and geographical distance, no longer factored into trade and commerce.

Size alone put the railroad in a class all by itself. Never had there been a business in which so much money was invested. The fact that the railroad's business took place across an entire country was another first. Management structures and strategies that worked for traditional businesses would not do for the railroad. Its efficiency and safety would depend on a continuous stream of information and accurate recordkeeping. The railroad's success relied on expensive equipment that had to be constantly maintained in safe, working condition. People were required to do that job, while others were needed in areas of accounting, purchasing, customer service, and train operation. In custom and batch firms, one person might handle purchasing and customer service while another took care of the bookkeeping and shop maintenance. This doubling-up of responsibilities was not an option with a company the size and nature of the railroad.

The railroad found that the most efficient means of operation was to divide management into geographical regions, with one central office staff. Each region operated independently but still had to report to the central office. This management structure offered a degree of freedom for each region but also ensured the security of having one staff that enforced the general rules and regulations.

America paid attention to how the railroad conducted business. Since big business was obviously a cornerstone of the Gilded Age society, it was important to determine what worked and what did not work in governing it. The railroad soon experienced a phenomenon that was new to commerce: large-scale competition. Although the railroad was considered one entity, in reality, there were several companies and lines. As soon as a geographic region was served by more than one line, the question became how to be the line most often chosen for transportation of goods and passengers. The obvious solution was to offer the lowest fare.

Competition leads to corruption On the surface, it made sense to lower fares. But as soon as one railroad line did that, the others did, too. However, an operation as large in scale as a railroad had numerous fixed costs just to keep the business going. If fares were lowered, that money had to be compensated for somewhere else; otherwise, profits decreased, and eventually the line would go bankrupt.

Some competitors began reducing prices secretly. They negotiated with large shipping companies, firms the railroads knew could take their business elsewhere. The deal usually included what was called a kickback. The shipper would promise to work with just one particular railroad company, no matter how low the competitors' prices were. In return, the railroad gave the shipper kickbacks in the form of money. This way, the railroad line was guaranteed a certain amount of business, and it had only to provide a rebate—often a percentage of the total bill—to the shipper. This was an unethical way to conduct business, but most railroads were guilty of such practices.

One unforeseen consequence of these kickbacks and competitive pricing schemes was a rapid decline in shipping rates. Near the end of the nineteenth century, rates got so low that railroads were claiming bankruptcy on a regular basis. Management from competing railroads came up with the idea to develop pools. These pools were ways in which competing railroads could cooperate to share business. With pools in place, rates became fixed, as competing railroads agreed they would not go below a specific price. The problem with this solution was that the railroad shipping rates got out of hand. Farmers and other businesses that relied on shipping protested the astronomical rates demanded by the railroads. These protests, in turn, led to government regulatory commissions. Never before in the American

economy did the government judge the situation serious enough to step in and limit the power of commerce.

Government to the rescue? When state governments realized the railroads were taking advantage of the public's need for their services, regulatory commissions were formed. These commissions publicized information about railroad operations in the hopes of educating the public. The theory was that if the public had knowledge of how the railroads operated, citizens and business owners could make more informed choices.

Throughout the 1870s, many states attempted to regulate the power of the railroads. Hesitant to tread where federal government had never gone before, President Ulysses S. Grant (1822–1885; served 1869–77) and the U.S. Supreme Court rarely upheld the ruling of these state-level commissions. Not until 1886 did the U.S. Supreme Court rule that only Congress had the power to regulate commerce between the states. This ruling led to a national movement for federal regulations regarding interstate commerce.

In 1887, under the leadership of President Grover Cleveland (1837–1908; served 1885–89 and 1893–97), Congress passed the Interstate Commerce Act. This act created the Interstate Commerce Commission (ICC), the first federal regulatory agency. The sole purpose of the Commission was to address railroad abuses. The Commission declared that shipping rates had to be "reasonable and just" and that the rates had to be publicly published. Kickbacks and secret rebates were made illegal, and price discrimination against small markets was outlawed.

The last of these four requirements was the hardest to enforce. Railroads traditionally offered lower rates for longer hauls, a practice that worked against many farmers and smaller companies. The ICC had the authority to investigate such discriminatory tactics, but it became immediately clear that determining which prices were discriminatory was hard. The ICC had no specific measures or standards, making the determination politically difficult. The idea of having an ICC was logical, but the reality was not helpful to many of those who relied on the railroads to do business; they continued to be charged unfair rates.

The ICC started out with five members; by 1920, there were eleven members, each of whom served a six-year term. The U.S. president elected members, but he could not remove them. Although the ICC was created to ensure fair play, the reforms it claimed to uphold only went so far, as later presidents appointed commissioners who were pro-railroad.

Big business: I'll do it myself

In addition to management structure, another difference between the batch and custom firms and big business was the actual business strategy itself. The smaller firms usually specialized in one aspect of production. For example, in furniture making, one company supplied the wood, whereas another was responsible for assembling or building the pieces.

Almost without exception, big business owners found success using a strategy called vertical integration. This strategy requires one company to become involved in all aspects of production. This practice cuts costs and allows for better production control. One of the most famous examples of a company that embraced vertical integration was the Carnegie Steel Company. Founded by robber baron Andrew Carnegie (see "America's Robber Barons" box), Carnegie Steel dominated the steel industry. Not only did Carnegie own all the steel mills but also he controlled the iron ore barges, the coal and iron fields, and part of the railroads. His desire to keep operating costs down led him to sell directly to the user whenever possible, rather than to a sales person or a middleman.

Singer, the sewing machine manufacturer, was another company that successfully implemented vertical integration. When Isaac Singer (1811–1875) sold his first sewing machines in 1853 under the company name Singer Manufacturing Company, he knew he had a machine that was considered expensive ($100) by many consumers' standards. To get his machines into the hands of the average housewife, he needed to make it affordable. He set up an installment plan, in which money could be paid toward the account on a regular basis until it was completely paid off. Because the sewing machine was new, Singer's employees had to be ready to give demonstrations to potential buyers and teach them how to use it. Singer recognized the importance of having replacement parts and repairmen readily available.

Rather than rely on other firms to take care of sales and maintenance or to provide instruction to consumers on how to use the sewing machine, Singer took control of all aspects of getting this product into the hands of the Americans who would benefit most from it. His company advertised heavily to build brand-name recognition. The company mass-produced the machines to save on production costs, and it provided its own sales and service personnel. By the 1870s, Singer had sales operations outside North America. Singer was one

Carnegie's Gospel of Wealth

Wealthy Scottish-born businessman Andrew Carnegie believed in using his power and wealth to advance the common good. In this caricature, he is shown wearing Scottish kilts and throwing his money. © THE GRANGER COLLECTION, NEW YORK.

In June 1889, Andrew Carnegie published an article titled "Wealth" in the magazine *North American Review.* Carnegie's philosophy was that men of great wealth were not robber barons but rather trustees of wealth whose duty it was to use their power and good fortune to advance the common good. He believed some men attained wealth because it was God's will. Carnegie claimed, "The man who dies thus rich dies disgraced." Carnegie obviously lived out his beliefs, as by the time of his death, he had given away 95 percent of his wealth.

The Gospel of Wealth was not the first philosophy of its kind. It was actually a more acceptable and politically correct version of an earlier philosophy promoted by social philosopher Herbert Spencer (1820–1903) in 1857. Spencer proposed his philosophy two years before Charles Darwin (1809–1882) publicly presented his theory of evolution. Darwin's proclamation greatly supported Spencer's philosophy, which said that the strong and mighty in society should survive and thrive while the poor and weak be allowed to die. Spencer's idea became known as Social Darwinism.

Social Darwinism upheld the elitist view that colonialism was just; native peoples were naturally weaker and less fit to survive, so white men were doing them a favor by confiscating their land and putting them to work. The theory was applied to military action: The mightiest militaries would be victorious, and the casualties on the losing side were a result of the losers' inability to survive. In the first half of the twentieth century, Social Darwinism was used to uphold the concept of eugenics, in which millions of mentally and physically disabled people were sterilized so that they could not contribute to the national gene pool and produce offspring.

Carnegie's Gospel of Wealth differed from Social Darwinism in that it called on the wealthy to give back to the society that made them rich. Because Carnegie represented the American Dream—a boy born into poverty who worked his way up to society's elite class through hard work and determination—his philosophy was popular throughout the Gilded Age. That is not to say all wealthy men were philanthropists (men who give their money away to worthy causes); nothing could be further from the truth. But his was a rags-to-riches story, and people respected Carnegie's wisdom.

Sewing machine executive Isaac M. Singer.

of the first companies to achieve that degree of expansion.

If you can't beat 'em, join 'em

With competition becoming a major factor of doing business in the early years of the Gilded Age, some corporations determined that vertical integration was not going to give them the power they needed to turn the highest profit. The way to conduct business, then, was to merge companies (bring different companies together as one company). This practice became known as horizontal integration. The Standard Oil Company set the pattern for business mergers. By the late 1870s, Standard owned 90 percent of America's oil refineries. By buying out the competition, Standard overwhelmingly dominated the market.

Standard Oil: an American empire

Prior to the Civil War, there was little need for oil. But the Industrial Revolution created a high demand for oil to run factories' machines, ships, and eventually, automobiles. Oil became a profitable industry. John D. Rockefeller became involved in the oil business in 1863, when he and two partners built a refinery in Cleveland, Ohio. Two years later, Rockefeller bought out his partners and founded Rockefeller & Andrew, Cleveland's largest refinery.

In 1868, Rockefeller negotiated a deal with Jay Gould, owner of the Erie Railroad. Rockefeller guaranteed Gould his business in exchange for rebates (money given back to businesses who used particular railroad companies for all their shipping needs; the money, in effect, acted as a refund of shipping fees), a practice that was eventually outlawed. This was the first of many such deals Rockefeller would make throughout his years as the oil king.

With one million dollars in capital, Rockefeller established Standard Oil Company in 1870. He now owned the largest corporation in the world as well as 10 percent of American oil refineries. Within two years, he was involved in a scandal called the South Improvement Company scheme. This was a secret alliance between the major refiners and the railroads. Although his reputation suffered, Rockefeller took advantage of the scandal to convince other Cleveland refiners to sell him their companies. When the scandal had died down, Rockefeller owned twenty-two of the twenty-six refineries located in Cleveland.

The year 1873 was a disaster for businessmen in America. September 18 of that year was known as Black Thursday, the day the stock exchange crashed and began an economic depression that lasted six years. On that day, the nation's largest financing operation, Jay Cooke & Company, failed due to problems financing the Northern Pacific Railroad. When it failed, fifty-seven more companies involved in stocks and bonds also failed. Millions of people lost millions of dollars in the crash. Rockefeller managed to come out of the nationwide tragedy wealthier than he was when it began. Depending on his colleagues' misfortune, the oil magnate bought refineries throughout Pennsylvania and New York.

By 1877, Rockefeller owned nearly 90 percent of America's oil refineries. In 1879, the forty-year-old was among the country's twenty richest men.

In 1881, journalist/activist Henry Demarest Lloyd (1847–1903) wrote an article for the *Atlantic Monthly* entitled "Story of a Great Monopoly." In it, Lloyd criticized the business strategies and ethics of Rockefeller. A monopoly is created when one company or person controls an entire industry, as Rockefeller basically did in America's oil industry. Monopolies prohibit smaller businesses and companies from operating because they cannot compete with the giant industrialists. Nobody profits from a monopoly except for the company or person in control. Lloyd's article led to a book called *Wealth against Commonwealth* (1894).

Rockefeller created Standard Oil trust in 1882. The trust was incredibly powerful, but the legalities of its existence were shaky at best. A handful of men invested in the trust, thereby becoming trustees. These trustees held all the stock at Standard Oil and so reaped all the profits. Like monopolies, trusts did not work in the favor of consumers. Trusts were built on mergers and fixed prices. Because oil

A political cartoon showing John D. Rockefeller sitting on his monopoly barrel, depicting him as "king of the world." © BETTMANN/CORBIS.

was necessary for daily living at all levels, consumers were forced to pay the prices demanded by Standard.

Americans were quickly becoming disenchanted and distrustful of monopolies. The topic was a major issue in the platforms of both candidates in the 1888 presidential campaign. Both the Democratic candidate, President Grover Cleveland, and the ultimate victor, Republican Benjamin Harrison (1833–1901; served 1889–1893), condemned the creation of monopolies. It would be two years before a law was passed making monopolies and trusts illegal.

The year 1888 also saw a state investigation into Standard Oil and its business practices. Rockefeller was called to the witness stand by the state of New York, but his testimony was evasive. The state could not prove, based on evidence and testimony, that Rockefeller was actually involved in any illegal activity. As a result, Rockefeller continued to conduct business as he always had, despite the fact that his dishonesty and unethical behavior were common knowledge. The following year, Rockefeller made his first charitable donation when he agreed to help found the University of Chicago.

The Sherman Antitrust Act On July 2, 1890, U.S. Congress passed the Sherman Antitrust Act, named after U.S. senator John Sherman (1823–1900) of Ohio, the Republican who introduced it. Prior to the Sherman Act, several states had already passed laws restricting the use of trusts. The laws, however, applied to business conducted only within those states. The Sherman Act declared it illegal to form trusts and monopolies both within states and when dealing with foreign trade. Like many of the laws passed in the Gilded Age, the theory was more promising than reality. With a maximum fine of just $5,000 and one year imprisonment, the consequence of building a trust was not so harsh as to detract those who would be inclined to do so. Although the federal government was now authorized to dissolve trusts, Supreme Court rulings kept them from implementing the Act for years. It was not until Theodore Roosevelt (1858–1919; served 1901–9) was president and enforced his "trust-busting" campaigns that the Sherman Act actually did any good. Future presidents enacted further antitrust legislation. In 1914, President Woodrow Wilson (1856–1924; served 1913–21) established the

Microsoft: Monopoly or Fair Play?

Antitrust laws are still aggressively pursued in America's modern economy. In May 1998, the United States filed a suit against Microsoft Corporation. The United States charged that the computer software company abused monopoly legislation in the way it handled its operating system and web browser sales. After two years of litigation, Microsoft was found guilty of violating the Sherman Act. The judge in charge of the case ordered Microsoft to divide itself into two units: one to produce the operating system, the other to produce software.

Microsoft appealed the verdict, and in November 2001 reached a settlement with the U.S. Department of Justice. Instead of dividing the company into two separate units of operation, Microsoft was ordered to share its application programming interfaces with third-party companies. It would also be required to appoint a panel of three people who would have unlimited access to Microsoft's systems, records, and source code for five years in order to ensure that the company complied (acted in agreement) with the settlement. Nine states and the District of Columbia fought against this settlement, claiming that it did not go far enough to fight the Microsoft monopoly. But on June 30, 2004, the U.S. appeals court approved the settlement. The case has been publicly criticized for not imposing harsher consequences. Others criticized the government for even pursuing Microsoft on terms of business monopoly. They claimed the suit was the result of government joining with smaller competitors against Microsoft to obstruct the bigger company's ability to profit. These critics believe antitrust laws go against the concept of a free marketplace, where all businesses share an equal chance to succeed.

Federal Trade Commission (FTC), a government department designed solely to protect the public from unfair business practices.

John D. Rockefeller decided to retire from Standard Oil in 1895. He did so on a gradual basis (it would take years) and without announcing it publicly. He did not want the public or the press to know of his retirement so that business could continue as usual. Retirement did not keep Rockefeller from being involved in his oil business. In 1896, he contributed $250,000 to the presidential campaign of the Republican candidate, Ohio governor William McKinley (1843–1901). McKinley's Democratic opponent, U.S. representative William Jennings Bryan (1860–1925) of Nebraska, was a staunch supporter of antitrust legislation. The candidates' views on the issue of trusts divided public opinion on the issue as well. In general, Democrats favored antitrust legislation and Republicans were against it. McKinley won the election with 271 electoral votes, leaving the Democrats with just 176.

Between 1898 and 1902, 198 trusts were formed in sugar, coal, and other industries. One of the biggest trusts formed was U.S. Steel, the first billion-dollar corporation. J. P. Morgan bought Carnegie Steel and took over the steel industry.

Rockefeller exposed by muckraker Ida M. Tarbell (1857–1944) was a journalist for *McClure's Magazine*. During the Gilded Age, journalism was a field dominated by men, but Tarbell won acclaim as a muckraker. Newspapers and magazines competed with one another to see who could print the most outrageous stories. During this time, big business was in the habit of ignoring laws that prohibited them from expanding. These two factors led to the development of a type of journalism called muckraking.

Robber Baron with Integrity

J. P. Morgan (1837–1913) was the most powerful force in the business of financing in his lifetime. Morgan was born into a wealthy family. From an early age, he was exposed to international banking. Unlike some of the other robber barons, Morgan was a man of character who considered personal integrity more important than financial success. He opened his own financial services firm on New York's Wall Street in 1862 and joined with the Drexel financing firm nine years later. The new firm was called Drexel, Morgan and Co. Today, Morgan's company is known as JPMorgan, and it owns Chase Bank.

Morgan's bank was responsible for keeping many of the railroads in business when competition began forcing some of them into bankruptcy. Morgan saved, among others, the Baltimore and Ohio, Chesapeake and Ohio, and the Erie lines. Because he conducted business honestly and with a natural sense of authority, people trusted him and took his advice without question. By the time of the Industrial Revolution, Morgan was the man business owners turned to for financing. His list of clients included General Electric and U.S. Steel. Morgan became the leader in America's financial community. When a banking panic threatened the security of big business in 1907, it was Morgan who took control and restored order.

Muckrakers were writers who made it their job to expose scandals, usually involving public figures such as politicians and businessmen. Muckraking was a major type of journalism from 1902 through 1912.

Although President Theodore Roosevelt was not in favor of muckraking and publicly denounced it, Tarbell and others like her continued the practice. Tarbell had already earned a solid reputation as a journalist for a series of articles she wrote for the magazine on the late president Abraham Lincoln (1809–1865; served 1861–65) shortly after she was hired in 1894. That series alone doubled the circulation of *McClure's*. Realizing the power of the press, Tarbell went after Standard Oil with a determination to expose Rockefeller for the sort of businessman many consumers believed him to be but which no one had been able to prove.

For two years, Tarbell researched Standard Oil through court documents, newspapers, and state and federal reports. Through her research, she got an idea of how Rockefeller did business, both publicly and in private. As impressive as her detailed research was, what was even more remarkable was her ability to translate those documents and the information they revealed in terms that the average American consumer could not only understand but find interesting.

"The History of the Standard Oil Company" was a nineteen-part series published over the course of two years, from 1902 to 1904. Tarbell exposed Rockefeller's unethical business tactics while at the same time showing what a brilliant businessman he was. She ended her study of Rockefeller and his empire with a two-part personal exposé. In it, she accused him of being a money-mad hypocrite. "Our national life is on every side distinctly poorer, uglier, meaner, for the kind of influence he exercises," she wrote. Rockefeller was offended by Tarbell's personal attack, but he refused to issue a public response.

Tarbell's series is considered a landmark of investigative journalism. It was among the top five on a 1999 list of the top one hundred works of twentieth-century American journalism.

Journalist Ida M. Tarbell, whose exposés on the Standard Oil Company earned her much praise. THE LIBRARY OF CONGRESS.

The beginning of the end Although President Roosevelt may not have appreciated Tarbell's muckraking, he was in favor of dismantling trusts. By 1906, his public attacks on Standard Oil were increasing in both number and intensity. Public anti-Rockefeller sentiment was also at a peak. People had had enough of Rockefeller's bullying. By 1907, the U.S. government had seven lawsuits pending against Standard Oil. At that time, the company was more than twenty times the size of its nearest competitor. The next year, the government launched its largest antitrust suit to date. Standard Oil was the defendant. It took two years, but in 1911, the U.S. Supreme Court demanded the dismantling of Standard Oil. The company was ordered to rid itself of its subsidiaries (smaller companies owned by Standard) within six months.

By this time, Rockefeller had left the company completely. His worth in 1913 reached its peak at $900 million, due in part to the selling of Standard Oil.

Although Rockefeller's business heyday was past, he continued to be burdened by problems. The later years would find him in another lawsuit, this time regarding the deaths of miners at one of the mines he owned in Colorado (see Chapter 3). Rockefeller died in 1937, leaving the bulk of his wealth to his son, John D. Rockefeller Jr. (1874–1960).

A tragic and uncertain future

Although some progress had been made in regulating big business, the government tended to stay out of the business of running a business in the late nineteenth century. The term for this concept of nonintervention is *laissez faire,* a French expression that means "to leave alone."

Laissez faire clearly was not working during this time of great transition. For the first time in history, industry had taken over the American way of life. Billion-dollar corporations were taking hold and taking over. Products were being mass-produced at a rate never imagined. With the growth in industry and opportunity came an increase in the incidence of corruption and greed. Big business owners soon learned that competition was something to overcome and trample. At a time when government should have been thinking about how to best usher in this new movement of a wage-earning society, it was, instead, turning its collective head and ignoring the escalating economic crisis.

People can be ignored only for so long before taking matters into their own hands. It was only a matter of time before violence would erupt as workers and management pitted against one another in what has become known as the Labor Movement.

For More Information
BOOKS

Baker, James T. *Andrew Carnegie: Robber Baron as American Hero.* Belmont, CA: Wadsworth Publishing, 2002.

Calhoun, Charles W. *The Gilded Age: Essays on the Origins of Modern America.* Wilmington, DE: Scholarly Resources, 1996.

Painter, Nell Irvin. *Standing at Armageddon: The United States, 1877–1919.* New York: W. W. Norton & Co., 1987.

WEB SITES

"Andrew Carnegie: The Gilded Age." *PBS.org.* http://www.pbs.org/wgbh/amex/carnegie/gildedage.html (accessed on April 3, 2006).

Carnegie, Andrew. "Wealth." *Internet Modern History Sourcebook.* http://www.fordham.edu/halsall/mod/1889carnegie.html (accessed on April 3, 2006).

"History." *Singer: At Home Worldwide.* http://www.singerco.com/company/history.html (accessed on April 3, 2006).

"The Rockefellers: People & Events: Ida Tarbell, 1857–1944." *PBS.org.* http://www.pbs.org/wgbh/amex/rockefellers/peopleevents/p_tarbell.html (accessed on April 3, 2006).

"The Rockefellers: Rockefellers Timeline." *PBS.org.* http://www.pbs.org/wgbh/amex/rockefellers/timeline/index.html (accessed on April 3, 2006).

Spencer, Herbert. "Progress: Its Law and Causes." *Internet Modern History Sourcebook.* http://www.fordham.edu/halsall/mod/spencer-darwin.html (accessed on April 3, 2006).

Tarbell, Ida M. *The History of the Standard Oil Company.* http://www.history.rochester.edu/fuels/tarbell/MAIN.HTM (accessed on April 3, 2006).

3

Heartaches and Hardships of the Labor Movement

Discontent among laborers and employees was not a concept unique to the Gilded Age. The Gilded Age was the period in history following the American Civil War (1861–65) and Reconstruction (roughly the final twenty-three years of the nineteenth century), characterized by a ruthless pursuit of profit, an exterior of showiness and grandeur, and immeasurable political corruption. For as long as people have worked for other people, labor conditions and wages have been issues. This unrest among workers intensified in the late nineteenth century because more people were earning wages.

Between 1860 and 1900, the number of workers in manufacturing quadrupled to six million. The 1870 U.S. census (a periodic count of the country's population, and related statistics as well) revealed that 67 percent of productivity relied on human labor. The Industrial Revolution (1877–1900) served only to increase that percentage and made America a nation of wage earners. When people are paid for their work by other people, it is called the wages system.

Coal mining: industry of sorrow

The primary industry of Pennsylvania in the 1860s was coal mining. The number of mine workers in 1870 peaked at around fifty-three thousand, compared with twenty-five thousand in 1860. Of these thousands, a full third were Irish immigrants.

The Irish were targets of discrimination and prejudice during those days, in America and elsewhere. (For more information, see Chapter 4.) Many people disliked the Irish because of their Catholic roots and because they were the least educated of all the immigrant groups in general. In addition, unlike other foreign workers in the coal mines, the Irish did not accept unfair treatment as just another part of the job. Instead, they

WORDS TO KNOW

Ancient Order of Hibernians (AOH): A Catholic organization formed in America in 1836. Some of its members came from various organizations created centuries earlier in Ireland. The purpose of the AOH was to help Irish Catholic immigrants settle in America and to defend them from persecution. One way the AOH defended its members was to keep its meetings and actions secret.

Gilded Age: The period in history following the Civil War and Reconstruction (roughly the final twenty-three years of the nineteenth century), characterized by a ruthless pursuit of profit, an exterior of showiness and grandeur, and immeasurable political corruption.

labor union: A formally organized association of workers that advances its members' views on wages, work hours, and labor conditions.

Molly Maguires: A secret society of workers established in Ireland in the 1840s whose mission was to fight discrimination. Some of its members immigrated to America later in the century. The Mollies were blamed for violence in the coal regions, though evidence against them was nonexistent.

socialism: An economic system in which the government owns and operates business and production as well as controls the distribution of wealth.

strike: A work stoppage by employees in protest of unfair treatment.

strikebreakers: Companies or individual employees who provide work during a strike; sometimes called scabs.

wages system: An economic system in which people rely on other people to earn a living. Employees are paid money for their services.

---

fought back when anyone tried to take advantage of them. They did not hesitate to speak out in their own defense because they knew no one else would.

Some of the biggest mines in the coal regions were British owned. The English stockholders appointed white, American Protestants (Christians, but not Catholics) as the officials in these mines. These white Protestants, in turn, hired Welsh and English miners to work the mines. These miners worked on a contract basis, meaning they were paid by the ton of coal mined. The more coal mined, the higher the wage. These contract miners hired laborers to do the hardest work. Most of the laborers were Irish, and they were paid only a fraction of what the contract miners received.

Mine superintendents (bosses) were usually Welsh, though some were English. When a top mining job opened up, these superintendents filled it with another Welshman or Englishman. The Irish laborers, whose work was harder and yet who received lower pay, constantly saw others being promoted while they remained in the lowest positions. Normally, a worker can go to a boss to complain of unfair treatment. In the case of the Irish mineworkers, those Irishmen who complained were blacklisted (had their names put on a list that was shared among all mines throughout the coal region) and could not get a job at all. They had no way to change policy and procedures.

No life of leisure Regardless of a miner's ethnic roots, his life was one of intense hardship. Some men began working the mines at the age of eight. (See more about the hardships of mining in Chapter 8.) Before the advent of electricity, they worked in mines 1,200 feet below the ground in total darkness except for the tiny flame on the front of their helmets. Those mine shafts were cold, so much so that miners' fingers would crack and bleed daily.

Each mine had a heated office or shed for the superintendent. Each mine also had an emergency hospital or first aid room. If a miner was injured, he was immediately taken to this room before being sent to the surface. These hospitals contained one or two stretchers and basic first aid supplies.

Miners faced great danger every day. The lamp on a miner's cap was fueled with fish or whale oil. Its light was poor and dangerous. Mines were filled with the earth's natural gases, and many gas explosions were ignited by the flame from a miner's cap. In addition, miners had to grow accustomed to being burned with dripping oil from their caps. Shortly after the beginning of the twentieth century, the carbide lamp appeared. This lamp used flint (quartz that sparks when steel strikes it) to produce a bright, white flame. While the carbide was a vast improvement over the old oil flame, it still produced an open flame that could cause an explosion.

Ventilation (the free flow of air) in mines was essential but difficult to provide because of the great depths at which the shafts lay below the earth's surface. Mines were damp, filled with carbon dioxide, gas, dust, and smoke. Miners in general did not live long lives. Many died of black lung, a disease that results from breathing coal dust. For the most part, the younger the man was when he began working the mines as a boy, the younger he was when he died.

Miners lived in small towns called patches. Mining companies owned these towns, and the families who lived there were never given the opportunity to own the homes. All rent money went directly back to the mine company. One such town still exists today in Stroudsburg, Pennsylvania. The town is called Eckley, and it consists of one partially paved road. Eckley was built in 1854 and is home to 150 buildings. Population peaked at nearly two thousand people in the 1880s, with up to fifteen people living in one double-family home. In the twenty-first century, just twenty residents remain, most of them descendants of miners who once lived there. They are still not allowed to own their homes because the town is owned by the Commonwealth of Pennsylvania. In an effort to maintain its historical accuracy, Pennsylvania forbids private ownership of any of Eckley's buildings. Given this protection, the now-historic village is a slice of life from an era long gone.

Perhaps the biggest injustice of all was the miner's wage. The average laborer earned less than twenty-five cents an hour until 1913, when his wage was raised to a quarter an hour. With this money, he had to buy all his own mining tools and supplies, including lamp oil, clothing, gloves, and picks. There was little left to buy his family food and other necessities. To make matters worse, wages at some mines were paid in script. Script was redeemable only at mine-owned company stores, where prices for basic goods were higher than at regular general stores and shops. These miners earned less money than

A two-family dwelling in the Eckley Miners' Village in Stroudsburg, Pennsylvania. The entire village was owned by coal companies in the mid-1800s. REBECCA VALENTINE.

laborers in many other industries, and they were forced to pay higher prices for everyday items.

One conflict leads to another The first significant conflict involving the Irish occurred during the Civil War. President Abraham Lincoln (1809–1865; served 1861–65) had passed a law allowing men to be free from service in the military if they paid a sum of $300. Irish laborers considered this a violation of their civil rights because they barely had enough money to feed and clothe their families. Antidraft riots broke out all

over the nation and included citizens of all nationalities.

In the years to come, a secret organization called the Ancient Order of Hibernians would be blamed for the riots. The blame came mainly from a newspaper owned by Welsh-American Benjamin Bannan (1807–1875). Bannan did not bother to hide his hatred of the Catholic Church or Irish immigrants. He openly sided with the Welsh and English miners in all matters. He wrote an article for his *Miner's Journal* in which he claimed that the only thing the Irish were good for was opening saloons and hanging out in them. It was Bannan who first blamed all crime and violence on the Irish, and it was he who almost singlehandedly started the American legend of a secret society called the Molly Maguires. This group, started in Ireland in the 1840s, was established with the goal of fighting discrimination. Some of its members immigrated to America later in the century. The Mollies were blamed for violence in the coal regions, though evidence against them was nonexistent.

There was a high incidence of crime in the coal regions throughout the 1860s and 1870s. The Irish were involved in riots, arson, and murder. But crime statistics from that era indicate that the crime rate was as high before the Molly Maguires supposedly took over as it was after they came on the scene. Neither did the crime rate drop even after twenty alleged Mollies were hanged and hundreds of others imprisoned. Other coal mining areas in America also experienced similar levels of crime during those decades, leading historians to believe that the crime was a result of the mining industry conditions, not the Irish discontent.

The Ancient Order of Hibernians The Ancient Order of Hibernians (AOH) is the oldest Catholic organization in America. (Hibernia is the Latin name for Ireland.) It was formed in 1836 in New York and by several organizations that were themselves formed centuries earlier in Ireland. As the members of these organizations immigrated to America, they reformed old alliances and renamed themselves the Ancient Order of Hibernians.

As immigration increased, so did prejudice against the Irish. In every city, shopkeepers hung signs in windows that read "No Irish Need Apply," to let these immigrants know

they had no chance of being hired for a job. After the Irish and even their churches became targets of violence in some cities, members of AOH felt they would have to resort to tactics once used in Ireland, mainly violence and sabotage (damage done on purpose). But that did not come to pass, as physical attacks against them were, in fact, few.

The AOH remained a secret organization in its early years in America. Its outreach included giving Irish immigrant members money when they arrived in America. It also gave them aid in finding housing and jobs.

Railroads versus the mines

Franklin Gowen (1836–1889) was the president of the Reading Railroad in 1866. This line was the main transporter of coal between Schuylkill (pronounced SKOO-kul) County and Philadelphia, Pennsylvania. Within two years of becoming president, Gowen purchased 200,000 acres of coal mining land for the Reading Railroad. Now that he owned a large percentage of the coal mines in that region, Gowen focused his attention to turning a profit from the mines.

Gowen became concerned with an Irish immigrant named John Siney (1831–1879). In 1868, Siney formed the Workers Benevolent Association (WBA), a labor union for miners. (A labor union is a formally organized association of workers that advances its members' views on wages, work hours, and labor conditions.) Even though Siney strictly forbid the use of violence by WBA members, Gowen became suspicious of Siney when a few mine bosses were found murdered in the Schuylkill region.

Gowen was not the only big business owner who was worried about the mining regions of Pennsylvania. Asa Packer (1805–1879) owned

The Conflict between Protestants and Catholics

Until the mid-1800s, the Roman Catholic population in America tended to be wealthy and enjoy a comfortable lifestyle. In the 1840s, millions of Irish Catholics left Ireland in search of a better life in America. Their appearance in the United States changed the Catholic population forever. American Catholics, once educated members of the aristocracy, or upper class, now included poverty-stricken immigrants from various countries—primarily Ireland—who spoke many languages. Although immigrants of other religions came to the shores of America, their appearance did not have the same impact as that of their Catholic peers. In 1850, Catholics comprised just 5 percent of the American population. By 1906, they made up 17 percent and were the largest religious denomination in the United States.

Immigration brought to the surface the fears and insecurities of many Americans. Citizens were coming to terms with accepting major shifts in life as they knew it. With the arrival of so many Catholics, upper-class American Catholics were expected to embrace lower-class immigrant Catholics. This was no easy task for aristocratic society, whose members enjoyed the class differences and the benefits associated with those differences. For non-Catholic Americans, they had to deal with an influx of people who did not share their beliefs. Catholic churches were being built in every American neighborhood. To some, it must have seemed as if Catholicism was taking over America.

Many Americans had mixed feelings about immigration anyway. Yes, immigrants would provide cheap labor to keep alive industrialism (an economy based on business and industry rather than agriculture). But they viewed immigrants as different. They had foreign manners and behavior. They were not American. Immigrants came to the shores of New York with great hopes of a

Lehigh Railroad, another major transporter in the region. Charles Parrish (1826–1896) owned the Lehigh & Wilkes Barre Coal Company. Gowen, Packer, and Parrish were among the wealthiest men in the country in the 1870s. Their financial security depended on increased coal production, which in turn meant increased use of the railroads. The three men bought large interests in the mines so that they could control the shipping of the coal. The plan was to ship as much coal out of the region as quickly as possible to ensure quick profit.

In an effort to improve relations between the union miners and the mine owners, Siney negotiated an agreement with Gowen. If the price of coal rose, so did the wages of the workers.

There was nothing said about a situation where the price of coal might decrease, and when the market became oversupplied with coal due to the plan of Packer, Gowen, and Parrish, the price of coal fell. Miners watched helplessly as their wages were cut by 50 percent. Even after working sixty hours a week, they did not have enough money to feed their families.

"Wildcat" strikes—those not sponsored by a formal organization but undertaken by miners on their own—took place in the mines owned by Gowen, Parrish, and Packer. The Irish led these strikes. Although Siney and most Welsh miners were against the strikes, the Irish and some other laborers felt it was time to demand a guaranteed wage.

better life, but they must have been terrified at the prospect of coming to a foreign land with no knowledge of the language or customs.

Feelings about immigration from both immigrants and Americans were expressed in their religious views. Catholicism gave immigrants a feeling of comfort and security. It was something they were able to bring over with them to a new land. Americans blamed Catholicism for the foreign invasion of their own comfort and familiarity. Yet it was the Catholic Church that made the greatest effort to welcome immigrants to America. The Church helped them find jobs and homes. It taught their children the basics of the English language. It looked out for their political interests.

Although Protestants and Catholics are Christian denominations, they differ in certain ways. For example, Protestants did not agree with the strict hierarchy (chain of command) in the church structure. Catholicism relies heavily on the authority of its leaders, beginning with the Pope in Rome. Protestants believed the Bible was the source of God's word; Catholics used rituals like confession and Mass to keep in contact with God. Protestants considered Jesus to be the only link between themselves and God; Catholics believed prayers should be offered to the saints. These few differences pitted Catholics against Protestants for four centuries before immigrants arrived in America.

Beyond these doctrinal, or policy, differences, the conflict also involved social class. Many upper-class Americans considered immigrants lazy and dangerous simply because they were poor and had different customs and ways of doing things. For lower-class Americans, immigrants competed for jobs and a place in society they considered belonged to them by right of birth. Eventually, Congress passed immigration restriction laws that limited the number of people allowed into America. Catholic immigration came to a standstill by 1924. (See Chapter 4 for more on immigration.)

Packer, Gowen, and Parrish recognized a business opportunity when they saw it and they seized it. While mining conditions were chaotic, the three men drove the smaller mines out of business. Those smaller mines could not handle the demands for higher wages from workers as well as demands for higher freight charges from the railroads. Soon the small mines were forced out of business and bought by Gowen, Parrish, and Packer. They now owned all the mines and railroads in the Schuylkill and nearby Carbon County region. They agreed not to compete with one another and met with other mine owners and railroad tycoons in 1873 to set the wholesale cost of coal.

The only uncontrollable factor in their successful mining equation was the WBA, especially the Irish membership. Gowen had big plans to build a monopoly in the mining industry, not only in the Pennsylvania regions but throughout the country. The WBA and AOH were the only obstacles in his way. Gowen hired the Pinkerton Detective Agency (see box) in 1873 to help him destroy the union and the AOH. Gowen (and possibly Parrish and Packer, although no hard evidence of it exists) paid Pinkerton $100,000 to gain access to the WBA with spies. Pinkerton sent Irish immigrant James McParland (1843–c. 1918) into Schuylkill County.

For two years, McParland lived under the alias James McKenna. He joined the AOH and the WBA and found work as a laborer. Within months of beginning his undercover work,

Pinkerton's National Detective Agency

Pinkerton's National Detective Agency was founded by Allan Pinkerton (1819–1884) in 1850. The Scottish-born Pinkerton emigrated to the Chicago area at the age of twenty-three in 1842. The Pinkerton Agency was one of the first private detective agencies in the United States and was the model used in the development of the Federal Bureau of Investigation (FBI).

America's law enforcement forces during the mid-1880s were, at best, capable of handling ordinary crimes such as theft and arson. For crimes involving murder, or those committed against the government, authorities relied on Pinkerton to solve the mystery. (In fact, Pinkerton was involved in thwarting an assassination plot against President-elect Abraham Lincoln in 1861.) Much of Pinkerton's business came from banks and shipping organizations such as railroads. As America became more industrialized, the agency accepted assignments from big businesses as well. Agents often infiltrated companies as spies. They also worked with strikebreakers, companies that provided cheap labor for industries when regular workers went on strike. In the 1880s alone, the agency provided services for seventy labor disputes, including the infamous Homestead Strike of 1892 (see later in this chapter). Soon, the

Pinkerton Detective Agency was considered the enemy of the common laborer.

The agency advertised itself as the "all-seeing eye." The company's logo included the eye; its motto was "We never sleep." This logo and motto eventually led to the establishment of the term "private eye."

The Pinkerton Agency depended on armed guards as well as spies like James McParland. Although the agency was highly regarded throughout the Gilded Age, modern historians have acknowledged that the detectives' methods were not always ethical. It is generally accepted, for example, that the testimony provided by McParland against the alleged Molly Maguires was made up. Evidence has never been found to prove any truth to McParland's claims. Pinkerton himself knew his detectives were not always truthful, but he felt the results justified the means; that is, if criminals were taken off the streets, then it did not matter how they were removed. This attitude does not take into consideration the imprisonment and death of innocent people.

When the Pinkerton Agency was established, there were fifteen operatives (detectives). By the early 1890s, there were two thousand active

McParland reported to Pinkerton that he believed the AOH was involved with a secret society called the Molly Maguires. The origins of the Mollies are not certain; even the history behind the name is unclear. What is known is that the society was formed in Ireland in the 1840s to fight worker discrimination, and some of its members emigrated to America later in the century. In order to join the Mollies in America,

Irishmen had to first join the AOH. But very few AOH members were Mollies. The Molly Maguires relied on terrorist tactics, including murder, to reach their goals. McParland—and eventually Gowen, Packer, and Parrish, along with the help of newspaper publisher Bannan—tried to convince authorities that all AOH members were Mollies. Because most AOH members were also involved in the agents and several thousand reservists (agents called upon only in time of need). When Allan Pinkerton died in 1884, his sons took over management of the company, which brought in nearly $2 million a year in the 1920s.

When Robert Pinkerton II (1904–1967), great-grandson of the founder, took over, he ended the agency's antiunion operations. The company's name changed to Pinkerton's Incorporated in the 1960s, and its headquarters moved to California. The agency had seventy branch offices throughout the United States and included about thirteen thousand full-time employees. In 1999, Pinkerton's was bought by a Swedish security company called Securitas.

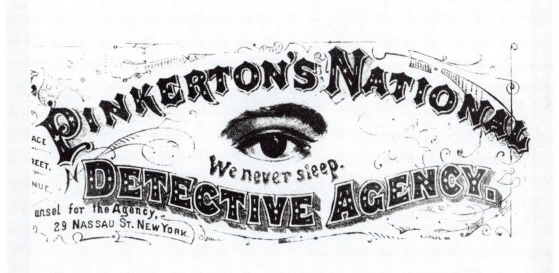

The logo of Pinkerton's National Detective Agency. The eye in the firm's logo led to the term "private eye."
© THE GRANGER COLLECTION, NEW YORK.

WBA, argued McParland and Bannan, both organizations had to be eliminated in order to destroy their power. McParland knew there was no truth to this claim, but that fact was merely an inconvenience.

Wrongful deaths? It took several years of undercover work by McParland, hundreds of pages of false court testimony on the part of police and citizens, and the cooperation of the wealthiest men in America to finally destroy the WBA, but in 1877 and 1878, twenty Irish Americans alleged to be Molly Maguires were hanged for the murders of sixteen or seventeen men (historical accounts vary), most of them mining officials. One of the executed, Alexander Campbell, claimed his innocence until the day he died. Hours before his execution, Campbell placed a dirt-covered hand on the wall of his prison cell and declared his handprint would be a constant reminder that the Pennsylvania town of Mauch Chunk (now called Jim Thorpe) had hanged an innocent man. Legend has it that despite every attempt of prison authorities to remove the handprint, including the destruction of that cell wall in 1930 and its subsequent rebuilding, a faint handprint remains visible to the naked eye. Natives of the town swear it is Campbell's handprint. Others call it a hoax. Regardless, the prison is now a historic landmark visited by thousands of tourists annually.

The AOH suffered from the Molly Maguire scandal, but it was not destroyed. The scandal did not give Parrish, Gowen, and Packer the results they had hoped for, either. Each of the men was affected when an economic recession hit in 1878. (An economic recession is a time of reduced business activity that usually results in rising unemployment rates and a drop in prices for goods and services.) Gowen declared bankruptcy in 1880 and shot himself to death nine years later. Parrish went bankrupt in 1878 and died the following year. Packer died in 1879, and within two years, his company went bankrupt as well. McParland became a Pinkerton manager and continued his union-busting business. He slowly slid into a paranoid insanity, existing under the fear that the descendants of the Molly Maguires were out to assassinate him for revenge. He died alone in a Denver, Colorado, hospital bed in either 1918 or 1919 (records vary).

Knights of Labor

The Molly Maguire scandal in Pennsylvania was not the only one of its kind. But it is representative of all the many issues that led to the labor disputes of the Gilded Age: prejudice against

immigrants; greed of big business owners versus the rights of workers; social class distinctions. That scandal illustrates well the reasons American and immigrant workers alike were willing to risk their lives to form labor unions. Without the unions, and sometimes, even with them, laborers' rights were difficult to demand and enforce.

Pennsylvania in particular was a place of intense labor union efforts. As far back as the 1790s, shoemakers in Philadelphia joined efforts to fix a pricing structure and keep out cheap competition. In the 1820s, a mechanics' union was formed. In 1869, one of the most powerful labor unions ever formed was organized in Philadelphia. Under the leadership of Uriah S. Stephens (1821–1882), nine tailors established the Noble Order of the Knights of Labor (KOL). The KOL differed from previous unions in that it allowed both unskilled and skilled laborers to join. Prior to the Industrial Revolution, most laborers were skilled craftsmen. But with the advent of machinery that could do the work of many men, businesses did not need to hire (or pay the higher wages for) as many skilled laborers. Much of the workforce of the late nineteenth century was unskilled. The KOL also welcomed women and African Americans into its ranks. During its early years, the KOL met in secrecy. By the 1880s, it had become a national force.

Among other goals, the KOL negotiated for an eight-hour work day (ten- or twelve-hour shifts had been the norm), an end to child labor, equal pay for equal work (which meant that regardless of sex and race, people who performed the same task would be paid the same wage), and an income tax that would require higher taxes to be paid by those who earned more. The KOL also worked to have the telegraph and railroad industries become government-owned so that private businessmen could not gouge workers with high prices.

Because the KOL was open to all workers, its membership grew rapidly. In 1884, fifty thousand laborers were Knights. By 1886, that number had jumped to seven hundred thousand. Membership was open to all craft and trade occupations, such as machinist, blacksmith, and carpenter. Workers in the professional sector, such as lawyers and doctors, could not join.

The KOL did not support worker strikes in the early years of its existence. In 1877, the same year as the first of the Molly Maguire hangings, the Great Railroad Strike occurred. The violence in the mining regions of Pennsylvania was not merely a state issue; people across the country knew what had been going on. They knew of the mine officials' murders, the Molly Maguire scandal, and the railroad forces that were behind the executions of ten (soon to be twenty) men who many believed were innocent of the charges against them. The mood among laborers across America was one of bitter resentment. Pennsylvania would soon find itself home to yet another industry scandal.

The Great Railroad Strike

The year 1873 was one of economic depression in America. (An economic depression is a period of low production and sales and high rates of unemployment and business failures.) The root cause of the 1873 depression was the collapse of the mighty railroad. The main reason for the collapse was simple: The railroad had overextended itself. With the last spike driven into the Transcontinental Railroad in 1869, America's obsession with the railroad began. In its excitement, railroad tracks were being built in every

direction. Two-thirds of the track headed west, an area still largely unsettled. So by 1873, there were thousands of miles of railroad tracks going virtually nowhere, at least nowhere that could be profitable to shippers or the railroads. Just one year prior, two-thirds of all railroads were unable to pay their stockholders dividends (the amount of money an investor makes off a company).

In 1873, Jay Cooke & Company failed. Jay Cooke (1821–1905) had been the chief financier of the railroads. With branches closing in New York and Philadelphia, railroad construction came to an abrupt halt. Railroad workers suddenly found themselves without jobs; by 1874, five hundred thousand railroad employees were out of work. By the end of 1873 alone, more than five thousand businesses had failed.

By 1877, 20 percent of the entire labor force in America was unemployed. Another 20 percent was working regular hours; the remaining 60 percent worked irregular hours and took work when it was available. Railroad workers were laboring at wages a full 35 percent below what they had made prior to the depression. The Pennsylvania Railroad announced it would reduce wages another 10 percent effective June 1, 1877. Soon, other eastern railroads announced similar cuts. Workers could take no more. At a time when they were already making next to nothing and working fifteen to eighteen hours a day to earn it, they were expected to accept even less.

On July 16, 1877, forty firemen and brakemen from the Baltimore & Ohio Railroad went on strike in Maryland. Police quickly broke up the crowd. A second strike took place the next day in West Virginia, and this time, strikers seized control of the train depot. Trains were

The Union Depot and Hotel in Pittsburgh, Pennsylvania, burn during the Great Railroad Strike of 1877. © CORBIS.

not coming in or leaving. Police arrested strike leaders, but the crowd managed to release them. President Rutherford B. Hayes (1822–1893; served 1877–81) sent in federal troops to take control. It was the first time a U.S. president took federal action against strikers.

On July 19, strikers of the Pennsylvania Railroad marched at Pittsburgh. This strike led to rioting. Federal troops were sent in from Philadelphia, and when they fired into the crowd, twenty-five people were killed and more were wounded. This event served only to infuriate the strikers further. They set fire to freight cars and sent them into the roundhouse (garage for trains) where soldiers were gathered. Though

the forces escaped, they were not able to prevent the angry mob, which had grown to somewhere between four and five thousand people, from destroying the depot. Five hundred train cars, over one hundred locomotives, and thirty-nine buildings were destroyed. While all this was happening, similar riots were taking place at depots across Pennsylvania. Freight was going nowhere; trains could not run. Federal troops restored order one city at a time. Strikers returned to work; though not victorious, they had caused more than $10 million in property damages.

Although the railroad crisis lasted just one month, the consequences were influential for years. The public had sided with the railroad laborers; they knew these men were working in unsatisfactory conditions and with very little pay. But after the Great Strike, middle- and upper-class Americans now felt the necessity to take a stand against labor. They felt these men, and not just railroad workers, must be controlled by any means available. Miners, sewer workers, and millhands all joined in on the side of the railroad strikers. It was America against the laborer, and the battle had just taken a drastic turn. For the first time, workers realized they had true power.

Terence V. Powderly and the KOL

In September 1879, a machinist and union organizer, Terence V. Powderly (1849–1924), became grand master workman, the highest position in the KOL. Powderly was an Irishman living in Pennsylvania. In addition to being a laborer, he practiced law and managed a grocery store.

Powderly was a small, dainty man. He did not fit the image of a strong union leader. But his political skills were such that he kept his grand master position for fourteen years. Powderly was a skilled public speaker, able to inspire his listeners and move them to action. His vision for the KOL was of the skilled worker defending the unskilled worker as well. That blend of skill levels was one of the reasons the KOL attracted so many members, but it would also be one of the main reasons for its end.

Most skilled workers did not want to join forces with the unskilled. They felt they had nothing to gain from such a union. That is why traditional labor unions did not allow unskilled workmen to join. It was only a matter of time before the traditional unions pitted themselves against the KOL.

The Knights played important roles in a number of strikes throughout the winter of 1883–84. In 1885, they found themselves involved in a major railroad strike involving the Wabash line. Financier Jay Gould (1836–1892) owned and controlled much of the Southwest railroad system, including the Wabash line. Gould was known for his unethical business tactics, which included blackmail (demanding money in exchange for withholding potentially damaging information). Workers of the Wabash line, some of whom were Knights, were not happy with their work situation and went on strike. Without them, Gould's entire system could not operate. He was forced to deal with the Knights, and the KOL's "victory" over the railroad's most celebrated businessman earned them the leadership of the labor movement. Total membership increased, and Powderly was the undisputed king. The honor proved to be short-lived.

The Haymarket Square riot

In early 1886, labor unions throughout the country began coordinating a movement for the eight-hour workday. On May 1, laborers from many industries went on strike. On May 3, strikers at the McCormick Reaper Works factory encountered police who attacked the unarmed strikers, killing several of them.

Events got out of control on May 4 in Chicago's Haymarket Square. A peaceful protest meeting was being held in the square. Participants were publicly denouncing the police brutality that led to the tragic events of the day before. As the Haymarket meeting was finishing, police arrived to break up the crowd, which was already dispersing of its own accord. Someone from the crowd threw a bomb into the group

A scene from the Haymarket Riot in Chicago, Illinois, in 1866. © BETTMANN/CORBIS.

of police officers. One officer was killed immediately, and seven more died later as a result of their injuries. A riot broke out and shots from both sides were fired. No one knows for certain how many protesters were killed in the riot. As soon as they fell, friends and coworkers dragged them to safety. The bomber was never identified.

The Haymarket Square riot did not help the laborers achieve their goal. Instead, it served to intensify the disgust of middle- and upper-class society toward the working class. Americans were demanding justice for the fallen police officers. Newspapers encouraged the ill will toward the strikers in particular, laborers in general. Eight Chicago anarchists (proponents of a society without rules) were eventually arrested and

charged with conspiracy to murder. A jury comprised primarily of businessmen and clerks found all the defendants guilty, even though no physical evidence tied them to the bombing. One defendant was sentenced to fifteen years in prison; the rest were hanged on November 11, 1887.

The Haymarket Square riot turned out to be the turning point for the Knights. With the events in Chicago, public opinion of labor unions hit a low point. Citizens were vocal in their hatred of the labor organizations, including the KOL. During the eight-hour-day movement, the Knights aborted a strike effort in a Chicago stockyard. Although workers had already convinced officials that negotiations among management and labor were necessary, Powderly ordered the Knights back to work, and the control reverted to management. Any authority the KOL once had was quickly disintegrating. By 1900, membership in the KOL had dropped to one hundred thousand workers.

Formation of the American Federation of Labor

New York in the 1880s had a large immigrant population. Immigrants lived in crowded slums (poor neighborhoods) and worked in sweatshops (factories known for unsafe working conditions and low wages). Often, the sweatshops also served as immigrants' apartments.

One industry that was made up of a large number of immigrants was cigar production. Several cigar-making shops employed nearly one hundred people, including sales clerks and managers. The actual work, however, was done by thousands in the sweatshops.

One worker, Samuel Gompers (1850–1924), worked at one of the bigger cigar shops in New York. Gompers was born in London, England, to Jewish parents who had emigrated to Holland. He learned how to make cigars at a young age. When he moved with his family to America in 1863, he relied on his skills to earn a living. By 1885, having earned a reputation as a dependable worker with a serious mind, Gompers was elected president of Cigar Makers International Union Local 144.

In 1886, the New York Cigar Manufacturers' Association cut wages. Local 144 of the Cigar Makers Union and the other cigar union, Progressive No. 1 of KOL, protested. When cigar manufacturers ordered a lockout of ten thousand workers, Progressive No. 1 negotiated and settled with the employers. Local 144 did not give in. As president, Gompers felt betrayed by Powderly and the KOL and accused them of not having the best interests of the workers in mind. Gompers persuaded the Cigar Makers to boycott all other cigars.

The conflict between the two unions gave the crafters unions (skilled laborers) the opportunity they had been waiting for to confront the KOL. The Knights, still focused on improving the rights of the unskilled laborer, ordered all members of the Cigar Makers International to resign or give up their KOL membership. On December 8, 1886, forty-two members from twenty-five different labor unions met and formed the American Federation of Labor (AFL). The labor movement had a new leader.

Unlike the KOL, the AFL acknowledged that each trade within its membership had autonomy (the ability to make its own specific rules and regulations). The executive committee would not interfere in each trade union's internal affairs, but it would have the right to resolve disputes. The AFL demanded dues (regular payments) to create a strike fund. That money would be paid to workers on strike, though the amount would not equal their usual pay. Soon city and state federations of the AFL were formed to promote labor legislation.

Gompers was elected the AFL's first president in 1886. With the exception of one year, he kept that position until his death thirty-eight years later. His office was a very small room; in it were his "chair" (an overturned shipping crate), his "desk" (a kitchen table), and his "filing cabinet" (a set of tomato boxes). From these humble surroundings, he drafted charters, collected monies, organized conventions, and edited the AFL's newspaper. He was a popular

American Federation of Labor president Samuel Gompers.
© AP IMAGES.

president who never lost communication with the laborers.

Despite Gompers's popularity, the AFL's growth was slow. The membership in 1886 was 150,000. By 1892, it had increased by just another hundred thousand. Despite the slow rise in membership, however, the AFL offered the first real stability to labor unions in existence. That stability attracted four railway brotherhoods, which had learned their lesson in the Great Railroad Strike of 1877. Other labor unions joined because the AFL offered health insurance and other benefits that many laborers considered as important, if not more so, than mere wages. Those laborers who disagreed with the philosophy and mission of the KOL left the Knights in favor of the AFL. With its lowest membership ever in 1900, the KOL eventually disappeared.

The strikes of the decade

The labor movement of the 1890s was marked by two major strikes: one in the steel mills of Pennsylvania, the other in the railroad industries of Chicago.

The Homestead Strike Homestead, Pennsylvania, was a steel mill town with a population of more than ten thousand people. Of those inhabitants, just over thirty-four hundred were employed by Carnegie Steel Company. Of those employees, eight hundred were skilled and earned an average of $2.43 for a twelve-hour shift, or roughly twenty cents an hour. Unskilled laborers earned fourteen cents an hour.

In 1889, these wages were paid on a sliding scale that was dependent on the market price being paid for steel. This means that the higher the market price (the price paid to the steel companies by other businesses who bought their product) being paid, the higher the wages would be. If the market price dropped, so did wages. But twenty and fourteen cents an hour was the average.

This agreement between management and labor was due to expire on June 30, 1892. Of the eight hundred skilled workers, all but twenty were members of the Amalgamated Association of Iron, Steel and Tin Workers. These union members were expecting better terms upon expiration of the old contract. Their expectations did not seem unrealistic. Andrew Carnegie (1835–1919), owner of the mill, had publicly empathized with (claimed to understand) strikers in other industries. He even implied that he understood how their frustration led to violence.

Carnegie was out of the country in 1892 visiting his homeland of Scotland. Negotiations were in the hands of Henry Clay Frick (1849–1919), chairman of Carnegie Steel. Frick was known for his hard-hearted antiunion attitude. He had no patience for workers who complained and would not tolerate rebellion in any form.

The union would not accept the new contract proposed by Carnegie Steel as it required workers to accept an 18 to 26 percent decrease in wages. Union leader Hugh O'Donnell (c. 1863–?) met with Frick throughout June in the hopes of reaching a compromise that both sides could accept. Frick refused to consider any negotiations. Instead, he ordered the construction of a solid-wood fence topped with barbed wire built around the mill. Workers soon called it "Fort Frick."

As meetings continued to be held without progress, frustrated workers made dummies that looked like Frick and superintendent J. A. Potter and hung them on mill property. Potter sent men to tear down the dummies, but Carnegie employees turned the water hoses on them. Frick used this event as an excuse to order a lockout (an event in which workers are forbidden to work and are refused pay). In addition to the 3 miles of fencing he had built, Frick contacted Pinkerton National Detective Agency. He paid $5 a day to each of three hundred detectives to act as guards at the mill. The detectives arrived on July 6. By this time, workers had already barricaded themselves inside the steel plant.

Frick never had the chance to carry out his plan to hire strikebreakers. Citizens of the town joined Carnegie Steel's displaced workers and confronted the Pinkerton detectives just outside the mill. With both sides armed, they battled on July 6 from 4 AM until 5 PM. It is not clear who fired the first shot but when gunfire had ceased,

seven strikers and three detectives were dead, with numerous others injured. The strikers surrendered, and on July 12, eight thousand state troops marched into Homestead and took control.

Public opinion initially presumed that Carnegie Steel was at fault in this dispute. In truth, both sides were guilty of taking the law into their own hands. America was disturbed that a labor-management disagreement could escalate into bloody warfare between one of the nation's most powerful companies and one of the most highly respected labor unions. However, as details of the strike were reported to the public, sentiment turned against the labor union. Most citizens believed the workers behaved brutally and used unnecessary violence in the confrontation.

The tension between company and union worsened on July 23, when anarchist Alexander Berkman (1870–1936) shot and stabbed Frick in his office. Frick was not seriously injured, and Berkman was caught. That incident put an end to the steel union. Even though Berkman was not a union member, the public was unaware of this fact and perceived his attack on Frick as merely another strategy waged by the union against management. It would be another forty years before the steel industry formed a new labor union.

Carnegie's Homestead plant reopened on July 27 with a thousand new workers under the protection of the military. The company pressed charges against O'Donnell and the strikers, but no jury would find them guilty. Both sides decided to drop the matter. The strike officially ended on November 20, 1892. Three hundred locked-out employees were rehired and joined the newly hired workers in the mill. Under their new contract, former employees worked longer hours at a lower hourly wage than they had before the strike. Most of the strikers who were not rehired were blacklisted and found themselves unable to get jobs in the steel industry. The strike did nothing but hurt the reputation of labor unions throughout the country.

Although Carnegie privately wrote letters to Frick in support of Frick's handling of the affair, Carnegie publicly implied that Frick was responsible for the tragic events stemming from the strike and asked him to resign as chairman. In spite of his departure from the steel firm, Frick was rewarded handsomely when Carnegie bought Frick's stocks in the company for $15 million.

The Pullman strike Two years after the Homestead strike, Chicago workers in the railway industry found themselves facing a similar situation. George Pullman (1831–1897) founded the town of Pullman, Illinois (just south of Chicago), in 1880. He opened a railroad-car manufacturing plant there. Pullman was just 300 acres in size, but it was home to factories, mills, and a foundry (where iron and steel are made into usable products) as well as homes, public buildings, and shops. Pullman's twelve hundred residents had no choices in their lives. The money they spent on rent (Pullman's homes could be rented, not owned), food, gas, and anything else went directly to the Pullman Palace Car Company. As in the patch towns miners lived in, prices in Pullman were higher than they were elsewhere.

Pullman's company was successful. At the end of 1893, he was paying $7.22 million in wages and another $2.52 million in dividends (monies paid to stockholders). America was hit with another economic depression that year,

and it would last until 1897. During that time, Pullman fired more than three thousand workers and cut the wages of those still in his employment. He did not lower the cost of housing or services, though. Once those deductions were taken from wages, most employees were left with $6 a week on which to live. One worker was left with two cents each week. And yet the company continued to pay its shareholders the regular dividend amounts.

In May 1894, Pullman listened as a committee of dissatisfied employees complained about the situation. He refused to consider raising wages or lowering prices of rent and services in the town. Pullman insisted that what he did as an employer should have no bearing on his role as a landlord. Then, against a promise he had made earlier, he fired three of the workers on the committee. This breach of promise led to the Pullman local union strike on May 11.

When the union declared the strike, Pullman immediately fired the six hundred workers who were not involved and closed its doors. History was on the side of business when it came to labor disputes. Pullman was prepared to wait out the strike, which he believed would not last long. Pullman workers realized how serious the situation was and approached the American Railway Union (ARU) for help. The ARU, under the leadership of Eugene V. Debs (1855–1926; see box), called for a boycott of all Pullman cars on June 26, 1894. One hundred fifty thousand railway workers across the country complied, and within a couple days, trains were not leaving Chicago.

Business was negatively affected by the Pullman strike, as was mail delivery and transportation in general. This strike affected not just Chicago or even all of Illinois, but the entire nation. Railroad companies had no choice but to call on the government for assistance in breaking the strike. When Illinois governor John Altgeld (1847–1902) refused to summon military troops and made clear his sympathies lay with the strikers, the railroads went directly to the federal level. When a federal circuit court order demanding workers return to their jobs was ignored by Debs, he was arrested and found guilty of contempt of court and conspiracy to interfere with the mail and served a six-month jail sentence.

President Grover Cleveland (1837–1908; served 1885–89 and 1893–97) did what no president before him had ever done: He intervened in a labor strike. On July 4, he sent in twenty-five hundred federal troops to halt the strike. Rioting occurred on July 7–9 when strikers attacked the military troops. Soldiers responded with gunfire at point-blank range. About thirty strikers were killed and many more were wounded. What began as twenty-five hundred federal troops soon totaled fourteen thousand as state and other federal troops joined in the confrontation. The strikers were defeated within the week. After several weeks of negotiating, the Pullman Palace Car Company reopened its doors on August 2. As part of the agreement, strikers were allowed to return to work unless they had been convicted of a crime during the strike.

Again, the conflict did not benefit the workers. Debs went to prison, the ARU disbanded, and American society supported big business and management more unwaveringly than ever before. It seemed that no matter how they tried to improve their conditions, trade unions were not going to win the favor of the American people.

Promises of the future

Laissez faire (lack of government interference) capitalism was America's reality in the late nineteenth and early twentieth centuries, and unless they found a way to effectively fight for justice, the working class could never hope for a better future. The Molly Maguire scandal, the Haymarket Square riot, the Homestead and Pullman strikes: These were reminders that power was in the hands of the wealthy. The majority of laborers still worked between fifty-four and sixty-three hours each week, sometimes even longer.

The American Federation of Labor (AFL) offered hope. By 1901, 75 percent of all trade union members were also members of the AFL. Its leader, Samuel Gompers, remained opposed to allowing unskilled workers into the AFL, partly because the socialists favored it.

Socialists in America continued to fight capitalism. When the Socialist Labor Party (SLP) tried to take over the KOL and the AFL in the 1890s, it failed. Jewish laborers, tired of the authoritarian (controlling) attitude of the SLP, severed ties with the organization in 1897 and 1898. Their leaders joined Eugene Debs in founding the Socialist Party of America in 1901.

Although progress was slow for the labor movement, most of the important gains were made in state and federal legislation. Congress passed the Erdman Act in 1898, which stated that railroads could not discriminate against union members. Between 1886 and the end of the century, reform took place in areas that included child labor, women's labor, negotiation guidelines, the eight-hour workday, safety conditions, and responsibility for accidents. (See Chapter 8 for more on labor reform.)

Before reforms were made, there was one industry still plagued by bitter and often violent

Eugene Debs: Energetic Socialist

Eugene Victor Debs was born on November 5, 1855, in Terre Haute, Indiana. He left school in his midteens to work the Indiana railroad yards and soon became a locomotive fireman and leader of the Brotherhood of Locomotive Firemen (BLF), a labor union. Debs was laid off during the 1873 depression and took a job in the grocery business. He kept this position until 1879, when he was elected city clerk. He would remain in the clerkship for four years before his work with the labor union took all of his time. Although he remained fond of the railroads and those who worked them, Debs never worked for the railroad again.

Debs was active as an officer in the BLF even after his job with the railroad ended. He was recording secretary of the Terre Haute chapter of the union and was named associate editor of its magazine in 1878. In 1880, he was elected as national grand secretary-treasurer of the BLF as well as editor-in-chief of the magazine.

Debs was a gifted speaker and used his skill to convince laborers of the advantages of cooperating with management and government up until the mid-1880s. His philosophy changed in 1886 when the Chicago, Burlington, and Quincy Railroads endured a year-long strike. Debs began to question the effectiveness of unions that were developed by individual craft lines (rather than along industry lines). Debs came to the conclusion that industry unions were more powerful in the struggle against giant corporations and big business.

With renewed energy, Debs resigned from his position and organized the American Railway Union (ARU). The ARU was open to anyone in the railway industry, regardless of skill level. Debs's involvement in the Pullman strike of 1894 as leader of the ARU landed him a six-month jail sentence for conspiracy to interfere with mail and contempt of court. This marked a turning point in Debs's life, one that led him from cooperationist (someone with an attitude of cooperation) to revolutionary (a citizen who organizes with other like-minded citizens to fight the government and/or society).

Debs's new philosophy was based on socialism. Socialism is a system in which the government owns and operates business and production as well as the distribution of wealth. It is the opposite of capitalism (which is what the American economy is based on), a competitive system in which business and production are privately owned and profit is the motive. Debs helped establish the Social Democratic Party in 1897 as an alternative to the more traditional political parties, the Republicans and the Democrats. The Social Democratic Party eventually was renamed the Socialist Party of America. Debs ran for president four times in the early twentieth century. Though unsuccessful, the Socialists did manage to win many state and local elections. By 1916, however, the Socialist Party lost what little influence it had on American politics.

Debs publicly spoke out against World War I (1914–18) when to do so was a violation of the Espionage Act. During that time, it was against the law to incite opposition to U.S. involvement in any conflict. Debs was arrested, convicted, and sentenced to ten years in prison. From his cell, he ran for president for a fifth and final time in 1920. For the second time, he received nearly one million votes.

Debs was pardoned (freed from penalty) and released from prison on December 25, 1921, by President Warren G. Harding (1865–1923; served 1921–23). The president freed a total of twenty-four prisoners of conscience (people imprisoned because of their beliefs, as long as they did not promote violence) that day. The socialist movement of which Debs had been a part no longer existed. A new generation of social reformers was established in the 1930s, however. Historians credit Debs and his followers for the socialist policies that made up the economic plan, called the New Deal, of President Franklin Roosevelt (1882–1945; served 1933–45). Debs suffered from deteriorating health while in prison and after his release; he died on October 20, 1926.

Eugene Debs speaks at a labor convention during the 1910s. © CORBIS.

disputes: coal mining. The slaughter of the alleged Molly Maguires did nothing to suppress miners and laborers from striking. If anything, it only increased their determination to be treated fairly. In the late 1890s, miners' wages had been cut due to a price war between competing mines. In 1897, the United Mine Workers of America (UMWA) union tried to restore wages. Most mine operators were willing to negotiate, but some were not. At that point, the UMWA ordered miners throughout the state to strike. Membership in the UMWA was at ten thousand, but nearly one hundred thousand miners joined the strike.

The anthracite coal strikes of 1900 and 1902

Anthracite (hard) coal mining was much more treacherous and difficult than bituminous (soft) coal mining. Anthracite coal lay deeper beneath the earth's surface, and it was harder to pick out of the mines. Records of miners' deaths were not kept until 1870, but they show that between thirty-two thousand and thirty-five thousand men died in Pennsylvania anthracite coal mines between 1870 and the early twentieth century. John Mitchell (1870–1919) was a bituminous coal miner from Illinois when he was elected president of the UMWA in 1898. He had taken part in the successful strike of 1897, which resulted in better wages and working conditions for the miners.

As president of the UMWA in 1900, Mitchell tried to negotiate with anthracite coal mine operators in Pennsylvania for a settlement similar to the bituminous coal miners' settlement three years before. The mine operators refused to negotiate, so Mitchell called for a strike on September 17. Eighty percent of all anthracite

coal miners joined in the strike. It did not last for long. On October 29, 1900, the strike ended in victory for the miners, who received a 10 percent wage increase, their first in twenty years. Still, mine operators refused to recognize the UMWA as their employees' representative.

By 1902, the UMWA was ready to order another strike. The 10-percent wage increase granted in 1900 was only a temporary solution to the grievances of the miners. Work conditions were still poor and dangerous, and the days were still long. The UMWA was still not officially recognized by mine operators.

On May 12, 1902, anthracite coal miners walked off the job; the strike had officially begun. This bold move had far-reaching effects. Anthracite coal was used as fuel for trains, running factories, and heating homes and businesses. The strike may have been limited to Pennsylvania, but all of America would feel the consequences.

Newspaper coverage of the strike only fed into America's fears of a coal shortage for the coming winter. Cartoonists and journalists alike focused on the power struggle between mine management and laborers. October arrived, and it was apparent the strikers were not going to give up; America knew drastic measures had to be taken.

On October 3, President Theodore Roosevelt (1858–1919; served 1901–9) called union leaders and mine operators to a meeting at the White House. UMWA president Mitchell agreed to negotiate, but the mine operators refused. Weeks passed and no progress was made on either side. America needed its coal to survive the impending winter and keep its factories and trains running. Roosevelt made history by becoming the first president to get involved in the arbitration of a labor dispute. He threatened to have the U.S.

Mother Jones: Fearless Activist

Activist Mother Jones. © BETTMANN/CORBIS.

Mary Harris Jones (1837–1930) was born in Ireland and came to the United States as a young woman. She met and married George Jones, who, along with their four children, died of yellow fever in 1867. Jones moved to Chicago and lost everything she owned four years later in the Great Chicago Fire.

Jones needed to support herself so she joined the Knights of Labor. In 1905, she helped found a union called Industrial Workers of the World (IWW), also known as the Wobblies. Jones was an organizer of labor strikes throughout America but had a particular fondness for miners and their cause.

Jones worked not only with miners themselves but with their wives and children. She would organize mining families to participate in demonstrations and protests on behalf of the miners. Women and children carrying mops and brooms marched at the mines, preventing strikebreakers from crossing the line into the mine shafts. Jones earned the nickname "Mother" when she began calling the miners her "boys."

Mother Jones embraced socialism and worked closely with American Railway Union leader Eugene Debs. An enthusiastic public speaker, she was known for organizing public events to get the media focused on striking workers. Her tireless efforts on behalf of working men and women took her to the coal mines of Pennsylvania, where she encouraged miners to join the union.

Opponents of Jones called her the most dangerous woman in America; her physical courage was known throughout the nation. She joined in protests, many of which ultimately resulted in her arrest. Jones spent time in more jails throughout the country than any other labor activist in history.

It may be surprising to know that Jones was against women's suffrage (the right to vote). She believed that a focus on winning the vote would take away much-needed attention to the economic situation of working-class women. Jones discussed this in her autobiography, *The Autobiography of Mother Jones.* "You don't need a vote to raise hell, you need convictions and a voice."

Mother Jones died in 1930 at the age of ninety-three, though she claimed she was one hundred years old. She was buried in the Union Miners Cemetery in Mount Olive, Illinois, and thousands of miners and their families attended her funeral. Her name lives on as the title of a political magazine that supports socialism. Jones is remembered as the "Grandmother of All Agitators."

Colorado state militia keep an eye on the tent camp of miners and their families in Ludlow, Colorado, in April 1914. The militiamen eventually opened fire on the camp, killing twenty people, including two women and eleven children. © BETTMANN/ CORBIS.

Army seize the coal mines and operate them until the owners agreed to negotiate. Mine management did not want this to happen, so they backed down and agreed to arbitration (discussion with the laborers). Roosevelt appointed financier J. P. Morgan (1837–1913) to head a commission to arbitrate the dispute. On October 23, after 164 days of striking, miners returned to work. They received a 10 percent increase in wages and a reduction in the number of hours worked each day. To their disappointment, their union was still not recognized as their representative, and the issues of hazardous working conditions and child labor were not addressed.

The strike marked a major turning point in history. It was the first time the federal government elected to settle a strike rather than break it. Although it would be another decade before labor reform truly took hold, the laborers finally felt they were beginning to be heard.

The Ludlow massacre

Unfortunately, the 1902 coal strike was not the last. In September 1913, more than ten thousand coal miners went on strike in Ludlow, Colorado. Led by the UMWA, the workers demanded, among other things, union recognition, a wage increase, enforcement of the eight-hour-day law as well as state mining laws, and the right to choose where they shop and live.

The leader among mine operators was Colorado Fuel & Iron Company, owned by John D. Rockefeller (1839–1937). (See more about Rockefeller in Chapter 2.) Rockefeller had the miners and their families evicted from company housing and used the National Guard to keep the mines operating.

Without shelter, the mining families set up tents in the hills and continued striking throughout the winter. Conditions were harsh, and food was scarce. But Rockefeller showed no sign of changing his mind; arbitration would not take place.

April 20, 1914, was Easter on the calendar of the Greek Orthodox Church, and the Greek immigrants among the miners were celebrating. Despite the strike, the mood around the tent camp that morning was festive. At 10 AM, however, Colorado troops surrounded the camp and opened fire on the miners' tent colony, which had been set up on public property. Company guards, strikebreakers, private detectives, and soldiers had planned the attack. They brought with them an armored car mounted with a machine gun called the Death Special. As bullets sprayed through the colony, tents caught on fire. Later, investigations revealed that kerosene had been poured on the tents.

By day's end, twenty people, including two women and eleven children, were dead. Three strikers were taken prisoner and executed. None of the attackers were ever punished, although hundreds of the miners were arrested and blacklisted (forbidden to find work) in the coal industry. John D. Rockefeller Jr. (1874–1960), who by this time was in charge of the

mine, denied the massacre ever occurred and publicly stated that no women or children died in what he called a fight that was started by the miners. He spent the next decade trying to repair the damage done by the Ludlow massacre to the Rockefeller name. Gradually, he came to acknowledge the atrocity of the massacre, and through his efforts to right the wrongs that had been done, Rockefeller increased the social awareness of his entire family. The Rockefellers would eventually become one of the most philanthropic (generous, through charitable donations) families in America.

For More Information

BOOKS

Calhoun, Charles W., ed. *The Gilded Age: Essays on the Origins of Modern America*. Wilmington, DE: Scholarly Press, 1996.

Campbell, Patrick. *A Molly Maguire Story*. Jersey City, NJ: P. H. Campbell, 1992.

Cashman, Sean Dennis. *America in the Gilded Age*. New York: New York University Press, 1993.

Kuchta, David. *Once a Man, Twice a Boy*. Nesquehoning, PA: Kiwi Publishing, 1999.

Painter, Nell Irvin. *Standing at Armageddon: The United States, 1877–1919*. New York: W. W. Norton & Co., 1987.

Poliniak, Louis. *When Coal Was King*. Lancaster, PA: Applied Arts Publishers, 2004.

WEB SITES

Byrne, Julie. "Roman Catholics and Immigration in Nineteenth-Century America." *National Humanities Center*. http://www.nhc.rtp.nc.us:8080/tserve/nineteen/nkeyinfo/nromcath.htm (accessed on April 7, 2006).

Eckley Miners' Village. http://www.eckleyminers.org/ (accessed on June 26, 2006).

"1886: The Haymarket Riot." *Chicago Public Library*. http://cpl.lib.uic.edu/004chicago/timeline/haymarket.html (accessed on April 7, 2006).

Heartaches and Hardships of the Labor Movement

"The Haymarket Affair Digital Collection." *Chicago Historical Society.* http://www.chicagohistory.org/hadc/intro.html (accessed on April 7, 2006).

"History: Eugene Victor Debs." *AFL-CIO: America's Union Movement.* http://www.aflcio.org/aboutus/history/history/debs.cfm (accessed on April 7, 2006).

"History: Mother Jones." *AFL-CIO: America's Union Movement.* http://www.aflcio.org/aboutus/history/history/jones.cfm (accessed on April 7, 2006).

Library of Congress. "Today in History: October 3: Anthracite Coal Strike." *American Memory.* http://memory.loc.gov/ammem/today/oct03.html (accessed on November 29, 2005).

"The Ludlow Massacre." *UMWA: United Mine Workers of America.* http://www.umwa.org/history/ludlow.shtml (accessed on April 7, 2006).

McCormack, Mike. "National History: The Ancient Order of Hibernians." *Ancient Order of Hibernians of America.* http://www.aoh.com/history/index.htm (accessed on April 7, 2006).

"Samuel Gompers." *Illinois Labor History Society.* http://www.kentlaw.edu/ilhs/gompers.htm (accessed on April 7, 2006).

"Spies for Hire: Advertising by the Pinkerton Agency." *History Matters.* http://historymatters.gmu.edu/d/5313/ (accessed on April 7, 2006).

4

"Give Me Your Tired, Your Poor..."

Immigration (the leaving of one's homeland to build a life in another country) was not a new concept at the dawn of the Gilded Age. The Gilded Age was the period in history following the American Civil War (1861–65) and Reconstruction (roughly the final twenty-three years of the nineteenth century), characterized by a ruthless pursuit of profit, an exterior of showiness and grandeur, and immeasurable political corruption. Foreigners had been leaving their homelands for America for centuries before the late 1800s. Historians of immigration generally divide immigration into three waves. The first wave crossed the Atlantic Ocean from 1815 to 1860; the second between 1860 and 1890. Immigrants of the first two waves were mostly British, Irish, German, Scandinavian, Dutch, and Swedish. The third wave crossed between 1890 and 1914. Immigrants of the third wave came primarily from Greece, Turkey, Italy, Russia, Austria-Hungary, and Rumania.

It is important to understand immigration to the United States as a process, not as an event. It did not have an actual "start" date, nor will it have an "end" date. Still, immigration reached its peak during the Gilded Age and Progressive Era when nearly twelve million people entered the United States between 1890 and 1910. (The Progressive Era was a period in American history [approximately the first twenty years of the twentieth century] marked by reform and the development of a national cultural identity.) This influx (flowing in) of foreigners to the shores of America changed the nation's face forever.

Immigration records

Although immigration records dating back to the nineteenth century do exist, the numbers are not accurate either in terms of how many immigrants arrived in America or their ethnicity. This is so for a number of reasons.

Ellis Island was the major port (point of entry) for immigrants crossing the Atlantic Ocean to America. However, it was not the only

WORDS TO KNOW

anti-Semitism: Prejudice against Jewish people.

coolies: Unskilled Asian workers.

Gilded Age: The period in history following the Civil War and Reconstruction (roughly the final twenty-three years of the nineteenth century), characterized by a ruthless pursuit of profit, an exterior of showiness and grandeur, and immeasurable political corruption.

immigration: Leaving one's country to live in another.

labor union: A formally organized association of workers that advances its members' views on wages, work hours, and labor conditions.

naturalization: The process by which a person becomes a citizen of a country other than the one in which he or she was born.

port: For an immigrant, point of entry into a country.

sojourners: Immigrants who planned to stay in the United States temporarily; they usually stayed for a particular season or for a predetermined number of years before returning to their homeland.

port. Smaller ports dotted the shoreline, but those ports did not keep consistent or reliable records. The same can be said of overland immigrants from Canada and Mexico; some immigrants were counted, others were not.

Even after the immigration procedures were in place (see sidebar), immigrants were recorded according to their presumed nationality, not their ethnicity. This gives a distorted picture of who was coming to America's shores. For example, sizable portions of the millions of people emigrating from Britain were Irish. But because they came from Britain, they were recorded as British, not Irish. The only Irish in the records were those from Ireland. Likewise, "Jewish" was not a recognized ethnicity until after 1948. Before that, the word referred only to a person's religious belief. So the number of Jewish immigrants was highly underreported.

Still, the records—as imperfect as they are—provide a glimpse into the ethnic makeup of America during the Gilded Age and the Progressive Era (see table).

Immigration peaked between 1900 and 1915, when fifteen million people entered the United States. That is as many as in the previous forty years combined. Immigrants accounted for almost one-third of America's population growth during that time.

Coming to America

Contrary to popular myth, most Gilded Age and Progressive Era immigrants were not the poorest people in their society. They paid their own way or had their journey funded by a relative, a friend, or even a prospective employer. Most of these immigrants were young adult males, single or married with wives back home, who planned to work in America for a few years, save money, and return home. Immigrants who did not plan to stay in the United States permanently were called sojourners. Other immigrants, usually single women or men with families in the United States, stayed permanently. Plans often depended on the immigrant's experience in America.

Immigrants walk on a bridge on Ellis Island after arriving there in 1902. THE LIBRARY OF CONGRESS.

Again, recordkeeping was not consistent, and statistics of those who returned to their country of origin were not kept until 1909. It is impossible to know, therefore, how many immigrants were sojourners who returned to America time and again.

The long voyage European immigrants had to cross the Atlantic Ocean to reach America's shores. Prior to the mid-1850s, the only method of transportation was the sailing ship. The trip took anywhere from one to three months, and it was a voyage of great discomfort.

Sailing ships were designed to carry cargo, not passengers. Captains, intent on making a profit by crowding as many passengers on

board as possible, did little to adapt their ships. Flour, potatoes, tea, oatmeal, and maybe fish were provided. Water was provided too, but often it was stored in containers previously used to store oil and other liquids not intended for human consumption. Drinking that water put one's health at great risk.

Passengers often had only a few square feet of space per person. Narrow beds similar to bunk beds were poorly constructed, with a focus on quick dismantling rather than on comfort. There were no toilets or windows, which made sanitation a major problem. Passengers relieved themselves on deck, a habit that made conditions even worse. When a storm would hit, the ship would violently pitch, tossing around

Welcome to Ellis Island

Ellis Island is located near the shores of New York and New Jersey. A man named Samuel Ellis owned the island in the late eighteenth century, and the U.S. federal government bought it from him in 1808 for $10,000. The Army used the island from 1812 to 1814 and the Navy was there in 1876. In 1890, the House Committee on Immigration chose Ellis Island to be the site for an immigrant screening station. The old location for evaluating incoming immigrants, Castle Garden, which was located in lower Manhattan, was too small to handle the growing numbers of immigrants.

The government enlarged Ellis Island from just over three acres to fourteen acres and erected an immigration depot and several support buildings. The first immigrants passed through Ellis Island on January 1, 1892. The main depot was a two-story-structure built of pine, with a blue slate roof.

Once immigrants disembarked from the ship, they filed into the registry room, an impressive room that measured 200 feet by 100 feet and had a 56-foot-high ceiling. The room itself was divided into twelve narrow aisles separated by iron bars. Doctors examined new arrivals at the front of the room. These doctors, in addition to other immigration officials, complained about the leaky roof and other structural problems.

Inspectors determined that the building would probably last less than five years. The roof was in danger of collapsing under heavy snowfall or high winds. The doors were poorly hung and sometimes fell off their hinges. Architects estimated repairs at $150,000.

Nothing was done about the problems until 1895, when architect John J. Clark was sent to inspect the building. Clark assured officials that the roof did not need repair, a report that angered Ellis Island employees who knew it was leaky. In addition to the architectural flaws, the building was not able to handle the heavy flow of immigrants. The inspection process was slow, and there was nowhere to house immigrants while they were awaited its completion. In 1897, the government decided to add a 250-bed dormitory to the main building.

Before the dorm could be built, a fire burned most of the buildings to the ground. No one was hurt, but there were two hundred immigrants on the island at the time of the fire. It took three hours to destroy the station. Three years later, on December 17, 1900, a new reception hall opened its doors to new immigrants. Sixty-five hundred immigrants completed the inspection process in nine hours. This efficiency was possible because the new building was modeled after the train stations of the time, which handled thousands of people and tons of cargo every day.

Ellis Island was expanded to seventeen acres in 1898, and a second island was added by using the dirt and rock removed during nearby

food, passengers, human waste, and anything else that was not secured to the deck.

Epidemics (widespread outbreaks of disease) were common and were the primary cause of death on immigrant ships. Typhus, a disease spread by head lice, was fatal if left untreated. Cholera was another deadly disease. Caused by infected drinking water, cholera victims became dehydrated to the point of death. Bodies were either thrown subway construction. A third island was added and completed by 1906. Dormitories, hospitals, kitchens, a baggage station, a bathhouse, an electrical plant, and the hiring of personnel to staff the depot raised the cost of renovations to a half million dollars. In 1954, the Immigration Services shut down Ellis Island, and activity resumed at the Manhattan immigration depot.

In 1885, the Statue of Liberty was given to America by the French. The statue—made up of 350 pieces and transported in 214 crates—arrived in the United States in June 1885; con-

struction was completed in October of the following year. "Lady Liberty" was placed on Bedloe's Island (next to Ellis Island), where she became the symbol of freedom and hope for millions of immigrants. Bedloe's Island was renamed Liberty Island in 1956.

Jewish American poet Emma Lazarus (1849–1887) wrote the sonnet "The New Colossus" in 1883. It is engraved on a plaque at the base of the Statue of Liberty. The poem contains the famous line, "Give me your tired, your poor, Your huddled masses yearning to breathe free...."

Ellis Island. © AP IMAGES.

overboard or left on deck until the ship reached shore.

With the invention of the steamship came a shorter, more comfortable trip for immigrants. By 1867, the journey took just fourteen days;

within forty years, that time was shortened to five-and-one-half days. The new ships were built specifically to carry passengers. Permanent beds were provided, and improved boilers allowed for reliable heating during the colder

The Immigration Process

First- and second-class immigrants passed through Ellis Island easily. Only the lowest classes were forced to endure a rigorous inspection. Even if these foreigners had nothing to hide, the process was stressful.

Immigrants were asked to give their names, ages, country of origin, and legal status in that country. Because many immigrants had last names that were difficult for inspectors to pronounce and spell, a great number of them were given new, more Americanized, names for their new lives. For people to whom family tradition held great value, this enforced name change was devastating.

After giving their occupation and work history, immigrants were asked questions about their religious and political beliefs. A health inspection followed this inquiry, and this was probably the most worrisome aspect of the process because immigrants had just spent weeks on board immigrant ships full of filth and disease. Many of the passengers left the ships ill. Immigrants were marked according to their condition: "P" indicated a pregnant woman; "X" was given to the mentally disabled. Anyone incurably ill was deported (sent home) immediately.

Immigrants who successfully cleared the inspection process then took an oath of loyalty to the United States and were allowed to enter. Where they went from Ellis Island depended on the plans they had made before the trip. A great many of them simply stayed in New York, at least temporarily, until they found work and saved money to move on.

three hundred passengers in first class and another thousand in steerage (the bottom level of the ship, always the least expensive fare).

In 1882, Congress imposed stricter laws regarding passenger ships. Adults and older children required 100 cubic feet each, 120 if sailing on the lowest deck. All passengers had to be given three daily meals. Captains were required to set standards of hygiene and discipline among his passengers; for every death at sea, the company was charged $10. While the laws were a good beginning, most historians agree that they were nearly impossible to enforce.

During the 1880s, the immigrant trade became fiercely competitive. By 1882, there were forty-eight steamship companies fighting each other for business. All these companies were German- or British-owned; the United States never managed to break into this particular industry. The competition, however, worked in the favor of the immigrants for a short time. In 1875, rates on one of the most popular steamship lines were as low as $20 (steerage) and as high as $300 (first class). By the early 1880s, fares were reduced in order to attract passengers and could be bought for $10 to $20. This is the equivalent of about $193 to $386 in modern currency. Company owners soon conducted business the same way the railroads did, by forming "pools" and fixing prices so that no one company could undersell another.

The role of the railroads

Steamship companies brought immigrants to America, but the railroads were responsible for providing the motivation to make the journey. They owned thousands of acres of land they

months. Health risks were greatly reduced as well, and throughout the Gilded Age, the average number of deaths at sea was less than 1 percent of all immigrants. Ships could hold around

Major Sources of Gilded Age Immigration

	Dates	Number	% of all Immigrants		Dates	Number	% of all Immigrants
Germany	1866–1870	554,416	36.6	Austria-Hungary	1866–1870	6,901	0.5
	1871–1880	718,182	25.5		1871–1880	72,969	2.6
	1881–1890	1,452,970	27.7		1881–1890	353,719	6.7
	1891–1900	505,152	13.7		1891–1900	592,707	16.1
	Total	3,230,720	24.7		Total	1,026,296	7.7
Ireland	1866–1870	239,419	15.8	Russia	1866–1870	1,883	0.1
	1871–1880	436,871	15.5		1871–1880	39,284	1.4
	1881–1890	655,482	12.5		1881–1890	213,282	4.1
	1891–1900	388,416	10.5		1891–1900	505,290	13.7
	Total	1,720,188	13.0		Total	759,739	5.7
Scandinavia	1866–1870	109,654	7.0	**Southeastern Europe Total**		**2,971,898**	**22.4**
	1871–1880	243,016	8.6				
	1881–1890	645,494	12.5	Canada	1866–1870	119,848	7.9
	1891–1900	371,512	10.1		1871–1880	383,640	13.6
	Total	1,380,676	10.4		1881–1890	393,304	7.5
Britain	1866–1870	359,807	23.8		1891–1900[2]	3,311	0.1
	1871–1880	548,043	19.5		Total	900,103	6.8
	1881–1890	807,357	15.4	China	1866–1870	40,019	2.6
	1891–1900	271,538	7.4		1871–1880	123,201	4.4
	Total	1,986,745	15.0		1881–1890	61,711	1.2
Western Europe Total		**8,318,329**	**62.7**		1891–1900	14,799	0.4
Italy	1866–1870	8,277	0.5		Total	239,730	1.8
	1871–1880	55,759	2.0				
	1881–1890	307,309	5.9				
	1891–1900	651,893	17.7				
	Total	1,023,238	7.7				
Poland[1]	1866–1870	1,129	0.1				
	1871–1880	12,970	0.5				
	1881–1890	51,806	0.4				
	1891–1900	96,720	2.6				
	Total	162,625	1.2				

(1) Polish data is also included in the figures for Austria-Hungary, Germany, and Russia for the years 1899 and 1900.
(2) Data for 1882–1893 is unavailable.

SOURCE: *Historical Statistics of the United States*, 1975.

no longer wanted and could provide immigrants something other promotional agencies could not: transportation to get to the land, and the opportunity to buy the land once they arrived. The railroads published booklets advertising America and making offers too good to be true. They tempted immigrants with reduced transportation fees by land and sea, low-interest loans, classes in farming, and even the promise to build churches and schools. Some railroad lines assured immigrants that they would be hired for railroad construction at $30 a month plus board. By the end of the nineteenth century, the railroads ended their recruitment campaigns. They had run out of land to sell at prices immigrants could afford.

Railroads offered just one option, however. After the American Civil War, the United States, northwestern states and territories in particular, had vast amounts of unsold land they wanted

Immigrants travel on the S.S. Patricia *in December 1906.* THE LIBRARY OF CONGRESS.

to get rid of. Realizing that an increase in population was the surest way to sell the land, state immigration bureaus focused their efforts on Germany, Britain, and Scandinavia. Pamphlets and newspapers advertised America as a land of great opportunity. One 1872 pamphlet, titled *Colorado, A Statement of Facts,* gave great encouragement to foreigners of all socioeconomic statuses. "The poor should come to Colorado, because here they can by industry and frugality better their condition. The rich should come here because they can more advantageously invest their means than in any other region. The young should come here to get an early start on the road to wealth."

The South also wanted cheap labor to replace the slaves it had recently lost following the North's victory in the Civil War. (Slavery had been outlawed.) Immigrants, however, were not attracted to the southern United States because it had virtually no unsold land and very little large-scale industry. Without these attractions, immigrants would have difficulty finding shelter as well as work.

Why they left

Although each immigrant had his or her own individual reasons for emigrating, the primary reasons for leaving home, regardless of region, were economic, political, or religious. For the

The Potato Famine of the 1840s

By the mid-1800s, potatoes had been a standard crop in Ireland for more than two hundred years. The lower classes had become dependent on them for several reasons. They were easy to grow and required only one tool, a spade. They were easy to store and provided more calories per acre than any other crop grown in northern Europe. Potatoes were versatile and could be prepared in countless ways. Because they were nutritious, they helped keep disease at a minimum. In every way, potatoes were the ideal crop for people with little money to spare.

To increase the harvest, Irish farmers favored the lumper, one of the most fertile varieties of potato. By planting lumpers, farmers could grow more potatoes on less land. So year after year, the same crop was planted in the same fields.

Modern agriculture technique is based on the knowledge that crops must be rotated on a regular basis. To plant the same crop in the same soil year after year depletes the soil of necessary nutrients and guarantees crop failure. The Irish in the nineteenth century did not know about crop rotation. All they knew was that potatoes were inexpensive to grow, easy to store and prepare, and nutritious.

In 1845, Irish crops became infested with fungus. The weather turned warm and wet, which served only to cause the fungus to thrive and spread. Potatoes rotted in the fields throughout the country. The blight (infestation) continued,

and soon the Irish found their potato surplus depleted. They had very little to eat. The few potatoes that did survive were replanted the following spring. And though they seemed healthy, some harbored strong strains of the fungus. As soon as the rains came, the blight began again. It took just weeks to strip Ireland of its potato crops for a second time.

Although the country's potato crops were ruined, other crops were untouched by the infestation. Farmers grew most of those crops in order to be exported to England, so they were not about to sell their food to their neighbors when they could get higher prices from England. Many Irish starved to death not because there was no food, but because the food that could be found was too expensive for them to buy.

In order to buy food to feed their families, potato farmers sold everything they owned—furniture, animals, and farming tools. Money that could have gone toward paying the rent was spent on food, and thousands of families were evicted (forced out of their homes). By the following spring, farmers had nothing to plant and nowhere to plant it. Very few potatoes survived the blight.

Irish farmers never again relied so heavily on one crop. In 1845, potato crops accounted for more than 2 million acres of land in Ireland. By 1847, only 300,000 acres of potato crops were planted.

early Irish immigrants, who left Ireland in the late 1840s to escape the potato famine (severe shortage because of crop failure; see box), the reason was economic. A combination of bad weather, questionable agricultural practices,

and poor economic conditions caused the famine, which lasted five years. The famine left a million dead of starvation. Those Irish who left wanted little else than the promise of a steady supply of food.

The Irish

Nearly two million Irish from Ireland came to the United States in the 1840s. As they found steady work that allowed them to save money, they sent for friends and relatives. This kept a continuous flow of Irish coming into America. In total, about 3.5 million Irish from Ireland immigrated to the United States between 1820 and 1880. In the years between 1820 and 1860, the Irish accounted for one-third of all immigrants to America. Many more Irish emigrated from Britain, but because Britain was the point of departure, they were counted as British, not Irish, in immigration records.

Though not the poorest in Irish society, those who came to America were incredibly poor by American standards. Many of them did not have money beyond the ship fare, so they settled in the port at which they arrived. The main port of entry was Ellis Island, near New York City. Other major ports for European immigrants were Philadelphia, Pennsylvania; Boston, Massachusetts; and Baltimore, Maryland. New York City eventually was home to more Irishmen than was Dublin, Ireland.

An 1870 census (a periodic count of the population) revealed that the Irish comprised 14.5 percent of the populations of large American cities. They dominated the population in New England and accounted for 22 percent of New York's population that year. They, along with the Germans, were the largest immigrant group in 1870.

Housing Like most immigrants, the Irish moved into subdivided homes that were built for single families. These buildings were called tenements (see "Home Sweet Home" box later in this chapter, and Chapters 3 and 8). In

these dwellings, the Irish crowded together and lived in attics, cellars, and alleyways—areas usually meant for storage. Many of the Irish had spent their lives living in mud huts in Ireland, so their expectations were not as high as those of Americans, or even other immigrants. Still, conditions in the tenements were horrible.

Sewage systems did not exist in the Gilded Age. In addition, tenement housing lacked running water. The combination of these two factors made cleanliness and hygiene impossible. As a result, disease was widespread throughout the crowded tenements. The Irish quickly gained a reputation for being dirty and disease-ridden; when they moved into neighborhoods, other families moved out for fear of illness. Other immigrant groups and Americans also came to equate the Irish with increased levels of crime and social deviance such as alcoholism. This was due, in part, to the fact that while other immigrant groups tended to tolerate unfair treatment by other people, the Irish did not. They fought back, and if they thought violence was necessary, they engaged in it. An important facet of Irish culture in the homeland was the pub or saloon. This is where people went to socialize and discuss work, politics, and current events. This cultural norm worked against the Irish during a time when alcohol consumption was considered by many to be immoral. This stereotype of the Irish would be promoted in cartoons and media for decades to come.

Labor Irish immigrants were laborers who took dangerous jobs that no one else wanted. The men worked the coal mines (see Chapter 3) and built railroads and canals while the women worked as domestic (household) help. American businesses wasted no time in taking advantage of the cheap labor supplied by the Irish. Companies threatened to replace uncooperative employees with cheap Irish workers; this led to more tension between the Irish and the rest of the population.

Second- and third-generation Irish immigrants (children and grandchildren of those who sailed to America) often took jobs as policemen, firemen, and schoolteachers. These generations achieved higher levels of education, which allowed them to earn more money. One of the most famous examples of a successful Irishman from an immigrant family was President John F. Kennedy (1917–1963; served 1961–63). The first Kennedy arrived in America as a laborer in 1848. Several generations later, one of them was president of the United States.

Religion The Irish were disliked by nearly every other ethnic group, and also by Americans, because of their poor living conditions, their willingness to work for low wages, and for their religion. (See "The Conflict between Protestants and Catholics" box in Chapter 3 for more detail.) Protestants (Christians who are not Catholics) and Catholics had a long history of conflict. The Irish were Catholic. In America, most Catholics were members of upper-class society. They were not accustomed to having to include or accept members of the lower class. The tension created by these class differences was an obstacle not easily overcome.

Protestant Americans watched as millions of Catholics flooded their shores. Catholic churches were appearing on every street corner in some neighborhoods. It seemed to some as though Protestant neighborhoods were being overrun with Catholics. These Irish Catholics brought with them foreign customs and rituals that Americans and other ethnic groups did not understand. Conflict was virtually unavoidable.

Although Catholics and Protestants are both part of the Christian religion, they differ in some basic beliefs. For example, Catholics operate under a hierarchy of leaders (chain of command), starting with the pope. These leaders provide authority in the Church; they make rules and decree what is morally right and wrong. Protestants believe the Bible is the only source of God's word.

The Irish in search of jobs were greeted with signs in storefront windows reading "No Irish Need Apply." They became the target of violence in big cities throughout the northeast. Catholic churches were burned, and riots broke out.

As the years went by Persecution was not new to the Irish. Ireland was under British rule, so most Irish immigrants had never known freedom as Americans understood it. In their homeland, the Irish were controlled politically, economically, and religiously. They often formed secret organizations, usually with the help of their village priest, to meet their educational and economic needs. These societies allowed the Irish to form a strong identity. They stuck together for the sake of survival. This experience helped them as immigrants in America as well.

The Irish were excellent organizers. They recognized the value of teamwork, and their ability allowed them to break into the American political system. Since most of them lived in big cities, they were able to take control of politics like no other ethnic group had ever done. The Irish put the power into the hands of the working class and established loyalty among that large voting group. They formed political machines (organized political groups that insure loyalty of voters by repaying them for their votes with favors such as money, jobs, or gifts) that took

Nativism in America

Anti-immigrant sentiment became such an ingrained part of American culture during the Gilded Age that it had its own name: nativism. By the early 1850s, nativism was so strong a sentiment that nativists formed their own political party. It was formally named the American Party, but the common name for it was the Know-Nothing Party. The party got its name from the policy that, when asked about their nativist organizations, members were supposed to reply that they knew nothing. A former U.S. president, Millard Fillmore (1800–1874; served 1850–53), even ran as the party's presidential nominee in 1856; he finished a distant third behind the Democratic and Republican candidates. By 1860, the Know-Nothings had disbanded.

The main targets of nativism were the Irish and Germans. These groups, both Catholic in religious belief, were considered the most dangerous threat to the American way of life not only in terms of religious and moral values but in economic terms as well. Millions of "outsiders" were doing the work many citizens believed should be done by Americans. Nativists considered immigrants a drain on the economy.

Although the Catholics were the most discriminated against in terms of religion, no ethnic group was spared. All Italians were suspected of being involved in the Mafia (organized crime). The Chinese who settled in California were resented because they established their own welfare associations to take care of their poor and impose order in Chinatowns. But the Jews were the victims of the most intense discrimination. They were stereotyped as being greedy. Anti-Semitism (Jewish discrimination) influenced laws, and Jews were prohibited by law from voting until the middle of the nineteenth century. Anti-Semitism was the driving force behind General Order No. 11, published in 1862, which stated all Jews were to be thrown out of the Union military, led by General Ulysses S. Grant (1822–1885). The order was revoked by President Abraham Lincoln (1809–1865; served 1861–65) after just eighteen days, but its passage reflected the rampant anti-Semitic attitude of America at the time. By the time of the Gilded Age, laws had changed, but the Jews continued to be blamed for many of the ills in society. Socially, they remained outcast well into the next century.

Nativism eventually led to the development of immigration laws that limited or completely prevented certain immigrants from coming to America.

---

over major American cities, from the mid-eighteenth into the twentieth century.

The most well-known political machine was New York City's Tammany Hall, which was controlled by the Irish for fifty years. (See Chapter 1.) William "Boss" Tweed (1823–1878) was elected chairman of the Democratic Party in New York in 1860. His headquarters were known as Tammany Hall. Tweed and his men became known as the Tweed Ring, and in the years Tweed was in office, they swindled hundreds of millions of dollars from the city.

Although there is no doubt Tweed was corrupt, he gave new immigrants a voice in a world that despised them. The Irish and other immigrants knew if they voted to keep Tweed in office, he would ensure that they had work, shelter, and a say in New York politics.

The Chinese

The Chinese emigrated to the United States in large numbers even before the Gilded Age. The major difference between the Chinese and other ethnic groups was that the Chinese crossed the Pacific Ocean and landed on the shores of California at Angel Island. They began emigrating in large numbers in the mid-1800s, largely to take part in the 1849 California gold rush.

The Chinese immigrants who arrived in America prior to 1849 received a warm welcome. Most of them were wealthy, and if they were not successful merchants, they brought other skills to America. These Chinese were artists, craftsmen, fishermen, and hotel and restaurant owners. They quickly earned a reputation for being dependable, hard workers.

By 1851, twenty-five thousand Chinese were living in and around the San Francisco region. That area was home to over half the Chinese immigration population of the United States at the time. Most of these immigrants were unskilled laborers who worked for low wages. Americans referred to these Chinese as "coolies." The offensive term comes from the Chinese words *koo* (meaning "to rent") and *lee* (meaning "muscle").

Chinatown

The Chinese workers formed urban clusters within larger cities. These clusters were called Chinatowns, and they operated independently of the larger cities around them. The Chinese, like the Irish, found strength in numbers, and they relied upon each other to create a cultural identity that would protect them against the harsh attitudes of Americans.

The Chinese not only lived in Chinatown, they also shopped and socialized there. The culture of Chinatown was much like that of the home these Chinese had left behind. Although these cities-within-cities were originally overcrowded slums (ghettos) full of crime and violence, many turned into tourist attractions by the mid-1900s.

Change of heart

Along with the Chinese, and to a lesser extent, Mexicans and French Canadians, came thousands of Americans from the east. These men hoped to find their fortune in the gold rush of 1849. Most miners were disappointed; gold was not to be found just lying around in streams and gulches. Mining was hard work, and many men gave up after weeks or months of finding nothing.

Gold seekers felt they had been misled. Disappointment led to resentment, as Americans considered their Chinese peers competition for the gold. Soon the Chinese were accused of stealing the Americans' wealth. Even when they were welcomed to America's shores, there was no denying that the Chinese race was different from that with whom any American had ever come in contact. Their physical appearance and language, their dress and hair—all of it set the Chinese apart from everyone else.

One other aspect of the Chinese workers frustrated Americans: They would not fight back. They were a peaceful group of immigrants and accepted their fate in America. Whereas other groups might respond with violence, the Chinese instead drew strength from each other. Having developed Chinatowns as their home base, they lived largely separate from the larger cities around them. By limiting their interactions

Chinese laborers working on the railroad in the Sierra Nevada Mountains of California in 1877. © BETTMANN/CORBIS.

with non-Chinese, they did not often confront racial hatred face-to-face.

The Chinese also found work in railroad construction with the Central Pacific Railroad (CPR). Railroad construction was dangerous, backbreaking work. No one wanted to do it. Because so few men willingly worked the lines, the railroad company sent an agent to China to hire Chinese laborers. In order to get the Chinese to America, the CPR gave them money in advance for their ship fare and immediate living expenses. Each laborer signed a contract promising to pay back the money over a period of seven months. In return, the laborers were guaranteed a monthly wage of $35.

Of that $35, about half went toward food. Since the railroad paid for shelter, that left nearly $20 every month for savings, much more than most laborers during the 1860s received. But many did not survive the work. More than one thousand Chinese railroad builders had their bones shipped back to China for burial.

Although ten thousand Chinese worked for the CPR in the 1860s, they were publicly denied any credit for their years of labor. A famous photo taken at Promontory Point, Utah, records the celebration over the last spike being driven into the Transcontinental Railroad. That golden spike connected the east and west by railway. Not one Chinese worker appears in that photo.

A difference in moral values

At a time when decent wages were hard to come by even for skilled laborers, this contract work only increased America's intolerance toward the Chinese. The emergence of the Chinese Consolidated Benevolent Association, a group of organizations better known as the Chinese Six Companies, did not help the situation from an American point of view, either. Like the Irish, the Chinese formed organizations to help new immigrants survive. The powerful Six Companies represented six different districts in Chinatown. The group often contracted with American companies to provide Chinese workers. The laborers did not work *for* the Six Companies. The group acted as a clearinghouse through which most transactions between Americans and Chinese were processed; it also dealt with immigration issues with local, state, and federal governments. The organized Chinese found this method the most convenient for handling life in a strange land.

As anti-Chinese sentiment grew, work became harder to find for the immigrants. Many Chinese started their own businesses in an effort to survive. They opened up laundries and restaurants, and it soon became obvious that these could be successful endeavors for the immigrants. Other Chinese found steady work as gardeners and domestic servants.

Americans resorted to violence to vent their frustration. In 1862 alone, eighty-eight Chinese were reported murdered. In all probability, that number was much higher, but the immigrants did not want to further antagonize authorities and so did not report every incident. Soon, even those businesses that employed Chinese workers were in danger of becoming victims of mob violence.

The most violent opposition began in the South. Many American Southerners believed other races were natural servants whose only purpose was to uphold the Southerners. Having to work at all was often more than they could tolerate. Having to work side-by-side with Chinese immigrants was the greatest insult. Was it not enough that they were given U.S. citizenship and all its privileges when they entered the country?

More than prejudice fueled anti-Chinese sentiment. Americans prided themselves on their moral values and ability to resist temptation, and they viewed the Chinese as highly immoral people. Chinese prostitutes (women who sell sex) comprised a large portion of the female population in Chinatowns (see box). In fact, there were no more Chinese prostitutes than there were in any other ethnic group, including Americans. It *seemed* there were more because there were fewer Chinese women in the United States than there were in other ethnic groups. In addition to prostitution, the Chinese were looked upon as gambling addicts. Again, the Chinese did not gamble any more than any other group of people. The reason behind the assumption that they did was that the Chinese provided gambling houses and venues that were visited by American and other immigrant gamblers. The same was true of prostitution: The Chinese provided the women, but their clients were of other ethnicities. This fact did not eliminate the stereotype. To most people, the Chinese were people of inferior moral values.

Immigration restriction laws

A person born in one country who emigrates to another country can become a citizen of that new country through a process called naturalization. Naturalization usually requires that

Women in Chinatown

Most Chinese who emigrated to America in the first half of the nineteenth century did not plan to stay. These temporary immigrants, known as sojourners, were escaping war and poverty in China, and hoped to save enough money to return to their families one day. So most of the Chinese immigrants at that time were young men.

As restrictions were placed on immigration laws, the Chinese population in America became even more imbalanced. In 1860, the ratio of Chinese males to females was 19 to 1; by 1890, it was 27 to 1. Throughout the century, women never made up more than 8 percent of the total Chinese population in America. This imbalance, coupled with laws that prevented Chinese men from marrying white women, created a demand for prostitution.

Whereas white prostitutes worked for wages either independently or in brothels (buildings where prostitutes work and sometimes live), Chinese prostitutes were women who were kidnapped or purchased from poor families in China and resold in America. This was a profitable business, but not for the women. Most of them were considered property and abused so badly that they rarely lived longer than five years in the States. In 1860, 85 percent of Chinese women in San Francisco were prostitutes; that number fell to 71 percent in 1870.

Those who escaped a life of prostitution were usually wives who lived with their husbands. True to Chinese custom, these women rarely left their homes. They cared for their children, did the housework, and often found other low-paying work, such as sewing, washing, and rolling cigars. Rural (country) wives also tended gardens and livestock, or caught fish and sold it to markets.

After the passage of the Chinese Exclusion Act in 1882, which allowed only Chinese in the merchant class to enter America, many of the women immigrants settled in cities and small towns where the Chinese were not so despised. Without the ability to speak English, and with few or no job skills, they took jobs in garment (clothing) shops and fruit orchards. Some worked in their husbands' laundries or grocery stores.

As difficult as life was for Chinese men, it was more so for the women, who remained subservient to (legally a class beneath) men, and were valued more for the services they provided than as individuals with rights.

---

the immigrant live in the new country for a specific number of years. During the early nineteenth century, members of any race could become citizens of the United States. In 1870, Congress passed the Naturalization Act, which restricted citizenship to "white persons and persons of African descent"—Asians, therefore, were refused the right to naturalize. This law was the first restriction placed on free immigration in American history. The Chinese would be ineligible for citizenship until the law was repealed in 1943.

The Naturalization Act of 1870 was only the beginning of America's attempt to keep the Chinese from its shores. On May 6, 1882, President Chester A. Arthur (1829–1886; served 1881–85) signed into law the Chinese Exclusion Act. This law prohibited Chinese laborers from immigrating to the United States for ten years. It was renewed for another ten years in 1892, and became permanent in

Political cartoon about the Chinese Exclusion Act of 1882. Men are shown using "congressional mortar" to construct an "anti-Chinese wall." THE LIBRARY OF CONGRESS.

1904. Although Chinese merchants (businessmen and those in skilled trades) could still emigrate, they were not allowed to become U.S. citizens. Those Chinese already in America were allowed to stay. An estimated twenty thousand returned to China, however, in fear that if they did not, they would never be allowed to go home again. Their fears of restricted movement came true in 1888 with the passage of the Scott Act, named after U.S. representative William Scott (1828–1891) of Pennsylvania. As punishment for those Chinese who had returned to their homeland, as well as a way to further restrict immigration, this new law forbid the return of any Chinese to America. These immigration restrictions permanently separated untold numbers of Chinese families who would never see one another again.

The Chinese Exclusion Act marked the beginning of an illegal immigration movement that involved an "underground railroad," much like the one used by African American slaves earlier in the century. People secretly worked together to smuggle Chinese citizens into the United States via Texas. The Chinese would be safely hidden and transported by various men and women on their journey to the United States. Once in Texas, these aliens attended a secret school that taught them enough English to help them find work. Chinatowns became even more important to the immigrants, as they needed to find shelter and steady work.

In spite of the Chinese Exclusion Act, the illegal immigration movement caused the Chinese population in America to increase. It peaked in

1890 at around 107,488 people. After that, the number decreased, mostly because the majority of Chinese immigrants were sojourners who never planned to stay. Using the Chinese underground railroad, they returned to their native land.

Immigration was restricted further in 1891, when a law was passed excluding convicts, the mentally retarded, the insane, the destitute (poorest of the poor), diseased people, and polygamists (people with more than one spouse). This law was not effective, as it affected only seven-tenths of 1 percent of all immigrants from 1892 through 1900.

The Chinese were legally forbidden to emigrate to the United States until 1943, when China became America's ally (partner) in World War II (1939–45). At that time, the Chinese fell under regular immigration law. Most Chinese immigrants who entered the United States after the war were women, many of them wives of Chinese men already in America.

Immigration Restriction League Clearly, America was threatened by a growing sense of disorder at the turn of the century. The Industrial Revolution (a period from approximately 1850 through 1940 that saw a shift from the use of simple tools to more elaborate machinery), the transcontinental railroad, unstable economic conditions, an influx of immigrants—all these events forced major change on American society. People were searching for control in any form they could find. One of these attempts to control conditions was the formation in 1894 of the Immigration Restriction League (IRL).

The Boston-based IRL was founded by attorney Prescott Hall (1868–1921). Hall and his followers believed some of the less desirable immigrants would negatively affect American culture. They encouraged Congress to pass a law that required potential immigrants to take a literacy (reading and comprehension) test. Those who passed would be allowed into America. The House of Representatives passed the literacy bill five times: in 1895, 1897, 1913, 1915, and 1917. The Senate seconded the House's motion all years except the first. Every president in office during those years, including Grover Cleveland (1837–1908; served 1885–89 and 1893–97), William Howard Taft (1857–1930; served 1909–13), and Woodrow Wilson (1856–1924; served 1913–21), vetoed the bill. The veto was overridden in 1917, and the immigration process of the twenty-first century still requires the successful completion of a literacy test.

Other immigrant groups

The Irish and Chinese stand out in the history of immigration during the Gilded Age and just before. Both groups were targets of intense prejudice and intolerance, even violence. Both groups formed a strong national and cultural identity in the midst of their new home, and that identity helped them survive in America. Chinese immigration and America's response to it changed the immigration landscape forever. Xenophobia (fear of foreigners) swept the nation, and society's response was to try to control immigration for the first time through restrictive laws.

Other groups of immigrants came to the shores of New York whose hardships were suffered in silence. One of the most persecuted of these groups was the Jews. Since Americans considered Jewish affiliation a religion rather than an ethnicity until 1948, records do not show accurate numbers regarding how many Jews crossed the Atlantic Ocean during the Gilded Age and Progressive Era.

Could You Pass the Immigration Test?

The following questions are just a handful of those included in the 2006 literacy test that potential immigrants must pass:

What did the Emancipation Proclamation do?

Where does Congress meet?

What is the head executive of a city government called?

Who said "Give me liberty or give me death"?

How many times may a congressman be reelected?

How many representatives are there in Congress?

What are the duties of Congress?

Who is the chief justice of the Supreme Court?

Can you name the thirteen original states?

How many Supreme Court justices are there?

Jews

Most of the early Jewish immigrants came from Central Europe. Like most other immigrant groups, they settled in larger cities, including Philadelphia, New York, and Baltimore. German-speaking Jews built their communities in cities such as Cincinnati and Cleveland, Ohio; Albany, New York; San Francisco; and numerous small towns across America. The country's Jewish population rose steadily, from about three thousand people in 1820 to three hundred thousand in 1880.

The Jews who emigrated between 1881 and 1924 were mostly from eastern Europe. These immigrants fled persecution and economic hardship and settled in the cities that other Jews had already established.

As was the case with the Irish and the Chinese, the Jews set up neighborhoods and built networks of social, cultural, and spiritual organizations. These associations helped welcome new immigrants and gave all Jews a sense of cultural identity. (The oldest volunteer Jewish women's organization, the National Council of Jewish Women, was formed in 1893 and continues to work to improve the quality of life for people of all races throughout the world in the twenty-first century.) For instance, the Jews quickly established themselves in the theater, and their productions were popular with all Americans. By the turn of the century, about two million playgoers attended Yiddish (a language that is a mixture of Hebrew and German, with some Polish and Russian) productions in New York.

Religion was the guiding force in every aspect of daily life for the traditional Jew. It was a major factor in the Jews' ability to remain unified. By 1860, twenty-seven synagogues had been built in New York. The synagogues were the center of much social activity within Jewish settlements.

New York was one of the most well-known Jewish settlement areas. In particular, Manhattan's Lower East Side is symbolic for the Jewish immigration experience in America. While other ethnic and religious groups lived there, the majority of the East Side's residents were eastern European Jews.

Home Sweet Home

Reports of the first tenement, located in lower Manhattan, date back to 1833. The building was unique in that it was built of cheap materials and designed for multiple families. Up until that point, most landlords preferred to build more expensive dwellings in an effort to boost property values.

As hundreds of thousands of immigrants flooded the cities beginning in the 1840s, businessmen and landlords recognized a market for cheap housing. These buildings could be constructed quickly and at little expense. They offered poor immigrants affordable housing and a chance to make an urban (city) home. By 1864, more than 62 percent of New York's residents lived in tenement homes.

A woman knits in her New York City tenement in the 1890s. PHOTOGRAPH BY JACOB RIIS. © BETTMANN/CORBIS.

Hardships on the East Side Like other immigrants, the Jews crowded into tenement buildings. Most tenement units consisted of three rooms: a kitchen, a front room, and a backroom. The backroom was used as the bedroom, and families with as many as ten members stuffed themselves into these cramped quarters. Often, family members worked in their tenement apartments as well. It was common to see tailoring and sewing in a back room during the day and people sleeping there at night. (See Chapter 8 for more on tenements and housing reform.)

Tenements offered little more than shelter from the weather. They lacked toilets and running water, which led to the spread of disease. Poor ventilation made them hazardous to live in, especially since they were located in industrialized areas where pollution was intense. Like the Irish, the Jews were unfairly stereotyped as filthy and diseased people.

Anti-Semitism finds its roots in America

Hygiene issues were just one factor that led to America's feelings of anti-Semitism. Like other desperate immigrants, the Jews were willing to accept low wages just to have work. American men and women were already being paid meager wages; the Jews replaced them because they were willing to work sixteen-hour shifts for even less pay. This bred a hatred and resentment toward the Jews.

A sizeable portion of the early Jewish population arrived in America with skills as tailors, seamstresses, and textile (fabric) merchants. For the cost of a few sewing machines, they were able to set up their own businesses in the garment (sewing) industry. Others found work in American-owned sewing factories. The garment industry, regardless of who owned and managed the shop, gave Jews something other industries could not: a chance to maintain a cultural and self-identity while still maintaining economic independence. Between 1881 and 1888, weekly wages never rose above $6, even though sixteen-hour shifts were common. The garment industry had its busy seasons, and the busier seasons forced them to work even longer shifts. Factory conditions were unbearable (see Chapter 8) and unsafe. Before labor reforms were implemented in the twentieth century, factories all over America were hazardous to human health and safety. One of the worst tragedies in labor history happened in the garment industry. The

Triangle Shirtwaist Company Fire claimed the lives of more than 145 of its 500 employees in 1911, most of them young women between the ages of sixteen and twenty-three. Located in Manhattan, the company employed mostly Jews. (See more on the fire in Chapter 8.) Throughout the Gilded Age and Progressive Era, the garment industry employed hundreds of thousands of Jewish immigrants, the majority of them women and young girls.

The Jews were among the first immigrants to form effective labor unions (a formally organized association of workers that advances its members' views on wages, work hours, and labor conditions). Their participation in the labor unions intensified America's distrust and resentment of them. Educated Hebrew students led the establishment of these labor unions; these students had emigrated from Russia when their country issued a decree limiting the number of Jews who could attend college. When these educated men joined working-class Jews in America, they realized that the degree of persecution was no different than what they experienced at home. They acted to change treatment of their race.

The cloakmaker's union was one of the first organized. It boasted seven to eight thousand members, workers who endured some of the worst treatment in the factories. After a long struggle, they won shorter hours (from anywhere up to sixteen hours a day, seven days a week to no more than ten hours a day, six days a week), better wages, and improved work conditions. Theirs was a great victory for the entire Jewish working class. It encouraged them to continue to keep trying, no matter how hard the battle. Soon, Jewish labor unions were forming throughout the country. One successful union was the United Hebrew Trades, formed on the

Lower East Side in 1888. The federation included twenty-five organizations and more than ten thousand members within the first year.

The success of the Jews led to resentment among Americans, yet they were among some of the model citizens of their day. Jews placed a high value on education, and attendance records show that their children attended school more regularly than those of other ethnic groups. Their grades were higher overall as well. Jews favored coffee and tea over liquor and beer; coffeehouses were popular meeting places in Jewish neighborhoods. Here, even the working class could meet to discuss labor activity and literature; no one was excluded from conversation. Crime was not widespread among the Jewish race. The state of New York held only 360 Jewish prisoners in 1893, an amazingly low percentage of a large Jewish population. The majority of those men were arrested for petty (small) crimes related to gambling.

Despite these facts, the Jews were a hated race throughout the Gilded Age and Progressive Era. After the Irish, they were the immigrant group most frequently caricatured (represented in cartoons that exaggerate features for comic effect). They were satirized (made fun of) with big noses and kinky black hair. Cartoons of the era depicted Jews as greedy and dishonest, with a tendency to show off their wealth by wearing diamonds and furs.

The main reason for anti-Semitism in America in the late nineteenth and early twentieth centuries was that the Jews refused to assimilate. Assimilation is the process by which a cultural group takes on the qualities and values of another cultural group. Immigrants who came to America were expected to assimilate: Americans believed these newcomers should adopt American ways, practice American rituals, and uphold American values. They wanted them to dress like Americans, eat American food, and act American. Jewish immigrants instead formed communities that allowed them to celebrate and live out their unique cultural beliefs. In the face of great hatred, they managed to thrive.

Germans

Germans made up the largest immigrant group in the Gilded Age. Through 1900, Germans made up one-fourth of all foreign-born citizens. The Irish left their homeland because of starvation; the Chinese left in time of war; and the Jews left amidst violent persecution. Unlike these three groups, the Germans emigrated because industrialization was taking over their jobs. All of Europe was experiencing industrialization, but the structure of German society was changing faster than anywhere else.

Some Germans settled in eastern cities like New York City and Buffalo, New York. Most of the Germans who established themselves in cities, however, headed for what historians call the "German Triangle": St. Louis, Missouri; Cincinnati, Ohio; and Milwaukee, Wisconsin. About 40 percent of all German immigrants lived in American cities. The rest settled in rural regions throughout the East and into the Midwest. Some went into Texas, others as far as California.

Urban Germans followed the same pattern as the other immigrant groups and established communities. Such a neighborhood, often referred to as a "Little Germany," closely resembled the typical Chinatown and served as cities within cities. The German segments featured traditional German businesses such as beer breweries, butchers, cabinetmakers, tailors, machinists, and cigar makers. German women

Jacob Riis on the New York Jew

Jacob Riis (1849–1914) achieved fame with photograph and pen as he exposed tenement slums in the late nineteenth century. He was directly responsible for bringing to the public's attention the undeniably wretched living conditions of the urban poor.

One of Riis's essays, "The Jews of New York" (1896), focused on the prejudice against Manhattan's Lower East Side Jews. Riis defended them as a race and highlighted their many achievements and virtues:

> The system of Jewish charities is altogether admirable. There is no overlapping or waste of effort. Before charity organization had been accepted as a principle by Christian philanthropy [charitable giving] the Jews had in their United Hebrew Charities the necessary clearing house for the speeding and simplifying of the business of helping the poor to help themselves. Their asylums [hospitals], their nurseries and kindergartens are models of their kind. Their great hospital, the Mount Sinai, stands in the front rank in a city full of renowned asylums. Of the 3,000 patients it harbored last year 89 per cent were treated gratuitously [for free]. The Aguilar Free Library circulated last year 253,349 books, mainly on the East Side, and after ten years' existence has nearly 10,000 volumes. The managers of the Baron de Hirsch Fund have demonstrated the claim that he will not till the soil to be a libel on the immigrant Jew. Their great farm of 5,100 acres at Woodbine, N.J., is blossoming into a model village in which there are no idlers and no tramps. At the New York end of the line hundreds of children who come unable to understand any other language than their own jargon, are taught English daily, and men and women nightly, with the Declaration of Independence for their reader and the starry banner ever in their sight. In a marvelously short space of time they are delivered over to the public school, where they receive the heartiest welcome as among their best and brightest pupils.
>
> The Jew in New York has his faults, no doubt, and sometimes he has to be considered in his historic aspect in order that the proper allowance may be made for him. It is a good deal better perspective, too, than the religious one to view him in, as a neighbor and a fellow citizen. I am a Christian and hold that in his belief the Jew is sadly in error. So that he may learn to respect mine, I insist on fair play for him all round. That he has received in New York, and no one has cause to regret it except those he left behind. I am very sure that our city has to-day no better and more loyal citizen than the Jew, be he poor or rich—and none she has less need to be ashamed of.

tended not to enter the work force. When they did, they took jobs as nurses, hotel and saloon keepers, janitors, and household servants.

German immigrants experienced a difference other groups did not. Within the German population, people tended to divide among religious lines. Approximately two-thirds of all Germans were Protestant, with Lutheranism being the most dominant denomination. A third were Catholic, and a small population

Milwaukee's German Heritage

In 1910, Milwaukee, Wisconsin, was known as the "Workingmen's City." Although it ranked twelfth in population, it was third among American cities based on the percentage of its workforce population. Buffalo, New York, and Detroit, Michigan, were first and second.

Milwaukee had a high German and Polish population in the Gilded Age and Progressive Era. The Poles established neighborhoods throughout the city but had the most impact on the

South Side. Germans settled on the city's North Side. The more prosperous built homes along Highland Boulevard.

Some of the most famous German companies had factories in Milwaukee's North Side, including the breweries Pabst and Schlitz and the sausage company Usinger's. Their owners built mansions along Highland Boulevard, which was nicknamed "Sauerkraut Boulevard" because of its primarily German population.

was scattered throughout other various religions, including Jewish, Methodist, and even Amish and Mennonite.

The Lutheran community experienced the most conflict. The newly arrived German Lutherans disapproved of the existing German Lutheran churches in the United States. The new immigrants felt these churches had become too Americanized. The services were conducted in English instead of German, and the church's rules had become too liberal for traditional German Lutherans' liking.

Italians

Fewer than 4,000 Italian immigrants were living in the United States in 1850. That number increased to 44,000 by 1880 and soared to 484,027 by 1900. Most Italian immigrants were from southern Italy.

Although most Italian immigrants had agricultural backgrounds, they were forced to live in urban America because inexpensive land was no longer to be found. Like other immigrants, they lived in clusters, but they did not dominate

neighborhoods as did the Jews or Irish. Instead they lived in smaller groups among other immigrant populations. They tended to relocate in America according to where they lived in Italy. For example, northern Italians lived primarily in California, while Sicilians (who had lived in southern Italy) lived in New Orleans, Louisiana. However, most Italians settled in the mid-Atlantic states (New York, Pennsylvania, Delaware, New Jersey, Maryland, West Virginia, and Virginia) and Washington, D.C., where the geography and weather most closely mirrored that of their home regions in Italy.

Italians lived in conditions similar to those of the Irish and Jews. They were forced into overcrowded tenements that lacked the necessities of healthy living. In an attempt to save money, Italian laborers often went without food. This, combined with the diseased living conditions, took a toll on their health.

One of the reasons for such skimping was that the Italians were sojourners. Their plan was to save as much money in as short a time as possible and then return home. Like other sojourners, many of these immigrants were

An Italian immigrant mother and her three children at Ellis Island in the early twentieth century. © BETTMANN/ CORBIS.

young men who left behind families, wives, and children. Before 1900, about 78 percent of all Italian immigrants were men who traveled to America in the spring, worked until fall was over, and then returned home. Historians estimate that 20 to 30 percent of all Italians returned to Italy permanently.

Italians entered the workforce in the lowest positions, as shoe shiners, sewage cleaners, and ragpickers (unskilled people who pick out rags and other garbage from trash cans and public dumps and sell them). Italian children were often expected to give up their education in order to take a job and contribute to the survival of their families. Italians in America kept the social patterns they knew in Italy and rarely accepted charity. Women worked, but rarely outside the home. They preferred jobs that allowed them to take work home, such as laundry and sewing, so that they could be with their children.

Male workers favored construction jobs when they could get them. Similar to the Six Companies association that helped the Chinese find work, the Italians found work through a labor broker known as a padrone. The padrone found Italian laborers work digging tunnels, building railroads and bridges, and constructing the first skyscrapers. In 1890, 90 percent of New York City's public works employees were Italian, as were 99 percent of Chicago's street workers.

Whereas the Irish were able to break into politics in the United States, the Italians found such activity difficult. They lacked the cultural unity to form a strong identity among all the other ethnicities. They were particularly successful in areas that did not require education, however, such as small business ownership and sales.

Other immigrant groups

Scandinavians The majority of the 1.4 million Scandinavian (Swedish, Norwegian, and Danish) immigrants settled in rural areas, mostly in Minnesota, Iowa, Nebraska, and North and South Dakota. By the end of the nineteenth century, they were migrating (moving from one region to another) to the Pacific Northwest (Washington, Oregon, and Idaho). Eventually, this group established themselves in urban regions, including Chicago and New York City.

In the earlier immigration years, at least, the Scandinavians were pioneers. They built sod houses on the prairies of those western and northcentral states, and the life they dreamed

of was soon replaced by the never-ending hardships unique to pioneers. Long hours of toil in the fields coupled with harsh and unpredictable weather conditions made prairie life unbearable for many. By 1910, 61 percent of the Scandinavians had moved to the cities.

The urban Scandinavians followed the patterns of other immigrant groups and settled their own communities, complete with charitable organizations, cultural events, religious affiliations, and newspapers. Men took jobs as unskilled laborers, while women found mostly domestic work. They did not speak any English, which hindered the Scandinavians' ability to assimilate. Some returned home or became involved in a world of crime and violence.

British Fifteen percent of all immigrants who landed on America's shores in the Gilded Age were British. It is impossible to generalize about this group, so diverse were its settlement patterns and habits. Unlike other immigrant groups, the British did not settle in particular regions, states, or neighborhoods. They did not tend to work in one or two particular industries, nor did they affiliate themselves as a group with one religion. As a result, one historian, Charlotte Erickson, labeled them the "invisible immigrants."

Although some Britons found work in industry, the majority of them made their living as skilled workers or professional workers.

Canadians Canadians had the shortest journey to America. Canadians emigrated via the railroad. Tickets cost $10 per person, and the trip took less than one week. Most Canadians emigrated as families whose plans were to save enough money to return to Canada and buy a farm. Adults earned as much as $1.22 a day; children were paid as little as twenty-eight cents each day. They worked six days, sixty hours a week.

Some Famous and Not-so-famous Immigrants

Asian Americans

James Wong Howe (1899–1976): Cinematographer who made more than 130 films. He was the first Asian American to win an Academy Award (Oscar).

Amy Tan (1952–): Tan is the daughter of Chinese immigrants who arrived in America after the Chinese Exclusion Act was repealed. She is an international best-selling author whose novels include *The Joy Luck Club*. She has written several children's books as well.

Anna May Wong (1905–1961): Wong was the first Chinese American actress to attain stardom in American cinema; she was the sister of James Wong Howe.

German Americans

Emile Berliner (1851–1929): Invented several machines, including the microphone and the gramophone. Invented acoustic tiles (used in concert halls and music venues) that improve sound reception and quality.

Thomas Nast (1840–1902): Famous for his political cartoons that appeared throughout the Gilded Age in the magazine *Harper's Weekly*.

Joseph Pulitzer (1847–1911): Journalist and newspaper owner who contributed the money in 1903 for the establishment of the Pulitzer Prize.

Irish Americans

Henry Ford (1863–1947): Son of an Irish immigrant, Ford established the Ford Motor Company in 1903 and introduced the Model T automobile in 1908. Five years later, Ford invented the assembly line.

John Philip Holland (1841–1914): Submarine inventor who convinced the U.S. Navy to use submarines in 1900.

Mary Anne Sadlier (c. 1820–1903): Wrote sixty volumes of work including children's and adult novels, romances, and children's religious texts.

Italian Americans

Chef Boyardee (1897–1985): Born Ettore Boiardi, became famous for his canned pasta and sauce dinners.

John Rapetti (1862–1936): Worked in France as one of the creators of the Statue of Liberty. His name is carved into the crown.

Rudolph Valentino (1895–1926): Silent film star.

Jewish Americans

Emma Lazarus (1849–1883): Poet and author of the sonnet that appears at the base of the Statue of Liberty.

Hannah Solomon (1858–1942): Founder of the National Jewish Council for Women.

Julius Stieglitz (1867–1937): Chemist who invented gases and chemicals used for warfare in World War I.

Polish Americans

Stanley Ketchel (1896–1910): Born Stanislaw Kiecal to immigrant parents, he is considered by many to be the greatest middleweight boxer of all time.

Albert Michelson (1852–1931): Became first American to win a Nobel Prize; he discovered a way to measure the speed of light.

Artur Rodzinski (1902–1958): Conductor of several American symphonies, including the famous New York Philharmonic.

The Schoolchildren's Blizzard

Most of the settlers on the Dakota-Nebraska prairie in 1888 were Scandinavian and German immigrants. Every day brought new lessons in how to survive the harsh weather conditions and the difficult demands of farming prairie land. It was not an easy life in any way. It most definitely was not the life they were promised by the railroads and other promotional agencies that encouraged them to settle here.

January 12, 1888, started out as a mild winter day, one of sunshine and blue sky. Children left their homes for school that morning with light jackets; some wore no coat at all. Most wore no hats or mittens. After months of unforgiving cold that forced them to stay indoors, these students were eager for the long walk to school.

Entirely without warning, gray clouds crowded the sky in the early afternoon. The temperature dropped 18 degrees Fahrenheit in three minutes. Hurricane winds forced their way across the prairie, and snow began a horizontal descent. Survivors recall hearing an explosion, a sound others compared to the roar of an oncoming train. It was the sound of a murderous blizzard.

As windowpanes shattered and winds tore through the prairie's one-room schoolhouses, children and teachers alike had to make the most important decision of their lives: Should they stay or should they try to make their way home? Those who chose to journey home did not live through the night. But even those who chose to stay in the frigid schools suffered.

By dawn on January 13, the prairie was littered with frozen corpses, most of them children who had tried to reach their families. Estimates of the dead run from 250 to 500; some bodies were never recovered. Others were discovered during the spring thaw.

Sisters were found side by side, their faces frozen to the earth. Fathers gave their lives trying to search for their children and were found with their coats and arms wrapped around those young bodies. One group of five brothers was found in a cluster. Three of them were kneeling in the traditional prayer position. Nearby, the eldest brother was found with his entire body wrapped around the youngest. All five had frozen to death, probably even before nightfall. Corpses were found with their hands frozen to barbed-wire fences. Mothers died sitting up, surrounded by the bodies of their frozen children. Firewood had run out, and no one dared leave the shelter of the house. Some bodies were found just a few feet outside the front door of their homes. The blizzard had prevented them from knowing where they were.

The sudden, heavy snowfall became known as the Schoolchildren's Blizzard. It was a freak of nature; never before or since has a storm of such magnitude occurred without warning. The blizzard that took the lives of hundreds of immigrants tore families apart and permanently crippled or otherwise traumatized many of its survivors. For many, many families, the memories of the blizzard have become family stories that are passed from one generation to the next.

Most French-Canadians settled in New England, though smaller concentrations could be found in New York, Michigan, Wisconsin, and Illinois.

Mexicans Official records indicate that fewer than ten thousand Mexicans emigrated to America prior to 1900. Many historians believe the real numbers are twice that figure.

Mexicans crossed the border at El Paso, Texas, because three railroads went through that city. These trains could transport the immigrants to jobs on nearby farms and in mines. Some railroads hired the Mexicans to construct more railway.

Japanese Hawaii in the 1870s and 1880s was home to vast sugar plantations whose owners needed cheap labor to work the fields. Between 1885 and 1894, more than twenty-eight thousand Japanese traveled to Hawaii to work on these plantations. After Hawaii was annexed (became a territory of the United States) in 1898, Japanese began emigrating in even larger numbers. By that time, Japan was a society of high unemployment rates and civil disorder. Making the decision to leave Japan was not difficult, and by 1900, half of all Japanese immigrants lived in Hawaii.

Most Japanese immigrants were single men, sojourners who planned to return home. Three-quarters of them did, at first. By 1900, only about one-quarter ever left Hawaii to go back to Japan. Plantation owners imported more than twenty-six thousand Japanese in 1899 alone. Never again would so many Japanese enter the United States in a single year.

The Japanese enjoyed fairly friendly race relations in Hawaii. This was not so on the mainland. Even the federal government recognized the difference in attitudes toward the Japanese and ceased issuing passports to the mainland. The primary reason for the prejudice against Japanese on the mainland was that they immigrated so soon after the Chinese. To many Americans, there was no difference between the two races. To make matters worse, the Japanese proved to be astute businessmen.

Although they started as laborers, they soon earned more money by working harder and working longer hours. Their pay increased beyond that of even white laborers, and many Japanese were able to buy their own farms, even though they had to pay higher prices than whites. Soon, they added competition to the American market. This only increased America's resentment.

Soon, even Hawaii rejected the Japanese, and laws were passed there to keep them from moving into skilled occupations. Later, race relations hit an all-time low during World War II, when Japan bombed Pearl Harbor. Anti-Japanese sentiment exploded, and Japanese Americans were rounded up and imprisoned in internment camps. Their homes and businesses were taken from them. Many lives and careers were irreparably damaged.

The urbanization of America

Immigration was supposed to make America a "melting pot;" that is, a place that welcomed various races in the hopes that what would result was an interconnected population that was different yet somehow American. The idea did not work out that way, as immigrants brought their cultural customs and values with them to the new land, and did not let go of them even in the midst of great pressure and hatred.

Immigration brought about many changes to the American landscape, most notably, urbanization. Rural America was quickly becoming a thing of the past, to be replaced with cities full of skyscrapers, bridges, and overcrowding.

America's rural and urban populations were both growing throughout the Gilded Age. But the rate of urban population growth was greater than that of rural growth. (See table.)

Rural vs. Urban Populations during the Gilded Age

Year	Total U.S. population (in thousands)	% Urban	% Rural	% Increase in urban population	% Increase rural population
1870	38,558	25.7	74.3	59.3	13.6
1880	50,156	28.2	71.8	42.7	25.7
1890	62,947	35.1	64.9	56.4	13.4
1900	75,995	39.7	60.3	36.4	12.2

SOURCE: U.S. Bureau of the Census, *Historical Statistics of the United States: Colonial Times to 1970.* Washington, DC, 1975.

As the chart illustrates, the urbanization rate was more than four times greater than the increase in the rural population in 1890. An urban area is defined as one that has more than twenty-five hundred residents. In 1860, America had 392 urban places; by 1900, that number jumped 343 percent, to 1,737 places. The reason for the increase was the development of older towns and cities as well as westward expansion.

Cities were considered "big" if they were home to more than one hundred thousand residents. In 1860, America had nine such big cities. By 1900, there were thirty-eight. New York was the first city to claim one million residents, and it did so in 1880. This increase was directly due to the immigration movement.

By 1900, America as a country was still just two-fifths urban. But the Northeast states (Maine, New Hampshire, Vermont, New York, Pennsylvania, Massachusetts, Rhode Island, Connecticut, and New Jersey) were two-thirds urban. The American South (Texas, Oklahoma, Arkansas, Louisiana, Mississippi, Alabama, Tennessee, Kentucky, West Virginia, Virginia, North Carolina, South Carolina, Georgia, and Florida) had the smallest urban population, with just 18 percent of its residents in cities. The North Central (Illinois, Indiana, Michigan, Minnesota, Nebraska, Ohio, and Wisconsin) and Western (New Mexico, Colorado, Wyoming, Montana, South Dakota, North Dakota, Idaho, Utah, Arizona, Nevada, Washington, Oregon, and California) regions had urbanization rates somewhere in between these two extremes.

Moving on Foreign immigration was responsible for half of the era's urbanization. The rest of the increase was due to Americans who left the countryside in hopes of a more prosperous life in the city. Economic depressions in the 1870s and 1890s forced many farms into bankruptcy (complete financial failure). Farmers joined the escape to the cities.

Another group that contributed to the urbanization of America was the African Americans. Throughout the 1870s, approximately 68,000 southern African Americans migrated to northern cities. These cities offered African Americans what no place in the South could: enforced civil rights and the opportunity to earn a living independently. Although slaves had been freed with the victory of the North in the Civil War, most white Southerners continued to look upon African Americans as an inferior race. In addition, nearly all land was still owned by whites. African Americans could work on that land, but they would probably never own it or reap the profits of their hard labor. Moving to the North gave African Americans the chance to begin life anew, in an atmosphere of freedom. By the end of the nineteenth century, that number increased to 185,000. This group was not attracted to the largest cities such as New York and Chicago but chose instead smaller urban areas. These smaller towns and cities were more like their homes in the South, and the familiarity made the transition to a new region more comfortable.

Southern cities increased in size owing to the African American migration as well. Not all rural residents went directly north, though most eventually did. In the last twenty years of the 1900s, the African American populations of Savannah, Georgia, and Nashville, Tennessee, nearly doubled. The Atlanta, Georgia, African American population also experienced a dramatic increase, from sixteen thousand to thirty-six thousand.

Urban growth brings change

As cities became more crowded, their environment changed out of necessity. Before industrialization, urban areas were "walking" cities; because of this, there were no specialized districts. Commercial, governmental, educational, industrial, residential, and religious buildings were built next to each other so that walkers could navigate the city conveniently. The wealthy lived just a short distance from the poor.

Urban development was influenced mostly by the advent of the streetcar. Streetcars moved along iron rails like trains. By the mid-1880s, three hundred cities benefited from street railway lines. Horses and mules pulled these streetcars, but at the turn of the century, cables replaced the animals. The streetcars were attached to the cables by grips, which allowed

them to move faster and more smoothly thanks to a nonmoving engine that powered an underground cable. The downfall of cable cars was that they broke down often and repairs were costly. Electrified streetcars called trolleys eventually replaced them. Introduced in Richmond, Virginia, in 1888, they quickly caught on throughout the United States. By the beginning of the twentieth century, most urban mass transit systems were based on electricity. The underground subway in New York opened on October 27, 1904. On the first day of operation, 150,000 passengers rode the subway at a cost of five cents a ride. By the 1940s, New York City's subway lines provided more than eight million rides a day.

As transportation improved, the cities grew. They no longer had to be compact so that foot traffic could manage daily travel. Trolley lines went from one end of the city to the other, with many stops in between. Residents could now move to outlying urban areas because they knew they could travel easily throughout the city. Before the trolley, the most sought-after city residences were often near the city's center (because of the convenience); mass transit, however, completely turned that pattern around. People began to divide themselves according to social class, ethnicity, and race. The middle of the city became home to society's lower classes, and the further toward the city limits one traveled, the more expensive the homes became.

Mass transit also encouraged the building of suburbs, or neighborhoods composed of the same "types" of people. Well before zoning laws and building codes were developed, construction companies were building entire neighborhoods of homes that were

San Francisco cable cars in 1873. © BETTMANN/CORBIS.

architecturally and structurally alike. Suburbs were built seemingly overnight on the outskirts of cities.

While suburbs sorted themselves out according to income and wealth, the core of the city divided itself into districts according to function. For example, New York's Wall Street was known—and still is—as the financial district. Other districts became known as the garment, entertainment, railroad, or government districts. Every large city followed this pattern. During this time, property taxes rose, as did the real estate value in these specialized districts. With few exceptions, single-family homes still in existence in the center of the city were forced out by the beginning of the twentieth century.

Birth of the skyscraper

As cities grew, so did buildings in order to accommodate the increase in people. Older buildings had been made of brick and masonry. These materials suited one-to-five-story structures well. Beyond that, the buildings would weigh too much and require incredibly thick lower walls and foundations. Railways allowed for horizontal urban expansion, but it took improved building techniques and materials to allow for vertical expansion.

Steel was the material of choice for urban building construction. A steel skeleton covered with light masonry marked the birth of the skyscraper in the mid-1880s. Chicago became home to the original skyscraper in 1885. The ten-story

Home Insurance Building was erected, and soon thirty- and forty-story buildings were being constructed throughout the nation. Housing soon followed suit, with the arrival of apartment houses for the upper class and tenement housing for the working class.

For a number of years, the towers of the Brooklyn Bridge dominated the New York skyline. It opened to traffic in 1883. By the end of the century, however, the city's new skyscrapers dwarfed the bridge's towers.

A need to be clean

Engineering became a profitable occupation as cities hired engineers to design reliable water and sewage systems. The last twenty years of the nineteenth century saw vast improvement in technology that cut down on the number of diseases carried by water. Between 1890 and 1914, the population served by filtered water grew from 310,000 to more than 17 million.

Sanitary engineers designed filters and built sewage treatment plants that relied on new chemicals to keep urban America clean and healthy. Running water and indoor toilets became standard features in the urban homes being constructed in the 1890s. Before the first decade of the twentieth century had ended, many cities had gas, electric, and telephone service.

As urban centers became home to business districts, large industries and factories were forced to move. Larger industries like railroads and steel mills required vast amounts of land, and the center of the Gilded Age cities simply did not have it. The cost of land was much higher in the city, too. So industry was pushed to the outskirts, and in the late 1800s, industrial suburbs emerged.

These suburbs were built around a particular industry. Employees of that industry lived in the suburbs because the cost of commuting every day by trolley was more than they could afford. Soon, shops, restaurants, and entertainment venues were built, and residents of the industrial suburbs had little reason to travel outside the town limits for their daily needs.

Is bigger better?

Many Americans welcomed the changes created by industrialism (an economy based on business and industry rather than agriculture). Housing was better. Life was made easier by the invention of electricity and the way its availability in homes and businesses improved transportation, communication, and daily life. Buildings were bigger, cities more exciting.

As urban areas continued to grow, so did the more bleak aspects of human nature. More people meant more crime. Cities were not accustomed to enforcing their own laws; that had always been the responsibility of state or federal governments. Mayors were elected but in reality had very little authority over city governments. Instead, corrupt political machines like Tammany Hall (see Chapters 1 and 3) ruled urban America. Crime and violence increased, as did social problems such as overcrowding. The labor movement, already in progress, continued to pit workers against management. Education was neglected as children headed for factories and mills to help families survive.

Reform was needed in virtually every imaginable way by the turn of the century. It would come from some of the most unexpected places. Women would rise up, their voices shouting for rights not only for themselves, but also for their families. So-called muckraking journalists would courageously expose public figures and industries for their corruption and lack of integrity. Education would become a national issue as African Americans demanded their fair shot at higher learning.

As cities were growing and changing on an almost daily basis, America's western frontier was entering its final phase. Before the dawn of the twentieth century, the Wild West would be known only in legends. A new movement would be ushered in as Americans discovered the beauty of its natural resources and treasures.

For More Information

BOOKS

Calhoun, Charles W., ed. *The Gilded Age: Essays on the Origins of Modern America*. Wilmington, DE: Scholarly Resources, 1996.

Cashman, Sean Dennis. *America in the Gilded Age*. New York: New York University Press, 1993.

Laskin, David. *The Children's Blizzard*. New York: HarperCollins, 2004.

Painter, Nell Irvin. *Standing at Armageddon: The United States, 1877–1919*. New York: W. W. Norton & Co., 1987.

WEB SITES

"Big Apple History: Coming to America." *PBS.org*. http://pbskids.org/bigapplehistory/immigration/topic2.html (accessed on April 17, 2006).

Brody, Seymour. "Jewish Heroes and Heroines of America." *Florida Atlantic University Libraries*. http://www.fau.edu/library/brodytoc.htm (accessed on April 17, 2006).

Center for the History & Ethics of Public Health. *The Living City*. http://www.tlcarchive.org/htm/home.htm (accessed on April 17, 2006).

"From Haven to Home: A Century of Immigration, 1820–1924." *Library of Congress*. http://www.loc.gov/exhibits/haventohome/haven-century.html (accessed on April 17, 2006).

"Immigration: Irish." *Library of Congress*. http://memory.loc.gov/learn/features/immig/irish2.html (accessed on April 17, 2006).

"Immigration: The Living Mosaic of People, Culture, & Hope." *ThinkQuest.org*. http://library.thinkquest.org/20619/index.html (accessed on April 17, 2006).

Libo, Kenneth, and Michael Skakun. "The Industrial Removal Office: German Jewry's Response to an Overcrowded East Side." *Center for Jewish History*. http://www.cjh.org/about/Forward/view_Forward.cfm?Forwardid=39 (accessed on April 17, 2006).

Libo, Kenneth, and Michael Skakun. "A Perfect Fit: The Garment Industry and American Jewry." *Center for Jewish History*. http://www.cjh.org/education/essays.php?action=show&id=41 (accessed on April 17, 2006).

"Literacy Test." *Institute of Texan Cultures*. http://www.texancultures.utsa.edu/newtexans/literacy.htm (accessed on April 17, 2006).

Lower East Side Tenement Museum. http://www.tenement.org/index.htm (accessed on April 17, 2006).

"Milwaukee Neighborhoods: Photos & Maps 1885–1992." *University Wisconsin-Milwaukee Libraries*. http://www.uwm.edu/Library/digilib/Milwaukee/records/picture.html (accessed on April 17, 2006).

Norton, Henry Kittredge. "The Chinese." *The Virtual Museum of the City of San Francisco*. http://www.sfmuseum.org/hist6/chinhate.html (accessed on April 17, 2006).

Smith, Marian L. "'Any Woman Who Is Now or May Hereafter Be Married...': Women and Naturalization, ca. 1802–1940." *Prologue: Quarterly of the National Archives and Records Administration*. http://www.archives.gov/publications/prologue/1998/summer/women-and-naturalization-1.html (accessed on April 17, 2006).

Smith, Marian L. "Overview of INS History." *U.S. Citizenship and Immigration Services*. http://uscis.gov/graphics/aboutus/history/articles/OVIEW.htm (accessed on April 17, 2006).

"Subway Centennial." *Metropolitan Transit Authority*. http://www.mta.nyc.ny.us/mta/centennial.htm (accessed on June 26, 2006).

5

Expansion into the West

As industrialism (an economy based on business and industry rather than agriculture) took over the Eastern states at the dawn of the Gilded Age, immigrants (people who leave one region to permanently live in another) came by the millions to build new lives in their new land. (The Gilded Age was the period in history following the American Civil War [1861–65] and Reconstruction [roughly the final twenty-three years of the nineteenth century], characterized by a ruthless pursuit of profit, an exterior of showiness and grandeur, and immeasurable political corruption.) Most of the immigrants settled in the East. The Southern states were populated largely with African Americans who had been freed from the bondage of slavery. Because the South was not as intensely affected by the Industrial Revolution (an era when business and industry replaced America's agricultural economy, approximately 1878–1900) as was the East, the population growth in that region was not as explosive.

The region of the United States that was still relatively open was the West. California was home to hundreds of thousands of Chinese immigrants who crossed the Pacific Ocean to work as servants and railroad laborers and in other positions most workers considered too dirty or dangerous. Mexican immigrants crossed the border into Texas and worked mostly as field hands, taking jobs where they could find them. For the most part, the West was still wild in the minds of Americans.

The Wild West: home of the Native American

The phrase "Wild West" conjured images of dusty plains and ferocious Indians, as Native Americans were called. They were also referred to as savages, known for their brutality in war.

Clashes between Native Americans and the rest of America had been occurring since the 1600s. Tribes in the Northeast forged respectful relationships with fur traders and missionaries, but English settlers lived

WORDS TO KNOW

Gilded Age: The period in history following the Civil War and Reconstruction (roughly the final twenty-three years of the nineteenth century), characterized by a ruthless pursuit of profit, an exterior of showiness and grandeur, and immeasurable political corruption.

Indian agents: Representatives of the U.S. government who worked with Native Americans. Their responsibility was to resolve conflicts and take the Native Americans' concerns to the government.

reservations: Specific land allotted to the Native Americans by the U.S. government, as part of

the solution to the "Indian Problem." The tribes did not own the land, but they managed it. These areas were the only places the Native Americans were allowed to live in the nineteenth century.

rustlers: Cattle thieves.

severalty: Individual ownership of land, as opposed to tribal ownership.

transcontinental railroad: The railroad system that traveled across the entire United States; this included five routes through the West. The last stake was driven into the railroad on May 10, 1869.

---

in constant fear of attacks. After the American Revolution (1775–83), the new government had to deal with a major problem: how to convince the Native American tribes in the Northwest Territory (land north of the Ohio River and east of the Mississippi River) to leave their land so white settlers could move in.

After many battles, the Treaty of Greenville was signed in 1795 and the tribes left Ohio for Indiana. The treaty allowed tribes to retain hunting rights to the land, and it promised them $20,000 in immediate payment in the form of goods needed for everyday living. Tribes would also receive another $9,500 in goods annually to be split among them. That did not satisfy the government, as settlers soon began moving in on Native American lands in Indiana, too. This breach of contract angered the tribes, and they formed a confederacy led by Shawnee chief Tecumseh (c. 1768–1813). The great warrior was killed in the War of 1812 (1812–15). His death ended the threat from the Northwest

Territory, and the U.S. government was able to develop a policy for removing Native Americans from the region.

By 1860, most Native Americans had been relocated across the Mississippi River. The tribes did not leave their homeland willingly or without a struggle. In addition to many smaller conflicts, the relocation program resulted in the first Seminole War (1817–18), the Black Hawk War (1832), and the second Seminole War (1835–42). These wars were a foreshadowing of what would be more than twenty years of battles between Native Americans and whites.

The Plains Indian Wars

Relocating the Native Americans did not produce the results for which the government hoped. The conflicts between the tribes and the settlers and military did not end. The only difference was the setting: The battles were now taking place west of the Mississippi River, primarily on the Great Plains. These wars make up what is now historically known as the Plains Indian Wars (1866–90).

Plains tribes were mostly peaceful and lived together with little conflict. But as white settlers moved into the region, the Native Americans grew increasingly distraught and angry. The settlers slaughtered buffalo herds to the point of near extinction. The tribal peoples depended on the buffalo for their way of life. The Native Americans respected the buffalo and hunted it with great appreciation. They killed only what they needed and used every part of the animal for food, clothing, and weapons. The mindless slaughter by white settlers led to the first conflicts between the tribes and the white men.

Hunting was not the only point of contention between the two groups. Corruption among Indian agents (representatives of the U.S. government who worked with Native Americans) fostered distrust and resentment between the Native Americans and outsiders. The responsibility of these agents was to respond to Native American concerns, but some agents stole supplies intended for the reservations (federal land allotted to and managed by Native Americans). Others stole money that was supposed to go to the Native Americans as outlined in various treaties and agreements.

In addition to corrupt agents, the Native Americans were expected to tolerate prospectors (gold miners) trespassing on sacred tribal grounds. Railroads posed another problem when they began interfering with traditional hunting practices. Overall, the Native Americans' way of life was destroyed.

Hostilities peaked between 1869 and 1878. More than two hundred battles were fought during those years. By the late 1870s, the goal of the

Who Were the Buffalo Soldiers?

Throughout the Plains Indian Wars, approximately 20 percent of the U.S. Cavalry were African American soldiers. These soldiers made up the Ninth and Tenth U.S. Cavalry Regiments. The Cheyenne and Comanche tribes nicknamed these men "Buffalo Soldiers" because they were courageous and strong, qualities shared by the buffalo. The hair of the Buffalo Soldiers reminded Native Americans of the tuft of hair between a buffalo's horns, as well. These soldiers wore their nickname with pride as they fought in more than 177 conflicts against the Native Americans. At least seventeen Medals of Honor were awarded the Buffalo Soldiers throughout the Indian Wars.

In addition to their military duties, the Buffalo Soldiers mapped miles of southwest frontier (wilderness at the edge of a settled area or region) territory and strung hundreds of miles of telegraph lines. Without the protection of the Buffalo Soldiers, construction crews could not have survived long enough to build the railroads throughout the American frontier.

The Buffalo Soldiers participated in many other wars, including the American Civil War, the Spanish-American War (1898), and both World War I (1914–18) and World War II (1939–45).

federal government became the Americanization of what Hiram Price (1814–1901), commissioner of Indian Affairs, called the "savages." In his 1881 annual report, Price wrote that to "allow them to drag along year after year . . . in their old superstitions, laziness, and filth . . . would be a lasting disgrace to our government."

Helen Hunt Jackson: Unlikely Activist

Activist Helen Hunt Jackson. © BETTMANN/CORBIS.

While many Native American rights activists joined organizations to further their cause, some, like writer Helen Hunt Jackson (1830–1885), acted alone. Jackson's parents died while

Jackson was a teen. She was sent to live with an aunt and received a high-class education at Ipswich Female Seminary in Massachusetts and then Abbott Institute (a boarding school) in New York City. At Abbott, she befriended future poet Emily Dickinson (1830–1886).

Jackson married U.S. Army captain Edward Bissell Hunt (1822–1863) in 1852, but their life together was marked by tragedy. She lost her husband and two sons within eleven years.

A grief-stricken Jackson moved to Newport, Rhode Island, a city she and her husband had spent time in years before. She renewed her friendship with Dickinson. It was during this time that Jackson decided to pursue a writing career. She initially wrote children's stories, poems, and travel sketches under pseudonyms (false names) like "H. H." and "Saxe Holm." Female writers of the day usually used pen names to conceal their true identity because writing was not considered a "proper" thing for women to do.

Jackson spent the winter of 1873–74 in Colorado Springs, Colorado, where she was seeking a cure for a breathing disorder she had. There, she

Taming the savages

The 1880s was a decade of reform in the federal Indian policy in the United States. Advocacy (support) groups for Native American rights were formed. Some groups worked together. The Women's National Indian Association, the Indian Rights Association, the National Indian Defense Association, and other organizations were collectively known as the "Friends of the Indian." Their goal was to succeed where

reservation life had failed the Native Americans. They believed tribal members could become productive members of society if they had education, U.S. citizenship, and their own land. It would seem that it never occurred to any of these activists that the Native Americans were the oldest citizens of the United States, having lived there longer than anyone else. The irony of the idea of "giving" land to the very people from whom they took land was lost on these well-meaning people.

met a wealthy banker named William Sharpless Jackson (1836–1919). They married in the fall of 1875, and the new bride was able to focus on her writing without worrying about finances. Jackson's time in Colorado nurtured her interest in the American West in general and in Native Americans in particular.

Jackson attended a lecture in Boston in 1879. She listened to Chief Standing Bear (1829?–1908) talk about the government's removal of the Ponca Indians from their reservation in Nebraska to Indian Territory. Jackson was so moved by the chief's words that she instantly became a tireless crusader for the remaining tribes. She used her writing skills to expose the government's mistreatment of Native Americans and was an active fund-raiser. Jackson was a determined reformer whose talents would sway public opinion.

Jackson published *A Century of Dishonor* in 1881. The book was not a balanced history, but a plea for mercy on behalf of Native Americans throughout the country. The book created a scandal by exposing dishonest government officials and practices, broken treaties, and general government corruption and mismanagement. Jackson gave every member of Congress a copy of her book.

As a result of *A Century of Dishonor,* the U.S. Department of the Interior authorized her and a translator to investigate the condition and needs of the Mission Indians in California. However, government authorities largely ignored the report she wrote in 1883. President Chester A. Arthur (1830–1886; served 1881–85) had made her the first woman to hold the position of commissioner of Indian Affairs in 1882, but Jackson's true gift lay in reaching the public rather than moving the government to action.

In 1884, Jackson wrote a novel called *Ramona.* The hastily written book was based on her experiences with the Mission Indians. The novel turned out to be the highlight of her career and has been compared with the famous antislavery novel by Harriet Beecher Stowe (1811–1896), *Uncle Tom's Cabin.* Stowe's novel shed light on the physical and psychological horrors of slavery.

Ramona has been credited by some historians as the inspiration for the enactment of the Dawes Severalty Act of 1887 (see later in this chapter). Although the legislation did more harm than good, Jackson's ability to exert such influence at a time when men ruled politics was impressive.

In an effort to transform the Native Americans into "civilized" people, the government developed programs designed to teach them how to farm and raise livestock. Unfortunately, the reservation lands the tribes were forced to live on were mostly infertile (unproductive). No matter how skilled they would become as farmers or cattle ranchers, the land would prevent them from succeeding to any great degree.

Educational reform was another challenge for the government. A federal school system was developed, and more than twenty thousand Native American children went through that system. They were taught English and vocational skills. For the boys, this meant farming and a knowledge of common trades such as laborers, carpenters, and office clerks. Girls were taught domestic skills such as sewing, cooking, and anything else that would help them manage a household. The main objective of the government was to make the Native Americans self-sufficient.

Another reform effort involved two off-reservation experiments. A boarding school was set up in Carlisle, Pennsylvania, in 1879. Eighty-four boys and girls from the Dakota territory attended. By the mid-1890s, 769 students attended. These students were under strict surveillance and completely cut off from relatives on the reservations. Some went years without seeing their families. Reformers considered the Carlisle school so successful that the Indian Office built eighteen more similar institutions by 1895.

The other experiment, begun in 1890, involved sending reservation children to public schools in California, Oregon, Washington, Utah, Nebraska, Oklahoma, Wisconsin, and Michigan. Again, this experiment was successful in the eyes of the whites, and by 1895 there were sixty-two off-reservation public schools for reservation children. These schools, added to the 19 boarding schools and the 185 reservation schools, made up the educational system for Native Americans at the end of the nineteenth century.

Native American response to these experiments and the Americanized educational system was mixed. Many resented having this system imposed upon them and their children. In addition to breaking up families, it instilled in students values that were not necessarily those of Native Americans. The most obvious of these values were religious in nature. Christianity was a white religion. Other Native Americans understood that their children were going to need the education forced upon them if they were to live in white man's society. Although they disliked having their children separated from their families, they accepted the imposition as just one more change in a changing society. What they could not foresee was that education alone was not going to allow their children to fit in to a mostly white society.

No studies were ever conducted to determine the long-term effects of these experiments on reservation children. Historians do know that most of these off-reservation students returned home once they completed their education. Because work was difficult to find on reservations, many reverted back to their old way of life. Those who did seek work outside the reservation often took low-paying jobs with the Bureau of Indian Affairs (BIA), which was established within the War Department in 1824. Measured against the goals set by the boarding school system, these educational experiments were failures; they did not convert the Native Americans to Christianity, nor did they make them self-sufficient.

The Native Americans did not have a choice about where they lived or how they were educated. But they would not let the white man take away their customs, languages, or political structures. This stance was a threat to the federal government, and by 1871, Congress was legislating programs without consulting the tribes. The BIA was designed to regulate and settle disputes with the tribes, but by the 1870s the BIA was less concerned with justice for the Native Americans than it was with keeping order. Tribes no longer were allowed to act as their own authority figures; they became wards of the government and were subject to laws and regulations imposed upon them. The programs and people that were supposed to protect the Native Americans were now the very groups that were persecuting them.

Life on the reservation

Reaction to reservation life among Native Americans was mixed. This is not to say that some preferred the reservation way of life. Without exception, the tribes would have preferred to continue their traditional way of life, a lifestyle that had been handed down to them through generations. But some Native Americans abandoned the hope of ever returning to their traditional lifestyle. They dedicated themselves to making the most of reservation life since tradition was no longer an option.

These tribal members learned to farm. Some took jobs as reservation police and judges or worked in various capacities with the Indian Affairs agencies. Others found work outside the reservation, usually in the Wild West shows (see box) or in traveling medicine shows (shows where Native Americans performed tribal dances and sold crafts and fake medicines). Some worked in lumber camps, mines, and railroad companies. They sent their children to school. They attended Christian church and dressed like "civilized" (Americanized) members of society. In every way, they tried to assimilate (become similar to their environment) in order to build a life for themselves.

Other Native Americans refused to be "Americanized." Many of these were older male members of tribes, warriors who fought against the United States and lost. Reservations were places of despair and hopelessness for many Native Americans. Many took to drinking liquor supplied by white men. This habit impeded their ability to think clearly, and soon reservation tribes were considered lazy drunks. As noted in Charles Calhoun's *The Gilded Age,* the famous warrior Sitting Bull (1831–1890) said, "I do not wish to be shut up in a corral. It is bad for young men to be fed by an agent. It makes them lazy and drunken. All agency Indians I have seen were worthless. They are neither red warriors nor white farmers. They are neither wolf nor dog."

The Dawes Severalty Act

The failure of reservations forced the U.S. government to reconsider its Indian policy. U.S. senator Henry L. Dawes (1816–1903) of Massachusetts led the effort for passing a general allotment act in which individual Native Americans would own their own land. This would take away the last factor keeping tribes together. Forcing them to live separately would weaken tribal ties and theoretically make assimilation easier. Dawes was supported not only by reformers but also by railroads, settlers, and other business owners. More than 60 million acres of surplus (extra) reservation lands would be for sale if the allotment act passed.

On February 8, 1887, the Dawes Severalty Act passed. The Act provided Native American families with 160 acres of land; single adults received 80 acres. Along with the land came full U.S. citizenship. There was a catch: citizenship would not be granted until a twenty-five-year trust had expired. Native Americans would lose their legal standing as a tribe but also would not have individual legal standing for an additional twenty-five years.

The Act was implemented gradually; reservations did not disappear entirely. Section 8 of the Act listed specific tribes that would be exempt from the law. These groups included Cherokees, Creeks, Choctaws, Chickasaws, Seminoles, Osage, Miamies and Peorias, and Sacs and Foxes. Also exempt were the Seneca Nation of New York Indians in the state of New York and tribes in the territory of Nebraska that adjoined the Sioux Nation to the South. The Dawes Act's provisions eventually extended to these groups as well, but not until 1893.

The Dawes Act did very little to help Native Americans assimilate. They were not prepared to

Entertainment in the Wild, Wild West

The West's reputation as a wild and dangerous frontier was due in part to entertainment shows that traveled from town to town. These performances showcased legendary figures such as Annie Oakley (1830–1926) and Calamity Jane (1852?–1903). The most famous traveling show belonged to Buffalo Bill Cody (1846–1917). Iowa native William Cody held many jobs throughout his life, but the job he considered his career was that of a scout. He also worked for the Kansas Pacific Railroad; one of his duties included finding meat for the workers. Cody calculated that he killed more than four thousand buffalo for the railroad. Whether or not this estimate is true will never be known, but this is what earned him the name Buffalo Bill.

After his stint with the railroad was over, Cody returned to scouting, working again for the U.S. Army. In 1869, he found himself leading forty men into battle. Though surrounded by more than two hundred Native American warriors, Cody remained calm and managed to keep most of his soldiers alive. Exploits like this brought Buffalo Bill fame and respect throughout the West.

Cody met a writer named Ned Buntline (1821–1886), who soon published a series of books and magazines featuring the adventurous scout. The completion of the transcontinental railroad (the railroad system that traveled across the entire United States) in May 1869 sealed Cody's fate; he took advantage of his fame and began work as a hunting guide for the wealthy. Hunters came from all over the world and rode the rails throughout the West in search of animals they had never seen in person.

Thanks to Buntline's novels, Cody had built a reputation throughout the country as a folk hero. The living legend enjoyed his hero status and used it to make money. By 1872, Cody was traveling across the country, starring in productions written by Buntline. The applause was addicting to Cody, who made up his mind to remain in show business forever. He continued to travel but still managed to engage in scouting adventures. In 1882, Cody joined forces with play producer Nate Salisbury. That partnership resulted in "Buffalo Bill's Wild West," a show that would take Cody overseas to Europe and bring him riches he never imagined.

The show itself was made of reenactments of specific historical scenes, such as those from battles, or of general events, such as wagon trains crossing the plains. Between scenes, Buffalo Bill would entertain the crowd with displays of his sharpshooting or rodeo abilities.

Throughout the 1880s, Cody hired approximately one hundred Native Americans for his shows. They would take part in battle reenactments and in staged Indian races. The Native Americans were paid for their work and enjoyed the travel. Some of the more famous warriors of the day, including Sitting Bull (1831–1890) and Geronimo (1829–1909), took part in the show. Despite the fact that Cody used the exploitation of the Native Americans to his advantage, by every account he always treated the Native Americans he hired with respect and refused to allow anyone in the audience to degrade them.

Buffalo Bill's show was an international success because it vividly portrayed the dangers of the West in a safe environment. The lifestyle imposed on him by the show took its toll. Endless travel kept him from his home and family,

A poster promoting Buffalo Bill's Wild West circus.
© CORBIS.

and years of hard drinking led to a general decline in his health. Cody was ready to quit the show by the 1890s, but poor investments of his wealth left him with little money. He continued to tour with the show until 1916. Cody died at the age of seventy on January 10, 1917.

live life as individual, small family groups. They had been brought up to depend on one another and live as a community. When the Act passed in 1887, tribes owned about 138 million acres of land. By 1900, they had just 78 million acres, and that number would drop to 48 million by 1934. Millions of acres that were not allotted to the Native Americans were considered surplus land and made available for sale to the highest bidder.

On paper, the Dawes Act may have seemed like a solid idea. In reality, however, it was anything but. Not only did the tribes lose much of their surplus land, they lost the individual allotments because they lacked the training to farm and access to credit to buy machinery necessary to operating a farm. They were not allowed to use their land as collateral (something of value pledged to assure repayment of debt), and the federal government had set aside just $30,000 for machinery, livestock, seeds, and other necessities. Rather than compete with their white neighbors, many Native Americans just sold their land to them instead. By 1934, when the Act was abandoned, Native Americans' dependence on the government had not been eliminated in any way. The Dawes Act accomplished the opposite of its intention; dependence on the U.S. government had increased.

The Ghost Dance

Even as the Dawes Act was being implemented, the Native Americans on reservations grew increasingly dissatisfied and unhappy. Many populations were starving. In 1888, a religious phenomena swept the American West. A Paiute tribe holy man named Wovoka (c. 1856–1932) from Nevada experienced a vision during an eclipse (overshadowing) of the sun. The result

of his vision was a religion called the Ghost Dance. According to the Ghost Dance, the earth as it was would soon die. New soil would cover the earth and bury the white men, leaving only Native Americans to enjoy the wild horses, buffalo, green grasses, and running water. Even those who had already died in this lifetime would enjoy an existence free from suffering.

In order to earn the right to this next life, Native Americans had to live honestly and embrace their culture's traditions. This meant turning their backs on the white men's ways, especially the use of alcohol. Wovoka instructed tribes to turn to prayer and chanting. He taught them the Ghost Dance, a dance in which dancers might die for a moment to get a brief glimpse into the paradise that awaited them. Part of the Ghost Dance involved the wearing of a specially made shirt which was believed to protect the wearer from enemy bullets.

The Ghost Dance movement caught on throughout the West. All Sioux reservations were practicing this new religion. One Lakota, Kicking Bear (c. 1852–1904), and his brother-in-law, Short Bull (c. 1845–1915), traveled to Nevada to learn about the Ghost Dance. Kicking Bear then visited the great Sitting Bull (1831–1890) in October 1890 to tell him what he had learned. Sitting Bull was a highly respected Lakota chief whose visions of the defeat of General George Armstrong Custer (1839–1876) and his own death came true. Sitting Bull expressed doubt that the dead would be brought back to life, but he had no objections to allowing his people to dance the Ghost Dance.

Indian agents, however, had already reported to the federal government their fears about the strength and influence of the Ghost

Native Americans participate in a Ghost Dance. © CORBIS.

Dance movement. Now their fears were intensified, as they believed Sitting Bull would join the Ghost Dancers. To keep this from happening, forty-three Lakota policemen were sent to remove Sitting Bull from his home at Standing Rock, South Dakota. They entered his cabin on December 15 and woke the sleeping chief. He agreed to come with the police and asked that his horse be saddled while he dressed. Meanwhile, a large group of Ghost Dancers gathered outside the cabin, and when Sitting Bull and the police stepped outside, one of the dancers shot Lieutenant Henry Bull Head. Bull Head pulled his gun and shot back at the dancer but accidentally shot Sitting Bull instead.

Another policeman then killed Sitting Bull with a shot to the head. Before the morning was over, six police and seven warriors were dead.

Wounded Knee Massacre

The Ghost Dance was officially banned on Lakota reservations, yet the dancers continued with their rituals. Many of Sitting Bull's tribe had fled to find safety with another Lakota tribe led by chief Big Foot (c. 1820–1890). Wanting to avoid further violence, Big Foot led his people and the newcomers further south toward the reservation at Pine Ridge, South Dakota.

What Big Foot did not know is that officials had already ordered his arrest. The great chief was growing weaker with each hour as pneumonia set in. He had no intentions of fighting and was flying the white flag (symbol of truce, or peace) when he had his people set up camp for the night near Wounded Knee Creek on December 28, 1890. As they settled in for sleep, troops of the Seventh Cavalry surrounded them on all sides.

Soldiers entered the camp the following morning and demanded the Native Americans turn over all their weapons. One of the Native American warriors, Black Coyote, was deaf; he did not understand what was going on and was not willing to give up his weapon. A soldier tried to disarm him and the firearm discharged. Chaos immediately set in, as Native Americans ran for cover and soldiers began shooting them to try to control the disorder. Big Foot was among the first killed, and his corpse lay in the snow for three days before being tossed into a mass grave.

The massacre lasted less than one hour. When it was over, around three hundred Native Americans had been unnecessarily slaughtered; two-thirds of them were women and children. Twenty-five soldiers were dead, another thirty-nine wounded. As reported on the Web site *PBS: New Perspectives on the West,* Lakota warrior American Horse (c. 1840–1908) recalled the brutality:

> There was a woman with an infant in her arms who was killed as she almost touched the flag of truce. . . . A mother was shot down with her infant; the child not knowing that its mother was dead was still nursing. . . . The women as they were fleeing with their babies were killed together, shot right through . . . and after most of them had been killed a cry was made that all those who were not killed or wounded should come forth and they would be safe. Little boys . . . came out of their places of refuge, and as soon as they came in sight a number of soldiers surrounded them and butchered them.

Corpses of women and children were found scattered as far away as three miles from camp. On New Year's Day of 1891, soldiers dug a pit and piled into it the bodies they could find. Relatives had already removed other bodies. Some soldiers kept souvenirs of the massacre, items such as Ghost Dance shirts they could sell later as "relics" from the Ghost Dance movement.

Because of his actions at Wounded Knee, the man who ordered the slaughter, Colonel James Forsyth (1834–1906), was removed from command. His superior officer was disgusted that Forsyth had approved of the brutal killings of innocent women and children. It was also discovered that many Lakota warriors were unarmed. Forsyth failed to see the error of his ways and instead wrote a report praising his troops for their courage in the face of "religious fanaticism." Forsyth was later reinstated to his position and even rose to the rank of major general. The government further insulted the Native American community when it awarded three officers and fifteen soldiers with the Medal of Honor for their conduct at Wounded Knee.

Although fighting between the Native Americans and whites continued occasionally throughout January, the Wounded Knee Massacre is generally considered the end of the Indian Wars as well as the end of the American Frontier. In 1890, the Bureau of the Census (the government department responsible for collecting information and analyzing the population) announced the closing of the frontier, as there

Victims of the Wounded Knee uprising lie on the ground in South Dakota, December 29, 1890. © BETTMANN/CORBIS.

was no longer an obvious line dividing the wilderness from settlement.

Railroads usher in the end of the Frontier

Railroads, and the Pacific Railroad in particular, were the main factor in the closing of the American Frontier. In 1865, the West and the Great Plains had just 960 miles of track. That figured increased more than a hundredfold by 1900, when the region boasted over 90,000 miles of track. Five routes linked the East with the West.

Railroads made travel faster, cheaper, and safer as they moved not only passengers, but equipment, ore, and grain across the vast prairies and Rocky Mountains of the West. Railroads permanently changed the landscape as well. Where once buffalo and bison roamed the plains, by the late nineteenth century, railroad tracks had destroyed the animals' environment. Eager sport hunters from across the globe traveled to and across the West in search of the mighty bison. Their slaughter was thorough; only about one thousand buffalo were left by 1885.

Frederick Jackson Turner: Frontier Theorist

Historian Frederick Jackson Turner. THE LIBRARY OF CONGRESS.

Frederick Jackson Turner was born in Portage, Wisconsin, in 1861. He became a professional historian and taught at the University of Wisconsin as well as Harvard University.

Turner gave a lecture to fellow historians in 1893 in Chicago. The lecture, titled "The Significance of the Frontier in American History," was ignored at the time of its delivery. Eventually, it became so well known and studied that one modern scholar calls it "the single most influential piece of writing in the history of American history," according to the Web site *PBS: New Perspectives on the West.*

Turner's theory was that the frontier's past gave the best explanation of the history of the

United States as a whole. He called the frontier the "meeting point between savagery and civilization," and credited it with being the most influential factor on America's character and society. The closing of the frontier, for Turner, left the prospects of the future of the nation a mystery.

Although more than a century has passed since Turner delivered his speech, historians still debate his ideas. Most historians agree that his theory that the frontier is the key to American history as a whole is too simple. They argue that his assumption leaves out important factors such as slavery, immigration, industrialism, and major wars. Others point out that the frontier was not "free land," as Turner called it. If it had been free, there never would have been a need for an "Indian policy," and the Indian Wars would never have taken place.

More recent scholarship focuses on the West not offering the freedom and opportunity that popular Western mythology—and Turner— would have people believe. Turner and popular Western mythology both fail to take into consideration the price paid by Native Americans, Asians, Mexicans, and women who found themselves living in the West.

Turner's theory is debated and contested as a whole, but few critics reject it altogether. The thesis became the organizing principle of American history studies and even prompted the development of a new movement called "The New Western History." This scholarship movement seeks to tell the story of America's history from the viewpoint of those who were treated unjustly. Turner continued his research until his death in 1932.

Hunters shoot at bison on the Kansas-Pacific Railroad tracks in 1871. © BETTMANN/CORBIS.

Cattle drives As the American Civil War ended, the demand for beef in the East was great. The dry land of the West made growing many crops impossible, but it was perfect for raising cattle. The challenge was getting the cattle across the country. Before the Transcontinental Railroad was built, the only way to get the cattle from the West (primarily Texas) to the railroad in Kansas or Colorado was to make the cattle walk the distance, also called a cattle drive. The journey was long—1000 miles—and took six months of riding ten- or twelve-hour days.

Twenty to forty cowboys were joined by a cook, a trail boss, and several wranglers to herd several thousand cattle and keep them moving in the right direction. The average age of the cowboy was between fourteen and eighteen years, and most of them were Spanish-speaking sons of local farmers, Native Americans, or freed African Americans. The work was hard and the days were long, but cattle drives provided much-needed work for young men in the early 1800s.

By the end of the nineteenth century, cattle drives had become a thing of the past. Cattle was now transported via railroad car.

Barbed Wire: Small Invention with Big Results

As settlers moved into the West and began farming, one thing became clear: Something had to be done with the cattle that freely roamed the plains. Crops needed protection from the destructive animals, but materials for building fences—mainly stone, trees, thorny brush, and mud—were in short supply. Farmers sometimes dug ditches around their crops, but those usually only made the cattle's invasion of croplands more difficult, not impossible.

In 1874, De Kalb, Illinois, farmer Joseph Glidden (1813–1906) invented fencing material consisting of a strand of wire with barbs (sharp points) wrapped around it. The strand was held in place by twisting another strand around it. Glidden's design was just one of more than 570 that received patents (sets of rights granted by the government to show ownership). A friend of Glidden's, De Kalb hardware store owner Isaac Ellwood (1833–1910), bought half the interest in Glidden's patent, and the partners built a factory in 1875 to make the wire. Glidden sold his half of the business to the Washburn & Moen Company, which went on to acquire all but one of the many barbed-wire patents by 1876.

The remaining patent belonged to De Kalb carpenter Jacob Haish (1826–1926), a German immigrant. Haish had received the first barbed-wire patent but became involved in a three-year legal battle over rights with Glidden. In the end, the courts decided Glidden was the true father of barbed wire. Despite the ruling, Haish made a fortune off his patent. He left it all to charity upon his death at the age of ninety-nine.

The invention of barbed wire solved one problem but created another. As landowners used the wire to protect crops and cattle alike, cattle owners who preferred the free-range method (letting their cattle graze openly, without fencing) hated the way it kept their animals from moving about at will. Religious groups called barbed wire "the devil's rope" because of the pain the barbs inflicted on cattle. Cattle drivers disliked it because it got in the way of the drives. When those groups opposed to the use of barbed wire were refused help by the government, they turned to vandalism and violence. By 1882, the "fence cutter wars" were raging across the prairie, causing not only property damage and financial loss, but loss of life. Ranchers murdered fence cutters, fence cutters murdered ranchers. The wars ended in 1884 when a law was passed making cutting fences a felony.

The Pacific Railroad and the Federal Land Grant Program

Before the final stake was pounded in connecting East with West via the Transcontinental Railroad, passengers and freight could only go as far as Kansas and Colorado. While this was a major accomplishment, the lack of railroads in the West prohibited human settlement on a large scale. The development of the Pacific Railroad changed that.

Now that the West had a railroad, immigrants could realize the American Dream, one of great hope of prosperity and riches. European immigrants entered America mainly at Ellis Island in New York. Beginning in 1869, however, they now had the option of leaving the East and heading West, where land was more plentiful. The federal government knew there was a demand for land, since immigrant populations continued to rise throughout the last half of

Cattle rustlers cut a barbed-wire fence on a Nebraska ranch in the 1880s. © THE GRANGER COLLECTION, NEW YORK.

the nineteenth century. Beginning in the early 1800s, the government began giving grants (money that did not need to be repaid) to various groups, such as those who wanted to build homes in the West, before railroads made life on the prairies easier. As railroads were being built, these grants were extended to include the financing of railroad construction.

The plan was simple. The government designated strips of land in areas it wanted people to settle. It designated alternating strips of land to

railroad construction and gave that land to railroad companies that promised to build. The railroads then sold the settlement land to settlers, most of them European immigrants, and used the money to pay for railroad construction. Figures released by the American government in 1943 show that a total of 131,350,534 acres of land were granted to all railroads under the program. About 18,738 miles of railroad track were built using funds from the land grants, a figure that represents 8 percent of all U.S. railroad construction.

Historians look at the land grant program with mixed reaction. One of the clauses in the land grant program required the railroads to transport government troops and property at half the normal rate for passengers and freights. In 1945, a congressional committee determined that the government had received more than $900 million worth of transportation in return for lands that would have cost just $126 million to buy. Because those lands would have been worthless if the railroads could not settle them, the railroads were taking a risk. So although the program promoted settlement in the West and achieved that goal, scholars debate whether the means by which the goal was achieved were ethically pursued. The government seemed to get the better end of the deal, having, in essence, traded $126 million of land for $900 million worth of transportation.

A lesser known aspect of the Federal Land Grant Program was the promotion of the West by the railroads themselves. It is generally accepted that most immigrants left their homeland in search of a quality of life they knew they could never have at home. But American railroad companies fed on the immigrants' needs and desires by promoting their land in Europe. Many railroads hired clergy and prominent businessmen to help influence immigrants to come to the West. The railroads focused their efforts on the non-English-speaking countries of northern Europe. It was a common belief that these groups had better work ethics than others, and that they would work harder, complain less, and produce more. The railroads published promotional brochures and pamphlets in several languages. These advertisements promised wealth and success, many times to a degree not possible even for the hardest of workers. But

Europeans desperate to find security and comfort believed what they read, and they headed west by the thousands.

When the data is considered, the importance of the railroads in settling the West becomes obvious. Between 1607 and 1870, 409 million acres of land in the West had been settled. The people who ventured west were mostly miners and ranchers. Between 1870 (the year after completion of the Transcontinental Railroad) and 1900, 430 million acres were settled. Most of the settlers in this time period were farmers, both American and immigrant.

So while the railroads brought change in the form of hope to millions of settlers, it forced change in the form of devastation and desperation on Native American tribes who had lived in the West for hundreds of years. The "Iron Horse," as the steam train was known among Native Americans, was something to fear.

The Wild, Wild West

Fear took other forms in the West as well. Towns seemed to appear out of nowhere once settlers began their westward journey. With such large numbers of people settling in a relatively short period of time, many of them from different backgrounds, lawlessness was unavoidable.

The days of the Wild, Wild West included some of the most famous outlaws in American history. Although many people romanticize the lives of people like Jesse James (1847–1882) and Billy the Kid (1859?–1881), in truth these men were hardened criminals.

Jesse James Jesse James was born in Missouri in 1847. He was a soldier in the Civil War, and some say it was cruel treatment from the

Union soldiers that turned James into a killer. After the war, James and his brother, Frank James (1843–1915), pulled off the first daylight bank robbery in peace time. The James men robbed the Liberty Bank in their home state of Missouri. They managed to rob $60,000 and murder one man.

The brothers spent the next fifteen years robbing banks and trains. Both finally settled into married life and had children. Jesse assumed the name Tom Howard and moved to St. Joseph, Missouri, in 1881 with his family. There was a $10,000 reward on his head, so James lived a quiet life. Although he did not work for a living, he did attend church regularly. By all accounts, he was a loving father and husband.

James bought a small farm in Nebraska in the winter of 1882. By April, he was in need of money. Most of his old gang was dead, so he recruited two brothers, Bob and Charlie Ford, to help him rob a Nebraska bank. Plans fell through when Bob Ford could not resist the chance to collect the reward money. As James stood on a chair in his living room while hanging a picture on a wall, Ford shot him in the back of the head through the window. James was dead.

Ford never collected the reward money but was sentenced to hang instead on charges of murder. He was pardoned (forgiven and set free) before his sentence was carried out, and he later died in a bar room brawl in Colorado. His brother Charlie killed himself.

Jesse James's legend still lives on in American history. Some say he was a Robin Hood who took from the rich to give to the poor. No evidence has ever surfaced to prove that theory, and the fact that James never held a job but still managed to live a comfortable life suggests there is no truth in it. Settlers lived both in fear and awe of James, hoping never to run into him, while at the same time hoping to catch a glimpse of the famous bandit.

Billy the Kid Another of the most famous outlaws from the West was William Henry Bonney (or McCarty), better known as Billy the Kid. What set Billy the Kid apart from other outlaws was his age. He was killed before his twenty-first birthday.

The birth date and place of Billy the Kid is not certain. The same is true about much of his early life. No one knows for sure if he ever knew his father, but there was no father figure in the Kid's early life. His mother died in 1874, when the Kid was probably thirteen or fourteen years old. His stepfather placed him in foster care and was never heard from again. Within a year, the Kid got involved in theft and was arrested. He escaped jail and began life on the run.

He learned how to steal horses in Arizona but left quickly after killing a man who was bullying him. He joined a gang of rustlers (cattle thieves) and gunfighters called The Boys in New Mexico. The Kid did not stay with The Boys for long but joined the "enemy" side. He ran for a time with a group of deputized (authorized by the law) gunmen called The Regulators, but again, that stint did not last long. The Regulators broke up, but some of them—Billy the Kid included—maintained a life of crime. He was arrested for rustling in 1880 and sentenced to death. The Kid killed two prison guards in 1881 and escaped but was hunted down by Sheriff Pat Garrett (1850–1908). Garrett shot and killed the Kid in the dark on July 14, 1881. It is believed he was only about nineteen or twenty years old.

Outlaw Belle Starr. © HULTON ARCHIVE/GETTY IMAGES.

Remembering the women While most Wild West outlaws were men, there were plenty of women involved in crime as well. One of the most famous was Belle Starr (1848–1889), who rode with the Jesse James Gang for a while before marrying a horse thief named Jim Reed. After Reed was killed in a gunfight, Starr moved to Indian Territory where she entered into her second marriage, this time with a Cherokee named Sam Starr. The Starrs formed their own rustling and horse-thieving gang; Belle was the brains of the operation.

The Starrs made a lot of money stealing and making bootleg (illegal) whiskey. They were good at what they did and left behind no evidence to link them to their crimes. Belle's luck ran out in 1882 when she was caught stealing a neighbor's horse. She was sentenced to a year in prison but was released after nine months for good behavior. Immediately, she returned to her husband and their life of crime. Sam was soon killed at a party, and Belle got involved with an outlaw named Blue Duck. They never married, however. Her third marriage was to a much younger bandit named Jim July.

The marriage was violent, and Belle Starr died at the age of forty-one. She was ambushed (surprise attacked) while riding her horse along a country road. The attack came just days after July publicly promised to kill her.

The end of the outlaw era came in 1901, when another famous pair of outlaws, Butch Cassidy (1866–1908) and the Sundance Kid (1867–1908), fled to South America after a life of bank and train robberies.

Birth of a genre

In addition to the legends of the outlaws who terrorized the Wild West, the Frontier culture produced another phenomenon: Western literature.

Oral tradition The oldest Western literature did not begin with white settlers but with Native Americans. Each tribe had its unique stories, traditions, and legends, all of which were passed down through stories told during ceremonies and in songs. Each region—West, Northwest, Southwest—had its own common threads that were woven throughout the stories.

Settlers also had their own oral tradition. Like Native American tribes, each group had

Women in the West

Although life in the West was dangerous and uncertain, it held an appeal to some women in the nineteenth century. During that era, there were two distinct cultures: The one in the East was established and refined. Women were expected to adhere to very specific codes of conduct and value systems. Their "place" was in the home, and they were expected to marry young and raise a family. The culture in the West was the opposite of that in the East. Women were not considered "bad girls" if they smoked, danced, used foul language, or engaged in behavior traditionally reserved for men.

Women in the West found a freedom not available to them in the East. The ratio of men to women on the prairies was 10 to 1. Men were appreciative of women just because there were so few of them. Behavior and attitudes that were not tolerated among society in the East did not make women of the West less desirable in any way. Many women who moved to the West did so to build new lives. They left behind them bad reputations and unsuitable pasts. Many changed their names and enjoyed a life in a place where background and family ties meant very little. Since most settlers in the West were not native to the area, no one cared about family history.

stories, jokes, and songs shared only within its boundaries. Settlement doctors had their own; cowboys had theirs. Immigrant groups from Europe brought with them their own traditions and cultural stories, and those, too, were passed along to each new generation. What ties these various traditions of folklore together is that as the West was settled, new "facts" were added into the stories to reflect the changing landscape. Much of today's information about the West of yesterday comes through this folklore.

Travel journals Historians value the travel journals of explorers that give firsthand accounts of life in the West. One famous example of this genre comes from the journals of the explorations of Meriwether Lewis (1774–1809) and William Clark (1770–1838). Lewis and Clark were hired by President Thomas Jefferson (1743–1826; served 1801–9) to explore and map a route by land from Missouri to the Pacific Ocean in the early 1800s. Those journals give detailed accounts of many Native American tribes in the Northwest as well as glimpses into the lives of specific individuals like Sacagawea (1786–1812), the teenaged female Shoshone interpreter who helped make Lewis and Clark's expedition possible. Those same journals describe various and new plants, animals, and even medicines. As historical documents, travel narratives such as these are an indispensable contribution to Western history.

The Western novel Arguably the most popular genre of Western literature is the novel. Most scholars agree that one writer can be considered the Father of the Western novel. James Fenimore Cooper (1789–1851) was unique in that his novels explored two contrasting sets of values and cultures, the civilized notions of the East and the wilderness of the West. Though full of action scenes, Cooper's novels were also intended to make the reader reflect on prejudices and assumptions that formed his concept of right and wrong. One of his most famous novels, *The Last of the Mohicans,* was made into a motion picture in 1992.

Tall tales and legends Tall tales (fictitious stories involving superhuman characters and exaggerated events) were passed down mostly through oral tradition but found their way to paper with writers like Mark Twain (1835–1910). Although Twain (real name Samuel Clemens) is most famous in many circles for his tales involving Tom Sawyer and Huckleberry Finn, his earlier writings were more fantastic in nature and earned him a reputation as a master of the tall tale.

European westerns Some of the most influential writing about the West actually came from Europe. Karl May (1842–1912) was one of the most famous European writers of Western literature at the end of the nineteenth century. His novels (sixty in all) have sold more than one hundred million copies around the world. This German author had intended to write stories for children, but his novels became popular among adults. Most of his stories involve a noble chief named Winnetou and his German bloodbrother, Old Shatterhand. May's novels gave his fellow Germans a place to dream about, and notable people such as physicist Albert Einstein (1879–1955) and physician and musicologist Albert Schweitzer (1875–1965) considered May among their favorite novelists.

Western poetry Sharlot Hall (1870–1943) stands out in the archives of Western literature because she was a woman writing about life in what is considered a man's world. Hall's family moved west to Arizona in the early 1880s. During the trek, the young Hall was thrown from her horse and suffered a spinal injury that confined her to bed throughout the 1890s. During this time, she began writing poetry. She published her first volume of poetry in 1910 in Boston. The book sold out immediately. Hall used descriptive language and imagery to write about ordinary aspects of Western life, such as sheepherding. Some of her later poetry used cowboy dialect (vocabulary specific to cowboys). She is considered one of the finest Western poets in American history.

Nature essays As more people moved westward, more natural resources were being discovered. The beauty of the West became the subject of much writing toward the end of the nineteenth century. Although writers had been writing of nature long before the West was "tamed," nature writing truly came into its maturity with the writings of naturalist John Muir (1838–1914). Muir's earlier writings had focused more on the scientific aspects of nature, but as he spent more time outdoors, his appreciation for the natural beauty of what he saw developed. Muir was a key figure in the Conservation Movement that began in the late nineteenth century, and he would later be joined in the ranks of nature essayists by writers such as Aldo Leopold (1887–1948). Together with Ralph Waldo Emerson (1803–1882) and Henry David Thoreau (1817–1862), these men created a type of writing that brought the American West to light in a completely different way.

Although westward expansion increased America's interest in and appreciation of nature, it did not mark the beginning of the Conservation Movement. The movement had begun decades prior, in the late 1840s, when people began to realize that America's natural heritage must be protected if it was to be preserved. It must be acknowledged that even before then, Native Americans were practicing sustainable agriculture. Sustainable agriculture is an approach to farming that preserves the long-term fertility of the soil. It maintains the ecological balance and avoids overuse of natural resources. Conservation as a concept was a concern of the Native Americans long before it became a movement in white society.

The Conservation Movement

Prior to the dawn of the Gilded Age, America's federal government had already begun to recognize, thanks to concerned citizens, conservationists, and scientists, that steps must be taken to preserve the nation's natural resources. In 1872, for example, Congress passed an act to set aside a tract of land at the headwaters of Yellowstone River in Wyoming, thereby establishing Yellowstone National Park. It was the first park of its kind in the United States. There were other apparent motives for establishing such an attraction. The Union Pacific Railroad hoped the park would attract tourists from all over the world who would ride their trains and stay in their hotels. The company hired artists to paint grand pictures of the geysers and wilderness of Yellowstone. That same year, Arbor Day was founded when future secretary of agriculture Julius S. Morton (1832–1902), a member of the Nebraska state board of agriculture, declared April 10 "tree planting day." (Other states individually followed suit through the years, until President Richard Nixon [1913–1994; served 1969–74] declared Arbor Day an official national "day" in 1970.) These acts marked the beginning of a collective thought of preserving nature for beauty's sake.

One of the most influential figures in the Conservation Movement was naturalist John Muir. Born in Scotland, Muir emigrated to the United States at the age of eleven, where he spent his free time exploring the backwoods of Wisconsin. Muir worked long hours helping his family plow the land and dig wells. The work developed in him a strong sense of union with nature; he learned to respect and love the land.

Muir traveled to Yosemite in the late 1860s and took jobs that kept him close to nature. Even while working in the sawmills and the fields, he was studying his outdoor surroundings. He stayed in the mountains until 1880, at which time he married and moved to California. Though he traveled occasionally, Muir mostly stayed home, tending to his pear orchard and vineyard (grape crops). He acquired wealth through his farming, but as his riches increased, so did his discontentment. With each trip to the mountains, Muir realized something must be done to save the wilderness or it would not last.

Founding of the Sierra Club In an effort to awaken the public and the government to the importance of preserving nature, Muir began writing papers and essays. His writing brought him in contact with Robert Underwood Johnson (1853–1937), editor of *Century* magazine, one of the most influential conservation publications of the era. Muir published two essays on Yosemite in which he called for the establishment of a national park. Johnson supported Muir's idea, and the two men approached Congress with the idea. On October 1, 1890, Yosemite National Park was established. This was the first time a major conservation reform had come about because of the efforts and actions of a private citizen.

The friendship between Johnson and Muir produced another lasting organization, the Sierra Club. The club was established in 1892 with Muir as president. Its purpose was to preserve and make accessible the Sierra Nevada mountains.

Conservationist John Muir (right) and President Theodore Roosevelt stand atop a ridge overlooking the Yosemite Valley. © BETTMANN/ CORBIS.

The Sierra Club still thrives in the twenty-first century, and its efforts have extended to include conservation issues of all kinds.

Throughout the last two decades of the nineteenth century, other strides were made in the Conservation Movement. The first Audubon Society was formed in 1886 to protect birds (though it disbanded after two years and reformed in 1905 as the National Audubon Society). The following year, sportsmen concerned with conservation founded the Boone and Crockett Club. It was the first organization to include big-game (large animals) hunters in the Conservation Movement.

Other major changes included the passing of legislation in 1894 that prohibited hunting in national parks. The forest service shifted its focus from tree protection to scientific management of all forests. Scientific management was a policy that allowed natural resources (in this case, trees) to be used while protecting the resources in a way that allowed for timely regrowth and development. In 1898, President William McKinley (1843–1901; served 1897–1901) named conservationist Gifford Pinchot (1865–1946) as chief of the Division of Forestry (later called the Bureau of Forestry) within the U.S. Department of Agriculture. Pinchot helped shift public awareness from saving trees to managing their growth.

In 1900, the Lacey Act was passed. Named for U.S. representative John F. Lacey (1841–1913) of Iowa, the act outlawed the interstate shipment of wild animals and birds that had been killed or obtained illegally. That year also marked a milestone in women's activism in the Conservation Movement. The California Club, a San Francisco women's organization, urged Congress to pass an act allowing the government to purchase two endangered groves of giant sequoia trees (redwoods). Although the measure failed, it was evidence of the public's growing awareness of the importance of preserving and protecting resources as well as of the increased influence of women in politics.

The conservationist president

When Theodore Roosevelt (1858–1919; served 1901–9) took over the presidency in 1901 following the assassination of President McKinley, he made conservation a cornerstone of his administration. Roosevelt was an avid outdoorsman and big-game hunter. Under his leadership, five national parks were established, as were four big-game refuges (protected areas), fifty-one national bird refuges, and the National Forest Service (in 1905).

Conservation was more than just a way to preserve America's resources and landscape for Roosevelt. He believed big-game hunting was an elite, or upper-class, sport; he did not want game-animal stock depleted by subsistence hunters (those who hunted to feed their families, rather than for sport). So part of Roosevelt's motivation was to protect the leisure activities of he and his wealthy friends.

But there was more to it than that. For the president, conservation was directly related to American manhood. His idea of masculinity involved self-reliance, courage, and hard work. In his eyes, hunting taught these values better than any other endeavor. To lose the ability to hunt, Roosevelt believed, meant to lose the essence of masculinity. Conservation was the only sure way to keep that from happening.

Roosevelt also considered conservation a tool for maintaining democracy. With an eye on the future, he considered it morally irresponsible to exploit natural resources for immediate gain and chose instead to develop policies that would insure future generations the same benefits as what the present generation enjoyed. Conservation, then, was inherently democratic to Theodore Roosevelt's way of thinking.

Nature was an essential part of America's history for Roosevelt. Since the nation lacked the historic and cultural traditions of European countries, the land took on a greater significance in its relation to America's identity. The country's many monuments and diverse wildlife were a source of great national pride, worthy of preservation and protection. As noted by Daniel Filler in the Internet article "Theodore Roosevelt: Conservation as the Guardian of Democracy," the former president wrote in a 1916 essay titled "Bird Reserves at the Mouth of the Mississippi," "Birds should be saved because of utilitarian [practical] reasons; and, moreover, they should be saved because of reasons unconnected with any return in dollars and cents. A grove of giant redwoods or sequoias should be kept just as we keep a great and beautiful cathedral."

Regardless of his motives and personal opinions, Theodore Roosevelt had a major impact on the Conservation Movement, greater than any president before or since.

With a look to the future

Under Roosevelt's administration, Pinchot added millions of acres of land to the national forests. The government controlled these forests and determined how they would be used. Both Pinchot and Roosevelt agreed that public lands should never be used for private gain. Congress began caving in to pressure from the private sector, though, and in 1907, they refused to allow Roosevelt to purchase forest reserves in the Western states. When William Howard Taft (1857–1930; served 1909–13) took over the presidency in 1909, Pinchot lost much of his authority and was fired by the new president in 1910.

Taft was not against conservation; the issue simply was not one of his priorities. He did continue to establish national parks. In 1911, Congress passed the Weeks Act, named after U.S. representative John W. Weeks (1860–1926) of Massachusetts, which authorized states to work together to protect their water and forest supplies. The Act also provided funds to the U.S. Department of Agriculture to use with states in a cooperative effort for providing fire protection of watersheds of navigable streams (streams able to be traveled by boat).

The Conservation Movement would continue to grow. It remains an active movement throughout the United States in the first decade of the twenty-first century.

For More Information

BOOKS

Calhoun, Charles W., ed. *The Gilded Age: Essays on the Origins of Modern America.* Wilmington, DE: Scholarly Resources, 1996.

Commire, Anne. "Helen Hunt Jackson." In *Historic World Leaders.* Detroit: Gale, 1994.

Furbee, Mary Rodd. *Outrageous Women of the American Frontier.* New York: Wiley, 2002.

Galbreath, Lester. *Campfire Tales: True Stories from the Western Frontier.* Albany, TX: Bright Sky Press, 2005.

Marker, Sherry. *Plains Indian Wars.* New York: Facts on File, 2003.

Painter, Nell Irvin. *Standing at Armageddon: The United States, 1877–1919.* New York: W. W. Norton & Co., 1987.

Streissguth, Thomas. *Wounded Knee, 1890: The End of the Plains Indian Wars.* New York: Facts on File, 1998.

Torr, James D., ed. *The American Frontier.* San Diego: Greenhaven Press, 2002.

WEB SITES

"Belle Starr." *Outlaw Women.* http://www.outlawwomen.com/BelleStarr.htm (accessed on April 26, 2006).

"Buffalo Bill's Wild West Show and Exhibition." *Welcome to the Crystal City: 1890s in Bowling Green, Ohio.* http://www.bgsu.edu/departments/acs/1890s/buffalobill/bbwildwestshow.html (accessed on April 26, 2006).

Devil's Rope Museum. http://www.barbwiremuseum.com/ (accessed on April 26, 2006).

Filler, Daniel. *Theodore Roosevelt: Conservation as the Guardian of Democracy.* http://pantheon.cis.yale.edu/~thomast/essays/filler/filler.html (accessed on August 20, 2006).

"The Golden Age: 1900–1945." *National Railroad Museum.* http://www.nationalrrmuseum.org/collections-exhibits/outline/golden-age.php (accessed on April 26, 2006).

"Golden Spike." *National Park Service.* http://www.cr.nps.gov/history/online_books/hh/40/hh40s.htm. (accessed on April 26, 2006).

McCallum, Frances T., and James Mulkey Owens. "Barbed Wire." *The Handbook of Texas Online.* http://www.tsha.utexas.edu/handbook/online/articles/BB/aob1.html (accessed on April 26, 2006).

"Nation Building: 1860–1900." *National Railroad Museum.* http://www.nationalrrmuseum.org/collections-exhibits/outline/nation-building.php (accessed on April 26, 2006).

"New Perspectives on The West: People." *PBS.org.* http://www.pbs.org/weta/thewest/people/ (accessed on April 26, 2006).

Texas Christian University Press. *A Literary History of the American West.* http://www2.tcu.edu/depts/prs/amwest/ (accessed on April 26, 2006).

"Who Are the Buffalo Soldiers?" *Buffalo Soldiers.* http://www.buffalosoldiers.com/ (accessed on April 26, 2006).

6

Panic and Populism: Revolt in the 1890s

The year 1890 marked the beginning of ten years of hardship and rebellion in America. The 1890s decade would lead the country down a path of economic depression, political reform, labor unrest (see Chapter 3), and agrarian (relating to land and rural matters) revolt, and war. America, which had just reunified itself after the Civil War (1861–65) and its issues of slavery and the economy of the South, would once again find itself divided, this time by issues of politics and money.

The Panic of 1893

Not since the depression of 1873 had America experienced economic hardship like that felt by Americans of all socioeconomic classes in 1893. A depression is a long-term economic state characterized by high unemployment, minimal investment and spending, and low prices. This depression was one of the worst in American history. The unemployment rate (percentage of the total working population that was out of a job) exceeded 10 percent for half a decade, something that had never happened before and would not happen again until the Great Depression of the 1930s. No city or region was left unscarred. One of every four workers in Pennsylvania was unemployed; in Chicago, Illinois, one hundred thousand people were sleeping in the streets.

Causes of the depression The depression in 1893 was ushered in with financial panic as the value of America's currency (money) weakened. Since the time of President George Washington (1732–1799; served 1789–97), the U.S. monetary system had been based on bimetallism, or the use of both gold and silver coins. But the California Gold Rush in 1849 resulted in the discovery of such large quantities of gold that its value decreased. Before 1849, gold had been sixteen times more valuable than silver.

People soon began melting their silver dollars and using the metal for other purposes, such as jewelry. In 1873, Congress ceased making silver

WORDS TO KNOW

bimetallism: A movement of the late nineteenth century aimed at expanding the amount of money in circulation by backing it with silver as well as gold. Also sometimes referred to as free silver.

capitalism: An economic system in which property and goods are privately owned, produced, and distributed.

Democratic Party: One of the oldest political parties in the United States. Originally linked with the South and slavery, it transformed into one associated with urban voters and liberal policies.

depression: A long-term economic state characterized by high unemployment, minimal investment and spending, and low prices.

farm tenancy: An arrangement whereby farmers who no longer owned their own farm farmed someone else's land and were paid a share of the harvest.

Gilded Age: The period in history following the Civil War and Reconstruction (roughly the final twenty-three years of the nineteenth century), characterized by a ruthless pursuit of profit, an exterior of showiness and grandeur, and immeasurable political corruption.

labor union: A formally organized association of workers that advances its members'

views on wages, work hours, and labor conditions.

mortgage: A loan of money to purchase property, such as a farm. The property is used as security for repayment of the loan; that is, if the borrower fails to pay, the property is seized.

Republican Party: One of the oldest political parties in the United States. Founded as an antislavery party in the mid-1800s, it transformed into one associated with conservative fiscal and social policies.

"Separate but Equal" doctrine: A policy enacted throughout the South that theoretically promoted the same treatment and services for African Americans as for whites, but which required the two races to use separate facilities.

stock: A share of ownership in a business.

tariffs: Taxes imposed on goods imported from other countries.

temperance: A movement that campaigned for the public to refrain from drinking alcohol.

trust: The concept of several companies banding together to form an organization that limits competition by controlling the production and distribution of a product or service.

coins, and America was placed on a "gold standard." A series of silver strikes beginning in 1875 and continuing throughout the 1880s in the San Juan Mountains of Colorado and nearby regions caused the price of silver to fall even further. In spite of this decrease in value, silver mining as an industry continued to grow.

Farmers, however, were going further into debt as prices per bushel of their crops continued to decrease quickly due to increased foreign competition and supply. In order to remain competitive, farmers had to continue lowering their prices, yet they still had monthly payments to make on expensive farm equipment and mortgages.

AGAIN ON DECK.

Executive-Officer CLEVELAND Reports for Duty on the SHIP OF STATE & is Warmly Welcomed.

"Thanks, Captain! Glad to get back and never better in my life"

Editorial cartoon showing Grover Cleveland saluting Uncle Sam as Cleveland returns to the U.S. presidency in 1893 after being away from office for four years. © HULTON ARCHIVE/GETTY IMAGES.

The Sherman Silver Act To help balance the economy, President Benjamin Harrison (1833–1901; served 1889–93) agreed to buy 4.5 million ounces of silver every month at market price. The U.S. Treasury, in turn, would issue notes that could be redeemed in either gold or silver.

This plan was known as the Sherman Silver Purchase Act of 1890. The legislation was named after the Republican who initiated it, U.S. senator John Sherman (1823–1900) of Ohio. Although the idea may have been solid, in reality the Act did not work very well. The increased supply of silver forced down the market price. Mine owners tried to make up for their loss by cutting the wages of their miners and laborers, a move that led to unrest and violence throughout the mining regions. As holders of

the notes understandably redeemed them for gold rather than silver (thereby getting more money for each note), the federal gold reserve was steadily drained.

Three weeks after Grover Cleveland (1837–1908; served 1885–89 and 1893–97) was sworn in as president for the second time in 1893, the gold reserves dipped below $100 million. This event weakened an already unsteady trust in the federal government. The Sherman Act was repealed, but it was too late. Silver mines were shut down across the mining regions. The price of silver per ounce dropped from 83 cents to 62 cents in one four-day period. Banks failed by the hundreds, and property values decreased to nearly nothing. America's economy was in serious trouble.

Trouble on the rails Another factor in the 1893 depression was a decrease in the amount of money being invested in railroads. Between 1870 and 1890, railroads accounted for 15 to 20 percent of all federal investments. Tens of thousands of miles of track were laid, and loans were approved for additional construction and equipment purchase.

Private investors in America and Europe bought stock in U.S. railroads. It seemed like a sure thing, an easy way to make money. Stocks were bought for a particular amount, and if the company did well, each stock earned money. With the increase in immigration, the explosion in the railroad construction industry, and the increasing settlement of the West, investors believed they could not lose. But they did lose, and in a big way.

The railroad system was overbuilt and overfunded. Companies were often mismanaged. In 1892, just 44 percent of all railroad stocks offered investors received a return (profit) on their investment. European investors pulled out before the situation got worse. The Philadelphia and Reading Railroads were the first companies to file for bankruptcy (a legal declaration that a company cannot pay its debts. By May 1893, more railroads shut down; 156 railroads would fail before the crisis was over. Without the railroads, industries like iron, steel, and farming had no way of shipping their products. America fell into a serious economic depression marked by high unemployment rates and tens of thousands of business failures.

Plight of the farmer

Farmers were perhaps the hardest hit by the depression of 1893. Prior to that year, the agriculture industry had enjoyed expansion and increased profit, thanks to improved farming methods, the introduction of machinery that could do a worker's job in half the time, and the railroads, which opened new regions to business. Between 1870 and 1890, the number of U.S. farms rose by almost 80 percent, to 4.5 million. By the end of the nineteenth century, that number increased yet again by 25 percent. Across the nation, about 29 percent of farmers were paying on mortgage loans (money loaned to them by banks so that they could live on and farm their property). One expert estimated that by 1890, 2.3 million farm loans were worth more than $2.2 billion. During that year, Kansas, Minnesota, Nebraska, and the Dakotas had more farm mortgages than they did families.

But the depression was preceded with six years of bad weather and drought. Crop seasons were shortened, or in some cases, nonexistent. Before farmers understood the importance of sustainable farming methods (which includes crop rotation to decrease the chances of disease and to maximize crop output), they farmed land in such a way that it no longer produced healthy or big crops. The combination of nature and ignorance proved too much for many farmers. On top of that, they were expected to take into consideration the dismal economic conditions across the country and accept lower prices for their product. Wheat prices fell twenty cents per bushel in 1892. When crop prices dropped below the cost of production, farmers chose instead to use their crops for firewood.

Different regions, different hardships The depression did not affect all farmers in the same way. Those in the West and on the Plains suffered most in that they were unable to obtain credit from banks and stores. Weather in this

Coxey's Army

The Depression of 1893 affected Americans of various income levels in different ways. Many of those who found themselves unemployed became "tramps" who walked the countryside in search of work. Others became beggars who knocked on doors in search of food or work. The winter months were especially hard on families with children. Thrown out of their homes, with no income, they became wanderers who took food and shelter wherever they could find it.

Those without food, shelter, and work grew increasingly desperate. The middle class as well as the wealthy feared violence and chaos, in part because of the widespread—and sometimes violent—labor strikes (in which workers refuse to work until conditions improve) that swept the country (fourteen hundred strikes in 1894 alone). The middle class and wealthy blamed the unemployed for the nation's crisis and called them lazy. Some of the more unfortunate blamed themselves as well, despite the obvious reasons for the economic downturn. Daily newspapers regularly reported stories of suicide and despair.

The federal government did not seem to be in much of a hurry to find a solution to the country's woes. Many people complained, but one man took action. Civil War veteran Jacob Coxey (1854–1951) was a successful Ohio business-man who organized a protest in reaction to the government's apparent inaction. Coxey, along with approximately five hundred unemployed demonstrators, marched from Ohio to the U.S. Capitol building in Washington, D.C., in 1894. The group was nicknamed "Coxey's Army," and members were treated well along their journey to the Capitol. Coxey became somewhat of a folk hero, an ordinary guy who could have let things happen as they might but who chose instead to take a stand.

Coxey was marching in support of the Good Roads Bill and the Non-Interest-Bearing Bonds Bill, two acts that would establish public works projects he believed would provide relief for the poor. Although his ideas would eventually be considered worthwhile ventures and be included in the "New Deal," a series of economic programs that began during the administration of President Franklin D. Roosevelt (1882–1945; served 1933–45), Coxey was largely ignored by Congress in 1894. Instead, when he and his army arrived at the Capitol steps, he and two other leaders were arrested for trespassing.

Coxey led another march on Washington in 1914, and this time he was given a hearing at the Capitol, where he presented his proposals. His efforts failed, though, and he returned home to his life of business. Coxey served as mayor of Massillon, Ohio, from 1931 to 1933. He died there in 1951.

region was harsher than climates elsewhere, so the chances for making a profit were uncertain, and lenders knew that. They developed tougher standards regarding farm loans, and most farmers did not meet those standards. Unable to pay their existing loans, farmers knew it would be impossible to get new loans. Creditors began foreclosing on (taking away) farms. Between 1889 and 1893, more than eleven thousand Kansas farms went into foreclosure. Western farmers were being evicted from (thrown out of) their homes and farms; many were homeless.

Other farmers went into tenancy, meaning they no longer owned their own farm, but they farmed someone else's land and were paid a share of the harvest. Farm tenancy increased from 25 percent across the country in 1880 to 36 percent by 1900. The very farmers who had been encouraged to borrow money as the Plains and western regions were being settled spent the last decade of the nineteenth century losing their farms or farming for someone else. It was a miserable existence.

The situation in the South was somewhat different. Once slaves were freed after the Civil War, they usually refused to work land in gangs under the supervision of an overseer. It reminded them too much of the slave conditions they had just escaped. With this attitude, commercial farming was out of the question. Most wanted to own their own land and equipment. The problem was not that land was not available; it was. Huge plantations had been broken into smaller properties. The outlawing of slavery made money scarce, however, so freedmen had nothing with which to purchase a plot of land.

Many landowners let freedmen farm the land and agreed to accept a portion of the crop, rather than money, as rent. These owners also became merchants who sold farmers seed, equipment, and other necessities. As collateral (something of value used to insure repayment of debt), farmers signed a mortgage on their crop. Because the only crop most landowners wanted was cotton, that left farmers without food for their families. They had to buy food from local stores. After 1870, cotton prices fell, and farmers did not earn enough to settle their debt. The merchant landowners then forced them into signing yet another mortgage

on next year's crop. It was a never-ending cycle that led farmers only further into debt.

This system made tenant farmers of both African American and white men in the South. For the whites, tenancy was especially demeaning because it forced them into a status historically associated with slaves. It also represented a loss of freedom that hurt their pride. With credit nearly impossible to attain and few skilled laborers in the region, the South's economy was uncharacteristically hopeless.

Farmers in the Midwest and Northeast, though affected by the depression, faired better than those in other regions. These farmers had been able to pay off their mortgages because of the inflation of the Civil War economy. During the war, there was a general increase in the price of goods, including crops. Farmers were getting more money per bushel. Even though there was less money in circulation at the time, people still had to eat, so farmers were making money.

These farmers had another advantage because they lived among a more developed railroad system. They were less likely to be charged higher rates than their fellow farmers in the West and South. These lower rail costs allowed the farmers to plant grain, which grew well in nearly any soil. Because they lived near cities and growing urban areas, the farmers of the Midwest and Northeast were also able to engage in dairy farming. Cows could survive on land that had been overused. Milk could be transported before it had time to spoil, because the distance from the farms to the cities was short.

Obtaining credit was much easier in these regions as well. Most farmers had lived in the area their entire lives. They knew the bankers and the local agricultural conditions. They knew how to successfully farm in those local conditions and knew which crops would sell.

Recovery from the depression began in mid-1897, but the American economy was not prosperous again for another year.

Organizing for power

Farmers were not alone in their struggles during the crisis of 1893. The idea of labor unions and organizations (groups that protect and fight for the rights of workers) was not new in 1890. Labor organizations had been forming since the late 1870s (see Chapter 3). These unions provided individuals with the chance to lead large numbers of American workers for whom traditional political and social concepts of problem-solving did not work. In 1880, farmers joined in on the unionizing efforts and formed the National Farmers' Alliance. This group would eventually become one of the biggest political threats to Republicans and Democrats and be known as the Populists.

Before the Farmers' Alliance, there was the Order of Patrons of Husbandry. Seven disgruntled farmers established this group in 1867. Oliver Hudson Kelley (1826–1913) led the group, which was more commonly known as the Grange. ("Grange" means "outlying farm"; given that the founders were farmers whose political needs were more specific, or outside the realm of society in general, the Grange was an accurate description of the organization, and easier to remember.) Kelley and his group believed a national organization was needed to represent farmers much as labor unions were beginning to represent workers. Organization was arguably more important for farmers,

since they operated independently and were scattered throughout the country.

The Grange worked to promote cooperatives (smaller groups) in which farmers helped each other economically and educationally. They achieved their goals by establishing mills, stores, grain elevators, even banks. The Grange also tried to manufacture farming equipment, but that endeavor failed. Membership in the Grange grew slowly but steadily until the Panic of 1873. America suffered severe economic depression that year.

Laborers were exploited at the hands of their employers, but farmers suffered abuse from more than one opponent. Railroads were perhaps the worst abusers. They knew farmers had to transport their crops to buyers, so they charged astronomical shipping fees. The farmers had no choice but to pay them. They were further insulted by the ability of government officials and many politicians to travel at reduced rates or even for free. Banks were hard on the farmers, too, especially in the West where the land was more difficult to farm. This added uncertainty caused banks to hesitate on giving loans and credit to farmers, which in turn made turning a profit more difficult, if not impossible. When loans were approved, they usually had higher interest rates than business loans for other people.

The Grange was in favor of railroad regulations as well as rules for grain elevators. These elevators were actually storage bins located in railway sidings. The elevators deposited the grain directly into freight cars at stations along each route. Western railroads forbid farmers to load their grain themselves, and they provided just one grain elevator in each station. So farmers either had to sell grain to the elevator

An editorial cartoon showing people sleeping under railroad lines, while a farmer tries to warn them of the dangers of an approaching train. Farmers of the 1870s were known to be against the railroad system, whose practices they believed were antifarmer. Many farmers belonged to an organization known as the Grange, or the Order of Patrons of Husbandry.
© HULTON ARCHIVE/GETTY IMAGES.

operators, or they had to pay a fee to use the railroads' services. Owners of these elevators had a monopoly (complete control) of the

business. Farmers were treated unfairly not only by the railroads (which they relied on for shipping) but also by the owners of the grain elevators (which they required for storage). Political action on the part of the Grange resulted in the Granger laws that became effective in the Midwest. These laws regulated shipping rates as well as the rates imposed for grain elevator usage. The U.S. Supreme Court determined in 1886 that several of these regulations were unconstitutional. The basis for this ruling was that the laws violated the power over interstate commerce that only Congress had. The following year, these same regulations were legalized by the Interstate Commerce Act.

Membership in the Grange peaked in 1875 at around 850,000. The depression took its toll on farmers' abilities to continue their organizing efforts, and membership in the Grange eventually declined. It exists today with 3,600 local chapters in 37 states and a total membership of 350,000. The Grange also helped act as a model for future farm alliances.

Other parties

As Grange membership peaked in 1875, another party was founded. The Greenback Party was established much for the same agricultural reasons that motivated the Grange. Some of the Grangers actually joined forces with the Greenbackers, who took their name from the paper money printed during the Civil War. The Greenbackers supported the quantity theory of money, which says that if the amount of money in circulation grows more quickly than the economy, inflation will occur. If the opposite happens, deflation (falling prices) results. They also promoted the concept of fiat money, which says money has value only because the government says it does and not because it can be redeemed for gold. Bankers and other money experts criticized both theories as illogical.

Throughout the 1880s, the Greenback Party aligned itself (sided) with local and state labor parties. In 1887, they joined with the farm alliances and labor organizations to form the National Union Labor Party, or Union Labor Party (ULP). The ULP sought reform in land, railroad, and financial sectors.

Unfortunately for the ULP, it was perceived by the public to be closely aligned with the Knights of Labor (see Chapter 3), or KOL. The KOL was a national labor organization that was involved in most of the labor strikes in the late nineteenth century. Some of the strikes became violent, and the violence turned public opinion against the labor unions and organizations. ULP party growth was limited because of this affiliation with the KOL, and so its nominee in the 1888 presidential election, state senator Alson J. Streeter (1823–1901) of Illinois, did poorly.

Clearly, politicians were heavily influenced by the wealthy businessmen, and they supported legislation that advanced the businessmen's cause, primarily profit. The failure of the ULP to perform well in the 1888 election did nothing to stop the farmers and laborers from running for political office. These farmers and laborers saw an ever-widening gap between the producing class (workers, including themselves) and the rich. Most of the issues they faced were economic. The American economy was providing great wealth, but the money was being unfairly distributed. Capitalism (an economic system in which property and goods are privately owned, produced, and distributed) was not working for the working class, the very people upon whom it relied. The producers watched the rich get richer and were determined to empower the state and federal governments to take control and regulate the distribution of wealth. From the workers' point of view, America's economy was reliant on the millions of men and women who toiled in the fields, ran the machines, and worked the businesses. As the workers saw, the people who got the money were those who were already wealthy. Something had to change, and soon.

The final election of the nineteenth century

As the voices of this "new" voting population got louder, Republicans and Democrats alike realized they would have to at least give the impression they were listening. Democratic president Grover Cleveland publicly echoed the sentiments of the farmers and laborers when he expressed concern over the growing power and wealth of a select few. Cleveland called this concentration of wealth undemocratic. In particular, the president attacked the protective tariffs (taxes) that kept overseas competition from taking over an American market. These taxes were levied on certain goods that companies in other countries might want to sell in America. The taxes prevented most overseas competition from entering the American marketplace because doing so would cost them more money than it was worth. The protective tariffs made sure that American companies that sold the same items would have the business of American consumers. Cleveland believed this limited healthy competition and gave power to businesses that may not have the consumers' best interests at heart.

Generally speaking, Republicans were in favor of the tariffs (because they wanted to keep the American marketplace saturated with American-made products) while Democrats

were against them (because they believed foreign competition would keep the marketplace healthy and limit unethical business practices). Earlier in the 1880s, Congress had passed a tariff that protected the rights and goods of American producers who had strong ties to Congress. These producers donated money to political campaigns, and the politicians wanted to keep these men happy. Such favoritism only strengthened the suspicion that the federal government was more concerned with keeping big business happy than it was with protecting the interests of "regular" people.

No other issue divided Republicans and Democrats more than the tariffs. Traditionally, Democrats represented the working people in big cities like New York and Chicago as well as white Southern farmers. They considered themselves consumers who wanted to pay lower prices, and they believed economic wealth should be evenly distributed so that the country was not run by a handful of wealthy men. Republicans were traditionally farmers in the Midwest, workers in Philadelphia, Pennsylvania, and Cincinnati, Ohio, and African American Southerners. Their priority was protecting industry from foreign competition that would serve only to lower prices. Republicans focused on profits, with an emphasis on taxes, money, and banking. These issues were the foundation of the elections throughout the 1890s.

The McKinley Tariff

President Cleveland wanted to reduce tariffs, which he blamed for the uneven distribution of wealth. Manufacturers constantly lobbied Congress to keep tariffs high so that they would continue to prosper. Cleveland believed these companies were working together in an unethical way to ensure their own profit and success.

Democrats introduced several tariff-cutting measures, citing the conflict of interest between laborers and farmers on one side and manufacturers on the other. The Democrats called these big businesses monopolies or trusts. They made sure the public knew that these trusts made amazingly huge profits off the hard work of their employees. The trusts were the enemies of the working class.

Here is an example of how the "protective" tariff worked: Grain was stored in bags. The bags were subject to a tariff of 54 percent. So for every $100 worth of bags a farmer bought, he paid $154. But this was only part of the injustice of the tariffs. The bags produced in America might be able to be sold at a profit for $100 or $125, but the manufacturer could charge as much as $153.99, or whatever farmers would be willing to pay, sell imported bags for less, and pocket the additional profit. This unfair (but common) practice was perfectly legal under the protective tariffs. This sort of business ethic was greatly responsible for driving farmers out of business. Democrats stressed that tariffs were not protective of the workingman.

Although the extra money brought in by the tariffs went to the federal government, Democrats argued that the government could not spend as much money as the tariffs brought in. They supported a tariff that would be for revenue (income) only. This tariff would be lower and bring in only as much money as the government needed to function. Lowering the tariff became the remedy for the unequal distribution of wealth.

The first response among Republicans was to try to find a way to spend the surplus tax revenue. When their schemes failed even before they were put into practice, the Republicans turned to other ideas. One Republican in particular, U.S. representative William McKinley (1843–1901) of Ohio, shrewdly switched the focus from foreign competition to U.S. production. McKinley insisted that protection was in the best interests of all Americans, especially the poor. He gave speeches in which he stressed the notion that protection enriched all Americans, not just the wealthy. By buying only American-made products, Americans guaranteed prosperity because they kept their jobs and bought each others' goods and services. To accept foreign substitutes was un-American and would lead directly to unemployment and poverty.

McKinley was a skilled speaker; his ideas appealed to union workers and laborers who believed protective tariffs would provide more jobs. The tariff was the central issue of the 1888 presidential campaign, which put President Grover Cleveland against former U.S. senator Benjamin Harrison of Indiana. Harrison won the election, although Cleveland won one hundred thousand more popular votes than his opponent. The victory encouraged Republicans, who introduced the McKinley Tariff in 1890.

The McKinley Tariff was a tax that increased prices of most foreign goods by 49.5 percent. Some products, such as sugar, were untaxed. Because it was an important staple (basic item) in the American diet, sugar escaped taxation. But in order to allow sugar into the country, money from the tariff was used to pay a "bounty" to sugar growers in Louisiana and Kansas. This bounty was the first sugar subsidy (grant paid to an enterprise by the government for the benefit of the greater public).

The tariff caused prices to skyrocket, and Republicans fell out of favor with the general public. Cleveland ran for reelection in the 1892 campaign and beat Harrison. The Democrats immediately set to work to reduce tariffs. By that time, the economy's downward spiral was out of control, and the depression of 1893 was unavoidable.

Birth of Populism: power to the people

Members of the Farmers' Alliances, the KOL, the Labor parties, and other smaller groups realized that their concerns were never going to be addressed unless changes were made in the political landscape. In 1892, thirteen hundred delegates from these organizations met in Omaha, Nebraska, and formed an independent political party. Their formal name was the People's Party, but they became known as Populists.

The reforms supported by the Populists were not new; their underling issues had been the basis of major complaints among protest groups for years. The Populists supported government ownership of the railroads and telegraphs and believed government land grants should be given to actual settlers, not to railroads. They called on the government to issue more silver and paper currency in the hope that the increase of money in circulation would raise prices and help farmers pay off their debts. Populists campaigned for the graduated income tax (the more money people made, the more taxes they paid). The graduated tax would redistribute wealth by taxing the rich more heavily than the poor. Populists wanted postal savings banks, which would give the poor a safe place to deposit their money because the banks would be government-owned. This new party supported the direct election of U.S. senators (rather than having them appointed by state legislatures). Populists wanted a reduction in tariffs and called for an eight-hour workday.

Unlike the Republicans and the Democrats, the Populists were not influenced by big business or corporate America. They represented the working class and tried to give these voters a voice. To convince voters, they needed to establish national unity, so they sent representatives to all regions of the United States. These activists gave public speeches to enthusiastic crowds in which they denounced the major political parties as money-grubbing politicians. Although most would-be Populists agreed on the major issues, one strong factor kept them from unifying: racism.

Jim Crow laws

One of the most popular forms of entertainment in the 1850s was the minstrel show. Minstrel shows traveled the country and featured white entertainers in blackface (charcoal or burnt cork was smeared over one's face). These performers sang, danced, and provided audiences with comic skits. Often, the comedy was at the expense of the African American population.

One of the most popular minstrels was Thomas "Daddy" Rice (1808–1860), who created a character named Jim Crow for his song and dance routine. The story goes that Rice invented this character after traveling in the South and seeing a crippled African American dancing and singing. By the 1850s, virtually every American knew who Jim Crow was. The term "Jim Crow" became a racial slur, used for any African American.

Depiction of an African American as a "Jim Crow" minstrel. THE LIBRARY OF CONGRESS.

Despite the abolition of slavery, America established and defended many acts of racial discrimination. These various laws and regulations became known as Jim Crow laws. Prior to the 1890s, Jim Crow laws prohibited African Americans from enjoying the same public places as whites. For example, some restaurants refused to serve African American customers. Other restaurants forced them to eat at tables at the back of the establishments. African Americans were forbidden from drinking from the same water fountains as whites, and they could not use the same public restrooms, attend the same schools, go to the same churches, or use the same public transportation as whites. Although the Civil Rights Act of 1875 had ordered that all persons should be entitled to equal enjoyment of public facilities, the Supreme Court ruled the Act unconstitutional in 1883. The Court decided that the Fourteenth Amendment of the Constitution protected African Americans only from discrimination at the state level; private businesses and individuals could treat them as they saw fit.

Shortly after the Civil Rights Act of 1875 was overturned, southern states took advantage of the law and enforced the limitations on African Americans mentioned above.

Plessy v. Ferguson In 1890, Louisiana passed a law requiring African Americans to ride in separate railroad cars. To protest the law, a light-skinned African American named Homer Plessy (1862–1925) boarded a whites-only train car. He was immediately arrested and a local judge ruled against him.

Plessy appealed the ruling and his case went to the U.S. Supreme Court in 1896. The Court determined that Plessy's rights had not been denied him because the separate railroad car provided was equal in every way to the cars provided whites. The "separate but equal" accommodations did not act as evidence that African Americans were inferior to whites.

The separate-but-equal doctrine is what allowed states to restrict African Americans from public areas and services. Soon, signs reading "Whites Only" and "Colored" appeared everywhere. Curfews were established for African Americans, and they were forced to use separate entrances and exits at places like libraries and theaters.

Lynching: vigilante justice

With the legalization of Jim Crow laws that encouraged racism and segregation (separation of African Americans from whites), the year 1890 ushered in another violation of justice: the phenomenon of lynching (unlawful hanging by rope until death).

In the past, white supremacy groups (who believed other races to be inferior to whites) like the Ku Klux Klan (KKK) sometimes used lynching as a way to try to control and threaten African American communities and populations. Mostly, the KKK tried to keep the African American race submissive by restricting their right and ability to vote. Even if the law permitted them to vote, the KKK terrorized African Americans into giving up that right in order to stay alive. Those who refused to be intimidated often were the victims of KKK violence and torture.

Lynching gained momentum beginning in 1890. Historians estimate that 233 lynchings took place between 1880 and 1884; 381 from 1885 to 1889. But from 1890 to 1894, lynchings hit an all-time high (of the century) of 611.

Antilynching campaign gains momentum

Local and state governments did nothing to deter the lynchings of the South. One brave woman, a teacher named Ida B. Wells-Barnett (1862–1931), became known throughout the nation as leader of the antilynching campaign. Born in Mississippi, Wells experienced the Jim Crow laws firsthand. When a conductor tried to force Wells-Barnett to give up her first-class accommodations and move to the Jim Crow car of the train, she refused. As the conductor tried to physically remove her, Wells-Barnett bit his hand but was thrown off the train.

An African American man hangs in a tree following a lynching. THE LIBRARY OF CONGRESS.

Although she sued and won, the defendant eventually won in appeals court.

Wells-Barnett became co-owner of an African American newspaper in Memphis called "The Free Speech & Headlight." Her editorials and essays spoke out against racism and discrimination, and her writing got her fired from her teaching job. She turned to writing full time.

In 1892, three people, one a good friend of Wells-Barnett's, were lynched while defending their grocery store from white attackers who wanted to put the store out of business. In the scuffle, one of the owners shot one of the attackers. An outraged Wells-Barnett criticized

Journalist and civil rights activist Ida B. Wells-Barnett.
SCHOMBURG CENTER FOR RESEARCH IN BLACK CULTURE.

the event in her newspaper and specifically discussed the evils of lynching. She encouraged African Americans to leave town. While out of town herself, a white mob ransacked and destroyed her newspaper office and warned her not to return. Wells-Barnett took her campaign to England, where she founded the National Afro-American Council and served as chairman of its Anti-Lynching Bureau. Wells-Barnett eventually helped establish the National Association for the Advancement of Colored People (NAACP).

Lynching continued to be used as a terrorist weapon well into the twentieth century. Across the nation, nearly five thousand African Americans were lynched between the 1800s and 1955. Most of these victims were murdered because they were political activists or labor organizers. Others simply violated unspoken laws of how whites expected African Americans to behave.

African Americans and populism

Given the always-present racism of the final decade of the nineteenth century, it only made sense that southern African Americans would organize their own unions and alliances. The Colored Farmers' Alliance was formed in Texas in 1890 when two smaller organizations merged. By 1891, the Colored Alliance had a membership of more than one million. These men were prohibited from joining the white farmers' alliances.

Although the Colored Alliance sometimes cooperated with another group of organized farmers called the Southern Farmers' Alliance, they clashed on some major issues. One of those issues was voting rights. An election bill promised federal protection to safeguard voting rights in the South. The Colored Alliance recognized the value for African Americans in this bill and supported it. The Southern Alliance was against it. Formed in 1877, most members of the Southern Alliance were in cotton production. All of them were white.

The Colored Alliance disbanded after it called for a cotton picker strike in 1891. The strike failed to happen due to poor communication and leadership. One Arkansas community actually tried to strike, and fifteen strikers were killed in the process. The alliance fell apart in the months after the strike.

The Colored Farmers' Alliance was just one of several African American organizations that mobilized for reform. Historically, the concept of "black populism" has been considered an offshoot of a primarily white movement. But historian Omar H. Ali of Towson University suggests that black populism was actually a movement parallel with the Populist movement.

Ali argues that during the years 1886 to 1898, Southern African Americans led an independent economic reform movement to help improve schools, establish newspapers, lead labor strikes, and usher in political reform. These efforts were not born of the mainstream Populist movement, but occurred alongside it.

By the late 1890s, racism completely separated the white Populists from the African Americans, even though their goals were nearly the same. Without the support of the whites, and with the widespread physical attacks on African Americans that characterized the decade, the so-called black populist movement collapsed.

African American Populists and farmers' alliance members were victims of racism in ways that kept them from being effective activists. For example, members of the Mississippi Colored Alliance boycotted (stopped doing business with) unfair merchants in 1889. Boycotts were common tactics among activists. But the Colored Alliance boycotters suffered extreme consequences: They were murdered because their behavior went against the status quo (what exists in society at the time). Although one would think the murder of fellow alliance members (from various alliances) might upset other members, this was not the case. White alliancemen were not disturbed by the murders, as they believed the African Americans knew the risks they faced and made their choices anyway.

Hope for the hopeless

The Populist Party needed to get a leader in the White House. Its choice for the presidential candidate in the 1892 election was former U.S. representative James B. Weaver (1833–1912) of Iowa. Weaver had been active in the Greenback-Labor Party and had unsuccessfully run for president on its ticket in 1880. Weaver was a lawyer who had served admirably in the Civil War, then later in the House of Representatives (1879–81 and 1885–89).

Weaver campaigned across the country on a speaking tour in 1892. To the surprise of Democrats and Republicans alike, he won more than one million popular votes on Election Day. His twenty-two electoral votes were not enough to win the election, but it was the first time a third party had won any states in the Electoral College since 1860. (Each state is appointed a number of voters in the Electoral College. That number is determined based upon the population of the state. The electoral votes ultimately decide a presidential election.)

Weaver ran against Democrat Grover Cleveland and Republican Benjamin Harrison. Cleveland won 277 electoral votes, leaving Harrison with 145. Weaver won the states of Idaho, Colorado, Nevada, and North Dakota.

The Populist Party did not do as well as they had hoped in the election for several reasons. In the South, Populists sometimes aligned with Republicans in order to reach a larger voter population. (Most African American Southerners were Republican.) But in the states where Populists did not support Republicans, African American voters were reluctant to give up what little power they already had in the Republican Party. To vote Populist was a risk they were not willing to take. In many cases, disfranchisement (taking away the right to vote) and violence at the polls prohibited African Americans from voting at all. Populists in the Midwest and

Northeast did not do well because voters in those regions did not need a third political party; the close rivalries between Republicans and Democrats provided alternatives within the traditional two-party system. Also, recent immigration to these regions established a population of nonunion workers. The philosophies and goals of the Populist Party did not hold great appeal to foreign-speaking workers who would be satisfied with work of any kind.

In the congressional races of 1894, the Populists managed to get thirteen representatives into Washington. They increased their vote by 41 percent over the 1892 election when they garnered 1,471,000 votes. Although this was not enough to give them a majority in either the Senate or the House of Representatives, their success was impressive for a third political party.

The Election of 1896

In an effort to increase the party's appeal, the Populists decided in January 1895 to downplay some of the more radical reforms of their platform (for example, transportation and land reforms, for which some party members wanted government ownership of all railroads and a portion of public lands to be set aside for settlers) and focus on the money issue. Party leaders promoted free silver as a way to gain control of the federal government. Many Populists balked at the change in campaign strategy; they wanted the whole Populist platform or nothing at all and feared a change in focus would divert the movement from issues they considered equally important.

The Populists approached the election of 1896 as a split party. Those in favor of focusing on the issue of bimetallism to the exclusion of all other issues were also in favor of fusing their

platform with the Democrats, who shared their perspective on the money issue. Those who preferred to stay with the original platform established in 1892 remained committed to participating in the election as an independent political party. They were against the free silver (another term for bimetallism) stance because they did not believe it would change the existing system of commerce and banking. This faction of Populists felt the issue of industrial monopolies was more important than free silver.

With America still in the midst of economic depression, the idea of free silver caught on strongly. The Democrats in particular favored it because their party had been hurt by the depression as well as by President Cleveland's inability to fix it. Additionally, the farmers' revolt had led to labor parties and Populism, which took away seats in Congress and severely limited Democratic power. Cleveland had made it clear that he was committed to maintaining the gold standard, and his stance turned many Democrats against him.

In a surprising turn of events, the Democratic Party made their feelings clear to Cleveland when they nominated former U.S. representative William Jennings Bryan (1860–1925) of Nebraska as the Democratic candidate. Bryan had been elected to Congress twice, in 1890 and 1892, then lost in 1894 in his bid for election to the U.S. Senate. During his years in Congress, he had gained a reputation as a gifted speaker whose passion for bimetallism and opposition to high tariffs endeared him to Democrats and Populists alike.

Bryan spoke at the 1896 Democratic convention on July 9 and delivered a powerful speech that became known as the "Cross of Gold" speech. Bryan's words called for free

Political cartoon of former U.S. representative William Jennings Bryan of Nebraska giving his "Cross of Gold" speech at the 1896 Democratic Convention; the speech won him his party's presidential nomination. © BETTMANN/CORBIS.

coinage of silver at a ratio of silver to gold of sixteen to one (for every sixteen silver coins minted, one gold coin would be produced). As noted on the *1896: The Presidential Campaign* Web site, he concluded his speech with this declaration: "Having behind us the producing masses of this nation and the world, supported by the commercial interests, the laboring interests and the toilers everywhere, we will answer their demand for a gold standard by saying to them: You shall not press down upon the brow of labor this crown of thorns, you shall not crucify mankind upon a cross of gold."

Bryan was telling his audience that sticking to the gold standard would work against the very

people who built the great nation of America: the workers and laborers. When the thirty-six-year-old speaker finished his speech and sat down, the crowd exploded with clapping and cheering. Men tore off their vests and jackets and threw them high into the air. Women screamed while men waved their hats and canes back and forth. According to newspaper accounts of the event, the frenzy lasted for a full half hour after the speech had concluded. The next day, Bryan was nominated. Populists recognized the value in joining the Democrats in their support of Bryan as well as the fact that they had just lost their position as leader of reform. It was in their best interests to merge with the Democrats, so they did.

This merge did not please Southern Populists. They believed that Democrats had victimized them for years, and now their political mates in the West were embracing them. The fusion with the Democrats split the Populist Party forever, and was the beginning of the end of the once-hopeful third party.

Although many reformers supported Bryan in the 1896 election, Republican William McKinley defeated his Democratic opponent and was elected president that year. McKinley had the support of millions of dollars in campaign funds donated by big business and industry; Bryan could not compete with such financing. The gold standard was kept in place, and high tariffs ruled the day.

The end of Populism

Populism quickly came to an end after the 1896 election. A run of gold strikes in the late 1890s increased the volume of money even without the free silver the Populists demanded. Determined Populists nominated national tickets in 1900, 1904, and 1908, but public support had eroded and disappeared. There were no Populists in Congress after 1903.

Temperance movement

All of America was busy trying to survive drought and economic depression. African Americans were struggling to deal with racism and hatred in addition to the economic conditions. Yet another issue came to the forefront of the country's attention in the 1890s: temperance (a movement that campaigned for the public to refrain from drinking alcohol).

The movement was led by women concerned with the destructive effects of alcohol on families and values. A group of women in

Ohio met in 1874 and established the National Woman's Christian Temperance Union (WCTU). The WCTU did much more than advocate against drinking alcohol. Members promoted the concept of kindergartens and physical fitness for women. They donated money and time to beautifying public areas. The organization advocated for women speaking out for the rights of children, families, and themselves in public.

One of the most famous and effective presidents of the union was Frances E. Willard (1839–1898). Willard was the second president of the organization and took it to the next level by founding the World's WCTU.

Other organizations formed as the years passed, including the Anti-Saloon League in 1893. It started as a state-level organization in Ohio but became a powerful national organization after 1895. Unlike the WCTU, the League focused only on prohibition (the outlawing of alcohol). Although a small political party called the Prohibition Party had formed in 1869, the League did not join. Instead, it opposed or supported Republican or Democratic politicians according to their views on temperance and nothing else.

The Prohibition movement would not become official until the 1920s, but the temperance movement that preceded it had great national influence in America. The movement was directly responsible for the drafting and passage of the Eighteenth Amendment, which prohibited the sale and consumption of alcohol from 1918 to 1933.

By the time the decade was coming to a close, Americans were ready for some peace. But 1898 would take America to war with Spain, and William McKinley would be reelected

The Wonderful Wizard of Oz and Populism

A scene from the 1939 movie The Wizard of Oz, *showing (from left) the Cowardly Lion, Dorothy, the Tin Man, and the Scarecrow walking along the Yellow Brick Road to Oz.* THE KOBAL COLLECTION.

L. Frank Baum, author of the classic children's book *The Wonderful Wizard of Oz*, was not a political activist. He did live in the Great Plains, though, where Populism had its greatest influence.

In a 1964 issue of *American Quarterly*, scholar Henry Littlefield analyzed Baum's story from a Populist perspective and focused on Baum's use of symbolism. Littlefield's interpretation has Dorothy as the symbol of Everyman. She hails from the Midwest (Kansas), home of hard-working people with simple lifestyles and expectations. Not uncoincidentally, she comes from a farm family. The Scarecrow and Tin Man are symbolic of farmers and industrial workers. The Scarecrow is in search of a brain, symbolic of the societal prejudice that farmers were not intelligent enough to recognize their own interests. The Tin Man had been dehumanized by hard and callous factory labor. His rusting was symbolic of the closing of thousands of factories in the depression of 1893.

as president in 1900 only to be assassinated shortly after beginning his second term the following year. The Progressive Era was about to begin.

For More Information

BOOKS

Brands, H. W. *The Reckless Decade: America in the 1890s.* New York: St. Martin's Press, 1995.

Cashman, Sean Dennis. *America in the Gilded Age.* New York: New York University Press, 1993.

Chambers, John Whiteclay II. *The Tyranny of Change: America in the Progressive Era, 1890–1920.* 2nd ed.

New Brunswick, NJ: Rutgers University Press, 2000.

Howes, Kelly King. *Reconstruction Era: Almanac.* Detroit: UXL, 2005.

Miller, Worth Robert. "Farmers and Third-Party Politics." In *The Gilded Age: Essays on the Origins of Modern America.* Edited by Charles W. Calhoun. Wilmington, DE: Scholarly Resources, 1996.

Painter, Nell Irvin. *Standing at Armageddon: The United States, 1877–1919.* New York: W. W. Norton & Co., 1987.

Steeples, Douglas, and David O. Whitten. *Democracy in Desperation: The Depression of 1893.* Westport, CT: Greenwood Press, 1998.

The Cowardly Lion represents William Jennings Bryan. When he first meets Dorothy and her friends, he tries to hurt the Tin Man. He fails and does not even so much as dent the Tin Man's body, thereby symbolizing his failure to win over industrial labor populations.

According to Littlefield, Oz is actually Washington, D.C., and the Wizard is the president of the United States. The actual journey to Oz represents the march to Washington undertaken by Ohio businessman Jacob Coxey and his "army."

When Dorothy and her companions reach Oz, the Wizard instructs them to kill the Wicked Witch of the West, who is symbolic of the forces of nature. Dorothy does the job by dousing the witch with water, which symbolizes the end of the drought that had plagued the West for years. Once the four friends return to the Wizard, they discover he is nothing special, just a common man. The political Wizard promises everyone what they desire, except for Dorothy. Her wish to return home to comfort her family is selfless; the Wizard has no magic solution for her.

In Baum's novel, Dorothy's shoes were made of silver. The silver shoes symbolize the silver standard that the Populists so passionately demanded. They had magic powers to solve Dorothy's crisis (just as the silver standard was supposed to solve the farmers' dilemma). When the book was turned into a movie, however, technicolor was a new enhancement to film, and producing studio MGM wanted to highlight its abilities, so Dorothy's silver shoes became ruby slippers.

Dorothy, being just a simple gal, does not realize the power she possesses. Instead, she goes down the yellow brick road, which symbolized the gold standard and got her into all kinds of trouble. By the end of the story, Dorothy understands the power of her shoes, but they are gone when she awakens from her dream, in her own bed, in Kansas. The imagery of Oz faded from her memory, just as the free silver issue faded from the public's concern.

Some critics insist Baum never intended to write a political allegory (fable using symbolism) at all, that any similarities are strictly coincidental. But Littlefield's theory has increased in popularity over time.

WEB SITES

Ali, Omar H. "Black Populism in the New South: The Mothers, Daughters, and Sisters of the Movement." *Towson University.* http://pages.towson.edu/oali/SHA%20paper%202005.htm (accessed on April 28, 2006).

Ali, Omar H. "Black Populism in the South." *Towson University.* http://pages.towson.edu/oali/black_populism_in_the_new_south.htm (accessed on April 28, 2006).

Davis, Ronald L. F. "Creating Jim Crow: In-Depth Essay." *The History of Jim Crow.* http://www.jimcrowhistory.org/history/creating2.htm (accessed on April 28, 2006).

Edwards, Rebecca. "The Depression of 1893." *1896: The Presidential Campaign: Cartoons & Commentary.* http://projects.vassar.edu/1896/depression.html (accessed on April 28, 2006).

Edwards, Rebecca. "'No Cross of Gold'" *1896: The Presidential Campaign: Bryan's Cross of Gold Speech.* http://projects.vassar.edu/1896/crossofgold.html (accessed on June 27, 2006).

"Freedom, a History of US." *PBS.* http://www.pbs.org/wnet/historyofus/web10/segment6_p.html (accessed April 28, 2006).

Holmes, William F. "Colored Farmers' Alliance." *The Handbook of Texas Online.* http://www.tsha.utexas.edu/handbook/online/articles/CC/aac1.html (accessed on April 28, 2006).

Library of Congress. "African American Perspectives: Progress of a People: Ida B. Wells-Barnett." *American Memory.* http://memory.loc.gov/ammem/aap/idawells.html (accessed on April 28, 2006).

Marcum, Christopher Steven. "The Parable on Populism: An Autobiography of a Wizard." *University of Arizona.* http://www.u.arizona.edu/~marcum/wizard1.htm (accessed on April 28, 2006).

"The Rise and Fall of Jim Crow." *PBS.* http://www.pbs.org/wnet/jimcrow/index.html (accessed on April 28, 2006).

Whitten, David O. "The Depression of 1893." *EH.Net Encyclopedia.* http://eh.net/encyclopedia/article/whitten.panic.1893 (accessed on April 28, 2006).

Woman's Christian Temperance Union. http://www.wctu.org/ (accessed on April 28, 2006).

7

Steady Leadership, Transitional Times

Everything about America was changing throughout the Gilded Age (approximately 1878–99). The Gilded Age was the period in history following the American Civil War (1861–65) and Reconstruction (roughly the final twenty-three years of the nineteenth century), characterized by a ruthless pursuit of profit, an exterior of showiness and grandeur, and immeasurable political corruption. The landscape, the workplace, the population, cultural values, and societal behavior and expectations were shifting. The men who led the nation throughout much of that era faced many challenges and intense corruption in both politics and business. Being president of the United States in the last quarter of the nineteenth century required strong leadership and a willingness to make decisions and then act upon them. Some of these presidents are remembered for their abilities. Others are remembered more for their lack of them.

The Gilded Age took its name from a book of fiction of the same name, written by Mark Twain (1835–1910; real name, Samuel Clemens) and Charles Dudley Warner (1829–1900) in 1873. The authors wrote about a politically corrupt and materialistic America after the Civil War. That image fit the real America as well. On the outside, the United States seemed to be gilded (covered with gold) in its endless moneymaking opportunities. People came from across the globe to begin a new life in America. But the image of a golden land covered up the uglier aspects of society—greed and excess. Many of those who dreamed of wealth and success actually lived in poverty. The country was divided into those citizens who lived lives of luxury and those who were barely surviving.

Grover Cleveland

Grover Cleveland (1837–1908; served 1885–89 and 1893–97) was the first president ever to serve two nonconsecutive terms (terms not back-to-back) in the White House. In the 1884 election, he ran against

149

WORDS TO KNOW

civil service: The system in which civilians work for various government agencies and departments. Before civil service reform, people were appointed to positions depending on whom they knew in politics and business. After reform, people had to apply for a job and pass examinations in order to qualify.

Democratic Party: One of the oldest political parties in the United States. Originally linked with the South and slavery, it transformed into one associated with urban voters and liberal policies.

electoral votes: The votes a presidential candidate receives for having won a majority of a state's popular vote (citizens' votes). The candidate who receives the most popular votes in a particular state wins all of that state's electoral votes. Each state receives two electoral votes for its two U.S. senators and a figure for the number of U.S. representatives it has (which is determined by a state's population). A candidate must win a majority of electoral votes (over 50 percent) in order to win the presidency.

Gilded Age: The period in history following the Civil War and Reconstruction (roughly the final twenty-three years of the nineteenth century), characterized by a ruthless pursuit of profit, an exterior of showiness and grandeur, and immeasurable political corruption.

patronage system: Also known as the spoils system. In patronage, someone donates large sums of money to help ensure the election of a candidate. That candidate repays the favor by making job appointments or by passing and proposing legislation that safeguards the interests of the business or person who donated the money.

Republican Party: One of the oldest political parties in the United States. Founded as an antislavery party in the mid-1800s, it transformed into one associated with conservative fiscal and social policies.

tariffs: Taxes imposed on goods imported from other countries.

trust: The concept of several companies banding together to form an organization that limits the competition by controlling the production and distribution of a product or service.

Republican James G. Blaine (1830–1893), a former member of U.S. Congress from Maine. Blaine was one of the most powerful politicians of the late nineteenth century. In addition to serving in the U.S. Senate for five years (1876–81), he served in the U.S. House of Representatives for thirteen (1863–76), during which time he was elected Speaker of the House (the most influential political position after the president and vice president). He was named secretary of state twice in his career as well, serving three presidents. Blaine is also remembered as

one of the founders of the Republican Party (one of the oldest political parties in the United States, associated with conservative fiscal and social policies).

Of the two presidential candidates in 1884, Blaine had the most political experience in Washington. Cleveland had little in comparison. He had been elected mayor of Buffalo, New York, in 1881 and quickly moved into position as governor of the state of New York the following year. He clearly had the support of New York, which was an important state in any election

150

because it had a high population, which meant it carried a high number of electoral votes (thirty-six). A presidential candidate receives electoral votes for having won a majority of a state's popular vote (citizens' votes). The candidate who receives the most popular votes in a particular state wins all of that state's electoral votes. Each state receives two electoral votes for its two U.S. senators and a figure for the number of U.S. representatives it has (which is determined by a state's population). A candidate must win a majority of electoral votes (over 50 percent) in order to win the presidency. A political candidate can win more popular votes nationwide but still lose the election due to receiving less than 50 percent of the electoral votes.

New York's support of Cleveland was the main reason the Democrats chose him for their presidential candidate. He appealed to middle-class voters of both parties for several reasons. He was a huge man, so large that his nieces and nephews called him "Uncle Jumbo." Although he dressed appropriately for a politician, in suit and tie, his size prevented him from ever coming across as too perfect or better than anyone else. He was a candidate the average man could relate to. His politics served the middle class as well. Cleveland was against big business corruption and greed. He had built a reputation as an honest and hardworking political leader in New York and used his power to fight Tammany Hall (see Chapter 1), the most corrupt political machine of the era. (A political machine is a well-organized group of men who control a political party with their vote; in return for their support, the political party rewards them with favors such as money and jobs.) Cleveland fought Tammany Hall even though it had supported him in his election for governor.

Cleveland's scandal

The 1884 campaign turned nasty as both candidates focused on their opponent's failings. For Blaine, this meant his questionable ethics during his time as Speaker of the House. Cleveland's campaigners painted Blaine as an immoral politician who used his power to get favors from the railroads. Blaine was soon considered a puppet of the big business world, controlled by money and the interest of influential business owners. He had enemies in both parties because of his ethics.

Cleveland was not without his shortcomings. For someone who preached the value of honesty, he had some explaining to do when a story broke that he had fathered a son with a thirty-six-year-old woman named Maria Halpin in 1874. Although there was no way to prove Cleveland was the father of the boy, he accepted responsibility and helped pay the expenses of raising a child. He publicly admitted to the affair, which helped retain the loyalty of his supporters. The child was named Oscar Folsom Cleveland, after Cleveland and his law partner, Oscar Folsom (1837–1873), who also could have been the real father. Halpin eventually suffered a mental breakdown and was admitted to an insane asylum. Young Oscar was adopted by a couple and Cleveland never saw him again.

Cleveland instructed his friends and supporters to refrain from making excuses and to publicly acknowledge that he had given in to temptation, but only in that one instance. According to www.americanpresident.org, one supporter made this argument: "We are told that Mr. Blaine has been delinquent in office but blameless in public life, while Mr. Cleveland has been a model of official integrity but culpable [guilty] in personal relations. We should

Cover of the September 27, 1884, issue of The Judge *magazine shows a baby shouting, "I want my Pa" towards Democratic presidential candidate Grover Cleveland. Cleveland had accepted responsibility for fathering a child out of wedlock, which led to the famous campaign slogan exchange between parties: James Blaine's Republican Party: "Ma ma, where's my pa?" After Cleveland defeated Blaine, the Democrats' retort was: "Gone to the White House, ha ha ha."* THE LIBRARY OF CONGRESS.

therefore elect Mr. Cleveland to the public office for which he is so well qualified to fill, and re-mand [return] Mr. Blaine to the private station which he is admirably fitted to adorn."

That is exactly what happened. Cleveland won the election with 219 electoral votes to Blaine's 182. The new president did not, how-ever, win the state of New York by many votes, as was predicted. Cleveland got just twelve hundred more New York votes than did his op-ponent; had Blaine won New York, he would have won the election.

First term in the White House

Cleveland was the first Democrat elected to the presidency since James Buchanan (1791–1868; served 1857–1861) served just before the Civil War. Cleveland spent the majority of his first term just trying to keep Congress from granting special favors and privileges to big businesses. The patronage system was a major part of the political corruption throughout the Gilded Age. In patronage, someone donates large sums of money to help ensure the election of a candidate. That candidate repays the favor by making job appointments or by passing and proposing legislation that safeguards the interests of the business or person who donated the money.

Cleveland did not consider himself an activ-ist president with a plan or agenda to push. He did not introduce much legislation; instead, he spent his efforts on appointing qualified and ca-pable officials to head departments within the federal government. His style was to name the most suitable official, give him the necessary au-thority to do his job effectively, and then use him for advice. In Cleveland's opinion, the less involved federal government was in citizens' ev-eryday lives, the better.

Much to the dismay of thousands of Dem-ocrats, Cleveland refused their petitions and requests for jobs and continued to reform the civil service (the system by which civilians are appointed to positions in various government agencies and departments.) Where once men were given federal government positions based solely on their political beliefs or on their rela-tionship with those in power, now they were being selected on the basis of their abilities and qualifications alone. This approach angered many of Cleveland's supporters who had with-stood twenty-four years of Republican rule and were hoping for a chance to make some money. Congress repealed the Tenure of Office Act in 1887, which prohibited the president from removing any officials from office without the approval of the Senate. Cleveland used his newfound freedom to remove corrupt officials from office before their terms expired and enact reforms throughout government agencies.

The power of the veto One of the powers of the president is the veto, which is the ability to vote against any given bill or legislation. Presi-dent Cleveland used his veto power more than any other president in American history: 584 times.

One of the most controversial vetoes of Cleveland's first term occurred in 1887. The president refused to pass a bill that would give disabled Civil War Union (Northern) veterans a regular pension (an income or regular payment received based on prior service). Most veterans who became disabled because of military service applied for their pensions through the federal Pension Bureau. The bureau investigated each

Editorial cartoon shows President Grover Cleveland lighting fire to a "government farm," as he pushes through his plans for civil service reform. The cartoon shows locusts (symbolizing government workers getting their jobs based on their political beliefs or relationship to those in power) being burned away, in favor of employees who receive their jobs based solely on their qualifications. © BETTMANN/CORBIS.

case to confirm that the disability was war-related and to determine how much money the veteran should receive. Some veterans' pension applications, however, were made in a private bill. These cases were not usually investigated, so there were many chances for corruption. During the years 1885 to 1887, 40 percent of all bills passed by the House of Representatives and more than half of all those approved by the Senate were private pension bills. In the first four years of his presidency, Cleveland received 2,099 private pension bills and vetoed 288 of them. The president's refusal to pass such bills angered the veterans, who made up a large portion of the voting public. But Cleveland believed

that passing the 1887 proposal would serve only to create an expensive, endless, and corrupt form of charity.

Legislative impact Only two new major policies were enacted during Cleveland's first term in the White House: the Interstate Commerce Act and the Dawes Severalty Act. Both laws were passed in February 1887, and both began in Congress rather than in the White House.

The Interstate Commerce Act was passed on February 4. The act was the result of nationwide frustration over the lack of railroad regulations. Railroads were notorious for their mismanagement and corruption. They were among the first businesses to practice price fixing. Rather than compete among themselves, owners of different railroads met and developed a pricing structure. This agreement allowed them all to profit without seriously underpricing each other, a practice known as pooling. Railroads also charged higher freight rates to shippers sending goods a short distance than they did to those sending goods long distances. Their reasoning for pooling was that it cost less per mile to send freight a long distance, though that simply was not true. Whether traveling short or long distance, the cost to the railroad was the same. Rebates were given in the form of refunds, but only to shippers who did a great deal of business with a particular railroad or to large companies, such as Standard Oil, that agreed to send the majority of their shipping business to one particular railroad company.

All these practices were forms of rate discrimination. They made it very difficult for smaller companies and farmers to compete in a market where big business got all the discounts and benefits. Although the first rate-discrimination laws were passed in 1842, they were not very effective because there was no federal enforcement of the laws, and state governments had limited power. By the late 1870s, merchants were calling for regulations. By the 1880s, even some railroads were joining in because rate competition had become so fierce.

The Senate passed the Interstate Commerce Act, 50–20. Former railroad company presidents cast five of the votes against the regulation. As a direct result of the Interstate Commerce Act, the Interstate Commerce Commission (ICC) was formed. Each of its five members was to serve six-year terms, and no more than three of them could be from the same political party. The law forbid pooling and rebates and eliminated some of the rate differences for long and short hauls. It also demanded that rates be "reasonable and just." The ICC was powerless to set rates or punish companies that violated the law. When all aspects of the new policy were in place, neither railroads nor some farm groups were happy. The railroads believed the federal government was too involved, and the farmers believed the government was not involved enough.

The Dawes Severalty Act was passed four days later, on February 8. Also known as the Indian Emancipation Act, the law took away all tribal lands and divided them up for individual ownership. In doing so, the government took away the legal standing and rights of tribes. Native American individuals gave up their tribal status in exchange for American citizenship as well as a specific amount of land. Heads of families received 160 acres; single adults got 80 acres. But ownership was still restricted: Native Americans could not completely own the land they were "given" until twenty-five years had passed.

The purpose of the Dawes Act was to force Native Americans to assimilate (fit into and adapt similar ways of life) into American society. Reformers saw the tribes' nomadic (frequent moving around) lifestyle as an obstacle to be overcome in order to become Americanized. The Act seriously undermined the Native American way of life, but it did little to help anyone assimilate. After all land had been divided and given out, there were millions of acres of "leftover" land that was then sold to non–Native Americans. Before the Act, Native Americans owned about 138 million acres of land. After the law's passage, their holdings dwindled to about 78 million acres. It was not until 1934 that the policy was reversed and surplus lands returned to the Native Americans.

International diplomacy President Cleveland was against building relationships with other countries, and he did not support territorial expansion (gaining more land for the United States). He felt both efforts would only entangle the nation in more political issues. America was contending with enough conflict on the home front with the railroads and Native Americans. As a result, he withdrew the Frelinghuysen-Zavala Treaty, which would have given the United States the right to build a canal in Nicaragua that would be jointly owned by the two countries. The treaty had been proposed during the Chester A. Arthur (1829–1886; served 1881–85) presidency but had never been approved by Congress because it violated a treaty with Great Britain that was already in existence.

The president also got involved in the issue of U.S. fishing rights in the North Atlantic Ocean off the coasts of Canada and Newfoundland. At the time, Newfoundland was not a Canadian territory, but belonged to the British. Fishing rights in this area of the ocean had been a source of conflict in American-British relations for more than one hundred years. By the time Cleveland was in office, American fishermen had been allowed to fish in the waters if Canadian fishermen could export fish to the United States duty-free (without taxation). Congress revoked those rights because it believed in taxing imports. As a result of the abridged agreement, Canadian fishermen began seizing U.S. fishing boats, claiming they were violating the agreement.

In March 1887, Cleveland signed a bill that allowed him to forbid all Canadian imports of any kind if the harassment of American fishermen continued. This law was known as the Retaliation Act, and though he signed it, Cleveland chose not to enforce it. He felt relations with Britain were more important than fishing rights,

so he used the Act as leverage in negotiations with Britain. In February 1888, the Bayard-Chamberlain Treaty was signed. The provisions of the treaty allowed American fishermen to fish in the waters off Canada. They could dock their ships there to purchase supplies and ship their catch back home after buying a fishing license. In the event Congress ever decided to lift the duty on Canadian fish, the licenses would be free of charge, and American fishermen would receive other privileges.

The Bayard-Chamberlain Treaty satisfied both sides for the time being, and America's relations with Britain improved. Cleveland never had to enforce the Retaliation Act, and at the same time, he showed Britain that America was not going to be pushed around. Cleveland also tactfully negotiated with British Columbia in the boundary dispute between that Canadian province and the U.S. territory of Alaska.

On race, immigration, and women Cleveland believed African Americans were inferior to whites, and he sided with white Southerners who refused to treat African Americans as social or political equals. Cleveland made it a point to let whites in the South know they had an ally in him, and he voted against the integration (mixing of all races) of schools. The president considered civil rights a social issue and believed the federal government should not interfere, and so he not only did not actively try to improve conditions for African Americans, but personally and publicly opposed efforts to protect them.

On the other hand, during his first term, Cleveland spoke out *against* the prejudice toward the Chinese on the West Coast. He soon decided that the attitudes of Americans in that region were so deep, and the Chinese culture so foreign to Americans, that there would never be a place for Chinese immigrants in the United States. Cleveland worked to limit Chinese immigration. He explained that the difference between the Chinese and European immigrants was that the Europeans were willing to assimilate into American society. (See Chapter 5 for more on immigration.)

Cleveland considered himself an Indian reformer but looked at Native Americans as children in need of a caretaker. He made efforts to convince Native Americans to give up their tribal ways and traditions so that they could assimilate into white society. Cleveland supported the disastrous Dawes Severalty Act in 1887.

Women during Cleveland's reign did not have the right to vote, and the president had little to say on that topic. Cleveland never spoke out in support of or against the idea. He basically took a neutral position, making sure to neither offend nor encourage women. He recognized the importance of women's clubs and organizations because women had influence on the votes of their husbands and fathers.

The campaign of 1888

Cleveland was renominated as the Democratic candidate in the 1888 presidential election. His opponent was former Civil War general and former U.S. senator Benjamin Harrison (1833–1901) of Indiana. Although Harrison won one hundred thousand fewer popular votes than Cleveland, Harrison won more electoral votes and became the twenty-third president of the United States.

The Harrison administration

Benjamin Harrison was born in 1833 in North Bend, Ohio. The grandson of the ninth U.S.

President Benjamin Harrison. © BETTMANN/CORBIS.

president, William Henry Harrison (1773–1841; served 1841), became a lawyer and moved to Indiana, where he volunteered in campaigns for the Republican Party. Harrison fought in the Civil War as a colonel. When he returned home, he built a reputation as an excellent lawyer.

Harrison served in the U.S. Senate throughout most of the 1880s, where he supported Native Americans and Civil War veterans. In the 1888 presidential campaign, he defended high tariffs (taxes imposed on goods imported from other countries; this was the main issue of the race), conservation of wilderness lands, and limited civil service reform. He broke from traditional Republican viewpoint in his opposition to the Chinese Exclusion Act of 1882, which ended Chinese immigration to the United States.

Harrison was the first candidate to participate in what became known as "front porch speeches." People would visit him at his home in Indiana and listen to him speak from his front porch. This campaign style encouraged citizens to think of Harrison as one of them, a regular man with a regular home and family. These speeches were not as informal as they appeared; Harrison's campaign managers carefully selected which newspaper reporters and community members would attend. By comparison, Cleveland gave just one speech in the 1888 campaign.

Although he received fewer popular votes, Harrison won the electoral college, 233 to 168, primarily because of the votes he received from New York and Indiana. A Republican president was back in the White House, and Republicans increased the number of seats in the House of Representatives by fourteen. They controlled the Senate by a narrow margin. For the first time in years, the Republican Party dominated the executive and legislative branches of the federal government.

Historians generally do not rate Harrison as a gifted or unique leader, but his administration was efficient and productive. Some of the legislation that passed during his presidency had a major impact on American business. Harrison supported the McKinley Tariff of 1890, a law that raised tariff rates an average of 49.5 percent. The bill was proposed by U.S. representative William McKinley (1843–1901) of Ohio. In addition to raising tariff levels, the bill gave the president expanded powers in the area of foreign trade.

The American public hated giant corporations and big businesses that took over the economy and forced consumers into paying high fees and prices. Republicans and Democrats alike rallied together in the call for reform of dishonest business practices such as monopolies. (Monopolies are businesses that have total control over a certain sector of the economy, including prices; in a monopoly, there is no competition.) As a result of this public outcry, the Harrison administration supported and passed the Sherman Antitrust Act of 1890. It was the first federal law to regulate big business. The Sherman Antitrust Act made it a federal crime for businesses to form trusts (the concept of several companies banding together to form an organization that limits competition by controlling the production and distribution of a product or service). Although the law had flaws, it was an important first step. (See Chapter 3 for more on the Sherman Antitrust Act.)

Another important piece of legislation passed during Harrison's term was the Sherman Silver Purchase Act of 1890. (See Chapter 6 for more.) This bill, sponsored by U.S. senator John Sherman (1823–1900) of Ohio (the same man who sponsored the Sherman Antitrust Act), had the U.S. Treasury purchase 4.5 million ounces of silver at market price each month. The silver was bought with Treasury notes that could be redeemed in either gold or silver. Holders of these notes were so eager to turn them in for gold (because they got more money per note that way) that they nearly emptied the Treasury's supply. The act increased the production of silver, which sent silver prices down rather than up, which was the intent. The act was repealed in 1893, the year of the worst economic decline America had ever experienced. Historians point to several factors that contributed to the panic of 1893, including the Sherman Silver Purchase Act. In addition to the depletion of the nation's gold reserves and the decrease in silver prices, railroads went bankrupt and banks across the country began to fail. The result was high unemployment and a severe shortage of money circulating in the economy.

In keeping with his desire to protect wilderness lands, Harrison gave his full support to the Land Revision Act of 1891, which created national forests. The president authorized the first forest reserve in Yellowstone, Wyoming.

Harrison's foreign policy Benjamin Harrison was one of the most active presidents in the area of foreign diplomacy. Where American interests were concerned, he would stop at nearly nothing to protect them. He took America to the brink of war with Chile over an incident involving American sailors who were harmed in the port city of Valparaiso. After discussion between the countries' leaders, Chile apologized and paid the United States $75,000 for the incident.

In 1889, President Harrison called the first modern Pan-American Conference in Washington, D.C. Leaders from North, Central, and South America attended the conference in an effort to develop military, economic, social, political, and commercial cooperation among the regions. At the conference, treaties on how to resolve international conflicts were developed, and tariff levels were revised. In addition, an organization that would eventually be known as the Pan-American Union was established. The union offered technical and informational services to the Americas, and provided a safe place for official documents. By forming various councils, the union took on the responsibility for furthering cooperative relations throughout the Americas. Its founding is celebrated on Pan-American Day each year in April.

As successful as he was in other foreign endeavors, Harrison did not achieve his goal where Hawaii was concerned. Harrison was in favor of annexing (adding to America's territory) Hawaii, but he was unable to convince the Senate of the usefulness of such an addition. Still, because of his efforts and because Hawaii did eventually become part of the United States, modern historians credit the Harrison administration as the one that put America on its path to becoming an empire.

Harrison's popularity wanes Harrison's popularity among the public took a severe blow on three national issues. The first was his support of the McKinley Tariff. Millions of citizens lost trust in a president who seemed to be siding more with big-business interests than with the average working man. The second issue involved the dissatisfaction of farmers in the South and West. Harrison had done virtually nothing to improve the farmers' situation, so their support shifted to the newly formed Populist Party (see Chapter 6). Finally, a series of violent labor strikes (when workers refuse to work until negotiations are made) linked Harrison to monopoly industrialists and bankers. Voters did not feel represented in the White House.

Add to these feelings of betrayal the fact that Harrison passed a great deal of Republican legislation in his first year in office. Congress in the Harrison presidency soon became known as the "Billion Dollar" Congress, and its rampant Republican activism was a major cause in the reversal of voter support for the president.

Harrison could not undo the damage his image had suffered. He had never been known as an overly friendly man publicly, yet he put his family at the center of his life. On most days during his term, he left the office by noon to spend time with his family. He also enjoyed hunting in his free time and took secret hunting trips whenever possible to get away from Washington. His tendency to be a private man, coupled with the unpopular events throughout his term, led him directly out of the White House. America reelected Grover Cleveland in the 1892 election. Cleveland took 277 electoral votes (compared with Harrison's 145) and 46.1 percent of the popular vote (compared with 43 percent for Harrison). Upon learning of his defeat, Harrison told his family he felt like he had been freed from prison.

Cleveland returns

Cleveland's presence in the presidential campaign of 1892 marked only the second time a former president had run for that office again. (Former president Millard Fillmore [1800–1874; served 1850–53] ran as the American Party's presidential candidate in 1856 but lost easily.) Cleveland's reelection was also a first: Never before had a previously defeated president been elected to the presidency for a second term. (And never since: With only one other former president running again—Theodore Roosevelt [1858–1919; served 1901–9], unsuccessfully, in 1912—Cleveland's feat has held up.) The Democratic Party regained power of the White House as well as both the Senate and the House of Representatives.

America was entering a severe economic depression (a long-term economic state in which unemployment rates are high, prices and business activity are low, and people are fearful of the future). By 1894, almost 18 percent of the country's workers were unemployed. People were hungry and many were homeless because they could not pay their bills. Railroad

construction dropped off by 50 percent. Nearly two hundred railroad companies went into bankruptcy (legal declaration of a company's inability to repay debt, so the business closes), as did one in every ten banks and dozens of steel companies.

Cleveland held onto his belief that the government should not support charity with its dollars. With citizens starving, some reformers suggested setting up a system of work projects funded by the federal government. These projects would include building highways, dams, bridges, and other public works. Such a system would give hundreds of thousands of men and women badly needed jobs, and the nation would enjoy the benefits of their labor. But Cleveland dismissed the notion as a bad idea, and nothing anyone did or said could change his mind.

Instead, the president blamed the Sherman Silver Purchase Act for the depression. He called for a cancellation of the act and got it. But in doing so, he lost the support of Democrats in the South and West, who from that point on, considered him more Republican than most Republicans. Now the Democratic Party was split from within, which weakened its strength.

When the act was repealed, thousands of holders of government bonds and old silver certificates (once used by the government to purchase silver) began cashing them in for gold. This frenzy nearly depleted the nation's gold reserve, and Cleveland had to authorize four new government bonds between 1894 and 1896 to keep the government from failing to pay its international debts. In order to do this, he turned to well-known investment banker J. P. Morgan (1837–1913) to financially support the bonds. Morgan backed the bonds with sixty-two million dollars in gold, which helped to restore the national treasury. Morgan was not respected among the working population. He was deeply involved with, and in many ways, largely responsible for, the industrial monopolies and trusts. He almost single-handedly controlled America's industry. When Cleveland turned to Morgan for help, he was accused of siding with big-business interests and betraying the average working-class citizen.

Cleveland's failure to deal effectively with the depression had a direct impact on the congressional election of 1894. The Democrats lost in every region except the South. No longer were the Democrats in power, and Cleveland felt betrayed by his own party. He left the presidency in 1897 with resentment and bitterness.

Foreign policy

President Cleveland was against territorial expansion and gave up trying to resolve the conflict in Hawaii. Hawaii's queen had been overthrown in 1893, and the island was now controlled by a revolutionary government. Cleveland tried to convince the government to return power to the queen, but his efforts failed. When he approached the queen with the suggestion of forgiving the revolutionary leaders, she also refused and demanded they have their heads cut off. Frustrated, Cleveland refused to put any more effort into the situation and turned over the problem to Congress. The matter was not resolved until 1900, when President William McKinley negotiated to make Hawaii an American territory.

Although reluctant to expand the American empire, Cleveland did not hesitate to protect the nation's interest overseas when necessary. His most controversial foreign policy decision involved a boundary dispute between Venezuela and Britain. Britain laid claim to the Orinoco River, a profitable trade route that ran through Venezuela. Venezuela wanted control of its own region, but Britain refused, so Venezuela called on the United States to get involved and help solve the dispute.

Britain did not want America involved in the issue. Cleveland made it clear that the United States was involved whether Britain liked it or not. To prove his commitment, he sent U.S. Navy ships to confront British warships near Venezuela, a move that caused alarm in the States. There was no need for fear of war, however, because Britain agreed to negotiate.

Another foreign policy issue involved Cuba. Cuba was a country under Spanish rule in 1895. Reports were coming to the United States of Spanish troops treating the Cubans cruelly. Although President Cleveland supported Cuba's independence, he wanted to remain neutral, so he refused to support Cuba in its desire to rebel against Spanish rule. Instead, he urged Spain to adopt reforms that would allow Cuba to gain its independence gradually. Cleveland's stance on this issue was the opposite of that of the Senate, which supported more aggressive involvement and passed pro-Cuban legislation whenever possible. When Cleveland refused to change his mind, Congress threatened to recognize Cuba as an independent nation. The president was unmoved and informed his cabinet that any such decision would be considered an act of defiance against his authority. The issue remained unresolved at the end of Cleveland's second term (it was later handled by President McKinley).

On the homefront

In addition to the depression that began in 1893, Cleveland had to deal with serious labor unrest

Workmen pull spikes from switches during the Pullman Railroad Strike of 1894. President Grover Cleveland made history by involving federal military troops in a labor strike for the first time. © KEAN COLLECTION/GETTY IMAGES.

throughout his second term. In June 1894, a railroad strike in Pullman, Chicago (see Chapter 3), created problems throughout the entire state of Illinois. Railroads stopped running, which put a halt to any business that relied on the railways for shipping. This work stoppage included mail delivery service and passenger transportation. State authorities realized the strike was beyond their control and called on the federal government for assistance. Cleveland's response made history when, for the first time, federal military troops became involved in a labor strike.

On July 4, President Cleveland sent in twenty-five hundred federal troops in an attempt to end the strike. Rioting occurred from July 7 through 9, when strikers attacked the military troops.

These forces responded with gunfire at point-blank range. About thirty strikers were killed and many more wounded. The number of troops soon escalated to fourteen thousand as state and other federal troops joined in the confrontation. The strikers were defeated within the week, and after several weeks of negotiating, the Pullman Palace Car Company reopened its doors on August 2.

Cleveland's response to the strike reinforced the trust of American citizens in their president. However, it was not enough to erase the feelings of betrayal brought about by his lack of response during the depression. His party did not even nominate him as the Democratic candidate in the 1896 presidential election (see Chapter 6 for more on the election) but chose instead former U.S. representative William Jennings Bryan (1860–1925) of Nebraska. Bryan lost the election, however, to Ohio governor William McKinley; this ended what most historians consider the final phase of the Gilded Age.

McKinley leads the nation

For a while, it looked as if Bryan would win the election because he not only had the Democratic vote but had become the Populist Party's choice when members realized they could not win the election. The Populist Party was a third political party that grew out of discontent among farmers and laborers throughout the nation. These men felt that neither the Democrats nor Republicans had their best interests in mind, so they formed their own party. It became clear early in the 1896 campaign that the Populists would not get enough votes, so they merged with the Democrats.

The Republican Party, however, raised $4 million in campaign funds, primarily from big-business donations. Funding at that level made it possible for McKinley to print and distribute two hundred million pamphlets, a strategy that kept his name uppermost in voters' minds. He also delivered 350 speeches from his front porch to 750,000 delegates (many representing big business corporations).

Bryan traveled 18,000 miles in just three months to give speeches and condemn his opponent as a puppet of (someone easily controlled by) big business. McKinley supported a protective tariff and the use of gold coinage only (as opposed to silver and gold), but Bryan promoted bimetallism, or the use of silver and gold coinage (see Chapter 6). Halfway through his campaign, Bryan began losing support.

Some Democrats favored the gold standard, and city-dwelling progressives (people who favored more modern ideas) found the candidate's moral tone offensive. McKinley beat Bryan in both the popular (52.2 percent vs. 47.8 percent) and electoral vote (271 to 176).

Issues at home

By the time McKinley took office, the depression was all but over. People's fear was subsiding, and so was the uproar over bimetallism versus the gold standard. Although McKinley had supported the gold standard, he spent most of 1897 pursuing an international agreement to bimetallism with Italy, Russia, England, and France. When negotiations failed late in the year, McKinley endorsed a gold-based currency and signed the Gold Standard Act in 1900. With that legislation, all currency was backed by gold at a fixed price of $20.67 per ounce.

McKinley was known as an honest man, and throughout his campaign, he had promised to raise tariffs. In 1896, taxes on certain products used in the United States brought in fairly large amounts of money. Alcohol taxes brought in $114.5 million, tobacco another $30.7 million. McKinley wanted to increase tariff levels so that internal taxes could be reduced (allowing taxpayers to spend less on those items they used more often). A raise in tariff rates would also encourage the expansion of American industry and increase the number of jobs because people would not want to buy from abroad when doing so would cost more.

In 1897, U.S. congressman Nelson R. Dingley (1832–1899) of Maine sponsored the Dingley Tariff Act, which raised rates to an average of 49 percent. The bill also gave the president authority to negotiate reductions of up to 20 percent.

President William McKinley. LIBRARY OF CONGRESS.

He also could move items to what was called a "free list," which meant those items would not be subject to the tariff. Other items could be dropped completely if all those in positions of authority agreed upon it. McKinley remained a committed supporter of high tariffs until the end of his life. Just one day before he died, he announced his shift in attitude and gave his support to reciprocal trade treaties (in which both countries involved in the transaction get something beneficial out of the deal).

On the issue of trusts, McKinley categorized them as either good or bad. He believed trusts were useful in terms of international competition but not so desirable within the American market. He limited his support of legal suits against trusts to those that hurt interstate (within the nation) commerce only.

McKinley was a supporter of the labor movement, and his time in the White House increased his popularity among workers throughout the nation. He endorsed the Erdman Act of 1898, which developed a means for negotiating wage disputes involving international railroad companies. McKinley also favored the Chinese Exclusion Act, which prohibited Chinese immigrants from settling in America. He had strong professional relationships with a number of leaders in the labor movement as well. Despite his support of America's workers, McKinley sent in federal troops to keep order at a mining strike in Coeur d'Alene, Idaho, in 1899. The incident ended in the arrest of about five hundred miners, who were kept in a bullpen from the time of their arrest in April until September. In his four-and-a-half years as president, the detaining of miners for five months was the one incident in which McKinley angered the organized-labor voting population.

McKinley undid much of the reform work Cleveland had done within the civil service. Because Cleveland had depended on the merit system (which based appointment to positions on qualification rather than favors or political party affiliation only) to fill civil service positions, Republicans were unhappy that not enough of the most influential positions within the civil service included Republicans. McKinley bowed to Republican pressure and removed about four thousand positions from the list, a move that satisfied Republican congressmen but led many of his citizen supporters to change their minds about him. It now looked as though the president was being controlled by, rather than in charge of, the Republican Party.

President McKinley did almost nothing to improve race relations while in office. Although he spoke against lynching (illegal hanging) in his first presidential address in 1897, he did not condemn the practice formally with legislation or any other efforts. Nor did he take measures to limit the racial violence in the South. For the most part, McKinley's reaction to the race issue was to appear as if he was doing something about it. For example, he appointed thirty African Americans to official positions in diplomatic and records offices. This seemed to whites to be enough, but it fell far short of what African American voters had expected. McKinley also allowed African American soldiers to fight in the Spanish-American War (1898), which went against the wishes of the majority of the military. Still, these measures did little to help African Americans.

Bigger, but better?

As the twentieth century drew closer, many Americans believed that to increase the greatness of the nation, the nation ought to increase its size and power. Others believed just as strongly that expansionism would cost too much money and bring too many nonwhite people into the country. Their stance was called "anti-imperialism," and some of its better-known supporters were former president Benjamin Harrison, presidential candidate William Jennings Bryan, steel magnate Andrew Carnegie (1835–1919), and writer Mark Twain.

McKinley managed to do what Cleveland and Harrison did not. In 1897, he negotiated a treaty with Hawaii that would make it a U.S. territory. McKinley not only recognized the island's value as a military strategic point, but realized other world powers would want to lay claim to

THE RELUCTANT BRIDEGROOM.

An editorial cartoon from 1897 pertaining to U.S. attempts to annex Hawaii. In it, Secretary of State John Sherman officiates at a wedding ceremony, in which Hawaii is the bride. Sanford B. Dole, president of the Republic of Hawaii, is giving away the bride; Uncle Sam is the groom; and President William McKinley is the best man. © THE GRANGER COLLECTION, NEW YORK.

the land if the United States did not. Anti-imperialists and Democrats were against the annexation and delayed it until 1900. At that point, Congress successfully petitioned McKinley to pass the resolution for annexation with a simple majority (more than 50 percent) vote, rather than the usual two-thirds majority vote. (In 1959, Hawaii became the fiftieth state admitted to the Union.)

The Spanish-American War During this period of imperialism versus anti-imperialism, President McKinley had to deal with a problem he had inherited from the Cleveland administration: Cuba. Spanish rule in Cuba was based on repression (domination), and Cubans revolted in 1895. Spain's response was to round up three hundred thousand Cubans and put them in camps where they could not help the rebels. Spain's behavior angered many Americans, who believed Cuba should be independent of Spain's rule.

Throughout 1897, McKinley tried to convince Spain to give Cuba its independence. In November of that year, Spain gave Cuba limited independence (regarding political matters within Cuba, it could govern itself; international matters would still be governed by Spain) and closed the camps. The peace was short-lived, when in January 1898, pro-Spanish demonstrators rioted in the streets of Havana, Cuba. McKinley sent the U.S. battleship *Maine* to the Havana harbor to protect American citizens who had arrived to help Cuba as well as to let Spain know that America still valued its relationship with Cuba.

Spanish minister to the United States Enrique Dupuy de Lôme (1851–1904) wrote a private letter to a friend back in Spain that was intercepted by the Cubans. The Cubans, in turn, leaked the letter to the U.S. media. The letter described McKinley as weak and indicated that the Spanish were not negotiating in good faith with the United States. The letter, published in the *New York Journal,* infuriated Americans, who saw it as an attack on the honor of both their president and their nation.

The situation worsened when the *Maine* exploded and sank on February 15, 1898. The explosion killed 266 crew members. A Navy investigation concluded that the explosion had been caused by an outside source, presumably a Spanish mine. (More recent scholarship has shown, however, that the explosion more likely occurred due to internal problems with the ship itself.) Though McKinley did not want to go to war, he saw no alternative at this point. He ordered U.S. ships to block Cuba's ports; America and its president wanted an end to the Cuban crisis. On April 23, 1898, Spain declared war on the United States. Two days later, America declared war on Spain. The war lasted just over three months, and fewer than four hundred American soldiers died in battle. Many more died from disease.

The Spanish-American War ended with the signing of the Paris Peace Treaty on December 10, 1898. The treaty gave Guam and Puerto Rico to the United States and allowed America to buy the Philippine Islands for $20 million. Spain gave up its hold on Cuba, which would be a protectorate (under the protection and partial control) of the United States until 1934. The United States, under McKinley's leadership, had become one of the world's great colonial powers.

More action overseas

The war with Spain was barely over when a civil war broke out in the Philippines. McKinley sent in thousands of military troops, a move that ended in 1902 in massive bloodshed. The conflict cost more than five thousand American lives and two hundred thousand Filipino lives.

China soon became a concern to McKinley as well. He knew that other world powers, such as Japan, Germany, and France, were also trying to establish influence throughout the world. In an effort to guarantee that Chinese ports would remain open to U.S. business, the president authorized an "Open Door" policy to China. This policy put China on an equal status with America in terms of trade and business. There would be no restrictions or tariffs, and the United States would support an independent China. The policy became useless at the end of World War II (1939–45), when China was recognized as a sovereign (self-governing) nation. As such, no country had the right to influence or attempt to exclude it from trade. Despite its demise, the Open Door policy remains one of the most important ever issued by the federal government.

In June 1900, a group of Chinese rebels known as Boxers killed a number of western missionaries and Chinese converts to Christianity. The Boxers did not want foreign influences intruding on their country or national identity. The group also invaded foreign populations in the city of Peking. McKinley sent over twenty-five hundred troops and several gunboats to China without first getting congressional approval. In addition to U.S. military support, China was assisted by Russia, Britain, Germany, and Japan. The allied (combined) troops put down the Boxer Rebellion by August. China was forced to pay reparations (costs of war) of more than $300 million, $25 million of which went to America.

A life cut short

In 1900, the Republicans once again spent several million dollars on the presidential campaign. They printed 125 million campaign documents, including millions of inserts that were sent to more than 5,000 newspapers every week. They hired six hundred speakers and poll watchers. The president himself stayed home and gave more front porch speeches. His running mate was Theodore Roosevelt (1858–1919), who had recently returned home from the Spanish-American War a hero. (McKinley's vice president during his first term, Garret A. Hobart [1844–1899], had died in office.)

McKinley's opponent was, once again, William Jennings Bryan. Again, McKinley won both the popular and the electoral vote. He won by an even greater margin this time, receiving 114,000 more votes than in the 1896 election. In addition, the Republicans also held the power in Congress (197 House seats compared with the Democrats' 151, and 55 Senate seats compared with 31).

On September 5, 1901, McKinley delivered a speech at the Pan-American Exposition in Buffalo, New York. At its conclusion, he attended a reception where he got to meet and greet the public. Just after four o'clock, McKinley was shot by a twenty-eight-year-old Polish immigrant named Leon Czolgosz (1873–1901). The bullet hit McKinley in the chest and knocked the president to the ground. While lying in his blood, he told his bodyguards not to hurt his assailant. McKinley was rushed to a hospital, where doctors expected him to recover. Gangrene (decay of skin tissue due to blood loss) set in around his wounds, however, and the president died on September 14, 1901, just six months after his second term had begun. His assassin was put to death in the electric chair on October 29, 1901.

Well into the twentieth century, historians considered McKinley a weak president who caved in to pressure and was controlled by his own administration. More recent scholarship has revised its opinion and views the president as a man who did the best he could to avoid war but who also stood firm in his decision once it was made. During his time in office, America won a war, expanded its overseas territories, and extended trade regulations with China. Never before had the United States been so powerful in so many ways. Critics condemn McKinley's motives for his involvement in Cuba, claiming it was not morality that influenced his decision but a desire to make America an imperialistic power.

McKinley did not change the description of the presidential position so much as he enhanced it, paving the way for more modern presidents who would follow. He was the first president to make use of printed propaganda (information that is spread for the purpose of promoting a cause) and used the press to his full advantage by inviting them to briefings and meetings. McKinley recognized the value of good publicity and used the media to manage war and political campaigns. No president before him had traveled as much as he did, and he used his travels to make speeches and meet face to face with the public.

William McKinley may not have done anything great, but he did most things well enough and with enough individuality and success to set the stage for the twentieth-century leaders who would steer America through the following years, known as the Progressive Era.

For More Information

BOOKS

American Presidents in World History. Vol. 3. Westport, CT: Greenwood Press, 2003.

Cherny, Robert W. *American Politics in the Gilded Age: 1868–1900.* Wheeling, IL: Harlan Davidson, 1997.

Gaines, Ann. *Grover Cleveland: Our Twenty-Second and Twenty-Fourth President.* Chanhassen, MN: Child's World, 2001.

Kent, Zachary. *Grover Cleveland.* Chicago: Children's Press, 1988.

Kent, Zachary. *William McKinley.* Chicago: Children's Press, 1988.

Leech, Margaret. *In the Days of McKinley.* New York: Harper, 1959. Reprint, Westport, CT: Greenwood Press, 1975.

Stevens, Rita. *Benjamin Harrison, 23rd President of the United States.* Ada, OK: Garrett Educational Corp., 1989.

WEB SITES

"Benjamin Harrison." *AmericanPresident.org.* http://americanpresident.org/history/benjaminharrison/biography (accessed on May 4, 2006).

The President Benjamin Harrison Home. http://www.presidentbenjaminharrison.org/ (accessed on May 4, 2006).

"Stephen Grover Cleveland." *AmericanPresident.org.* http://americanpresident.org/history/grovercleveland/biography (accessed on May 4, 2006).

"William McKinley." *AmericanPresident.org.* http://americanpresident.org/history/williammckinley/biography (accessed on May 4, 2006).

8

Progressivism Sweeps the Nation

Throughout the first decade of the twentieth century, 40 percent of all wage earners in America lived in poverty. This meant they did not make the minimum amount of $600 that was necessary to pay bills, buy food, and have anything left over. In the 1904 book *Poverty,* sociologist Robert Hunter (1874–1942) provided evidence that six million people—one-fifth of all Americans in the industrial states—lived in intense poverty.

Judging by these statistics, Americans in the twentieth century were not doing any better than they were in the nineteenth century, when 90 percent of society was earning an average annual income of $380. Yet the wealthy of the late nineteenth century were wealthy beyond imagining. One New York socialite threw a birthday party for her dog. The canine wore a $15,000 diamond collar to its party.

The Progressive Era (generally the first two decades of the twentieth century) was a period of reform (change) that began in America's urban areas. The federal government passed laws regarding labor, women's rights, railroads, the food industry, politics, education, and housing. The Progressive Era was a departure from the previous years primarily in the attitude toward social class. In the Gilded Age (approximately 1878–99), the upper class generally believed that their wealth was God-given and that those who lived in poverty did so because they were immoral (in violation of what was accepted as proper behavior). This philosophy was called Social Darwinism. With the dawn of the Progressive Era came a subtle and gradual shift in attitude. As the number of Americans living in poverty increased and their circumstances became more visible in public society, some of the more powerful members of society began to realize that with good fortune came an obligation to help those in need. This belief was fostered primarily by steel magnate Andrew Carnegie (1835–1919), who wrote and published his philosophy, which he called "The Gospel of Wealth." In addition to believing that

WORDS TO KNOW

conspicuous consumption: The buying of expensive and unnecessary items as a way of displaying one's wealth.

Gilded Age: The period in history following the Civil War and Reconstruction (roughly the final twenty-three years of the nineteenth century), characterized by a ruthless pursuit of profit, an exterior of showiness and grandeur, and immeasurable political corruption.

labor strike: A refusal of workers to work until management agrees to improvements in working conditions, wages, and/or benefits.

Progressive Era: A period in American history (approximately the first twenty years of the twentieth century) marked by reform and the development of a national cultural identity.

reform: Change intended to improve a situation.

settlement house: A center that provides community services to the poor and underprivileged in urban areas.

suffrage: The right to vote.

wealth included responsibility for those without, Carnegie believed simply giving money to the poor did nothing more than continue the cycle of poverty. He felt, instead, that assistance should be given in ways that would help the poor help themselves, such as in establishing community-based services, training, and libraries. Philanthropy (charitable donations, community service, and volunteerism to promote human well being) fostered a general sense of reform that had an impact on nearly every social aspect of America. In his report on poverty, Hunter challenged the theory behind the Gospel of Wealth by arguing that poverty was the result of the failure of America's economic system to meet the needs of all individuals.

Class distinction

Class distinction (differences between lower, middle, and upper classes) was clear at the turn of the century. The lower class included a large portion of nonwhite citizens, both immigrant and native-born (those born in America). Many Americans considered this population inferior based on the color of their skin. Immigrants were criticized for their inability to speak English as well as for their cultural rituals, habits, and customs, which were unfamiliar to and considered odd by Americans. Regardless of cultural background, the income of the lower class reflected its status. Whites were judged by their ethnic background. Besides ethnicity, religion affected a person's status level. Jews and Catholics were usually among the lowest-paid Americans, and so they also often were relegated to the lowest class.

The poor lived miserably. They did not have enough to eat, and what they did have was not the best quality. Poor children suffered from rickets, a sometimes-inherited disease caused by a deficiency of vitamin D. Without vitamin D, calcium is not absorbed, and bones are too soft to support the weight of a human body.

Directly related to the level of poverty was the quality of health care. At the beginning of the Progressive Era, the life expectancy of an African American man was about thirty-three years, compared to about forty-six years for a white man.

The growing middle class was made up of native-born white Americans, those whose parents came from families of western and central Europe. This class included artists and skilled workers, craftsmen, farmers, small shopkeepers and business owners, lawyers, teachers, and doctors. New members of the middle class were people employed in offices and city businesses, a group that became known as white-collar workers. The middle class lived in row houses (small houses built in rows) throughout urban areas, in single-family homes in the suburbs, and on the more prosperous farms in the country.

Upper-class Americans came from families that had inherited their wealth or were those fortunate few who built their wealth during the Gilded Age in industry and big business. Some of the more recognizable names among the wealthy were the Rockefellers, the Vanderbilts, the Morgans, and the Fords.

Most of the upper class were Protestant (Christian, but not Catholic), though there were a few Catholics and Jews among the population. In general, the upper class or their families came from France, Germany, Britain, or Holland. The wealthy lived in mansions in the cities and suburbs and vacationed at their summer homes along the East Coast.

The wealth of the upper class was hard to believe. Although less than 2 percent of the American population was wealthy, it made up 60 percent of all the wealth in the country.

The poor and very poor totaled 65 percent of the population and made up about 5 percent of the wealth. The middle class, which comprised 33 percent of the American population, made up 35 percent of the total wealth.

Occasionally, people were able to improve their social status, but this was true almost exclusively for whites. For example, among the Italian and East European Jewish population in Manhattan, New York, 32 percent moved from lower-class (blue-collar) jobs to middle-class (white-collar) jobs between 1905 and 1915.

Despite some exceptions, poverty remained a major problem in early Progressive America. Even though some of the wealthy bowed to public pressures (for example, religious organizations that encouraged its wealthier members to donate money and/or resources; journalists who published newspaper articles that revealed the questionable ethics of some of the wealthier industrial institutions that made their profits off the underpaid labor of the poor) to donate money to charitable organizations and causes, there were simply too many people living in poverty. Donations and other charitable works could never be enough to significantly or permanently reduce the degree of poverty in an America that was just beginning to build a middle class. Even with men like Carnegie and the increase in charitable organizations, old attitudes about money and obligation were not going to drastically change overnight. The general attitude among not only the wealthy but also a sizeable portion of the working class remained that each individual was responsible for his or her situation without regard to economic or social environment. This belief made America the last advanced industrial nation (country in which society is based on industry rather than agriculture)

Margaret Sanger and the Birth Control Controversy

Feminist Margaret Sanger. © CORBIS.

Social activist Margaret Sanger (1879–1966) dedicated her life to improving the quality of life for women and children. As a young woman, the New York native Sanger became interested in women's rights. She graduated from the Hudson River Institute with a teaching degree but soon turned her attention to nursing.

After completing a nursing program at White Plains Hospital in New York in 1900, Sanger began working in some of the worst slums of New York City. Her job involved delivering babies and nursing weak mothers back to health. Many of these women's ailments were caused by having too many children. Others nearly bled to death when they tried to perform their own abortions (procedures in which a fetus is terminated and removed from the mother's womb). They would beg Sanger to help them find a way to keep from getting pregnant.

One young mother who had consulted Sanger for help died during childbirth. Sanger promised herself she would find a way for women to take control of their lives and thereby improve not only their own quality of life, but that of their children as well.

Sanger traveled to Europe to learn about family-planning techniques and returned to New York in 1914 with information for her patients. She

---

to offer its citizens some form of social (government-funded) welfare. Even when such a system was offered in the 1930s, progress was slow.

Changing families, changing roles

As more women left the home and headed to work in the newly industrialized nation, family size was shrinking. This reduction was due not only to reforms for women such as the right to education as well as to hold jobs outside the home, but also to improvements in medicine and living conditions, which allowed people to live longer: Advancements in medicine meant children were surviving illnesses that once killed them, so women did not feel compelled to give birth to as many children to ensure the survival of some. Statistics bear that out: In 1800, the average American family had seven or eight children; in 1900, that number decreased to three anticipated great opposition to her plans to teach about birth control. Her strategy was to educate the public, form an organization to help raise awareness and money, and then work for reform in federal legislation. She founded *Woman Rebel*, a magazine for mothers and young women that included birth control information. The first issue was published in March 1914, and it immediately caused a stir.

The Comstock Law of 1873 had restricted the sending of birth control information through the mail. Sanger's magazine was therefore considered obscene, and the U.S. Postal Service banned several issues. Sanger was charged with nine counts of breaking obscenity laws, which carried a maximum prison sentence of forty-five years. Sanger fled to London, where she lived without her husband and children for two years.

In 1915, charges against Sanger were dropped and she returned to New York, where she resumed her battle for birth control rights. She founded the National Birth Control League (now known as Planned Parenthood Federation of America) and began lecturing and raising money. When it became clear she would have to challenge obscenity laws directly, Sanger opened the first U.S. birth control clinic in 1916.

The clinic, located in a poor section of Brooklyn, was popular, but police raided and closed it within weeks of its opening. Sanger and two other nurses were arrested. Sanger refused to close her clinic, so she was sentenced to thirty days in a workhouse. Upon her release, she continued her mission and opened another clinic.

Sanger began publishing *The Birth Control Review* in 1921 and received more than one million letters from mothers across the country in the first five years alone. These letters detailed horrific accounts of dying children, and women bleeding to death. Many described lives of intense poverty as they had one child after another because they were not allowed to legally plan the size of their families. Sanger compiled five hundred of these letters into a book called *Mothers in Bondage*. The 1928 book was influential, but Sanger's fight was far from over. She spent the first half of the 1930s seeking reforms on a federal level.

The Supreme Court overturned the Comstock Law in 1936. Shortly after that, the American Medical Association announced that doctors had the right to distribute birth control information and devices to their patients. The fifty-seven-year-old Sanger had achieved victory.

or four; by 1920, the average mother gave birth to two or three children.

Educational reform was another factor in the decision to have fewer children. Whereas children once provided some of the family income, they now were required by law to attend school. A child attending school still had to be fed and clothed but no longer contributed money for the family. By using birth control (see box), families could improve their standard of living (see box). As birth control became a controversial issue, another, more morally questionable issue arose, that of eugenics (see box).

Divorce was another factor that affected families. Wives had traditionally been considered the property of their husbands. With the Progressive Era came a shift in how society viewed women. No longer generally thought of as "the second sex," women were seeking and receiving equality both in and outside of marriage.

Eugenics: Reform Gone Wrong

Eugenics is the theory of improving hereditary qualities such as physical strength and intellectual capacity by socially controlling human reproduction. The term comes from the Greek roots for "good" and "generation," and was first considered a true science around 1883.

Advocates (those in favor) of eugenics believed that in order to develop a superior human race, people with defects or imperfections should be forbidden to reproduce, or at the very least, separated from the rest of humanity. People who would qualify as those with serious imperfections included the mentally ill, the physically disabled, addicted people (alcoholics, opium addicts), epileptic people (those subject to physical seizures due to a medical condition), and even the very poor. African Americans were also victims of eugenics, as they were perceived as a race to be inferior to whites.

Eugenics was an extension of the philosophy known as Social Darwinism. Supporters of Social Darwinism held that the superior and worthy members of the human race prosper, while the less fortunate live lives of lower quality because of their immorality and laziness. Although many Americans recognized the ethical problems of eugenics, it was advocated by enough prominent scientists and biologists that the idea of eugenics gained popularity.

By the 1920s, eugenics was influencing all sectors of American society. State fairs and exhibitions held "Better Baby" competitions in which prizes were awarded for the finest human stock. Contestants were judged on the perfection of their genetic traits, such as the symmetry of their physical features. Judges also looked for dangerous conditions such as mental retardation and alcoholism. The American Eugenics Society was founded in 1923 and included twenty-nine chapters throughout the nation. The 1924 Im-migration Act limited immigrants of "inferior stock" from entering the country. President Calvin Coolidge (1872–1933; served 1923–29), who signed the bill into law, publicly declared that America should be kept American.

The medical community had difficulty keeping up with research to back the claims of the eugenics movement. Where the law allowed, people considered inferior were unknowingly sterilized so that they could not reproduce. Indiana was the first state to pass a sterilization law (1907), and at least thirty other states soon followed. More than three thousand people had been sterilized without their knowledge by the mid-1920s. These victims included orphans, the poor, the homeless, the chronically ill, and even those who scored poorly on IQ (intelligence quotient) tests. The sterilization law had another disturbing aspect: It extended to the offspring of these so-called inferior people. This means that sons and daughters of parents suffering from any of the perceived deficits could also be—and often were—forced into sterilization.

Eugenics lost its popularity in America in the 1930s, primarily because enough scientists and researchers began publicly questioning the ability to measure the value of certain traits. Eugenics as a science was doubted, but forced sterilizations continued into the 1970s.

It has been speculated through the years that birth control advocate Margaret Sanger was in favor of eugenics because birth control influences breeding. The reformer has been misquoted in order to support the claim of her eugenics philosophy. In fact, Sanger publicly denounced the racial exploitation of eugenics principles and made clear her stance that a woman should have full control over her reproductive rights. Forced sterilization and imprisonment were in direct opposition to her beliefs.

This shift in attitude naturally extended to the law. By 1909, civil marriage vows no longer demanded that women promise to obey their husbands. Divorce regulations became more female friendly. By 1900, one in every twelve marriages ended in divorce (compared with one in every twenty-one in 1880). By 1916, that statistic rose to one in every nine. (By 2006, it was one in every two.)

More traditional citizens, often led by clergy, saw the soaring divorce rate as a threat to social order and tried to restrict divorce legislation. Faced with a public majority who wanted increased freedoms and the opportunity for more equal marriages, the movement to restrict legislation failed.

Farewell to Victorianism

American society during the Gilded Age was based on what is known as Victorian ideals. Such standards had their roots in England at a time when the country was ruled by Queen Victoria (1837–1901; reigned 1837–1901). In England, this was referred to as the Victorian Era. Victorianism focused on morality and all things proper. Under Victorianism, the ideal woman was quiet, obedient to men, dutiful to her children and husband, and perfectly content to live a life that largely revolved around others. She was skilled in the art of sewing, and her clothing revealed not so much as an ankle. She did not drink liquor or laugh loudly, and she never disagreed with a man's point of view. A Victorian woman was the keeper of morality. Victorian children dressed in uniforms and played quietly. They did not speak unless spoken to, and they had very few rights. Only men seemed to be allowed any sort of independent life. They had their pursuits outside of the home, which might include a career and hunting. Men relied on women to uphold moral goodness and virtue, but they themselves were not held to the same standards.

Changes in marital law influenced Victorian ideals, but the main challenge to Victorianism came from the youth. Along with the extension of required education to the higher grades came coeducation, in which boys and girls were taught together. Public high schools had nearly equal populations of males and females. By 1910, about 40 percent of all college students were women. That was double the number of college women in 1870. Some of the more traditional colleges and universities—about 20 percent—refused to go coed.

Reforms for women

Women's lives were affected more than anyone else's in the Progressive Era. In addition to being seen as worthy of formal education, they were encouraged to have careers, marry later (if at all), and seek equality with men.

For the first time, sexuality became a social concern. Females were more visible in public, and opportunities that did not exist before to meet males became an everyday occurrence. No longer did young men and women socialize only at adult-supervised church gatherings and neighborhood picnics. They now met at dance halls, theaters, and amusement parks. Couples could choose from a number of activities, including bicycle riding, roller skating, and buggy rides.

Fashions changed in the Progressive Era, too. The Gibson Girl (see Chapter 9) no longer represented the ideal woman. The modern middle-class woman wore facial makeup (previously only worn by lower-class women) and skirts that no longer touched the ground. The new fashions allowed not only greater freedom of movement, but more exposure of skin.

New stereotypes replace the old Victorian women were believed to be the keeper of moral values, not only within the family but in society as a whole. As the Progressive Era evolved, all Victorian ideals were shattered. Taking their place were the stereotypes of the virgin (the "good" girl) and the vixen (the "bad" girl).

The good girl dressed properly and remained pure. She might be seen in public with the opposite sex, but she was the picture of good manners and purity. The bad girl adopted the latest fashion trends, smoked and drank with the boys, and turned flirting into a social art.

As motion pictures became a popular pastime in the mid-1910s, two actresses became symbolic of the virgin and the vixen. Mary Pickford (1893–1979) became "America's sweetheart" as she portrayed the child-woman. She was sweet and innocent, with long hair and wide eyes. At the other end of the spectrum was Theda Bara (1885–1955), whose dark, exotic looks landed her film roles as the sexual, dangerous temptress. Until censorship was imposed in the 1920s, films celebrated women's newfound sexual freedom.

The birth of feminism Women of the Progressive Era were in a conflicting position. Two major philosophies regarding women characterized the first two decades of the century. The first was inherited from the prior century and revolved around the idea that women must work together as a group if they are to survive in a man's world. This concept recognized the biological differences and experiences between

Despite her Canadian heritage, actress Mary Pickford was commonly referred to as "America's sweetheart" because of her on-screen innocence. © CORBIS.

men and women and maintained the moral superiority of the female sex.

The second philosophy placed less emphasis on gender differences and focused on equal rights and opportunities for women. This concept gained momentum throughout the twentieth century. Those who favored this feminist point of view focused not on solidarity, or power and unity as a group, but on the individuality and unique abilities of each woman. These early feminists believed in every woman's right to self-expression and self-fulfillment.

Each philosophy had its uses. Those who believed in the power of solidarity worked to improve conditions for women in dangerous, low-paying jobs. Working-class women fought for

With heavy makeup and exotic looks, actress Theda Bara was one of film's early sex symbols. © HULTON-DEUTSCH COLLECTION/CORBIS.

reforms in the workplace, and their efforts led to state laws forbidding long hours and dangerous work conditions. They did not rest until a law was passed to guarantee a minimum wage. Some activists took their effort further and encouraged women to join labor unions.

Despite their progress in getting recognition as valuable members of society, women continued to be victimized in the workplace. For example, women were usually restricted to the jobs that did not challenge society's traditional views of women as inferior. They were given unskilled or semiskilled positions in laundries, textile (fabric) mills, canneries, and tobacco factories. Immigrant women fared worse than their native-born peers, as the higher-paying jobs nearly always went to white, native-born females. Nonwhite workers had the lowest-paying jobs in every industry.

The Women's Trade Union League (WTUL) was founded in 1903 by several wage-earning women. The female wage-earning population and their middle- and upper-class support organized to promote labor legislation for women. The WTUL was most active in New York and Chicago, and it played a major role in the garment workers strikes of 1909–10 (see "Labor Reform" later in this chapter). The WTUL was also instrumental in providing support for the women's suffrage (right-to-vote) movement that began in the 1910s.

Votes for women During the first decade of the twentieth century, women's reforms were largely cultural and social. By 1910, women realized that true power would come only if they were given the right to vote. Also called suffrage, the right to vote became the goal of the women's movement throughout the second decade, while other reforms were pushed to the back of the agenda.

Some states had already granted women suffrage. Wyoming was the first, in 1869, followed by Colorado, Utah, and Idaho. Attitudes toward women in these western states were more progressive, less traditional, than those in eastern states. Women in the West were valued for their contributions to a largely male population, and so it seemed only natural that they be treated equally.

The suffrage movement gained strength as young college-educated women joined the ranks of activists. They brought with them enthusiasm and the attitude that solidarity need not stand separately from women's rights. Soon, the largely white, middle-class women's movement built

African American Women and Reform

African American women of the Progressive Era supported the women's reform movement, but the women's reform movement did not necessarily support African American women. Most of the organized reform associations either opposed or were divided over the issue of including and working with African American women.

As a result of the separate-but-equal (equal rights for African Americans, but separate from whites) doctrine, African American women focused their efforts on the National Association of Colored Women (NACW) and turned it into a well-organized group for the protection and advancement of African Americans. Most of these women, who were in the upper classes of society, agreed with their white counterparts' ideas: Women had their place (in the home) and were morally superior to men.

As the 1910s progressed, African American women joined African American men in forming local community institutions such as kindergartens, homes for the aged, and orphanages. They also helped build and maintain African American hospitals staffed by African Americans, a necessity since they were discriminated against in white hospitals.

One of the most influential and longest-lasting African American associations was formed in 1909. The National Association for the Advancement of Colored People (NAACP) was established by a group of about sixty activists, most of them white. Among them, however, were some of the most famous African American reformers in history, including Ida B. Wells-Barnett (1862–1931) and W. E. B. Du Bois (1868–1963). By 1917, the NAACP had nine thousand members, a number that grew to ninety thousand by 1919. The organization promoted equality for African Americans and quickly established itself as a resource for legal aid against discrimination. By the end of the twentieth century, the NAACP focused its efforts on educational programs for youth as well as development of better economic conditions for African Americans. Its membership going into the twenty-first century was nearly five hundred thousand.

solid relationships with working-class white women, and the number of people the movement could reach instantly increased. These women launched door-to-door campaigns throughout poor and working-class urban regions. Some of the more courageous women spoke publicly on street corners, something America had never experienced before. Others focused their reform efforts on farming communities or professional organizations.

In 1910, the state of Washington gave women the right to vote. Next came California and Oregon. Illinois was the first state east of the Mississippi River to grant suffrage (1913). By 1914, the movement included hundreds of thousands of women and their male friends, partners, and coworkers. Although some men were in favor of women's suffrage because they believed women were equal to men and thus should have the same rights, this was not true of all men. Some men recognized the value of the female vote only when suffragists pointed out that female voters would help reformers reduce political corruption because

Suffragettes march in a parade in New York City in May 1912. © BETTMANN/CORBIS.

they would vote for men who were truly qualified to hold an office and not because a candidate was owed a favor or had bribed them.

Not everyone was in favor of women's rights, especially the right to vote. Those who were against suffrage included some women, who believed the right to vote would threaten the basis of American society. For these women, the proper place for females was in the home, raising children and keeping house. Liquor-store owners feared the female vote because of the temperance (moderation of liquor consumption) movement. Should voters pass a law limiting liquor consumption (which they

ultimately did), business would slow down. What these businessmen could not foresee was Prohibition, when drinking and selling alcohol became illegal. Prohibition lasted throughout the 1920s and was directly responsible for an increase in organized crime and activities involving the illegal manufacturing and selling of liquor. Other people who opposed suffrage were business owners who feared the legislation of a minimum wage. These men made great profits by underpaying their employees; if women were allowed to vote, the practice of underpaying them because of their sex could be outlawed.

Conflict within the Movement

Women suffragists Elizabeth Cady Stanton (seated) and Susan B. Anthony. THE LIBRARY OF CONGRESS.

Although the goal of the suffrage movement was to secure the right to vote, the movement itself was not unified. Rather, it was made up of different organizations, each with its own philosophy and plan on how to achieve that goal. The movement suffered from years of internal conflict among leaders and organizations alike.

The movement consisted of two main rights organizations: the American Woman Suffrage Association (AWSA) and the National Woman Suffrage Association (NWSA). The AWSA was established in 1868 and was the first organization of its kind. Its strategy was to fight for suffrage one state at a time. The NWSA was formed in 1869 by two women whose names will be forever linked to women's rights: Elizabeth Cady Stanton (1815–1902) and Susan B. Anthony (1820–1906). The NWSA went after the vote on a federal level. The NWSA even proposed the argument that white women were more fit to vote than many African American men whose right to vote was guaranteed by the Fifteenth Amendment. The AWSA and NWSA, though united in a common goal, competed against one another for funding, members, and support. The other primary difference between the two associations was that the AWSA focused only on getting the vote, while the NWSA demanded many reforms.

As the movement grew, the two organizations realized that nothing would be achieved if they continued to fight each other. In 1890, they merged to form the National American Woman Suffrage Association (NAWSA), with Stanton as president and Anthony as vice president. Although the Gilded Age would see very little progress in women's rights, the NAWSA headed the movement in the Progressive Era. By the era's end, the association had secured women the right to vote.

On August 26, 1920, the federal government finally recognized women as men's equal in suffrage, and the Nineteenth Amendment was passed. Women throughout America were granted the right to vote.

Urban reform

Cities were the symbol of modernization in the Progressive Era. Chicago, New York, Pittsburgh, Detroit, and Cleveland doubled in size, and by 1920, 51 percent of America's population lived in urban areas. Immigration (see Chapter 4) was the main reason for the urban population explosion in urban America, but industrialism was another. Workers did not want to live too far from their jobs, so many native-born Americans left the country to settle in cities.

Whereas cities were proof of progress for some, others considered urbanization a sign of the evil that permeated the era. For these critics, urbanization led to overcrowding, poverty, violence, crime, and immoral behavior. Economist and social critic Henry George (1839–1897) was not impressed with the crowded cities. As reported in John Whiteclay Chambers II's book, *The Tyranny of Change,* George lamented, "This life of great cities is not the natural life of man. He must under such conditions deteriorate, physically, mentally, morally," he wrote in 1898. Other reformers blamed the problems of cities on an ineffective economic system and believed conditions could be improved through better planning.

As cities grew, so did the influence of government on their growth. Urban planners tried to combat overcrowding through garden cities (planned communities designed to keep green spaces) and zoning (division of cities into sections for homes, businesses, and factories). The first zoning law was passed in New York City in 1916 and gave the public control over the use of land and construction. Within ten years, more than one thousand cities across America would pass zoning laws in hopes of controlling not only how land was used, but also the height and use of buildings.

Although the passage of zoning laws signaled a major transition toward governmental intervention in the marketplace, the laws were largely negative in their results. The zoning laws did not encourage adequate housing, nor did they provide a basis for coordinating housing and city planning. The result, instead of well-planned cities, was major overcrowding and a type of residential (living) building called tenement housing.

Tenement houses Tenement housing was the first style of apartment buildings. By 1903, New York City's eighty-two thousand tenements housed nearly three million people, all of them among the lowest class of society.

Tenement housing had nothing going for it except cheap rent. The buildings were erected close together so that there were no lawns. The Lower East Side of New York at the turn of the century was a typical tenement ghetto (a poor, crime-ridden section of the city). There, the basic tenement buildings were five stories high and contained twenty three-room apartments, four to a floor. Each apartment or flat contained a front room, small bedroom, and kitchen, for a total of 325 square feet. The only room to receive light or ventilation (air) was the front room. As other tenement buildings were constructed around it, however, both light and ventilation were cut off.

Tenements built before 1867 did not have toilets, showers, or even running water. Common (used by all tenants) toilets were situated in between buildings, toward the rear of the lots, and may or may not have been connected to public sewage lines. Garbage was disposed of in a large box kept in front of the buildings, but it was not picked up on a regular basis. Many tenements were without heat. The buildings that had heat posed a serious health threat. The fumes and smoke from the coal-burning heaters had nowhere to go without proper ventilation (air passages).

A view of New York City tenements at the beginning of the twentieth century. © PHOTO COLLECTION ALEXANDER ALLAND, SR./CORBIS.

The first housing law, passed in 1867, required tenements to have one toilet for every twenty residents. Those toilets had to be connected to sewer lines whenever possible. The next law was passed in 1879 and required all new tenements (but not old) to be built so that every room received air. Under the old tenement floor plan, most existing inner rooms had no access to outside walls. Building engineers solved this problem by developing a type of blueprint that allowed for the air shaft to run through the building in such a way that air was provided to all rooms.

This same law required toilets in all tenements to be hooked up to sewage lines and equipped with a way to flush after use. It was not uncommon for raw sewage to be strewn throughout a tenement yard. As reported by Laurence Gerckens on *Plannersweb.com,* the first *Report of the Tenement House Department* of New York, published in 1903, indicated:

Some of the conditions which are found in these buildings surpass imagination. It does not seem possible that human beings can actually live under them and retain the least vestige [degree] of health. Many cases have been found where the plumbing fixtures have been removed and the pipes left open, permitting sewage gas to find its way into the apartments and permeate the building. . . . In some of these houses the water closets [toilets] have been stopped up for weeks, the bowls overflowing and the floors covered.

Despite the housing laws, tenement life remained dangerous and miserable. The most far-reaching bill was passed in 1901. The Tenement House Act not only required improvements on ventilation, toilets, and light but set standards that all but banned the construction of buildings on 25-foot-wide lots. Newly built tenements would have to be wider, with more space. The highly effective 1901 law required existing tenement buildings to upgrade to meet the new, stricter standards. With the passage of the law came the formation of the Tenement House Commission, a committee that inspected housing and ensured the laws were being followed.

Tenement landlords were furious over the passage of the 1901 act. They believed the law had come out of nowhere and that the new standards were too harsh. Their tenants, after all, were mostly poor Irish immigrants who were used to crowded living conditions. Landlords insisted their tenants did not mind living in poor conditions; to be forced to make improvements would cut down on the amount of profit made from each building. By 1902, as improvements were being made, landlords realized the imposed changes were not as drastic as they had feared.

To meet the new requirements, landlords had to update old buildings with skylights in the hallways, to provide natural light for as long as it was available. To assist residents once nighttime set in, landlords were required to make sure that a lamp burned from sunset to sunrise along first- and second-floor stairways. Inside the apartments, landlords had to cut out part of the wall that kept the inner rooms darkened twenty-four hours a day to allow for light from an outer room to enter.

The most controversial aspect of the 1901 act, because of its expense, was the requirement that all common toilets be removed. Every building now had to have one water closet for every two families. These closets had to be constructed inside the buildings whenever possible, whether in newly built tenements or those already in existence. Without exception, all toilets had to be connected to sewer lines, even if those lines had to be built. Most landlords ignored the law until they absolutely had to comply. There were reports even in 1918 of tenements with outdoor toilets still in use.

Every reform throughout the Progressive Era, whether in housing, labor, poverty, education, or women's rights, influenced other reform. For example, housing reform improved living conditions in urban areas. Even so, housing reform alone was not going to solve any major problems. Poverty, public health, and child labor were still issues. Without reform in each area, no real solutions were possible.

The establishment of settlement houses

People involved in the settlement house movement understood how reforms worked. Settlement houses were centers that provided community services for the poor and underprivileged. The philosophy behind the movement was that reform was the responsibility not only of the government but also of the people. Progressives believed that

Jacob Riis: Reporter-Turned-Reformer

American journalist Jacob Riis. © CORBIS.

Jacob Riis (1849–1914) emigrated from Denmark to America in 1870, at the age of twenty-one. He became a reporter for the *New York Evening Sun* and quickly became known as a pioneer of photojournalism. Riis took his own photographs to accompany the stories he wrote about situations he saw in the new country he immediately came to love.

Riis began photographing and documenting conditions in New York City's slums. He collected his work in a groundbreaking book titled *How the Other Half Lives.* Published in 1890, it brought Riis to the attention of an influential man who would one day be the twenty-sixth president of the United States. New York Police Board of Commissioners president Theodore Roosevelt (1858–1919) and Riis became fast friends, and together they spearheaded the housing reform movement. Riis is credited with bringing to the forefront the plight of America's urban poor. His two other photojournalism books are *Children of the Poor* (1892) and *Children of the Tenements* (1903).

Riis's photojournalism efforts were part of a new type of journalism called muckraking. Muckrakers exposed scandalous and unethical practices among established institutions in America. Some of the more famous muckrakers were Ida Tarbell (1857–1954), for her series on the Standard Oil Company; Upton Sinclair (1878–1968), for exposing the dangers and poor work conditions of the meatpacking industry in Chicago; and Lincoln Steffens (1866–1936), for his investigation of the scandals among city and state politicians. Muckrakers worked side by side with reformers during the Gilded Age and Progressive Era.

society as a whole could improve through organization, education, and willpower.

The first American settlement house, University Settlement, was established on New York's Lower East Side in 1886. By 1910, more than four hundred settlement houses operated across America's urban landscape. These settlements were really experiments not

in charity but in social organization. Historians consider settlement houses the first example of social services but emphasize a major difference: Social services provide specific services, whereas settlement houses aimed to improve neighborhood life as a whole. Those who ran the settlement houses did so on a voluntary basis. Women were the primary reformers in

Jane Addams: Woman on a Mission

Young children gather around child-labor activist Jane Addams. © UNDERWOOD & UNDERWOOD/CORBIS.

Jane Addams and friend and fellow labor activist Ellen Starr (1859–1940) founded Hull-House in the Chicago slums in 1889. Addams got the idea for Hull-House after visiting England and Toynbee Hall, the first settlement house in the world.

Addams was a personable woman whose intelligence and enthusiasm attracted people to her. She had no trouble finding funding or volunteers for Hull-House. When economic depression hit in 1893, Hull-House was serving two thousand people a week. That number increased as the depression made conditions worse throughout Chicago.

In addition to founding the settlement house, Addams worked tirelessly for legislation on behalf of child laborers, factory working conditions, and the juvenile justice system. She became the first vice president of the National American Women Suffrage Association (NAWSA) in 1911.

Addams received the Nobel Peace Prize in 1931 for her reform efforts, and her funeral in 1935 was attended by thousands. Hull-House still stands as the Jane Addams Hull-House Museum.

the settlement house movement, with Jane Addams (1860–1935) being the most famous (see box).

Settlement houses provided medical services and legal aid to a mostly immigrant population. The immigrants who came to America in the nineteenth and twentieth centuries knew nothing about the society into which they immersed themselves. Few could speak English, let alone read and write it. Settlement houses provided free education in which immigrants and other working-class poor could learn English as well as vocational (career) skills. They also provided kindergartens, library services, recreation clubs for boys and girls, and classes on nutrition and banking.

Settlement houses depended on volunteers not only to staff and operate them but for funding. Reformers used newspapers and clergy to spread the word about the houses and explain the movement's mission to the public. The women activists formed relationships with business and civic leaders and then approached them for assistance in the form of either money or time and skills.

In addition to providing social services, settlement houses became central locations for workers involved in political reform as it related to labor, women, and economics. Reformers worked toward legislation to protect children from labor and immigrants from exploitation (being used for someone else's benefit).

Settlement houses still exist, although they have become more specialized. Some of their services—providing libraries and kindergartens, for example—became the responsibility of municipal and state governments.

Labor reform

The Gilded Age and the Progressive Era were periods of great unrest among American laborers and workers (see Chapter 3). America's working class found itself at the mercy of big business, industry, and a government that did not want to get involved in labor disputes. Labor strikes (a refusal of workers to work until management agrees to improvements in working conditions, wages, and/or benefits) became common occurrences throughout the nation.

Although major federal reform legislation would not be passed until the 1930s, reformers of the Progressive Era were particularly concerned with child labor. Industrialism encouraged growth in child labor because children were considered easier to manage and cheaper to hire than their adult counterparts. They were also less likely to strike, a major advantage in a time of intense conflict between management and labor.

The 1900 census (a periodic count of the nation's population and related statistics) indicated that approximately 1.75 million (about 18.2 percent) children in the nation aged ten to

fifteen years old were working. Children even younger than that held jobs in mills, factories, and on the streets; they were not included in the census. If they had been, the number of child laborers in 1900 would have exceeded 2 million (about 21 percent).

Children's jobs Children held a variety of positions in a number of industries. Beginning as early as five years of age, boys and girls worked as newsies (kids who sold newspapers on the streets), a job that kept them out past midnight and in all kinds of foul weather. According to Digitalhistory.com, one ten-year-old newsie showed a reporter the marks on his arm where his father had bitten him for not selling more papers. Because of the long hours and bad weather, newsies often fell victim to pneumonia. Without proper nutrition and medicine, many died.

Because life on the streets was tough, newsies were a particularly tough bunch of children. In 1899, they proved just how tough they could be when they surprised everyone by going on strike against two newspapers: the *Evening World* and the *Evening Journal.* These papers had raised their prices from fifty to sixty cents per hundred papers during the Spanish-American War (1898). They did this because they could; the publisher knew people needed news, so they would willingly pay the increase. However, that price was not lowered after the war, and the newsies were the ones forced to pay that extra amount. To make a profit, they then had to sell more papers in order to make up for the increase. Newsies throughout New York joined the strike, which lasted about one week. In the end, a compromise was reached. The child laborers would still have to pay sixty cents per one hundred newspapers, but the publisher agreed to buy back any unsold papers. The success of the strike helped bring attention to the plight of child workers across the country.

Other young children worked in factories, running machines three times their size. They worked twelve- to fourteen-hour shifts, and the lucky ones brought food to eat in case they earned break time. Child laborers also rolled cigars, weaved baskets, picked fruit, worked with oysters and shrimp, and set bowling pins. Hours for these odd jobs were inconvenient. Some were expected to show up at work at 3:30 AM and stay until 5:00 PM.

Many children also worked in fabric mills. Most were never formally hired; many would show up with an older brother or sister. Average pay for these young children was forty-eight cents each twelve-hour day.

Another common practice was for businesses to pay poor families—usually immigrants who were desperate for more money—to take work back to their tenement homes and finish it overnight. Industries in which this was usual included textiles and laundries. After reform legislation, this practice was illegal because it kept children up late into the night, which then left them too exhausted to go to school. The practice of sending work home was illegal, but that did not keep it from happening. The law against it was nearly impossible to enforce.

Long hours, little pay

Most laborers and workers throughout the Gilded Age and the Progressive Era were grossly underpaid, but children fared the worst. The philosophy of the time embraced the idea that children should work because it developed a work ethic and strong spirit at a young age. Many greedy business and shop owners took

advantage of children and depended on the difference in age and size to work in their favor. Parents were not able to shield their children from the horrors of a life of hard labor; families needed every penny to survive.

Pay rates for children varied, but they were all appallingly low. According to child-labor activist and photographer Lewis Hine (1874–1940; see box), one boy working in a North Carolina mill made sixty cents a day for a twelve-hour shift. That would translate into about $10.69 a day in modern money. One Georgia family—consisting of the mother, four daughters, and one son—worked in a mill in 1909 and earned $9. Since the husband had died, the mother was responsible for providing for her family. That nine dollars had to support her and nine children. That amount translates into about $166.38 a week in modern currency.

Six-year-old Laura Petty was a berry picker in 1909. She earned two cents a box, but because she was so small, she only filled two boxes a day. Boys aged seven to twelve who cut fish in a Maine cannery in 1911 earned seventy-five cents to one dollar a day, even though they worked from 7:00 AM until midnight. Even in the twenty-first century, that amount translates to just $13.37 to $17.83 a day for a seventeen-hour shift.

Breaker Boys

Child labor in any form was a horrifying ordeal, but children working the anthracite (hard) coal mines suffered under particularly grim conditions. Mining families were traditionally large, with many children. Boys as young as eight or nine would lie about their age to the mine boss in hopes of getting a job in the breaker. A breaker is a huge factory where coal is

The Triangle Shirtwaist Factory Fire

Firefighters work hard to extinguish the flames at the Triangle Shirtwaist Factory building in New York City on March 25, 1911. © UNDERWOOD & UNDERWOOD/ CORBIS.

Working conditions in the Progressive Era were poor regardless of where the factory was and what it produced. Accidents were common. The worst situations became known as sweatshops (manufacturing workplaces that exploit their workers and operate under inhumane working conditions). One tragedy in particular—the Triangle Shirtwaist Factory fire—came to symbolize the struggle of labor against sweatshop management in early twentieth-century America.

The Triangle Shirtwaist Company building in New York City was the site of what many historians consider the worst industrial disaster of its era since the Industrial Revolution began. On March 25, 1911, fire broke out in the top three stories of the ten-story building. By the time the flames were extinguished, 146 of the 500 employees were dead, many of them immigrant girls around the age of fifteen.

The building was typical of most others in New York at the time—overcrowded and without a sufficient number of emergency exits. There was one fire escape for the entire building, which itself was fireproof and showed little exterior damage after the fire.

processed. The nickname given to these young boys, of which there were approximately sixteen thousand in Pennsylvania alone in 1902, was Breaker Boys.

For fifty to seventy cents per ten-hour shift (five to seven cents an hour), a Breaker Boy arose at 5:30 each morning, put on his work clothes, ate breakfast, and walked to the breaker by 7:00 AM. He sat on a hard wood bench built across a long chute. Underneath the bench passed a steady stream of broken coal mixed with slate rock. The Breaker Boy's job was to pick out the slate rock and leave only the coal. To do this, the boy had to be hunched over for hours at a time. A Breaker Boy's fingers were constantly bloody because most could not afford gloves. But even gloves offered little protection from the sharp and jagged slate. If the boys fell asleep, as they often did, or were not moving as quickly as the breaker boss felt

When the fire broke out around 4:40 PM, employees of other businesses in the building had already gone home. Had the fire begun ten minutes later, the Triangle Shirtwaist Company women also would have been gone, as indicated by the remnants of coats and cold-weather accessories found on the corpses.

When it became clear there was no way out of the flames because most of the doors were locked (as part of management's effort to keep employees from taking breaks or stealing), employees began jumping out of windows. Witnesses reported that many of them were already on fire, their hair and clothing in flames. With the exception of about a half a dozen people, those who jumped met their death by plunging through broken glass or crushing themselves on the sidewalks below. Firemen had to focus all their efforts on extinguishing the blaze, and bodies were left lying for hours in heaps on the ground where they had fallen.

According to a *New York Times* article published the day after the fire, one witness gave this account: "I only saw one man jump. All the rest were girls. They stood on the windowsills tearing their hair out in the handfuls and then they jumped. One girl held back after all the rest and clung to the window casing until the flames from the window below crept up to her and set her clothing on fire. Then she jumped far over the net and was killed instantly, like all the rest."

No one ever determined how the fire started. The building had gone through four recent fires before the one on March 25 and had been reported to the Building Department as unsafe. And yet it remained open for business. The final fire spread more rapidly than most because of the garments inside, which were made of flammable material. Furthermore, sewing machines were crammed together so closely that there were no paths to the doorways.

An investigation into the fire resulted in the two owners of the building being found innocent of any wrongdoing, despite the fact that they were aware of the fire hazards associated with their building. Families of the victims felt justice had not been served. Twenty-three families filed suits against the owners. In 1913, the owners settled by paying each family $75 for the loss of their loved one.

they should, he would hit them with a cane or a bullwhip.

There was a saying about coal miners: Once a man, twice a boy. Most miners began their careers as boys in the breakers. From there, they moved into the mines and worked as men. When black lung (a medical condition caused by breathing coal dust) forced them out of the mines, they returned to the breakers, right back where they had begun. The average age of death of a miner, whether from black lung, explosion, or machine accident, in the early 1900s was 32.13 years. Their job was considered so dangerous that no insurance company would give them coverage.

Labor reform, finally

Before federal legislation was passed to regulate labor laws, many states enacted their own laws. For example, by 1914, most states required

Lewis Hine: Child-labor Activist

A photograph by child-activist Lewis Hine of a West Virginia child miner in 1908. © BETTMANN/CORBIS.

louder than any written documentation, Hine approached welfare agencies with them in hopes of getting help for tenants and child laborers. He became a staff photographer for the National Child Labor Committee in 1908. In this position, he traveled throughout southern and eastern America, photographing child laborers in mills, factories, fields, mines, and anywhere else he could find them. He took more than five hundred photographs between 1908 and 1912.

Often, Hine was refused entry into a factory by its owner. When that happened, he would wait outside to photograph the children taking their lunch break or arriving to and leaving work. He would interview these little laborers, who often lied about their ages because the minimum legal age for working was fourteen. When he suspected he was being lied to, he would visit the homes of the children to talk with parents and find evidence of the children's true ages as listed in passports and the family Bible. In an effort to prove how physically harmful a life of labor was for children, Hine would secretly measure children's heights against the buttons on his coat. Everything he did, he documented. His work is how historians know so much about child labor in the Gilded Age and the Progressive Era.

Hine's photos and interviews with children proved to America that child labor robbed its victims of childhood, education, and health. His efforts led directly to the establishment of child labor and safety laws for all workers.

What journalist Jacob Riis did for housing reform, Lewis Hine did for child-labor reform. Hine was a photographer who began documenting immigrants arriving at Ellis Island in 1904. He became interested in the lives of immigrants as they struggled against all odds to build new lives for themselves and their families.

Using his camera, he documented the unsafe living and labor conditions of America's working class. With a belief that his photos could speak

children to be at least twelve or fourteen years old, and many had already limited a child's work day to ten hours. These laws were difficult to enforce, and families encouraged their

children to lie about their ages so that they could contribute to the household income.

Some states were more progressive than others. Maryland, for example, was the first

A 1911 photograph by Lewis Hine of a large group of male child miners, frequently referred to as "breaker boys."

state to pass (in 1902) workman's compensation laws; these laws assured workers injured on the job that they would receive some sort of income during the time they could not work. In 1904, the National Child Labor Committee (NCLC) formed. The NCLC campaigned aggressively for federal child labor law reform. The first federal child labor law was not passed until 1916 and was in effect only until 1918. The law prohibited the movement of goods across state lines if minimum age laws were violated. This law, like so many others, failed because it was nearly impossible to enforce.

It was not until 1938 that the Fair Labor Standards Act was passed. For the first time, minimum ages of employment and work hours for children were regulated by federal law.

Better education for more people

Reform depended on knowledge, and most reformers agreed that knowledge was best shared through formal education. Nevertheless, the people who needed education the most—women, children, immigrants, those who lived in poverty—were the least likely to be able to obtain it. Compulsory (mandatory) school attendance was not a law at the beginning of the twentieth century. Child laborers and their families placed a higher value on earning money than they did on learning to read and write. It became clear in the Progressive Era that education, though important, was not a priority over putting food on the table.

As America experienced a 49 percent increase in the number of school-aged children in the early twentieth century, the number of high schools doubled and the number of seventeen-year-old graduates tripled to 16 percent between 1900 and 1920.

Progressive education

John Dewey (1859–1952) was an educational reformer who believed school should reflect the real lives of society. Dewey wanted schools to take responsibility for helping immigrants assimilate (become successfully integrated) into American culture in addition to teaching academics.

Dewey's philosophy of education is known as pragmatism and focuses on students learning by doing rather than on being lectured to. In pragmatism, value is determined by practical results. If students do not remember what they learn and use it to better themselves and their quality of life, then the education they received has no value.

Pragmatism became part of a larger style of learning called progressive education. Advocates of progressive education believed that children learn best through experiences in which they have an active interest. This philosophy included the hands-on learning experiences promoted by Dewey and recognized the importance of individual learning differences. Progressive classrooms favored teachers who guided rather than taught.

Experimental schools Progressives sought to reorganize schools and classrooms, and experimental programs were used in some of the larger cities. Dewey's Laboratory School in Chicago used a program in which younger students worked in groups on a central project related to their own interests. The Gary plan (1908–15) was used in Gary, Indiana. The plan divided the school building into classrooms and space that included laboratories, shops, an auditorium, and a playground. Two schools operated at the same time in this space so that each area of the building was in constant use. School lasted for eight hours a day, six days a week. The Gary plan was successful and adopted in various forms throughout the nation.

Other respected experimental schools were developed in Chicago, New York, and Iowa. Progressive education was widely accepted throughout the Progressive Era, though it was never without its critics. Those opposed to this new style of education did not agree with the way it ignored or did not focus on such academic disciplines as reading, writing, and arithmetic. Despite the success of progressive education, traditional educators believed a student's individual interests should not influence the content of his or her education. By the late 1950s, progressive education fell out of favor with Americans. By that time, however, it had forever changed the way school was taught.

Education for all

In addition to changing the way students were taught, reforms opened educational doors for a more diverse student body. As society's idea of what women should be evolved, more girls were seeking education at an earlier age and going on to college. Progressive reformers pushed for compulsory education laws, and by 1918, every state had its own attendance law. This does not mean the law was obeyed. Immigrants and working-class families often lied about their children's ages so that they could work instead of attend school, but the laws did help reduce child labor.

The progressive education movement focused on education for white, middle-class Americans. It did little to improve education for African Americans in general. In 1887, only two-fifths of all eligible African American students were enrolled in school. Not much had changed by 1900. Some of the northern states contributed funding for African American schools in the South, but most of the actual reform in those schools came about as a result of the fund-raising efforts of African American men and women themselves. Poor rural African American farmers mortgaged their farms and land to pay for the construction of new schools. Mothers sponsored raffles, music programs, fish-fry dinners, and other activities to raise money for their children's education.

Booker T. Washington and Tuskegee Institute

One name stands out among African American educators of the Progressive Era. Booker T. Washington (1856–1915) founded the Tuskegee Normal and Industrial Institute in Alabama in 1881. The school's beginnings were humble. The state had donated $2,000 for teachers' salaries, but nothing for land, buildings, or equipment. The first classes, which were made up of thirty students, were held in a run-down church building.

As principal, Washington had three objectives for his school. First, he would travel throughout rural areas and share with those poor farmers new and improved ways to farm the land. While there, he would help them find ways to develop their moral and spiritual life as well. To accomplish this goal, Tuskegee developed an extension program that traveled the countryside, bringing training to those who could not attend class. Smaller schools founded and taught by Tuskegee alumni (graduates) were built throughout the South.

Washington's second objective was to develop craft and occupational skills such as woodworking, machinery operation, and farming so that students would be ready to take jobs in the trades (industry and production) and agriculture. To do this, Washington allowed students to help construct the buildings needed for the Institute, and in return they received credit toward their tuition and experience in a trade. These students ate the food they grew at the school's farm and learned about modern agricultural methods.

Third, Washington wanted to make Tuskegee what he called a "civilizing agent." Education would take place not only in the classroom but in the dining hall and dormitories as well. Washington insisted on developing moral character and a sense of personal pride in his students.

In 1882, Washington moved the school to 100 acres of abandoned farmland, which he purchased with a $200 loan. Tuskegee was a great success, partly because of the quality of its education, and partly because Washington traveled the country telling anyone who would listen about his school. He was able to secure donations from some of the country's wealthiest men, including

Tuskegee Institute founder Booker T. Washington. LIBRARY OF CONGRESS.

Andrew Carnegie and John D. Rockefeller (1839–1937). By the time of Washington's death in 1915, the campus included 161 buildings on 268 acres and a community of almost five thousand students, staff, and faculty.

Wide reform, mixed results

Hardly any aspect of American society was untouched by reform in the Progressive Era. While each effort and victory improved the quality of life, poverty and oppression remained widespread. Because Americans continued to

hold fast to the belief that those who worked hard would thrive, there was little public assistance for those in need. What little state and local government spending there was went mostly to institutions such as the almshouses (shelters for the very poor who could not survive on their own). Even in 1923, over two thousand almshouses sheltered nearly eighty-six thousand inmates.

Millions of urban poor barely continued to survive on irregular employment. Labor unions (see Chapter 3), which generally organized and assisted skilled workers, were not available for those workers considered semiskilled or unskilled. Many poor Americans were physically or mentally disabled, widowed (left without a husband) with children, or elderly. Reforms did little for this segment of America's population. In the South, poverty was equally intense, as the African American population remained largely unaffected by reform laws.

It would take a major economic depression in the 1930s for America's middle- and upper-class to understand the far-reaching effects of poverty and realize that public assistance was a necessary component of society.

For More Information

BOOKS

Bartoletti, Susan Campbell. *Kids on Strike!* Boston: Houghton Mifflin, 2003.

Calhoun, Charles W., ed. *The Gilded Age: Essays on the Origins of Modern America.* Wilmington, DE: Scholarly Resources, 1996.

Chambers, John Whiteclay II. *The Tyranny of Change: America in the Progressive Era, 1890–1920.* 2nd ed. New Brunswick, NJ: Rutgers University Press, 2000.

Cooper, John Milton, Jr. *Pivotal Decades: The United States, 1900–1920.* New York: W. W. Norton & Co., 1992.

Freedman, Russell. *Kids at Work: Lewis Hine and the Crusade Against Child Labor.* New York: Clarion Books, 1998.

Frost-Knappman, Elizabeth, and Kathryn Cullen-Dupont. *Women's Suffrage in America.* New York: Facts on File, 2004.

Harlan, Louis R. "Booker T. Washington, 1856–1915." In *Encyclopedia of Southern Culture.* Edited by Charles Reagan Wilson and William Ferris. Chapel Hill: University of North Carolina Press, 1989.

Hopkinson, Deborah. *Shutting Out the Sky: Life in the Tenements of New York, 1880–1915.* New York: Orchard Books, 2003.

Hughes, Pat. *The Breaker Boys.* New York: Farrar, Straus & Giroux, 2004.

Kuchta, David. *Once a Man, Twice a Boy.* Nesquehoning, PA: Kiwi Publishing, 1999.

Mele, Christopher. *Selling the Lower East Side.* Minneapolis: University of Minnesota Press, 2000.

Poliniak, Louis. *When Coal Was King.* Lancaster, PA: Applied Arts Publishers, 2004.

Riis, Jacob A. *How the Other Half Lives: Studies among the Tenements of New York.* New York: Charles Scribner's Sons, 1890. Reprint, New York: Barnes & Noble Books, 2004.

Sanger, Margaret. *Margaret Sanger: An Autobiography.* New York: W. W. Norton, 1938. Multiple reprints.

WEB SITES

"About Jacob Riis." *The Richmond Hill Historical Society.* http://www.richmondhillhistory.org/jriis.html (accessed on May 17, 2006).

"Anti-Saloon League of America." *Ohio History Central.* http://www.ohiohistorycentral.org/entry.php?rec=845 (accessed on May 17, 2006).

"Child Labor in America 1908–1912: Photographs of Lewis W. Hine." *The History Place.* http://www.historyplace.com/unitedstates/childlabor/ (accessed on May 17, 2006).

"Child Labor in U.S. History." *Child Labor Public Education Project.* http://www.continuetolearn.uiowa.edu/laborctr/child_labor/about/us_history.html (accessed on May 17, 2006).

DeMause, Neil. "Our House." *Here: The Stories Behind Where You Are.* http://www.heremagazine.com/ourhouse.html (accessed on May 17, 2006).

Dolkart, Andrew. "The Tenement House Act." *Lower East Side Tenement Museum.* http://www.tenement.org/features_dolkart.html (accessed on May 17, 2006).

Gerckens, Laurence. "Ten Events that Shaped the 20th Century American City." *Planning Commissioners Journal: PlannersWeb.* http://www.plannersweb.com/intl/excerpts10events.pdf (accessed on May 17, 2006).

"History of Tuskegee University." *Tuskegee University.* http://www.tuskegee.edu/Global/story.asp?S=1070392 (accessed on May 17, 2006).

"Jane Addams." *Women in History.* http://lkwdpl.org/wihohio/adda-jan.htm (accessed on May 17, 2006).

Mintz, S. "Problems of Youth." *Digital History.* http://www.digitalhistory.uh.edu/historyonline/us30.cfm (accessed on May 17, 2006).

Muncy, Robyn. "Women in the Progressive Era." *Places Where Women Made History.* http://www.cr.nps.gov/nr/travel/pwwmh/prog.htm (accessed on May 17, 2006).

"Progressive Era Reform." *Oswego City School District: Regents Exam Prep Center.* http://regentsprep.org/Regents/ushisgov/themes/reform/progressive.htm (accessed on May 17, 2006).

Scheuer, Jeffrey. "Legacy of Light: University Settlement's First Century." *Jeffrey Scheuer.* http://jscheuer.com/legacy.htm (accessed on May 17, 2006).

"The Triangle Factory Fire." *Cornell University ILR School.* http://www.ilr.cornell.edu/trianglefire/ (accessed on May 17, 2006).

"The Truth About Margaret Sanger." *Planned Parenthood.* http://www.plannedparenthood.org/pp2/portal/medicalinfo/birthcontrol/bio-margaret-sanger.xml#1132244666315::-5699605734901894369 (accessed on May 17, 2006).

"Tuskegee Institute." *National Park Service.* http://www.nps.gov/bowa/tuskin.html (accessed on May 17, 2006).

"Urban Experience in Chicago: Hull-House and Its Neighborhoods, 1889–1963." *University of Illinois at Chicago.* http://www.uic.edu/jaddams/hull/urbanexp/ (accessed on May 17, 2006).

9

Life in a Changing America

Robber barons, powerful industrialists who amassed personal fortunes usually through corrupt and unethical business practices, and powerful politicians led the country through the Gilded Age (approximately 1878–99) and into the Progressive Era (approximately the first two decades of the twentieth century). Other Americans used this time of change to introduce exciting new ideas and concepts in literature, music, and art. American culture was greatly affected by ground-breaking artists, performers, and athletes who took advantage of the changing times to give America what it had never had: a true identity.

The Gilded Age took its name from a book of the same name, written by Mark Twain, the pen name of Samuel Clemens (1835–1910), and Charles Dudley Warner (1829–1900) in 1873. The authors wrote about a post–Civil War (1861–65) America that was known for its political corruption and materialistic society. That image fit America well. On the outside, the United States seemed to be gilded (covered with gold) in its endless moneymaking opportunities. People from around the world came to America to begin a new life. But the gold covered up the unsightly parts of society—greed and excess. The country seemed to be divided into the luxuriously wealthy and the very poor.

The Progressive Era was a period of reform (change) that began in America's urban areas (cities). The federal government passed laws regarding labor, women's rights, railroads, the food industry, politics, education, and housing (see Chapter 8). The Progressive Era was a departure from the Gilded Age primarily in attitudes toward social class. In the Gilded Age, the upper class generally believed that their wealth was God given and that those who lived in poverty did so because it was their fate. With the dawn of the Progressive Era came a shift in attitude, and the wealthy (for the most part) began to realize that with good fortune came an obligation to help those in need. Philanthropy (community service, financial donations, and volunteerism to promote human well-being)

WORDS TO KNOW

conspicuous consumption: The buying of expensive and unnecessary items as a way of displaying one's wealth.

depression: A long-term economic state characterized by high unemployment, minimal investment or spending, and low prices.

Gilded Age: The period in history following the Civil War and Reconstruction (roughly the final twenty-three years of the nineteenth century), characterized by a ruthless pursuit of profit, an exterior of showiness and grandeur, and immeasurable political corruption.

muckraking: A style of journalism that seeks to

expose scandal and corruption among public figures and established institutions and businesses. The term was coined by President Theodore Roosevelt in 1906.

philanthropy: Community service, financial donations, and volunteerism to promote human well-being.

Progressive Era: A period in American history (approximately the first twenty years of the twentieth century) marked by reform and the development of a national cultural identity.

reform: Change intended to improve a situation.

---

fostered a general sense of reform that touched nearly every social aspect of America.

The appeal of the fair

Fairs were popular events at the turn of the century. Manufacturers used fairs to introduce new products and demonstrate their uses. States and provinces set up booths and competed for new citizens and investments. For the cost of fifty cents (about ten dollars in current money) for adults, twenty-five cents (about five dollars in current money) for children ages six through twelve, fairgoers could spend a day being simultaneously educated and entertained. It was the equivalent of Disney World, the Olympics, and the Super Bowl all rolled into one event. This is the impact fairs had on American culture in the Gilded Age and the Progressive Era.

One of the most famous and influential fairs of the Gilded Age was the World's Columbian Exposition, also known as the Chicago World's Fair. The Columbian Exposition was

held at Jackson Park in Chicago, Illinois, from May 1, 1893, through October 31 of that same year. It was not mere luck that Chicago was home to the fair. Many cities wanted to host the Columbian Exposition. Fairs attracted large numbers of people, and these people would spend their money outside the fair as well, such as for lodging. New York, St. Louis, Chicago, and Washington, D.C., competed for the privilege of hosting the exposition as well.

Each city submitted petitions to the U.S. House of Representatives. These petitions listed reasons why a particular city should be chosen as host of the fair. After months of consideration, the House selected Chicago, on the condition that the city raise an additional $5 million. This was easily done. Some of the most powerful men in business contributed to the effort, including railroad tycoon George Pullman (1831–1897), financier Charles Schwab (1862–1939), and book publisher Andrew McNally (1836–1904).

Trivia About the Chicago Fair

- The exposition took up 2 miles of coast-line along Lake Michigan and 633 acres.
- The cost to develop and produce the fair was $28 million, equal to about $535 million today.
- Nearly twenty-eight million people attended the fair.
- More than forty thousand skilled laborers and workers were employed to construct the fair.

- The fair boasted more than a quarter million exhibits and seventy thousand exhibitors.
- The fairgrounds included three thousand bathrooms, half of which cost a nickel to use.
- Two thousand security guards and eighteen hundred clean-up men were employed.

Because the selection process was written about frequently in newspapers and was talked about throughout the nation, the fair generated great interest among exhibitors, vendors (sellers of goods), and the public. The fair's theme was the four hundredth year anniversary of Christopher Columbus (1451–1506) discovering America. Fair developers realized at an early stage that the exposition was going to be profitable. They charged 25 cents a day to let people watch the workers construct the buildings and fairways. More than three thousand people did just that every week until completion.

The fair itself was huge (see box), with fourteen main buildings and two hundred additional buildings. The fairgrounds included a system of lagoons and waterways fed by Lake Michigan. Architects designed the layout, and the exposition was nicknamed "The White City" because all the buildings were painted white.

A day at the fair People came from all over the world to attend this cultural event, including royalty such as Archduke Franz Ferdinand (1863–1914) of Austria, Sultan Abū Bakar of Johore (c. 1843–1895), several native rulers of India,

and Princess Maria Eulalia (1864–1958) and her husband Antonio of Spain. Other visitors included famous Americans such as reformer Jane Addams (1860–1935) and musician Scott Joplin (1868–1917). Altogether, about 25 percent of America's population attended the exposition. The rest of the country experienced it via newspaper coverage, guidebooks, and family and friends who had attended.

Each main building at the fair was centered around a different sector of life. These included government, mining, machinery, agricultural, and manufacturing/liberal arts. In each building, fair-goers could see the latest trends and inventions. Several popular and enduring products made their debut at the fair: Juicy Fruit gum, Aunt Jemima syrup, Cracker Jack popcorn, Shredded Wheat cereal, Pabst beer, the hamburger, diet carbonated soda, postcards, and the Ferris wheel, among others.

Once attendees tired of walking through buildings, they could enjoy entertainment in the midway (amusement park), where countless rides, musicians, and refreshments enhanced the carnival-like atmosphere. In addition, the midway contained a hot air balloon ride, a zoo, re-creations of traditional Japanese and German villages, a swimming pool, and a wax museum. It was not possible to get through the entire fair in one day. To the delight of Chicago's innkeepers and hotel owners, millions of people stayed overnight for at least one day, and usually several more.

A lasting legacy The Columbian Exposition was a financial success. It earned back more than the $28 million spent on developing it; the concession stands alone brought in $4 million. The fair was in fact so successful that it became the model of most of the fairs to follow. The fair met its goals in other ways as well. The purpose of the exposition was to encourage American unity in the face of cultural change and to celebrate technology and commerce. By showing the American public that ethnic differences and the changes resulting from immigration and increased foreign relations have a positive impact on society, the fair had a major influence on cultural attitudes.

The fair affected consumerism and advertising as well. On the fairgrounds, millions of Americans were introduced to the vast array of choices they had in products ranging from food to soap to home decorating materials and beyond. This realization led directly to "conspicuous consumption," or the buying of expensive products as a way to display a person's wealth. Although the term was not coined until 1899, the fair set in motion the attitude that the higher the price, the better the product. For example, prior to the exposition, a housewife might have bought a generic (not brand named), inexpensive kind of coffee. Upon going to the fair, she discovered that there were many brands of coffee, some more expensive and claiming to be better tasting. From that point on, she bought the more expensive coffee. She believed that she

must be buying a higher-quality product, not because it actually tasted better but because its manufacturer said it was better and it cost more. Perhaps, she was led to believe, when her friends visit her, they will notice she buys the more expensive brand and think that she has more class.

Directly related to conspicuous consumerism was advertising. For months following the fair, advertisements for products that had won awards at the event used that fame to sell the products and gain brand recognition (in which consumers recognize a brand name and automatically link it to the idea of high quality or superior craftsmanship). Advertisers also took advantage of the new perception that buying products and items was fun. They subtly reinforced the idea that the more a consumer spent, the happier he or she would be.

The Chicago World's Fair was responsible for a new holiday—Columbus Day. Thanks to the fair, schoolchildren began each day in the classroom with a burst of patriotism by reciting the Pledge of Allegiance. Some historians claim that author L. Frank Baum (1856–1919) modeled his famous fictional city, Oz, on the glamour and sensory experience of the fair. The event found its way into novels as well as songs, and a new musical genre called ragtime was introduced on the fairgrounds by Scott Joplin.

The midway of the fair had a major impact on America's culture at the turn of the century. With its exotic foreign villages and native tribal performers featured in displays created to imitate their rural (primarily African) villages, the midway inspired the idea of a modern carnival with various forms of live entertainment. The first permanent midway was established at Coney Island, New York, in 1897. The hot dog was introduced into society there, and by

Racism at the Fair

Despite the 1893 publication of a pamphlet titled "The Reason Why the Colored American Is Not in the World's Columbian Exposition," in which the African American authors protested treatment of their race at the fair, a more modern account of the event provides evidence that African Americans were involved in many aspects of the exposition.

One of the most distinguished African Americans of his day, abolitionist (person against slavery) Frederick Douglass (1818–1895) served as a representative from Haiti. Other outspoken African Americans who exhibited at the fair included writers James Weldon Johnson (1871–1938) and Paul Lawrence Dunbar (1872–1906), activist Ida B. Wells (1862–1931), reformer Booker T. Washington (1856–1915), and Nancy Green (1834–1923), best known for her role as Aunt Jemima. Educational exhibits from highly respected African American colleges were on display throughout the months of the fair. African American educators, associations, and organizations gave powerful public speeches to emphasize the importance of education to African Americans everywhere.

The fair hired thousands of African Americans for positions such as waiters, laborers, and train porters. On the fairgrounds, however, the racist attitudes that prevailed during that era were obvious. African Americans were prohibited from becoming members of the Columbian guard, the police force of two thousand that was in charge of protecting the grounds. The fair hired more than one hundred of those who had been turned away as guards as janitors and chair men (workers who pushed wheeled chairs used by visitors who could not or would not walk around the grounds). The uniforms worn by these men were similar to those worn by the guardsmen, but their duties were completely different.

African American women gave lectures on the importance of women from all races joining forces in the fight for equal rights and suffrage (voting rights). Among them were journalist Fannie Barrier Williams (1855–1954) and feminist author Frances Watkins Harper (1825–1911). In regard to this particular issue, gender was more important than race, and thousands of American women heard these African American activists speak.

In August, the Congress on Africa met for an eight-day assembly at the fair. Leaders and speakers publicly discussed the future of African American public policy. Whites from America, Africa, and Europe attended the conference to collaborate with these African American political leaders in hopes of solving the problem of inequality and racism.

In addition, many African American performers entertained fairgoers on the midway. Some, like the Fisk Jubilee Singers, were musicians. Others were writers who read their works aloud.

In spite of these inclusions, some African Americans boycotted (refused to attend) the fair because of its racist policies, which included having African American exhibits approved by an all-white committee. Many exhibits were banned outright. Douglass disagreed with those African Americans who chose not to go to the fair and encouraged his race to participate to their full capability in an effort to show the world that skin color did not affect intelligence or creativity. Although the fair was attended by African Americans, and although they maintained exhibits and held jobs throughout the six months of the event, the separate-but-equal approach (give African Americans equal rights, but keep them apart from whites) to including them paved the way for what would be federal law by 1896.

A man and a woman stand at a fence looking down at the Columbian Exposition in Chicago in 1893. © CORBIS.

1910, thousands of amusement parks dotted the American landscape. All the parks were modeled on the Chicago Fair's midway. The most popular amusement parks of the twenty-first century—Disneyland and Disney World—were also modeled after the fair.

The rapid changes in technology and industry in the late 1870s and early 1880s led to fear among many Americans. The fair invited Americans to learn more about advancing technology, especially electricity, in a leisurely way. The fair, however, helped shift the nation's attitude toward technology in a more hopeful direction: More and more, technology was being viewed as the new symbol of progress. The Columbian

Exposition highlighted America's shift from an agrarian (agricultural-based) society to a more technological, consumer-based country.

Advertising changes America

Prior to the Gilded Age, general-store owners decided what products they would sell. They would choose the items that promised the most profit, and shoppers were at the mercy of their grocers' likes and dislikes. All that changed in the 1880s, when manufacturers began investing time and money into advertising their products.

The mission of advertising once was to make a product appealing to the customer.

With the Gilded Age came a shift in that goal: The job of any advertising campaign now was to turn customers into consumers. To do this, advertisements had to make shoppers believe they needed a particular brand. For example, everyone used soap. Thanks to an effective (and expensive) advertising campaign by the manufacturer Procter & Gamble, millions of Americans were requesting—demanding—Ivory soap. By 1909, Ivory had become so popular, it was as if no other soap existed.

Creating a need is what advertising was all about. By the early years of the Progressive Era, America had become a materialistic society (one that placed a high value on products, whether needed or not). Whereas consumers once got their information about products from those who made or sold them, they now relied on advertisements to inform them. Advertisements were developed by experts hired to persuade people into believing they needed—and could not live without—particular products and specific brand names.

The downside of consumerism

There were drawbacks to becoming a consumer society. Along with an increase in the number of choices one had at a supermarket came the blurring of the line between want and need. Advertisers were so skilled at their jobs that many Americans failed to understand that buying a particular brand of product would not necessarily bring them happiness. Many were not able to distinguish their true needs from their desires. According to David Blanke of Rosary College and Concordia University, historian William Cronon has made this point by using the example of the midwestern farmer who bought pancake mix from a Chicago mail-order firm. The mix consisted primarily of wheat—exactly what the farmer was growing in his own fields.

Another negative aspect of consumerism was the high level of greed of the corporations and manufacturers behind the products. Local store owners, once responsible for the safety of their locally obtained products, could no longer be held accountable for food shipped in from distant manufacturers. Fraud was common in the 1880s: Milk producers included embalming fluid (the substance that keeps a corpse from decaying) in the milk to keep it from souring. Chalk was added to flour, and animal feed included sawdust, two practices designed to increase the weight and bulk of a product to make consumers believe they were getting more for their money.

While manufacturers' ethics were being questioned, so were those of the advertising companies. Just as consumers could not be sure if the products they were buying were safe or legitimate, neither could they trust that the advertisements for such products were truthful. Before the first decade of the twentieth century was over, magazines and newspapers were telling advertisers that they had the right to refuse to run any advertisement they found objectionable or possibly fraudulent. The advertising agencies themselves were not making efforts to be truthful, but many individual businesses were.

It was not until 1906 that the Pure Food and Drug Act was passed, requiring all edible products to have a label listing ingredients. By 1910, groups such as the Association of Advertising Clubs of America had been established to encourage advertisers to uphold the truth. This was the beginning of what is known as the truth-in-advertising movement. These associations called for states to enact regulations upholding standards of truth. By the end of the 1920s, most states had enacted some form of advertising regulations, though standards varied.

Introducing Consumer Magazines

The cover of the October 1916 issue of McClure's *magazine.* SPECIAL COLLECTIONS LIBRARY, UNIVERSITY OF MICHIGAN.

Many factors influenced the development of advertising in the Gilded Age and the Progressive Era.

The rise of big business gave corporations great power both in terms of money and in determining what products and services they believed Americans would find valuable and necessary.

Technological inventions were also changing the way America lived. Housewives enjoyed innovations such as the washing machine, the sewing machine, and other appliances that eased the drudgery of housework. With more leisure time, entertainment such as fairs, amusement parks, sporting events, and theaters became more popular. Each of these pastimes encouraged consumerism.

Direct mail was another way manufacturers could advertise their products. In 1892, for example, Sears, Roebuck & Co. mailed eight thousand postcards advertising particular products to consumers across the country. The postcards looked as though they had been handwritten. Sears received two thousand orders directly from that advertising campaign. Newspapers were another advertising vehicle. Among the most influential innovations for advertisers (and buyers) were the consumer

The importance of political cartoons

In addition to advertising and muckraking, another aspect of printed media became important in the late nineteenth century: the political cartoon. These cartoons were a combination of pictorial editorial (opinion) and social commentary, and they influenced public opinion throughout the Gilded Age and the Progressive Era.

Politics were central to the American way of life in the Gilded Age. People's political beliefs were as important as their religious beliefs, and

newspapers were the main source for political discussions, news, and announcements. Political cartoons were effective because one did not need to be a skilled reader to understand what was being said. Citizens of all backgrounds could find meaning in the pictures. The most famous political cartoonist during this era was Thomas Nast (1840–1902). Nast worked for the popular magazine *Harper's Weekly*.

In the 1870s, a New York politician named William "Boss" Tweed (1823–1878) was involved in the disappearance of $200 million in magazines. In 1883, *Ladies Home Journal* and *Life Magazine* began publication. *McClure's* joined them in 1893, the first year of a severe economic depression (a long-term economic state characterized by high unemployment, minimal investment/spending, and low prices). The magazine lost $5,000 each month throughout its first sixteen months on the newsstands. *McClure's* managed to survive and within a short time became the most popular consumer magazine of the day. Whereas earlier magazines focused on traditional topics primarily aimed at women and mothers, *McClure's* appealed to a growing middle-class reader whose interests were of a progressive nature. The magazine became America's voice as it dealt with important and timely political, social, and economic issues. By June 1898, more than four hundred thousand people subscribed to the magazine, and it contained more advertising than any of its competitors.

In addition, *McClure's* featured articles on art and history, and illustrations were included throughout the 126-page periodical.

In keeping with the progressive times, *McClure's* began to specialize in what became known as

muckraking (a style of journalism that seeks to expose scandal and corruption among public figures and established institutions and businesses). One of the most important figures of the muckraking movement was a writer named Ida M. Tarbell (1857–1954). Tarbell wrote a nineteen-chapter series in which she exposed the corruption and greed of the Standard Oil Company. Her account detailed the questionable business ethics of company owner John D. Rockefeller (1839–1937) and helped America develop sympathy for independent oil workers. The series, entitled "The History of the Standard Oil Company," was published from November 1902 through October 1904 and is considered a landmark piece of investigative journalism.

Because of conflicts with the owner of the magazine, in 1906 the regular writing staff left *McClure's*. The quality of the magazine's writing was never the same again, and it was sold to pay off debt in 1911. At that point, it became a women's magazine. Readership steadily declined, and the magazine ceased publication in 1929. Even in the twenty-first century, *McClure's* is considered one of the most important magazines in the history of journalism.

taxpayers' money. Nast launched a series of cartoons depicting Tweed and his "Ring" of fellow politicians as bumbling, greedy, corrupt men who were in power only because they were feared by everyone (most of this was true). Nast's cartoons attracted a great deal of attention. As a result, people previously unaware of Tweed's corruption began demanding reform. Tweed was annoyed with Nast and offered to pay him a great deal of money to stop satirizing (making fun of) him in cartoons. When Nast declined, Tweed threatened *Harper's Weekly* if they did not fire Nast. None of his threats did

any good. Instead, Nast is credited with paving the way for the successful prosecution and imprisonment of Boss Tweed and his Ring. Nast's involvement as a cartoonist changed the course of political history and cemented the role of the political cartoon forever.

Literature: entertaining and educational

The late nineteenth and early twentieth centuries were exciting decades in terms of literature and writing. Writing prior to the Gilded Age was in

History of the Mail-Order Business

The cover of a Sears Roebuck catalog from the fall of 1900. © BETTMANN/CORBIS.

With millions of people moving westward into unsettled territories throughout the Gilded Age, the time was perfect for companies to invest in building a mail-order segment of business. The first business owner to do so was Aaron Montgomery Ward (1844–1913), in 1872. His company, Montgomery Ward, was located in Chicago, but he was once a traveling salesman who realized his rural customers would be better served by a new way of shopping. Instead of having a salesman come to their door with a limited supply of products, and since these customers had no way to get to the stores in the East, Ward revolutionized the retail industry with his idea of a mail-order business. Customers would receive a catalog from which they could order, and goods would be shipped directly to them.

Ward's first catalog was just one sheet of paper. With time, the catalogs grew in size, and until 1926, Montgomery Ward was strictly a mail-order business.

If Montgomery Ward was successful, Sears, Roebuck & Co. was unbeatable. Richard Sears (1863–1914) first sold watches by mail order in 1886. He hired A. C. Roebuck (1864–1948) to repair his watches, then sold that business in 1889. Upon completion of the sale, Sears established another mail-order firm to sell various types of jewelry. While Roebuck continued

the Romantic style or the Genteel Tradition. Romanticism was a literary movement that stressed, in part, individualism, a reverence for nature, and imagination over reason. Romantic authors include John Keats (1795–1821) and William Wordsworth (1770–1850). The Genteel Tradition stressed conventionality, or staying with what was considered normal and acceptable, in social, moral, and religious standards. Writers in the Genteel tradition include R. H. Stoddard (1825–1903) and Bayard Taylor (1825–1878).

Many writers of the Gilded Age and Progressive Era were part of a movement literary historians call Realism. Their writing was more realistic and reflective of American culture, to do repairs, Sears, Roebuck & Co. was incorporated in 1894 and became a general mail-order business that included a variety of goods ranging from food to farm machinery to household goods. By 1900, Sears surpassed Montgomery Ward with mail-order sales exceeding $10 million a year.

Farmers especially liked buying from mail-order businesses because they could choose from a larger selection of goods without ever having to make the long drive into the nearest town. That alone saved them hours of valuable time. Better yet were the prices, which were lower than what could be found at local merchants' stores. Richard Sears prided himself on his advertising slogans, and one of those was "Cheapest Supply House on Earth." Free delivery of mail in rural (country) areas began in the 1890s, making mail-order transactions even easier and more cost effective. Rural customers could order whatever they needed and have it delivered within days. In 1925, the year its first retail store opened, Sears sold around $243 million worth of goods, more than 95 percent of it by mail.

In 1908, Sears began what would be a most profitable business: It began selling entire houses by mail. In a separate catalog titled *The Book of Modern Homes and Building Plans,* the retailer offered twenty-two complete home building kits to anyone who could afford the $452 to $2,906 it would cost to purchase a particular model.

Sears provided not only the lumber and instructions but also the financing. This made owning a home a possibility for thousands of families who had never dared hope for such a thing before. When immigrants flooded the country, urban areas became overcrowded; mass transit helped alleviate that problem somewhat by allowing a growing middle class to leave the city and settle into suburbs (see Chapter 4). But the Sears Modern Homes program gave them the one necessity they lacked: affordable housing. This housing program, coupled with the introduction of mass transportation and the rise of industrialism, resulted in the expansion of the middle class.

Although no official document exists to indicate how many Modern Homes survive in the twenty-first century, it has been reported that more than one hundred thousand homes were sold between 1908 and 1940. When Richard Sears realized how popular the Modern Homes program was becoming, he added two more catalogs, one for farm buildings and another just for barns.

even when that reflection was ugly. These writers weaved social and political commentary and criticism into their work, and the tone of their work was matter-of-fact and sometimes comic or satirical (a blend of criticism and wit, sometimes combined with exaggeration, to scorn attitudes or problems). The writer most widely recognized as representative of the Gilded Age and the Progressive Era is Samuel Clemens, better known as Mark Twain.

Mark Twain

Twain was the man responsible for coining the phrase "Gilded Age." One evening at a dinner party, Clemens and his neighbor, novelist and editor Charles Dudley Warner (1829–1900), were complaining about the low quality of the novels their wives were reading. Someone challenged the men to write something better, and the collaboration resulted in the 1873 publication of the novel *The Gilded Age.* The book was

Drugs: Not a New Problem

Although modern Americans tend to think of drug use and abuse as a recent problem, drugs have been an issue of concern for centuries. By 1900, one in every two hundred Americans was addicted to opiates (pain killers) or cocaine. The use of opiates stemmed in large part from the Civil War. Wounded soldiers were treated with morphine and suffered the results of addiction for the rest of their lives. Even children's cough syrup contained morphine. By the end of the 1800s, opiates could be purchased at any drug store. Sears sold a 3-ounce bottle of laudanum (a form of opium) for 28 cents. Because it was inexpensive, it was considered a drug for the working class, though upper-class women often developed an addiction because their doctors prescribed it for nearly every "women's" ailment.

Cocaine was another drug of choice. By 1885, it was being used to treat every ailment from asthma to depression to hay fever. One medicinal label instructed users to "snuff very little up the nose five times a day until cured." The original Coca-Cola recipe contained cocaine (and influenced the name of the beverage). Advertisements for the soda called it an alternative to liquor (which, along with all alcohol, was outlawed during Prohibition [1920–33]) and boasted about it being "a valuable Brain Tonic."

about a time when America was run by powerful but corrupt politicians and big businesses. The wealthy got richer through their corruption while the poor got poorer. It would prove to be exactly how the late nineteenth century would be remembered.

Twain's more popular novels among young readers include *Tom Sawyer* (1876), *The Prince and the Pauper* (1881), and *The Adventures of Huckleberry Finn* (1884).

Twain's critical attitude toward societal norms was not always immediately evident in his novels. The book *The Adventures of Huckleberry Finn,* for example, can be read on many levels. From one perspective, it is nothing more than an adventure novel centering around a young country boy. Another assessment will reveal it as a coming-of-age novel in which the reader sees the main character literally grow from a boy to a man through various experiences. On a deeper level, Twain was commenting unfavorably on the racist attitudes of white Americans toward African Americans. The book has been banned from many schools and public libraries throughout the years because of its racial themes.

Other writers who shaped the era

Although Mark Twain was undoubtedly the most popular author of his day, other notable writers left their mark on the literature of the Gilded Age and the Progressive Era.

Kate Chopin Kate Chopin (1851–1904) was a regionalist writer; her stories almost always took place in the same region—in this case, Louisiana. Chopin's characters brought to life the values and even the dialects (specific language and slang) particular to the South. But the writer's voice broke away from traditional regionalist authors. She was a feminist who believed in the equality of women and men. Her most famous novel, *The Awakening* (1899), was published amid scandal. In the novel, the female protagonist (main character) rejects traditional Victorian values and enjoys discovering

Political cartoonist Thomas Nast portrays politician William "Boss" Tweed as a fallen emperor after corruption was revealed following his reelection to the New York state senate in 1871. © HULTON ARCHIVE/GETTY IMAGES.

there is more to being a woman than maintaining a clean house. The public and critics called the book vulgar and it immediately went out of print. Interest in the book resurfaced in the 1950s as women were once again trying to break free of the societal restraints that limited them both professionally and personally. As reported on *Kate Chopin: A Re-Awakening,* a PBS Web site, *The Awakening* is among the top five most-read American novels in colleges in the twenty-first century and is considered a prime example of American realism.

Jack London Jack London (1876–1916) was an American writer at the forefront of a new type of literature: the wilderness-adventure novel. This type of fiction was closely related to the newly popular western novel (see Chapter 5). Both the wilderness novel and the western novel involved adventure in an untamed land. London's style of writing departed from the western novel; his fiction was more realistic and less romantic. Although he wrote more than twenty novels, nearly as many short-story collections, and numerous works of nonfiction and journalism, the author is best remembered for his novels centering around sled dogs in the Yukon (a territory in northwest Canada). These titles include *The Call of the Wild* (1903), *The Sea-Wolf* (1904), and *White Fang* (1906).

In addition to the Yukon, London studied and wrote about two other regions and their cultures: California and the South Pacific. He spent the winter of 1897 in the Yukon, which gave him the material and ideas for his first stories. The stories were published in the *Overland Monthly* in 1899. America quickly realized that London was much more than an entertaining author. His works embodied his belief in socialism (an economic system based on public ownership of the means of production and distribution of wealth). Although he kept his social and political commentary out of most of his fiction, London did not hesitate to criticize what he considered the ills of society, including the use of liquor and the relationship between poverty and capitalism (a profit-motivated economic system in which capital is mostly owned by private individuals).

London was a highly publicized and influential figure throughout his adult lifetime. His novel *The Sea-Wolf* was the basis for the first American film. He was among the first celebrities ever used to endorse consumer products in advertising (grape juice and dress suits).

Henry James Henry James (1843–1916) was a master of the psychological novel (a story that relies more on what goes on inside the characters' minds than it does on action). Although he eventually moved to London (1876) and became a British citizen one year prior to his death, he is considered one of the great American novelists.

James combined his love of travel with his love of writing. He chose to write novels about the people he met in the places to which he traveled. Many of his novels compare sophisticated Europeans with somewhat crude Americans, though in midcareer he changed focus from international travel to revolutionaries and reformers. He would eventually return to international themes.

Some of James's most famous novels include *The American* (1877), *The Portrait of a Lady* (1881), *The Bostonians* (1886), and *The Turn of the Screw* (1891).

James was one of the first writers to narrate a novel from the point of view of a particular character, and he refined this technique throughout his career. For this, he is considered by many to be the father of the stream-of-consciousness novel, in which the narrative follows the thoughts and feelings of a character without thought to logic or sequence.

W. E. B. Du Bois William Edward Burghardt (W. E. B.) Du Bois (1868–1963) was born in Great Barrington, Massachusetts. Although he is considered more of a social activist and reformer than author, he is remembered as well for his famous 1903 book, *The Souls of Black Folk*.

In this book of fourteen essays, Du Bois detailed the history of the African American in America and talked about the idea of progress as it related to African Americans. Du Bois asserted that the role of African Americans and their leaders was not to accept with gratitude what little was handed to them in terms of rights and privileges, but to demand equal treatment.

Du Bois talked about the "double consciousness" of African Americans: that of being American, and that of being "Negro." Du Bois challenged his fellow African Americans to stop looking at themselves through the eyes of whites. *The Souls of Black Folk* was considered a groundbreaking book at the time of its publication and remains so in the twenty-first century.

Upton Sinclair Upton Sinclair (1878–1968) was born in Baltimore, Maryland, but moved with his family to New York when he was ten years old. By the age of fifteen, he was writing dime novels, and also helping to pay his college tuition by writing for pulp magazines (see box). He also wrote articles for various boys' weekly magazines during this time.

Sinclair's fame rests on one novel, published in 1906. *The Jungle* exposed the unsafe and filthy conditions of Chicago's meatpacking industry and led directly to the passage that same year of the Pure Food and Drug Act. This law created the Food and Drug Administration (FDA), which became responsible for insuring the safety of all food and medical products. Also passed in 1906 was the Meat Inspection Act, which set hygiene standards in all meatpacking plants and demanded that all animals pass inspection prior to slaughter.

For his novel, Sinclair was considered and remains in the twenty-first century one of the first muckrakers. Other muckraking journalism pieces of his include *King Coal* (1917), an expose of a Colorado coal strike, and *Boston* (1928), a discussion of the Sacco-Vanzetti case. Nicola Sacco (1891–1927) and Bartolomeo Vanzetti (1888–1927) were two Italian immigrants accused of murdering two Boston-area men. The immigrants were eventually executed for

the murders, though both men had alibis (excuses) for the night of the murder. The case and trial were among the most controversial in American history. Sinclair's treatment of the event caused national outrage because he portrayed the case as an example of American justice being sacrificed in the name of social class and wealth.

Other well-known, though not necessarily American, authors of the Gilded Age and the Progressive Era include poets Emily Dickinson (1830–1886) and Walt Whitman (1819–1892); Rudyard Kipling (1865–1936) of *Jungle Book* fame; Sir Arthur Conan Doyle (1859–1930), best known for his character Sherlock Holmes; and British playwright Oscar Wilde (1854–1900).

Newspapers and the print revolution

Newspapers were not new to the Gilded Age, but the years from 1886 to 1895 were of major importance to the spread of print journalism beyond the Midwest. At a time when radio and television had yet to be invented, newspapers were the public's main source of information.

New technologies allowed newspapers to cut production costs, set type faster with a machine rather than by hand, and hasten the printing of illustrations. Electricity was the main innovation that helped newspapers increase their production volume. Electrically run machines sped up all production processes, and costs were cut as manufacturers began to make paper out of wood pulp. The Linotype typesetting machine (1886) allowed typesetters to work line by line instead of letter by letter.

Dime Novels and Pulp Magazines

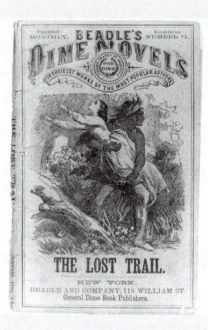

The cover of "The Lost Trail," one of Beadle's dime novels. THE LIBRARY OF CONGRESS.

Reading was once a pastime available only to the upper-middle and wealthy classes. Lower classes, in general, could not read well, if at all. Books were costly because paper and printing were expensive. Prior to the building of railroads, books were transported by riverboat. When the waters froze, the availability of books came to a halt until the spring thaw.

With the Gilded Age came new technologies that allowed for faster printing and cheaper resources. Free public education meant that more people were learning to read and write, regardless of social class. Railroads shipped books year round, which meant more affordable books were finding their way into the hands of a wider reading audience. More readers meant there was a demand for more publishers; this led to an opportunity for instant wealth in the publishing industry.

Dime novels, which got their name from the fact that they cost just ten cents each, first appeared in 1860. Their themes were usually patriotic and often featured conflicts between pioneers and

The new machine also created equal margins on both sides of a column of text.

Newspapers were now more visually appealing, and they could be offered to readers without raising costs. Wise investors saw an opportunity to make profits. Newspaper agencies easily found loans to buy faster machinery.

Perhaps the most remarkable development in the print revolution was the evening newspaper. Prior to the Gilded Age, newspapers were delivered in the morning. By 1890, two-thirds of all daily newspapers were evening editions. Newspapers in the West carried articles about events of the day, even when those events occurred in the East. Reporters could travel to cover a story, then report the news to the main office via telegraph (an early version of the telephone, except the user typed text into it instead of talking). By 1880, there were nearly 111,000 miles of telegraph wire running throughout the nation. Within three years, there were four intercontinental lines. Without westerners and Native Americans. By the mid-1890s, the covers of dime novels were printed in color, and many featured scenes of bloodshed and violence. At this point, the books appealed mostly to teenage boys.

Other dime novels were written specifically for young women. The covers of these books featured a well-dressed young lady wearing a stylish hat and holding a copy of a dime novel in her hands as she gazed out into the distance. The primary readers of these novels were working-class girls. Reading was a respectable activity, and the dime novels gave these young women a feeling of self-improvement, a way to close the gap between the lower and the middle classes.

It is not possible to say how many dime novels were published. One company, Beadle's Dime Novels, published more than five million dime novels between 1860 and 1865 alone.

Pulp magazines

Closely related to dime novels were pulp magazines, which began appearing in the 1880s. Many dime novels became pulp magazines by enlarging the format from a small book to a 7 x 10-inch magazine layout that included all-color illustrations. These magazines shifted their focus to an older reading audience.

Most pulp magazines featured stories involving supernatural, Wild West, and detective plots. Later, around the time of World War I, science-fiction stories were added. Other pulp magazines catered to female readers and included stories of love won and lost.

Some famous authors who got their start writing pulp fiction include western writer Louis L'Amour (1908–1988), detective-fiction writer Dashiell Hammett (1894–1961), and science-fiction writers Isaac Asimov (1920–1992) and Ray Bradbury (1920–).

Pulp fiction reached the height of its popularity in the 1930s, when it served to release America from the worries of war and economic depression.

technology, none of these advancements in print media could have occurred.

Art

Like literature, art was also part of the Realism movement, at least for a while. Women and children were the most commonly painted subjects, with both American and exotic landscapes coming in a close second.

Regarded by many artists and art historians alike to be the greatest painter of the nineteenth century is Winslow Homer (1836–1910). Although Homer painted and etched women and children as did most mid-nineteenth artists, he eventually expanded his focus to include both sexes. What interested the artist most was communicating the personality of his subjects. For example, in many paintings of hardworking fishermen and their families, Homer primarily focused on the women of the North Sea region of England, painting them as they mended nets, cared for children, and waited for their men to return home safely.

Winslow Homer's etching entitled "The Netmenders," which shows women mending their husbands' fishing nets. THE LIBRARY OF CONGRESS.

As he aged, Homer longed for solitude, and his paintings reflected this shift in lifestyle. His later paintings, mostly landscapes and seascapes, are the paintings most respected by modern artists and collectors.

Impressionism Art in the Gilded Age and the Progressive Era was a reflection of the values of American society. Those values in the late nineteenth century were changing. Industrialism had given birth to a new social class: the middle class. Where once society was made up mostly of lower and upper classes, it now found itself with a growing middle class. This middle class included managers in the new industries as well as teachers, lawyers, and doctors. Prior to the Gilded Age, art had generally represented the upper class and its experiences. This traditional approach to art was rapidly changing at the turn of the century.

A group of French artists called the Impressionists (for the way reality left its impression on their work) changed the art world in the 1890s. These painters painted people as they saw them in daily activities, rather than formally posed. Mary Cassatt (1844–1926) was an

American Impressionist living in France who is best remembered for her paintings of women and children. Like her Impressionist counterparts, Cassatt painted her subjects not in formally posed portraits but in relaxed positions and natural surroundings.

Another artist representative of the era was John Singer Sargent (1856–1925). He, too, was an American living abroad. Although Sargent was famous for the portraits he painted, by the 1880s he had moved to Impressionist landscapes. He was (and still is) criticized for maintaining a sense of superficiality (falseness) even in his Impressionism, but he is generally considered, at least in his later career, to be an Impressionist painter.

Although Impressionism in Europe faded out in the early twentieth century, some American Impressionists continued to paint in that style into the 1920s. But as America welcomed the new century, society was clearly moving toward urbanization and modern life. Cities were overcrowded with overworked adults and children, and the gap widened between the rich and the poor. Life in urban America was not pretty, and one group of artists dedicated themselves to depicting the hardships of life on canvas.

The Ashcan School Just as Mark Twain took literature to new heights by insisting it reflect reality, so did a group of painters move art into the real, if disturbing, realm of life. In 1891, artist Robert Henri (1865–1929) and seven others began a movement in Philadelphia, Pennsylvania. Known as "The Eight," these painters shocked America not by the way they painted but by their subject matter. These men created no seascapes or formal portraits. Instead, they

chose as their subjects the harsh realities of city life. The Eight used dark, dreary colors to capture the hopeless atmosphere of urban America and made the nation acknowledge that not all of life in the Gilded Age was touched with gold.

The Eight were given the nickname "Ashcan School" by a critic who was repulsed by their work. These rebellious artists did not care what the public thought.

The Eight took their rebellion one step further when they organized and widely publicized an art exhibit in 1913. The exhibit, held in New York's National Guard Armory and known as the Armory Show, was the first ever to be planned by artists. No judges were present and no awards given out. Five hundred thousand Americans attended the Armory Show. If the works by the Ashcan School were shocking, those by the new modern abstract artists such as Pablo Picasso (1881–1973) and Marcel Duchamp (1887–1968) were nothing short of appalling. These paintings were as far removed from reality as they could be, and critics dismissed these painters as insane. Within a few years, however, the abstract, modernist style would become firmly established in American art.

Photography

Photography emerged as an art form in the late nineteenth and early twentieth centuries (see Chapter 10 for the history of the camera). One man in particular is directly associated with photography as an art: Alfred Stieglitz (1864–1946). Stieglitz was born in New Jersey and developed an interest in photography at the age of eleven. He studied his craft in Berlin, Germany. By 1892, Stieglitz was known for his photographs of everyday life in Paris and New York.

Like the artists of the Ashcan School, Stieglitz found inspiration in the grittier aspects of urban life. His dedication to his craft was remarkable. For one particular photograph, "Winter, Fifth Avenue," Stieglitz stood in a snow storm for three hours, waiting for just the right moment to snap the shutter.

Stieglitz was a cofounder of the magazine *Camera Work,* a journal for new photographers. The world-famous publication ran from 1903 to 1917 and published the works of new and exciting photographers as well as photographs of groundbreaking European painters. Readers of the periodical knew who Picasso was well before the presentation of the Ashcan School's Armory Show.

Stieglitz himself was a gifted photographer, but he had a greater impact on the world of photography for the way he promoted it and elevated it to an art form.

Architecture

Henry H. Richardson (1838–1886) was the premiere architect of the Gilded Age. His buildings had a medieval influence mixed with Roman style—massive arches and imposing towers. Richardson designed many churches and cathedrals of the day. His style was so unique that it is sometimes referred to as Richardsonian.

The buildings of the Columbian Exposition of 1893 influenced architecture. Many buildings erected after the fair were in the classical style, with large pillars and flat rooftops. Architect Louis Sullivan (1856–1924) designed the Transportation Building for the exposition, and he remained a popular architect until the beginning of the twentieth century. History would prove that Sullivan's protégé (someone who studies under the direction of someone else) would

achieve a fame far greater than his teacher's, as Frank Lloyd Wright (1867–1959) became one of America's leading architects in the twentieth century.

Perhaps the most memorable aspect of Progressive Era architecture was the skyscraper. Until the 1880s, the height of buildings was limited by the construction techniques commonly used. The first skyscraper was built in Chicago in 1885 and stood ten stories high. Architects in that city considered the skyscraper's appearance a challenge and immediately set to work building even taller structures. As construction techniques improved—especially the advent of the metal frame, which would bear the weight of the walls—buildings got taller. Soon the skylines of all urban areas included towering skyscrapers.

Arts and Crafts movement

Improvements in architecture imposed changes to the outsides of buildings, but the Arts and Crafts movement (1880–1910) brought changes to the inside as well. In direct response to the fancy, lavish décor of the Gilded Age, a group of craftsmen and artists began what was called the Arts and Crafts movement. The idea behind the Arts and Crafts style was to return to a time when furniture and other household decorating items were made by hand. The movement's founder, William Morris (1834–1896), and his followers believed that the industrialization of America forced the country into a culture that was sterile and boring; it did not allow for designers and builders to make items of quality, one at a time. Even homes were being built from packages and kits. (Oddly enough, the bungalow-style home-building kits sold by Sears were considered part of the Arts and Crafts style.)

Furniture of the Arts and Crafts style was made of dark wood and simple construction. The elegance of the style of furnishings was in its simple understatement. To allow natural beauty to come through, wood furniture was sometimes left unfinished, the surfaces a bit rough. Fabric patterns were small and repetitive, in muted earth tones. Overall, the idea behind the movement was a return to a simpler time when people were more important than machines.

Cultural investments

Cultural organizations such as opera houses, museums, and libraries were funded by large donations from men such as Andrew Carnegie (1835–1919) and John D. Rockefeller. Carnegie donated hundreds of millions of dollars to build more than twenty-five hundred free public libraries throughout English-speaking lands across the world. Of these, more than sixteen hundred were built in America. His generosity stemmed from a belief that as someone who had made great wealth, he was obligated to give it away before his death. Libraries were especially important to him because he knew from experience what it was like to be a poor immigrant with little access to education. He believed libraries could help immigrants achieve a desirable level of education that would lead to a chance for prosperity.

John D. Rockefeller (owner of the Standard Oil Company) made millions of dollars in donations to various cultural and educational organizations. He donated $35 million to the University of Chicago and made donations to many other colleges, including Yale, Harvard, Vassar, and Spelman. In 1902, he established the General Education Board, which funded educational needs throughout the country in the amount of $325 million during the years of its existence (1902–1965).

Religion and the Social Gospel

Capitalism affected every segment of life, and religion was no exception. As people grew wealthier through aggressive competition and a focus on only themselves, religious leaders denounced capitalism and blamed it for all of society's problems. They argued that capitalism forced men into greed and selfishness and encouraged them to care only about their own well-being.

The message of the Social Gospel movement was that people should be as concerned about their neighbor as they are about themselves. Leading advocates of the Social Gospel were two ministers: Washington Gladden (1836–1918), regarded as the founder of the movement, and Walter Rauschenbusch (1861–1918). Rauschenbusch ministered to the German immigrant community in a section of New York City known as Hell's Kitchen. He saw first-hand how poverty led to other social problems. Like Gladden, he blamed capitalism as the root cause.

The Social Gospel movement declined in popularity after World War I, largely because of general disillusionment over the war itself. It did however influence many aspects of the reform movement, including women's suffrage, temperance (a movement that campaigned for the public to refrain from drinking alcohol), and settlement housing in the cities.

Sports: baseball is king, but boxing is big

The 1890s saw America begin an enthusiastic appreciation of physical activity. Biking became a popular craze among men and women alike. The discovery of nature as a place to be explored encouraged Americans to hike and camp. Spectator sports took over the nation as

Other Interesting Cultural Events of the Era

The first Coca-Cola was served at Jacob's Pharmacy in Atlanta, Georgia, on May 8, 1886. The store's bookkeeper came up with the name, and his handwriting is still used in the logo in the twenty-first century. Between 1890 and 1900, sales increased by 4,000 percent.

Originally established as a legislative library in 1800 when President John Adams (1735–1826; served 1797–1801) approved the spending of $5,000 to buy books for Congress to use, the Library of Congress initially included 740 books and 3 maps. In 1802, President Thomas Jefferson (1743–1826; served 1801–9) gave Congress the authority to develop the library as it saw fit. For nearly a century, the library's holdings were kept in the U.S. Capitol. But on November 1, 1897, the library's first official building opened its doors. Originally one room, the library in the twenty-first century consists of three buildings. If all the shelves were laid end to end, they would cover more than 500 miles. It is the largest library in the world.

The first New York subway opened for business to the public at seven o'clock PM on October 27, 1904. Before the night was over, 150,000 passengers had taken a ride underground. Construction took just four years.

Newspaper journalist Nellie Bly (1864–1922) completed a trip around the world in seventy-two days, six hours, and eleven minutes on January 25, 1890. She had read *Around the World in Eighty Days,* by Jules Verne (1828–1905), and announced to her readers that she could make the trip in less time. In order to complete the trip, Bly traveled by train, ship, horse, donkey, sampan (small riverboat), and jinrikisha (a seat on wheels pulled by a man). Never one to shy away from risks, Bly had once posed as a patient in an asylum (an institution for the insane) to get an insider's view of the horrible conditions. Her report on her experience led to reforms in the twentieth century.

Lizzie Borden (1860–1927) was accused in 1892 of murdering her father and stepmother with an axe (eleven blows to his head, nineteen to hers). Although she was later found innocent of the charges, her story remains one of the most popular unsolved mysteries in American culture. More recent scholarship suggests that Borden did in fact probably kill her father and stepmother. The evidence indicates the way in which the crime was carried out is in keeping with the classic profile of a child who has been sexually abused by a parent. A jump-rope rhyme of unknown authorship judges her as guilty:

> Lizzie Borden had an axe
> And gave her mother forty whacks.
> When she saw what she had done
> She gave her father forty-one.

The Federal Bureau of Investigation (FBI) was established within the Justice Department in 1908, although some members of Congress were not in favor of the development. The Bureau almost immediately embarrassed itself when it rounded up thousands of young men at the start of World War I and only a handful turned out to be draft dodgers (men trying to illegally escape going to war).

one of the most popular ways to spend one's free time.

The sudden increase in the popularity of sports was a direct reaction to the changes wrought by the industrialization of the country. Men and women found themselves on a regimented schedule during the workweek. They were bound by the time clock as well as the rules of the factory, mill, or shop. American society was very clear about its expectations regarding proper behavior, and industrial urban life forced Americans to conform to its restraints. Physical activity, then, was a way of breaking free of those restraints. Watching athletes amaze an audience with their talent and skill was another way to escape the routine of daily life.

Baseball Baseball became an organized sport in the 1840s and 1850s, but its popularity increased after the Civil War. By 1911, it was known as "America's pastime."

The first professional team, the Cincinnati Red Stockings, formed in 1869 and with it, major league baseball in America had begun. As more teams formed—eventually becoming the National League—players traveled by train from one city to the next, and team rivalries built loyalty among fans. With the development of the American League in 1901, Americans had two organized leagues of teams with which to fill their leisure time. The two leagues merged in 1903 and played the first World Series.

Baseball was more than just a sport for a nation that was still figuring out who it was at the turn of the century. At a time when economic depression, mass immigration, and industrialization gave Americans plenty to worry about, baseball offered an affordable escape (tickets were twenty-five cents for bleacher seats, fifty cents for the roofed grandstand), an inexpensive outing for a few hours to cheer for a favorite team or player. What became so interesting about this particular sport is that its evolution directly reflected the changes of the society in which it was developing. The story of baseball matches the American story of immigration and assimilation (fitting into a new culture): Many athletes were immigrants searching for a new life. Baseball contains the story of race relations in America: Racism forced African American athletes to form their own leagues, and yet some of the most famous and beloved baseball players in the history of the sport were African American. Not as commonly known, baseball has its own story of women and their struggle for equality: When forbidden to participate in the sport, they, like African Americans, formed their own teams. Baseball reflects the story of the struggle between labor (players) and management, as early managers of the teams were often corrupt in their practices and cared little for their players' welfare. Comparisons between the sport and reality were many. These common factors are one reason baseball is called America's pastime.

Late-nineteenth-century ballparks were usually located on the outskirts of town in middle-class neighborhoods. They were conveniently located next to inexpensive mass transit (street cars or trolleys) and often had to relocate because the wood structures burned down. In the 1890s alone, there were twenty-five fires at various ballparks across the country. Privately built and funded, these ballparks cost about $30,000 to develop and seated ten thousand fans. The first fireproof ballparks were built in 1909 in Pittsburgh and Philadelphia. These safer stadiums were built because owners recognized the growing popularity of the sport. They had a responsibility to make the game as safe and enjoyable as possible.

Boxing Baseball was not the only sport to capture America's attention. Basketball was invented in 1891, and the popularity of college football continued to grow. Golf and tennis had loyal fans, as did horse racing. But the only other sport to rival baseball in terms of popularity and devotion was boxing, or prizefighting, as it was called then.

Boxing began in eighteenth-century England. It was immediately popular because it combined two beloved pastimes: sports and gambling. Most boxers were working-class men sponsored by wealthy gentlemen. Almost from its beginning, the sport was marked by corruption and dishonesty.

The first American heavyweight champion was John Sullivan (1858–1918), who held the title from 1882 to 1892. Sullivan was champion when boxing made the drastic change from bare knuckles to gloves. Unlike most other sports, prizefighting was one sport African Americans were allowed to participate in, though many white boxers refused to fight them.

The first African American (and first Texan) heavyweight champion was Jack Johnson (1878–1946), whose reign lasted from 1908 to 1915. More than an athlete, Johnson was also the first African American cultural icon (symbol or hero). At a time when news of African Americans was not printed in newspapers or magazines, Johnson was photographed more often than any other African American and most whites, and his name appeared in print on a regular basis throughout his career.

Johnson was born in Texas in 1878. Not content to spend his life doing physical labor, he used his size (6 feet, 200 pounds) to his advantage and learned to box. As an African American boxer with a white manager, he was often unfairly treated. Johnson refused to be controlled by anyone, and he was not above firing a manager if he was unhappy with him. Despite the fact that boxers in that era lived among the lower classes of society, which included

African American icon and boxer Jack Johnson. © AP IMAGES.

prostitutes (women who are paid for sexual services), drug addicts and dealers, and criminals, Johnson's intelligence prevented him from giving in to temptation. He was determined to become champion of his craft.

When Johnson beat his opponent, Canadian Tommy Burns (1881–1955), on December 26, 1908, to become the first African American heavyweight champion, whites in the audience immediately began crying for a "great white hope" to take back the title. Johnson was not a favorite among whites because of his preference for socializing with (and eventually marrying) white women. This mixing of the races is called miscegenation, and it was illegal at the time. Even many fellow African Americans disliked Johnson for this reason. As one of the few

Gibson Girl: An Artistic Cultural Icon

One of the many Gibson Girl illustrations from Charles Dana Gibson; this one, "Patience," appeared in Collier's *magazine.* THE LIBRARY OF CONGRESS.

Some cultural icons are real people, such as athletes and celebrities. A different sort of icon, a drawing of a certain kind of girl, was the result of a vision belonging to an artist named Charles Dana Gibson (1867–1944). Gibson was an illustrator for several popular magazines. His pen-and-ink drawings came to represent the spirit of the Progressive Era.

Although Gibson created many illustrations, he was and remains most famous for his Gibson Girl. She was the embodiment of America's perfect woman: cultured, beautiful, innocent but with a twinkle in her eye. Always dressed in a flowing skirt, with her long, carefully arranged hair sometimes pulled up in back, the Gibson Girl was the ideal of early twentieth-century feminism. She became the inspiration for fashion and eventually appeared on non-print items such as wallpaper, dinner plates, and matchboxes.

America loved its Gibson Girl for the self-confidence she portrayed, and she remained a cultural icon until World War I. By then, America's hopefulness had faded to cynicism. The Gibson Girl no longer seemed appropriate for a country faced with war.

public representatives of his race, his behavior reflected on his entire race. To involve himself with white women during a time of deep racism was not only dangerous for Johnson himself but for other African Americans as well; his actions made other African American men targets for whites' anger at Johnson.

Morality was the basis for much of the reform laws being passed throughout the Progressive Era. With prostitution at an all-time high during this time, America needed someone to blame. Immorality became linked in the public's mind to miscegenation. At a time when reformers were beginning to label boxing as immoral because it was violent, Johnson became a man with two strikes against him: He was a boxer who preferred white women.

In 1912, Johnson's first (white) wife killed herself. Within three months, Johnson married another white woman, prostitute Lucille Cameron. Johnson was found guilty of violating the law and sentenced to serve

How Henry Ford Changed the World

When industrialist Henry Ford (1863–1947) introduced his now-famous Model T automobile in 1908, he changed the lives of millions of Americans.

The Model T was not Ford's first car; Ford did not even invent the automobile. His contribution was designing a car that was simple and affordable enough so that the average American could own one. The Model T was that car. More than ten thousand of them sold for $825 (the equivalent of about $17,300 in 2005 using the Consumer Price Index) each in the first year of production. Because of innovative production techniques that eventually included the moving assembly line, the price dropped to $575 (about $11,500 in 2005) within four years, and sales skyrocketed. By 1914, Ford owned 48 percent of the automobile market. His new car-manufacturing plant was turning out one Model T every ninety-three minutes. By 1927—years after the perfection of the assembly line—Ford was producing one car every twenty-four seconds. The price dropped to $300 (about $5,800 in 2005).

Ford made more than cars. He made it possible for Americans to live in the country and work in the city. For those who did not like city life, he allowed for the development of an entirely different lifestyle: the suburbs. His innovations created jobs and allowed for mobility on a scale never before known. Suddenly, distances between loved ones did not seem so great, and families could take summer vacations. Tourism became a major American industry. Weekend jaunts to the country became a popular pastime, whereas before, the furthest one could hope to travel in one trip was fifteen miles or so. Horses pulling wagons or carriages could not be expected to go farther than that.

Thanks to affordable cars, more people could attend colleges and universities, and hospitals were now more accessible. More cars meant the development and maintenance of new roads and a highway system that connected one region to the next. It was only a matter of time before interstate highways were built, connecting one end of the country to the other.

It can be argued that the introduction of Ford's economical Model T had the greatest effect on the lives of women. Where once their lives centered around the home, if for no other reason than that they had no means of

one year and one day in prison. He refused and fled to Europe, where he lived until 1920. At that time, he returned home to serve his time.

While overseas, Johnson continued to fight because he needed the money. However, he was not bringing in spectators like he once did, and his title meant very little because he was a fugitive from justice. Since he could not fight in the United States, he was not much good to any manager. He finally lost his title in 1915, to Cuban fighter Jess Willard (1881–1968). There would not be another African American heavyweight champion until Joe Louis (1914–1981) won the title twenty-two years later.

After serving his prison term, Johnson lived off his fame by fighting in exhibitions and telling his life's story. He continued to marry and divorce white women, but now that he was no longer a champion, no one gave it much thought. Johnson died in a car crash in 1946.

transportation at their disposal, they now could travel conveniently. Rural women could visit their neighbors miles away without having to leave an entire afternoon open for the walk or horse ride. They could shop at their local merchants or venture further where selection and price were more consumer friendly. The car made women more visible in towns and society in general, giving them an independence and power they had never had.

Automobile pioneer Henry Ford (right) sits in a 1905 Ford Model N runabout next to Ford official David Gray, circa 1905. © BETTMANN/CORBIS.

Entertainment

Opera houses first began appearing in American towns and cities in the 1880s. By the end of the nineteenth century, even small towns had them. Although the name conjures up images of luxurious curtains and gold-leaf balconies, most opera houses were little more than meeting halls with a stage. The exception to this was the Metropolitan Opera House in New York City, which opened in 1883 and actually hosted real operas. New Orleans, Louisiana, also boasted an authentic opera house. But in most places, these opera houses were a town's cultural-events center.

Minstrel shows and vaudeville

Prior to the Gilded Age, much popular music was serious and more classical and religious in style. The advent of fairs and of cultural events like Broadway musicals changed popular music as the middle and lower classes began to enjoy a variety of musical styles. Entertainment included traveling groups of actors, singers, comedians, and other performers who went from town to town. America had been enjoying traveling shows for years. These earlier performances began in the 1830s and were called minstrel shows. White performers would rub burnt cork or charcoal on their faces to indicate they were portraying African Americans. This was called blackface. Their performances would include song and dance styles from African American culture, but often the performers would savagely mimic what they considered behaviors typical of African Americans. For example, their dancing more closely resembled the antics of wild animals. Their movements were clumsy, and they portrayed African Americans as simple, unable to understand even the most basic concepts and ideas. To a white audience, this form of racism was comedy.

By the end of the nineteenth century, the minstrel show gave way to the more popular variety show. Each traveling company was made up of a variety of performers, usually one or two who were well known throughout the country. Booking agents figured these stars would attract an audience who would be forgiving of the other less-talented performers. These variety shows were known as vaudeville.

Vaudeville had something for everyone. Though one show was similar to the next, each had its own unique focus or act. Performances might include short theatrical sketches, song and dance routines, comedy routines, animal acts, sideshow oddities similar to those found at a circus or carnival, magic acts, and physical acts such as acrobatics or strongmen.

The amazing Harry Houdini One of the most famous acts in vaudeville was escape artist

Famous escape artist Harry Houdini. THE LIBRARY OF CONGRESS.

Harry Houdini (1874–1926). Like many vaudeville performers, Houdini was an immigrant. He left Hungary in 1878 and got his start in show business as a magician. In 1899, his agent advised him to leave behind traditional magic and concentrate on escapes. Houdini was an instant hit with his first vaudeville appearance. He left on a tour of Europe in 1900 and became a star.

Houdini returned to America in 1905 and amazed America the following year when he escaped from the locked jail cell of Charles Guiteau (c. 1840–1882), the man who had assassinated President James Garfield (1831–1881;

served 1881). This stunt confirmed Houdini's status as a celebrity, and America hailed him as a cultural hero. In 1913, he introduced a new dramatic escape demonstration called the upside-down water torture cell. His fans could not get enough of his straitjacket escapes made while hanging upside-down in a sealed water chamber.

Houdini continued his life of illusion and great escapes until 1926, when he died from an infection caused by a ruptured appendix.

Racism in vaudeville Immigrants found in vaudeville a place where they could fit in to this new American culture. They knew they were appreciated for their talents by the weekly paycheck and daily applause. African Americans were not so lucky.

Vaudeville was as racist as the rest of America. As in minstrelsy, blackface was a popular routine. African American performers were forced to use the blackface makeup to hide the fact that they actually were dark skinned. It was a humiliating experience for the performers, but nobody except African Americans gave much thought to the degrading experience. The attitude was handed down from the minstrel shows, which did not give a second thought to the racial stereotypes it promoted. Minstrelsy produced songs commonly referred to as "coon" songs, which reflected the hardships of African American culture. ("Coon" was considered an offensive word for African American.) The most popular title was "All Coons Look Alike to Me." In the 1890s alone, more than six hundred coon songs were published.

Bill "Bojangles" Robinson (1878–1949) was one of the most famous African American performers in vaudeville. A tall, thin man, Robinson was a talented tap dancer who made a name for himself with his "stair dance," which involved an intricate tap dance up a long flight of stairs. Even after vaudeville's popularity declined, Robinson remained a favorite with white audiences. He appeared in films with legendary stars such as Shirley Temple (1928–) and Will Rogers (1879–1935).

Movies

Films in the Gilded Age and Progressive Era were silent (sound on film had not yet been mastered). Most of the films were short, lasting just a few minutes. Live piano music would accompany the movie as theater-goers watched performers silently enact a story in black-and-white film. Movies were incorporated into vaudeville shows, but in 1905, a new kind of theater, the nickelodeon, appeared on the American scene.

Nickelodeons were small, storefront theaters that showed movies all day long for the cost of five cents a movie. The owner of several vaudeville shows built the first nickelodeon in Pittsburgh, Pennsylvania. By 1908, America boasted eight thousand nickelodeons. These tiny theaters attracted men, women, and children because no matter what time of day or night it was, a movie was playing. Nickelodeons declined in 1907 as bigger movie theaters with larger seating capacities were built.

Silent films were not considered a form of art until the 1910s. At that point, they increased in length, and film studios began marketing their best actors to attract a greater audience. Most of the famous silent-film stars reached the height of their popularity in the 1920s, including Charlie Chaplin (1889–1977), Theda Bara (1885–1955), and Mary Pickford (1892–1979).

Considered the first masterpiece of film, *Birth of a Nation* took the cinematic world by storm upon its release in 1915. Written and directed by D. W. Griffith (1875–1948), this movie elevated cinema to an art form and made Americans understand how it could be used to spark social change. It was Griffith's first major film; nevertheless, it earned him the title "father of film."

The film captured the violence and excitement of the Civil War through its innovative filming and editing techniques. African Americans throughout the nation were outraged at Griffith's deliberate racism and prejudice and accused him of recording a distorted history (many historians agree). The film caused riots in a number of African American communities.

The cinema was one of America's most popular recreational pastimes in a constantly-changing culture, but not everyone was pleased with the film craze. Many reformers viewed theaters as hotbeds of sin and crime. This was due to the content of films, which included romance and vampires (seen by reformers as sexually explicit), but also to the theaters themselves, which reformers believed encouraged viewers to act in ways considered immoral for the time. No one could police the activities taking place in a darkened theater. Reformers were concerned about the ease with which crimes such as theft and prostitution (the selling of sex for money) could occur. In 1907, Chicago established the nation's first censorship board to protect its citizens against immorality.

The era of silent films ended in 1926 when the first talking move (called "talkie") was produced.

Popular music

Vaudeville had a direct impact on the public's music tastes in the Gilded Age and the Progressive Era. Popular music was beginning to emerge as an industry in the 1890s, and most music centered around the piano. Owning a piano was a symbol of prestige and good taste in the 1890s. Young women and girls were the primary players.

Popular tunes were based on religious and ethnic themes as well as tales of love and sentimentality. Ballads (songs that tell a story) often ended in death or with one lover leaving the other. At the time, music was sold not as a record album but in the form of sheet music for piano. The first million-selling hit was "After the Ball," written in 1892 by Charles Harris (1867–1930). Tin Pan Alley in New York was the center of the sheet-music publishing business. Dozens of publishing houses competed to publish the best songs.

Ragtime Although the late nineteenth and early twentieth centuries are remembered as the Ragtime Era, that title is misleading. There was no one dominant style of music. Broadway tunes were popular and often sung in vaudeville acts. Traveling minstrel shows made coon songs popular. Amusement parks that featured marching bands had an impact on the music industry and led to a rise in the composition of patriotic songs. The reason for the emphasis on ragtime is that it was a fresh sound, and one that was wholly American.

Ragtime, or rags as the songs were called, was influenced by African American rhythms. They are lively, upbeat tunes with syncopated (off-the-beat) rhythms. Rags were originally written for piano, but the style was often transcribed for a variety of brass instruments and led directly to the style of music that gave its name to an entire era: jazz.

Invention of the Phonograph

Thomas Edison (1847–1931) invented the first phonograph in 1877. It used a tinfoil cylinder that recorded sound by pricking the tinfoil with a needle. Each different sound placed the needle pricks in a different position. During playback, the phonograph used a different needle to "read" the needle pricks. Various sounds were produced by the vibrations of the needle against the tinfoil. The mechanics and limitations of the machine made recording several instruments at once nearly impossible, and some instruments, such as the violin, could not be recorded at all because their sounds were complex and not easily picked up by the recording device. Horns, with their loud blasts, recorded the best.

In 1893, an inventor named Emile Berliner (1851–1929) released the first gramophone, or disc player. After years of research and development, Berliner found a method that performed better than the cylinder phonograph. His machine used a needle to play hard rubber discs that allowed up to three and one-half minutes of recording time. The public was not quick to give up their cylinder phonographs, so sales were slow at first. Berliner continued his research and found a more durable disc, and with that, sales increased.

Eldridge Johnson (1867–1945) was the Henry Ford of the recording industry; he changed the course of events forever when he founded the Victor Talking Machine Company in 1902. Johnson had been hired by Berliner to build components for the gramophone. When Berliner was found to be in violation of some patent laws (laws declaring formal rights of ownership) and could not sell his machine in the United States, Johnson bought some of the patents from Berliner and set to work improving the machine.

The result was the Victrola, available for $200 in 1905 (the equivalent of about $4,400 in 2005). Improvements in the production process and technology allowed Johnson to drop the price to a mere $15 by 1911 (the equivalent of about $300 in 2005). Americans in homes all across the country became the proud owners of a Victrola.

Rags were played in saloons, parlors, gambling halls, and juke joints (dance halls). The best-known ragtime composer and performer was Scott Joplin. Born in Texas, Joplin mastered the banjo and began playing piano at an early age. He was one of the few African Americans to perform at the Chicago's World Fair in 1893. In 1899, Joplin wrote and played "Maple Leaf Rag," considered the perfect model of a ragtime tune. He followed that a few years later with "The Entertainer," another popular rag that also reemerged in the 1970s as the popular theme song in the hit movie *The Sting*.

Joplin wrote an opera, *Treemonisha,* in 1911, but it was largely unsuccessful. He died in 1917. In 1976, his opera won the prestigious Pulitzer Prize.

Blues Blues, a music style with its roots in African American rhythms and slave spirituals, was born in the South shortly before the turn of the century. It developed from the suffering experienced by sharecroppers who were overworked in the fields. African Americans working on prison road crews and chain gangs conceived other blues tunes. As explained on PBS.org, jazz musician Sidney Bechet (1897–1959) remembered that the first time he heard the blues was by a prisoner in a jailhouse. "The way he sang it was more than just a man. He was like every man that's ever been done wrong. . . . The blues, like spirituals, were prayers."

As a written music, the blues did not appear until around 1911. African American composer W. C. Handy (1873–1958) popularized the style with his tune "Memphis Blues" in 1912. The blues gained in popularity and rivaled jazz as the dominant style of music in the 1920s.

Blues was not a style of music respectable white Americans appreciated. Its themes of lust and heartache were not aligned with white society's moral values. Aside from religious tunes, popular music for whites included themes of suffrage and temperance.

Cultural expression was vast and varied throughout the Gilded Age and the Progressive Era. From the fairs to the rise of popular music and consumerism, the Chautauqua to the Gibson Girl, America's optimism (positive outlook) was at the root of every segment of cultural development. Yet it was also a time of poverty; by 1904, one in every three people was close to starving. America's hope survived even as it suffered great economic depressions, political and business corruption, and war. More was better and there was little difference between need and want to a growing middle class. This attitude would lead the nation directly into the 1920s, the Roaring Twenties. If the Progressive Era was one of reform and hope, the Roaring Twenties were times of self-indulgence and moral wickedness.

For More Information

BOOKS

Brooke-Ball, Peter. *Champions of the Ring: The Great Fighters: Illustrated Biographies of the Biggest Names in Boxing History*. London: Southwater Publishing, 2001.

Brown, Joshua. *Beyond the Lines: Pictorial Reporting, Everyday Life, and the Crisis of Gilded-Age America*. Berkeley: University of California Press, 2002.

Espejo, Roman. *The Age of Reform and Industrialization, 1896–1920*. San Diego: Greenhaven Press, 2003.

Greenwood, Janette Thomas. *The Gilded Age: A History in Documents*. New York: Oxford University Press, 2000.

Smythe, Ted Curtis. *The Gilded Age Press, 1865–1900*. Westport, CT: Praeger, 2003.

Tygiel, Jules. *Past Time: Baseball as History*. New York: Oxford University Press, 2000.

WEB SITES

"American Cultural History: 19th Century—1890–1899." *Kingwood College Library*. http://kclibrary.nhmccd.edu/19thcentury1890.htm (accessed on June 6, 2006).

"American Political Cartoons: An Introduction." *Truman State University*. http://www2.truman.edu/parker/research/cartoons.html (accessed on June 6, 2006).

Blanke, David. "Consumer Culture During the Gilded Age and Progressive Era." *H-Net*. http://www.h-net.org/~shgape/bibs/consumer.html (accessed on June 30, 2006).

Dalkey, Victoria. "Art: The 'American Renaissance'." *Sacramento.com*. http://www.sacramento.com/portal/events/story/3848683p-4874088c.html (accessed on June 6, 2006).

Early, Gerald. "Rebel of the Progressive Era." *PBS: Unforgivable Blackness: The Rise and Fall of Jack Johnson*. http://www.pbs.org/unforgivableblackness/rebel/ (accessed on June 6, 2006).

"The Explosions of Our Fine Idealistic Undertakings, Chapter II." *Ida M. Tarbell*. http://tarbell.allegheny.edu/mc2.html (accessed on June 6, 2006).

Gibson-Girls. http://www.gibson-girls.com (accessed on June 6, 2006).

"History of the Sears Catalog." *Sears Archives*. http://www.searsarchives.com/catalogs/history.htm (accessed on June 6, 2006).

John W. Hartman Center for Sales, Advertising & Marketing History. *Emergence of Advertising in America: 1850–1920*. http://scriptorium.lib. duke. edu/eaa/index.html (accessed on June 6, 2006).

The Library of Congress. "Dime Novels." *American Treasures of the Library of Congress*. http://www.loc. gov/exhibits/treasures/tri015.html (accessed on June 6, 2006).

Library of Congress. "Houdini: A Biographical Chronology." *American Memory*. http://lcweb2. loc.gov/ammem/vshtml/vshchrn.html (accessed on June 6, 2006).

"The Movement." *Arts & Crafts Movement*. http:// anc.gray-cells.com/Intro.html (accessed on June 6, 2006).

Negro League Baseball. http://www.negroleaguebaseball. com/ (accessed on June 6, 2006).

"The New Woman." *True Women, New Women: Women in New York City, 1890–1940*. http://www. library.csi.cuny.edu/dept/history/lavender/386/ newwoman.html (accessed on June 6, 2006).

Paul V. Galvin Library Digital History Collection, Illinois Institute of Technology. "The Book of the Fair, by Hubert Howe Bancroft." *World's Columbian Exposition of 1893*. http://columbus. iit.edu/bookfair/ch27.html (accessed on June 30, 2006).

PBS. "About the Program." *Kate Chopin: A Re-Awakening*. http://www.pbs.org/katechopin/ program.html (accessed on June 30, 2006).

PBS. "Baseball." *Ken Burns*. http://www.pbs.org/ kenburns/baseball/ (accessed on June 6, 2006).

PBS. "The Birth of the Blues (1900–10)." *The Rise and Fall of Jim Crow*. http://www.pbs.org/wnet/ jimcrow/stories_events_blues.html (accessed on June 30, 2006).

Reed, Christopher Robert. "The Black Presence at 'White City': African and African American Participation at the World's Columbian Exposition, Chicago, May 1, 1893–October 31, 1893." *World's Columbian Exposition of 1893*. http:// columbus.gl.iit.edu/reed2.html (accessed on June 6, 2006).

Rose, Julie K. *The World's Columbian Exposition: Idea, Experience, Aftermath*. http://xroads.virginia.edu/ ~MA96/WCE/title.html (accessed on June 6, 2006).

Stasz, Clarice. "Jack [John Griffith] London." *The Jack London Online Collection*. http://london.sonoma. edu/jackbio.html (accessed on June 6, 2006).

Strasser, Susan. "Consumer to Customer: The New Consumption in the Progressive Era." *Organization of American Historians*. http://www.oah.org/pubs/ magazine/progressive/strasser.html (accessed on June 6, 2006).

"Winslow Homer (1836–1910)." *The Metropolitan Museum of Art*. http://www.metmuseum.org/ toah/hd/homr/hd_homr.htm (accessed on June 6, 2006).

"The World's Fair and Exposition Information and Reference Guide." *Earth Station 9*. http:// www.earthstation9.com/index.html?1893_chi.htm (accessed on June 6, 2006).

10

Adventure and Invention: An Era of Daring

Every era has its share of adventurers and heroes. The Gilded Age and the Progressive Era were no exception. (The Gilded Age was the period in history following the American Civil War [1861–65] and Reconstruction [roughly the final twenty-three years of the nineteenth century], characterized by a ruthless pursuit of profit, an exterior of showiness and grandeur, and immeasurable political corruption. The Progressive Era was a period in American history [approximately the first twenty years of the twentieth century] marked by reform and the development of a national cultural identity.) The years between 1878 and 1913 were a time of exploration and risk-taking. Although many seekers failed—even died—while trying to live their dream, there were those whose determination and perseverance were enough to let them achieve their goals. For some, that goal meant finding wealth. For others, the dream was to do something no one else had ever done before. Still others were simply curious, not ambitious. Their curiosity led them to discovery.

Unless they were members of the upper class during the Gilded Age, men and women worked very hard and earned very little. They had little if any savings because they could not earn enough income to put money aside. They lived in poverty-stricken neighborhoods where crime was uncontrolled and disease took the lives of both young and old.

In 1890, eleven million of America's twelve million families earned less than $1,200 a year. Of these families, the average annual income was about $380. This was far below the poverty line. For people living in these conditions, the thought of taking risks gave them hope. They might fail, but what if they did not?

Going for the gold

Hope is exactly what brought thousands of people—men and women—to Alaska and the Yukon. (Alaska was purchased from Russia in 1867, and became a U.S. territory in 1912 and the forty-ninth state of the

WORDS TO KNOW

aeronautics: The study of flight and aircraft.

boomtowns: Towns that were built quickly by gold-seekers.

Gilded Age: The period in history following the Civil War and Reconstruction (roughly the final twenty-three years of the nineteenth century), characterized by a ruthless pursuit of profit, an exterior of showiness and grandeur, and immeasurable political corruption.

grubstake: To advance money or supplies to miners in exchange for a percentage of profits from any discoveries.

patent: A grant by the government of the ownership of all rights of an invention to its creator.

poverty line: The least amount of income needed to secure the necessities of life. If someone lives below the poverty line, he or she cannot afford to purchase the basics needed to live, such as food, shelter, or medical care.

Progressive Era: A period in American history (approximately the first twenty years of the twentieth century) marked by reform and the development of a national cultural identity.

prospector: An explorer looking for minerals, such as gold.

sluice: A wooden trough for washing gold. Soil is shoveled into a steady stream of water. Gold and other larger particles get caught in the bottom. Smaller sluices called rockers were often used during the gold rush. These sluices could be rocked back and forth to hasten the process of separating the gold from the soil.

Smithsonian Institution: A government institution with most of its grounds located in Washington, D.C. It includes 16 museums, 7 research centers, and 142 million items in its collections.

stampeders: Gold-seekers.

Yukon: One of Canada's extreme northwest territories. Sixty percent of the territory's population lives in its current capital city, Whitehorse.

Union in 1959. The Yukon is one of Canada's extreme northwest territories.) Gold was first discovered in this region in 1849 by a Russian miner in the Kenai Peninsula of Alaska. Word traveled, and a few prospectors made their way to Alaska. The actual Alaska gold "rush" did not begin until around 1880. Gold had been found here and there up until that time. But in 1880, experienced prospectors Joseph Juneau (1836–1899) and Richard T. Harris (1833–1907) made a major gold strike. With the navigational help of Chief Kowee (c. 1817–1892), an Auk Indian and an Alaskan native, the two

men struck gold in Gold Creek. Accounts vary as to how much they found, but it is generally believed that the pair panned 1,000 pounds (454 kilograms) of gold from the creek.

A miner named George Pilz (1845–1926) grubstaked (advanced money in exchange for a percentage of profits from any discoveries) Juneau and Harris. But instead of returning to Pilz, the men loaded the gold on their canoe and headed for Canada. They were found by another one of Pilz's prospectors and brought back to Pilz at gunpoint. The find was the beginning of Alaska's first major gold rush. This rush would pale in comparison to the one that followed in the Klondike just sixteen years later.

Juneau and Harris staked out a 160-acre site and built a mining town near where they had discovered the gold. At first, the town was called Harrisburg (after Harris); then it was known as Pilzburg and Rockwell. In 1881, those living in the town met and voted on an official name for their town. They chose to name it Juneau, after Joe Juneau. The name stuck, and Juneau became Alaska's capital in 1900 (and continued as capital when Alaska became a U.S. territory in 1912 and a state in 1959).

A journey of hope In July 1897, two ships carrying miners docked in San Francisco, California, and Seattle, Washington. The miners had just returned from the Klondike, a vast region in Canada's Yukon territory. Accompanying the miners onboard one of the ships were endless bags of gold. The *Excelsior* docked in California with $200 worth of gold onboard. The *Portland* sailed into Seattle with more than $1.5 million in gold dust and nuggets. Newspapers were alerted, and soon everyone, everywhere knew of the gold awaiting them in the Klondike.

Within six months, approximately one hundred thousand gold-seekers (called "stampeders") set off for the Klondike. Only thirty thousand would reach their destination.

The decision to make the journey to the Klondike required careful planning and consideration. But the majority of stampeders had no idea where they were going, how they would get there, or how they would live once they arrived. They just set off, their heads full of promises of wealth. What they knew of the Klondike came from pamphlets and newspaper and magazine articles. These stories came from

stampeders who had already been to the Great White North and returned. Some came home with empty pockets, but that did not stop them from telling their tales. In many cases, those tales were greatly exaggerated, giving those back home false hopes of finding their life's riches. Other literature of the time focused on the adventure of traveling to the Klondike and living in the wilderness.

The trek into the Yukon The earliest stampeders were ill-prepared for a journey to the Yukon. They relied on maps and booklets for advice and directions. What they did not know then was that most of Alaska and Canada was wilderness. No one had accurately mapped those regions. Whatever literature they found was based on estimates and guesses at best. In an effort to get rich quick, some publishers provided maps that were made solely on what the mapmaker had heard from other people. These maps led thousands of people to their deaths, usually by starvation or exposure to the cold weather.

Out of necessity, a new career was born. Outfitters (commercial companies that sell "outfits"—wilderness survival equipment and supplies) seemed to spring up overnight. These operations provided necessities like food, clothing, tools, and camping equipment. In response to the unnecessary deaths of the earlier stampeders, the Northwest Mounted Police made a rule that stampeders had to have one year's worth of supplies and goods before they could cross the border into Canada. This came to about 1 ton (1 metric ton) of supplies per person. An outfit for two people cost anywhere from $250 to $500. For many, this was money they had saved specifically for the journey west.

Robert Service

One man in particular found great success in the gold rush, not from panning and discovering gold but from writing about life in the Yukon during that time. Robert Service (1874–1958) worked at a bank in the city of Whitehorse in the early 1900s. A British poet, Service had already published at least two poems before leaving for the Yukon, but few paid attention to them.

Soon, Service was asked to submit a poem to the local newspaper. He wrote "The Shooting of Dan McGrew." A month later, he wrote and published "The Cremation of Sam McGee." With these two poems, Service's life changed. By 1908, he no longer had to hold a day job; he quit and lived the rest of his life off his writing.

Here is the first verse of "The Cremation of Sam McGee":

There are strange things done in the midnight sun
By the men who moil for gold;
The Arctic trails have their secret tales
That would make your blood run cold;
The Northern Lights have seen queer sights,
But the queerest they ever did see
Was that night on the marge of Lake Lebarge
I cremated Sam McGee.

Other stampeders sold everything they owned to raise this money. Towns like Seattle made huge sums of money by outfitting the miners.

Once outfitted, stampeders had to decide which route they would take to the Klondike. There were five different routes to choose from, each with its own advantages and disadvantages. The route most commonly used was traveled by boat from the West Coast of the United States to Skagway, Alaska. From there, they took either the Chilkoot or White Pass to the Yukon River. Then they endured a 500-mile (804.5-kilometer) boat ride to Dawson City, the Yukon's capital city.

Both Chilkoot Pass and White Pass were dangerous. Chilkoot Pass was 32 miles (51.5 kilometers) long and rose 1,000 feet (304.8 meters) in the final half mile. Trekkers faced 60-mile-per-hour (96.5-kilometer-per-hour) winds in temperatures as low as −65 degrees Fahrenheit (−54 degrees Celsius). Fifteen hundred steps were carved out of ice and snow to help stampeders reach the top of the pass. These steps earned Chilkoot Pass the nickname "Golden Staircase." It was impossible for loaded packhorses to make their way up the steps. Stampeders had to unload the horses, lead them over the Golden Staircase, then come back for their belongings and move them piece by piece up and over the mountain trail. With so many people on the mountain trying to reach the same destination, each stampeder had to make about forty separate trips over this challenging section of the pass. This was the point where many stampeders gave up. Those who kept pressing on and made it to the Klondike could boast that they survived the 580-mile (933-kilometer) route.

White Pass was not as high as Chilkoot, but it was more hazardous. Conditions were slick and

Prospectors gather their gear in preparation for their hike up the steep Chilkoot Pass to the Klondike gold fields in the Alaska Territory in the late 1890s. © CORBIS.

narrow. Thousands of pack animals died on that trail. It became known as "Dead Horse Trail." By 1900, a railroad had been built that would make the Chilkoot trail useless. By that time, however, the mass rush to the Yukon was over.

If stampeders successfully made it over the passes, they were faced with a three-week trip down the Yukon River to the gold fields. After all they had been through, a boat trip may have not sounded so bad, but the river was wild with rapids. Many stampeders died or lost all of their possessions when their boats fell apart as they rode the rapids.

Other stampeders chose to ride a steamer ship for the 1,600-mile (2,500 kilometer) trip up the Yukon River. Those who chose this route often had to be rescued from ice.

However, this was the only way to reach Nome, Fairbanks, and St. Michael in Alaska.

By 1898, only thirty thousand stampeders made it to Dawson City. The reasons for not making it varied. Some gave up. Others died from disease from eating the meat of dead horses along the trail. Some died of malnutrition and exposure. Some went insane. Just three years later, the population of Dawson City dropped to nine thousand. The life of a gold miner was hard.

From Seattle, Washington, the Klondike was more than 1,000 miles (1,609 kilometers) away. Add to that the miles traveled by each stampeder to get to Seattle, and that is how long the journey was. Although other cities in Washington promoted themselves as departure points for the

Supply List from the Chilkoot Trail

Here is a list that pioneer Edmonton outfitters McDougall and Secord designed for stampeders heading off to the Chilkoot Trail in 1898. Each person was required to carry these general supplies:

2 suits heavy knit underwear

100 lbs. navy beans

6 pairs wool socks

150 lbs. bacon

1 pairs heavy moccasins

400 lbs. flour

2 pairs German stockings (stockings that were knit and then shrunk to be airtight)

40 lbs. rolled oats

2 heavy flannel overshirts

20 lbs. corn meal

1 heavy woollen sweater

10 lbs. rice

1 pair overalls

25 lbs. sugar

2 pairs 12-lb. blankets

10 lbs. tea

1 waterproof blanket

20 lbs. coffee

1 dozen bandana handkerchiefs

10 lbs. baking powder

1 stiff brim cowboy hat

20 lbs. salt

1 pair hip rubber boots

1 lb. pepper

1 pair prospectors' high land boots

2 lbs. baking soda

1 mackinaw, coat, pants, shirt

½ lb. mustard

1 pair heavy buck mitts, lined

¼ lb. vinegar

1 pair unlined leather gloves

2 doz. condensed milk

1 duck coat, pants, vest

20 lbs. evaporated potatoes

6 towels

5 lbs. evaporated onions

1 pocket matchbox, buttons, needles and thread

6 tins/4 oz. extract beef

comb, mirror, toothbrush etc.

75 lbs. evaporated fruits

mosquito netting/1 dunnage bag

4 pkgs. yeast cakes

1 sleeping bag/medicine chest

20 lbs. candles

pack saddles, complete horses

1 pkg. tin matches

flat sleighs

6 cakes borax

6 lbs. laundry soap

½ lb. ground ginger

25 lbs. hard tack

1 lb. citric acid

2 bottles jamaica ginger

"KLONDIKE GOLD RUSH, YUKON TERRITORY 1897." *ADVENTURE LEARNING FOUNDATION.* HTTP://WWW.QUESTCONNECT.ORG/ AK_KLONDIKE.HTM (ACCESSED ON JUNE 7, 2006).

Thousands of prospectors converge in 1898 at the base of Chilkoot Pass in Canada's Yukon Territory to pack their gear in preparation for their hike toward the Klondike gold fields. © CORBIS.

Klondike, the overwhelming majority left from Seattle.

Now what? Getting to the Klondike and Alaska was just half the battle. Once stampeders reached their destination, they needed to establish a home. They found flat land in places such as Nome, Alaska, and Dawson City in the Yukon. Here they quickly set up tents while they built shacks. They built general stores, saloons, and eateries. These towns became known as boomtowns. Some boomtowns lasted

only weeks. Once it was discovered that an area did not provide gold, miners moved on to the next place. The boomtown was left behind and quickly disappeared.

If miners thought the journey to the Klondike was rough, they may have been surprised that panning for gold was so difficult. Gold was not lying just beneath the water, ready to be scooped up. Most was at least 10 feet (3 meters) below the surface. To get it, miners had to dig through permafrost (a layer of ground that is always frozen). Before being able to dig, they had

A prospector pans for gold in the Klondike. © BETTMANN/CORBIS.

to thaw the ice. Then the miners used a sluice (a wooden trough for washing gold) to separate dirt from the gold. Miners could dig only in summer, when temperatures were warmer. The work was hard, and not always rewarding.

Empty promises, broken dreams Only the early gold miners—known as the Klondike Kings—made their fortune in the Klondike and Alaska regions. It has been estimated that those few men found over one billion dollars in gold (according to today's standards). Friedrich (Fred) Trump (1869–1918), the grandfather of

businessman Donald Trump (1946–), made his fortune running a hotel along the Chilkoot trail. Some of the women who joined in the gold rush made healthy profits running dance halls. Others earned good money by opening laundries, restaurants, or hotels.

For the majority of the stampeders, by the time they arrived, most of the creeks had been claimed. Those men who stayed on soon found themselves working for the Klondike Kings. Although they were paid anywhere from $1 to $10 a day (a decent wage in those days), they realized they were not going to amass the fortunes of

Women of the Rush

Men were not the only people to make the journey to the north. In fact, one of every ten people to join the gold rush was a woman. A number of them found their fortune, either by finding gold or working in other professions. Some found wealthy husbands during the rush.

Women trekked north as miners, teachers, writers, shopkeepers, medical professionals, cooks, entertainers, and prostitutes. Many owned and ran hotels throughout the mining towns of the Yukon. One such woman was Belinda Mulrooney (1872–1967). She headed to Dawson City in 1897 at the age of twenty-five. Mulrooney built the Grand Forks Hotel where the Yukon's Eldorado and Bonanza Creeks met. The hotel was an immediate success, and Mulrooney invested her profits in mining claims. In 1898, she built a first-class hotel, the Fairview, in Dawson City.

By the end of that first year, Mulrooney expanded her business and established a tele-phone company in Dawson City and Grand Forks. She also set up a water delivery company in Dawson City.

Mulrooney's story is unusual, but it is not the only one of its kind stemming from the gold rush. Women changed the boomtown way of life by bringing to the wilderness some aspects of life the miners had left behind. Women were responsible for establishing libraries, restaurants, churches, and families. Women also provided the men with encouragement and humor when their spirits were low.

If not for women, historians would know much less about the Klondike gold rush than what they know now. Although some men kept journals, women were more likely to keep diaries and recorded weather conditions, physical descriptions of camps and towns, and lively interpretations of life during the gold rush.

which they had dreamed. Working for the Klondike Kings was not why these stampeders made the treacherous six-month journey. Thinking they would have better luck in Nome, most of Dawson City packed its bags and left. Life in Nome was no better, however. By 1914, the Alaska-Klondike gold rush was over.

When curiosity becomes a way of life

Every day, people of great intelligence are born. Every day, people with a heightened sense of curiosity are born. Wilbur Wright (1871–1948) and Orville Wright (1867–1912) were brothers whose lives were entwined until death. Their flying machines and first successful flight in 1903 ensured their place in the history books.

The Wright brothers were quite different, but their personalities balanced each other. Both men were intelligent. Wilbur had an amazing memory, while Orville continually came up with new ideas and inventions. The two brothers together accomplished more than either of them likely could have as individuals. Where Wilbur used his analytical skills to figure out technical problems during the invention of the airplane, Orville's positive outlook and enthusiasm kept the pair from losing hope. They were a perfect match.

Orville Wright: the serious one Orville Wright was born on April 16, 1867, in Millville, Indiana. His father, Milton, was a minister who was against slavery and supportive of the outlawing of alcohol. The elder Wright gave all his children—four sons and one daughter—a sense of morality and strength of character that served them well throughout life. Orville's mother was also devoted to the church. Unlike most women of her time, Susan Wright had attended college. She had a mechanical mind and used her talent to make toys for her children. She even built small appliances for her home. When Orville or Wilbur needed advice for their inventions, they turned to their mother.

Orville Wright excelled in his school studies. In his senior year of high school, Orville and his family moved to Dayton, Ohio, for reasons related to Milton's position in the church. Orville did not graduate. He took preparatory classes at a high school in Dayton with the plan of studying at Yale and becoming a teacher.

In 1885, tragedy imposed itself upon the life of Orville Wright. The young Wright sustained an injury during an ice hockey game. His face and teeth eventually healed, but he was left with digestive disorders and a heart condition that would linger throughout his life. Orville became a withdrawn and depressed man. He gave up his plans for Yale and isolated himself from the world. He spent most of his time caring for his sick mother, who was dying from tuberculosis, a common bacterial infection. He remained devoted to her until her death in 1889.

A practical joker among his few close friends, Orville was a private and shy man with strangers. As life progressed and the Wright brothers found fame, Wilbur was the one to represent and then speak for them in public.

Wilbur Wright: the dreamer Wilbur Wright joined the family on August 19, 1871. Even as a young child he would take apart toys and machines in an effort to find out how they worked. Unlike his older brother Orville, Wilbur was impulsive, not given to thinking things through before jumping in. Accounts portray him as a perfect example of the nutty inventor, with several projects going on at once, ideas striking him in the middle of the night.

He also differed from his brother in how well he performed in school. With a mind every bit as sharp as Orville's, Wilbur was unable to focus on school work. He frequently got into mischief, and teachers complained that he did not apply himself to his full ability. He had the brains, but his interests were elsewhere. He did improve in high school, but he chose college preparatory classes for the junior year curriculum. This choice prevented him from qualifying for his diploma his senior year, so he decided to skip attending that year altogether. Wilbur Wright never graduated from high school. Neither brother suffered from their lack of formal education. They both spent much of their life in private study.

Whereas the two older Wright brothers, Reuchlin and Lorin, married and had families of their own, Wilbur, Orville, and their younger sister Katharine had an unspoken agreement between the three of them. They never had an interest in finding a mate, but chose to live their lives together. Only Katharine would break the pact, when she left Orville in 1926 to marry.

As brothers often do Wilbur and Orville lived as a team from the time they could communicate with one another. As noted on the Franklin Institute Web site, Wilbur was quoted as saying in

1912, "From the time we were little children my brother Orville and myself lived together. We usually owned all of our toys in the common [together], talked over our thoughts and aspirations [dreams] so that nearly everything that was done in our lives has been the result of conversations, suggestions and discussion between us."

The brothers also argued a lot. Wilbur called this "scrapping," and these intense discussions were an important part of the creative process when it came to inventing. The Wright children grew up in a home where intelligence was valued. Every one of the five siblings had a strong self-confidence. To be able to defend one's beliefs with passion helped Orville and Wilbur understand each other's perspective on any given project.

How it all began In 1878, Milton Wright gave Wilbur and Orville a toy helicopter. Designed by a French aviation enthusiast, the helicopter was powered by a rubber band. The brothers immediately began working on making copies of it in various sizes. They played with the toys for days, then moved on to the next activity. The brothers never forgot their introduction to flying machines, however.

Orville's first serious technical interest was printing. His father's office was in the same building as the United Brethren Printing Establishment. Orville enjoyed freedom in the printing office and his interest developed into a serious hobby. In 1888, and with young Wilbur's help, Orville built an even bigger printing press and began accepting jobs. This was the first time "the Wright brothers" would appear in print. Over the years, they took on numerous small printing jobs, including a small school newspaper called the *Midget,* pamphlets, and several local newspapers.

In 1889, the brothers published their own weekly newspaper. The *West Side News* gave Wilbur and Orville the chance to solidify their working relationship. The two men realized at this point that they could run a serious business if they collaborated and drew on each other's strengths. By the third issue, Wilbur was listed as the paper's editor and Orville was the publisher.

The Wright brothers sold their printing business ten years later to pursue a new dream—building bicycles.

Cashing in on the bike craze American consumers developed an interest in bicycles in the late 1880s. The English safety bike was introduced to the States in 1887. The safety bike had two wheels of equal size and was much easier to ride than the original high-front-wheel and low-back-wheel model. More people could enjoy bike riding than ever before. At the peak of the bike craze in the 1890s, more than three hundred bicycle companies were manufacturing more than one million bicycles a year.

Wilbur and Orville Wright opened a bicycle rental and repair shop in 1893 in Dayton. This was the perfect outlet to satisfy their mechanical interests. Although they did not know it then, the knowledge and practice they obtained through their work on bikes would be invaluable to them in their pursuit of building an airplane. The brothers were able to make a good living with their shop, and they became known throughout the community as trustworthy businessmen.

The Wright Cycle Company operated out of five separate locations throughout Dayton between 1893 and 1897. Competition was stiff by the mid-1890s; more than twenty-four bike repair shops had sprung up in the city. Orville and Wilbur decided to branch out into bicycle sales. They began carrying more than a dozen brands, but even this expansion did not seem to satisfy the two entrepreneurs.

The brothers began designing and building their own line of bicycles, which they offered to the public in 1896. Unlike the competition, the Wrights built their bicycles by hand, with the help of Ed Sines, who had assisted them in the day-to-day operations of their previous printing business. This traditional means of production gave the Wrights' bikes a certain appeal the other, more "modern" manufactured bikes were lacking.

Between 1896 and 1900, the peak years saw the Wrights building three hundred bicycles a year and earning between $2,000 and $3,000 annually. Today, only five bikes built by the Wright Cycle Company are known to exist.

Take to the Skies The Wrights moved their bike company one last time in 1897. The building was at 1127 West Third Street. Within a few years, they were involved in aerodynamics and began building experimental aircraft. They built the plane that made the first successful flight in 1903 in this bike shop.

The connection between building bicycles and inventing airplanes is not obvious, but a magazine article published in 1896 discussed the similarities between biking and flying. James Howard Means published the article "Wheeling and Flying" in his journal, *Aeronautical Annual*. The article stated that balance and control are of the utmost importance in both activities. It discussed the need for lightweight, yet strong, structures and chain-and-sprocket transmission systems (the same system used on bicycles, in which a chain moves around a toothed wheel) to propel the structure. The article maintained that wind resistance and the shape of the rider affected the success of the flight.

Given the brothers' mechanical ability, curiosity, and unceasing quest for knowledge, it should not be surprising that they began experimenting with aeronautics. Beginning in 1899, they used their bike shop to build and research aircraft. Although the men have been credited with genius for their invention, researchers and scientists through the ages have been in awe not only of the result (the first airplane) but also of the research process implemented by Wilbur and Orville. Their research and evaluation methods remain an important part of the aeronautical industry today.

From theory to reality Orville and Wilbur began by studying everything they could find on aeronautics. Wilbur wrote a letter to the Smithsonian Institution on May 30, 1899, expressing his interest in researching and learning all he could about flight. He closed the letter with a request for any materials or resources the institution might be able to share with him.

After thorough research, Orville and Wilbur decided it would be best to test their ideas using full-sized gliders. By studying how aerodynamics would affect such a simple machine, they figured they could slowly evolve their design, step-by-step. It would prove to be an excellent decision.

Eventually, the duo was able to reduce the known obstacles to flight to three broad points: wings, a way to balance and control the craft, and a means to propel it.

At this stage in their experiments, their knowledge of bicycles came in handy. Like an airplane, a bicycle is an unstable structure, but can be controlled. The brothers figured the same theory would apply to an airplane. They initially thought they could control the plane with a system of gears and pivoting shafts. Unfortunately, the sheer weight of such mechanisms would keep the plane from getting off the ground. Together they came up with the idea of wing-warping.

Wing-warping was a technique that twisted the wings so that the wing on one side of the plane would meet the oncoming airflow at a greater angle than that on the other side. The plane would rise on that side. By twisting the wings to various degrees, the plane could be controlled and balanced.

Wilbur tested the theory using a kite the brothers built in 1899. The wing-warping concept proved to be a sound theory in reality. Orville and Wilbur went back to the design table to build a glider. This was a huge step; building a small kite is one thing, but building an aircraft that will carry a man into the sky is another.

When complete, the glider weighed 52 pounds (24 kilograms) and had a wing span of 17 feet (5.2 meters). The Wrights wanted to build part of the wings with spruce, but they had to settle for pine because that is what was available. Pine is a soft, light wood, not ideal for aircraft structure, but it would have to do. The framework was covered with a sateen fabric (a midweight, strong material).

The future of aerodynamics was found at Kitty Hawk Now the brothers needed a place to test the glider, a place with wide open spaces and steady winds. They settled on a small fishing village in North Carolina called Kitty Hawk. The winds in Kitty Hawk proved to be even stronger than the brothers planned. They sent whirlwinds of sand through the air at any and all times of the day. According to the Smithsonian National Air and Space Museum Web site, Orville wrote in 1900, "We came down here for wind and sand, and we have got them.... The sand is the greatest thing in Kitty Hawk, and soon will be the only thing."

Wilbur and Orville took turns piloting the glider during the test flights at Kitty Hawk. This gave them both much-needed experience manning the craft. Repeated flights gave them the information necessary to take back to the drawing table when it came time to make the next new-and-improved aircraft.

The 1901 Wright glider had problems. When the Wrights returned to Kitty Hawk that year, the new glider performed worse than the first one. At least they could control the 1900 glider; this new one was erratic. Although they experienced glides of more than 300 feet (90 meters), the brothers were discouraged. They questioned the data they had collected from the 1900 tests. Instead of having only lift problems, they now had to rethink their method of control.

When Orville and Wilbur went over the old data yet again, they realized something. Some of the numbers were solid and would not change; they were measurements rather than calculations. Since they knew they had measured correctly, they were sure of the accuracy of those numbers, but they had been using other researchers' equations and formulas to figure some of the information, such as lift and drag (how high the craft would go, and the degree of wind resistance). Maybe they were relying on faulty research.

Orville Wright flies a glider over Kill Devil Hills, North Carolina, in October 1911. © BETTMANN/CORBIS.

Further research (using bicycles) led the brothers to conclude that the equations they had been using from other researchers' work were, indeed, inaccurate. They built a large wind tunnel in 1901 and tested their theories. What they learned in their wind-tunnel experiments solved their problems regarding balance and lift. They were still left with the question of control.

The Wrights built one more glider. They first flew it as a kite, just as before. The results were impressive; the lift and balance problems were gone. It was time to man the glider. Again, they took turns piloting. The Wrights had added a fixed vertical rudder (steering

mechanism) to the tail of the craft. This addition took care of the issue of control by giving the inventors a means to change the course of travel horizontally as well as vertically.

The Wright brothers had designed a three-axis control system: They already had achieved balance and pitch control, and the rudder gave them lateral control. In its final flying form, this 1902 glider was actually the invention of the first airplane. It was the first fully controllable aircraft ever built and flown.

Orville and Wilbur were encouraged by the success of their 1902 glider. It was not enough to have broken all records and made history with their aeronautical research. They set their sights on building the first engine-powered airplane.

The Wrights spent most of 1903 researching ideas for powering the plane. The engine they built was simple, even by the standards of their day. The two propellers were impressive. The Wrights built them to spin in opposite directions at the same time. The propellers were 8 feet (2.4 meters) in diameter and 1 inch (2.5 centimeters) thick. The propellers were powered by a chain-and-sprocket transmission system, inspired by what the brothers knew of the mechanics of bicycles.

The Wright brothers returned to Kitty Hawk in September 1903. Almost immediately, things started to go wrong, making the men question the sanity of their plan to take to the air. The weather was exceptionally bad, and they were experiencing technical difficulties with the airplane. They forged on, and on December 14, set out to test the 152-pound (69-kilogram) plane. They flipped a coin to determine who would fly first. Wilbur climbed aboard. The plane was airborne for just 3½ seconds before it crashed into the sand.

Three days later, the damage was repaired and the brothers set out to test the plane again. Orville sat in the pilot's seat this time. He kept the plane in the air for twelve seconds before it came to rest in the sand. It had flown a distance of 120 feet (3.7 meters). History had been made; a human had maintained flight for a significant amount of time that did not end with a crash.

They made three more flights that day. Wilbur made the longest flight on the final run. The plane was in the air for 59 seconds and flew 852 feet (260 meters). The world of aviation and aeronautics was changed forever.

Just after that final flight, a gust of wind caused the plane to roll over. It was so seriously damaged that it never flew again. It took three years for the Wrights to obtain a patent, but on May 22, 1906, U.S. Patent 821,393 was granted to Orville and Wilbur Wright. Due to a mix-up, the patent was given to the 1902 glider rather than the 1903 airplane. This would cause many patent infringements (violation of owners' rights) in the future.

Practical applications of the airplane The Wright brothers achieved their goal of inventing the first powered airplane, but it was not a practical plane. If they were to sell their planes, they had to design and build crafts that could be used in terrains other than wide, sandy spaces. So they set to work and built two more airplanes. By 1905, they were done building experimental aircraft. On October 5, Wilbur flew their latest plane for 39 minutes. He circled a field thirty times and flew a distance of 24.5 miles (39.4 kilometers).

Life without Wilbur Wilbur Wright, always the more fragile of the two brothers, died of typhoid fever (a bacterial disease concentrated in the bloodstream) in 1912. He was forty-five years old. Orville sold the Wright Company in 1916 and returned to the business of inventing. He built himself an aeronautics lab and became a member of the National Advisory Committee for Aeronautics (NACA). Wright remained a member for 28 years, until his death from a heart attack in 1948. Ten years later, NACA became NASA (the National Aeronautics and Space Administration).

Invention without adventure

Gold miners led adventurous lives, but the majority of them did not end up with results that

Aviator Wilbur Wright flies in his airplane over France in 1908. © BETTMANN/CORBIS.

showed their hard work and sacrifice. Then there were people like the Wright brothers, whose inventions included adventure. Without the life-endangering first flights those two men made, the first occurrence of humans in flight may not have taken place for several more years.

While the gold rush and the first successful flight represent the spirit of the Gilded Age and the Progressive Era, they were not the norm. Many inventions made during that time did not involve risk-taking.

What is that ringing? On March 10, 1876, Alexander Graham Bell (1847–1922) invented the telephone. He was just twenty-nine years old. Bell and his assistant, Thomas Watson (1854–1934), had been experimenting with sound in hopes of improving the telegraph. Already in use for thirty years, the telegraph sent one message at a time using a series of dots and dashes called Morse code. The telegraph worked properly, but Bell felt it would be more effective to have a system that allowed more than one message to be sent at a time, and

Alexander Graham Bell (left) and assistant Thomas Watson examine the first telephone. © CORBIS.

one that did not rely on typing out (and understanding) Morse code.

Bell was born into a family of men who were trained in elocution (the study of proper speaking in terms of voice control and sound). Having been trained to follow in their footsteps, Bell had a solid understanding of how sound is made and travels. This knowledge contributed to his success in inventing the telephone.

Bell and Watson knew that all they needed to do was find a way to transmit sound electrically. They built a transmitter capable of varying electronic currents and a receiver that would mimic these variations in frequencies human ears could hear. The first telephone was built, and Bell's notebooks from the experiment recall the first words ever spoken through a telephone: "Mr. Watson, come here, I want to see you."

The telephone changed the way the world communicated. Distance between people no longer mattered. Life became easier. By 1884, long-distance calls could be made between Boston, Massachusetts, and New York, New York. By 1892, long-distance service was available between New York and Chicago, a distance of 800 miles (1,287 kilometers).

Shedding light on an age-old debate Many people credit Thomas Edison (1847–1931) with the invention of the electric lightbulb. Although he is one of the most successful inventors in the world (with more than one thousand patents), he did not invent the lightbulb. In fact, most of his inventions were not original, but were improvements on devices already in existence.

What Edison did invent is the electric lamp, or incandescent lightbulb. This was an improvement over the lightbulb invented in 1854 by Heinrich Göbel (1818–1893). Göbel's lightbulb used a bamboo filament to get its light. The filament is the fiber within the lightbulb that glowed and provided light. Bamboo was used because it was lightweight and, at the time, maintained its light for what was considered a reasonable length of time. Within five years of experimentation, his bulb lasted for up to four hundred hours and was considered the first practical bulb. Edison's bulb used a carbon filament heated with electricity and lasted for up to one thousand hours.

In 1878, Edison established the Edison Electric Light Company in New York City. He made the first public demonstration of incandescent lighting on December 31, 1879, in New Jersey. His contribution revolutionized society. These bulbs required a central electric utility system, and soon the electric industry was born. This industry created entirely new employment opportunities for thousands of people. Ships, a primary mode of transportation, could now have electric lighting installed. Night-time no longer meant a decline in activity, or even productivity. Seemingly overnight, street lights

sprang up, and electric trolley cars took over the streets.

Who invented the radio? Nikola Tesla (1856–1943) was born in Croatia in 1856. In 1883, he designed an induction motor, which is a motor that operates on the principle of a rotating magnetic field. Tesla immigrated to America in 1884. He landed on the shores of New York with four cents in his pocket and a letter of recommendation from Charles Batchelor (1845–1910), an associate of Thomas Edison's. The letter read: "My Dear Edison: I know two great men and you are one of them. The other is this young man!"

Tesla initially worked with Edison in New Jersey. The two inventors came from different backgrounds and had very different work habits. These differences ultimately led to conflict. Tesla resigned from his job with Edison. Eventually, Tesla would invent the alternating current, several generators and transformers, fluorescent lighting, and the Tesla coil. His work with alternating currents actually brought him back into contact with Edison, who invented direct current. Edison favored direct current for electric power distribution. But alternating current was more efficient. Direct current required more power lines. Alternating current could transform the electricity into lower or higher voltage without extra lines. Tesla sold the rights of his alternating-current machinery to George Westinghouse (1846–1914) in 1885. The alternating current system became the industry standard and is still used today.

In 1895, Tesla was able to transmit a signal 50 miles (80 kilometers). He did this using his Tesla coil, which was used to magnify the incoming electrical energy. This was the first example of wireless communication. Unfortunately, Tesla's

lab burned to the ground before he was able to publicly demonstrate his discovery.

In the meantime, an Italian inventor named Guglielmo Marconi (1874–1937) had been working on his own wireless transmission system. He took out the first wireless telegraphy patent in England in 1896. Tesla applied for his own radio patent in 1897. The patents were granted in 1900. Marconi's first American patent was turned down that same year. He kept applying for the next three years, but was refused due to Tesla's patent.

Patents do not guarantee an inventor's rights are safe. In 1900, Marconi Wireless Telegraph Company stock jumped from $3 a share to $22 dollars a share. Suddenly, Marconi was famous throughout the world. Edison and millionaire industrialist Andrew Carnegie (1835–1919) invested in Marconi's business. On December 12, 1901, Marconi transmitted and received radio signals across the Atlantic Ocean. Even then, Tesla was not concerned. Although Marconi was using seventeen of Tesla's patents, Tesla knew he owned the patent on the first radio.

In a surprising move, the U.S. Patent Office reversed its previous decision and gave Marconi the patent for the invention of radio. No official explanation for this reversal has ever been given. Many believed the financial backing of Edison and Carnegie influenced the change.

Tesla was furious when Marconi won the 1911 Nobel Prize for the invention of the radio. He sued Marconi's company but had no money to take the case to court. A few months after Tesla's death in 1943, the U.S. Supreme Court reinstated Tesla's patent. Tesla was the true inventor of the radio. But even today, many people credit Marconi.

Kodak: "You press the button, we do the rest"

In 1888, George Eastman (1854–1932) introduced the first simple camera. His goal, according to his biography on *Kodak.com,* was to make photography "as convenient as the pencil."

Eastman was a New York high-school dropout. As a child from a poor family, he realized the need to work to help support his fatherless family, which included a mother and two sisters. Eastman went to work at the age of fourteen. His job as a messenger boy for an insurance firm paid him $3 a week. Not satisfied with the pay or the job, he took his services to another insurance company, where he began writing policies when not delivering messages. His pay increased to $5 a week. Eastman moved up the corporate ladder, and in 1874 was hired as a junior clerk, a position that earned him $15 a week.

When he was twenty-four years old, Eastman was planning a vacation. A friend suggested he take pictures to memorialize the trip. Eastman bought a camera and all the heavy equipment that went with it. The equipment was stunningly impractical; the camera alone was the size of a microwave oven. The outfit included wet plates, chemicals, glass tanks, and other items. Eastman never took that vacation, but he became determined to simplify the photography process.

It took three years of working nights to develop a formula to make gelatin emulsion, the chemicals that allow film to develop. In the past, the chemicals had to be carried around with the camera (hence, all the heavy equipment), and film was developed using wet plates. Eastman's formula used dry plates, which were coated with a gelatin that allowed photos to be safely processed at a later date (as opposed to having to process them at the time they were taken), and he invented the machine to manufacture those plates.

In 1880, Eastman rented an office in New York and began making dry plates to sell to photographers. The plates were made of glass, and because the process was still so new, those plates often failed to work once photographers bought them. The defect was not actually in the plates themselves, but in the gelatin emulsion that covered them. The emulsion was what made the images able to be processed into photographs. Because Eastman was still trying to perfect the balance of chemicals in that dry emulsion, the emulsion recipe sometimes was imbalanced and failed to develop the photos. Eastman nearly went broke making sure he replaced bad plates with working ones. But his integrity and ethics earned him a reputation as a solid, honest businessman.

Soon, Eastman began trying to find a lighter support than glass. He experimented with different types of film paper and was finally satisfied with paper that had the gelatin emulsion already on it. With this style of paper, he had eliminated the need to carry around the messy, heavy chemicals. He also invented the roll holder, which was similar to the mechanism that holds a roll of toilet paper in place. The roll holder was used instead of the glass plates to hold the film in place, and its invention made carrying and using the equipment and camera much easier because the whole system was lighter and more portable. His roll holder was an immediate success, but now he needed to find a way to get his product to the general public. Up to that point, only professional photographers took photos.

Eastman was a believer in the power of advertising, and he began to promote his products with ads he wrote himself. He first used the slogan, "You press the button, we do the rest" when he introduced his own camera design to the world in 1888. Within a year, the public was familiar with the phrase.

The name Kodak had absolutely no meaning to anyone; in fact, it was not even a real name. Eastman's favorite letter was K; he felt it was a strong letter. He wanted a name that began and ended with K. After much experimenting with various combinations of letters, he came up with Kodak. Eastman also chose the bright yellow color still used in the company's advertising and logo today.

Assembly line: simple idea, radical results The world of industry was forever changed in 1913, the year Henry Ford invented the assembly line. As is often the case with inventions, one might wonder why it took so long for anyone to come up with the idea of the assembly line. It is a logical way to build something.

Henry Ford was born July 30, 1863, in Michigan. Although he was born into a farming family, he showed an early interest in all things mechanical. He left home at the age of sixteen to work as an apprentice (student assistant) for a machinist in Detroit. In 1888, he married and supported his family by running a sawmill.

Ford took a job with the Edison Illuminating Company in Detroit in 1891. He began as an engineer and was promoted to chief engineer just two years later. During this time, he began spending his free hours experimenting with internal combustion engines. In 1896, he invented the Quadricycle. This vehicle had four large bicycle-like wheels, was steered with a system like that in a boat, and had two forward speeds.

Pleased with his progress, Ford established the Ford Motor Company in 1903. He was the

An assembly line at Ford Motor Company in March 1928. © HULTON ARCHIVE/GETTY IMAGES.

company's vice president and chief engineer. Ford introduced the Model T car five years later (see Chapter 8). Only two or three cars were made each day at the Ford plant. Small groups of men would work on each car using components purchased from outside manufacturers. It was not an efficient way to build vehicles.

The Model T changed the way America lived. Ford's cars were selling faster than he could build them, so he moved his factory to a bigger plant in the Detroit suburb of Highland Park, in 1910.

Ford was the first industrialist to manufacture interchangeable and standardized parts. He eventually made many models of automobiles, but many of the parts in each model were the same as those in other models. By making one part to fit all cars, Ford was able to lower the cost of his autos, thus making them more affordable for more consumers.

In keeping with that efficient spirit, Ford invented the assembly line. Workers stood in one place while a moving belt carried each car along. Every worker was responsible for incorporating one part onto the automobile. Parts were delivered to each worker by a carefully timed conveyor belt so that assembly was smooth and efficient. Again, this invention allowed Ford to lower the cost of his cars because it now took less time to assemble each one. Soon, he was the largest car manufacturer in the world.

Biology and life science advancements

The Gilded Age and the Progressive Era are remembered not only for their societal attitudes and philosophies, but also for the rapid gains made in a relatively short time period. In addition to the major inventions of the Wrights, Bell, Edison, Tesla, Eastman, and Ford, great strides were made in biology and the life sciences. A few examples follow.

- Biologist Jacob Loeb (1859–1924) was nicknamed "Dr. Frankenstein" for his belief that life could be engineered, or made by human hands. He experimented with parthenogenesis, a process that involves stimulating an egg to become an organism without fertilization. Loeb publicly declared that life could one day be created in a test tube. In 1978, Loeb's prediction came true with the first successful birth of a test-tube baby. A test-tube baby is a baby born from an egg that was fertilized in a test tube rather than in the mother's womb (the egg would be implanted into the womb at a later date).

- In 1900, Austrian psychologist Sigmund Freud (1856–1939) published *On the Interpretation of Dreams*. This text discussed the theory that human behavior is based on the unconscious mind. Freud believed that while people may repress (hold

back from consciousness) unpleasant thoughts or feelings, they never get rid of them entirely. Those thoughts show up in the unconscious mind and come back to the person as dreams. Freud's theory was controversial because he believed most suppressed thoughts (thoughts concealed from oneself) revolved around sex.

- Albert Einstein (1879–1955) introduced his special theory of relativity in 1905. This theory states that the speed of light stays constant in a vacuum, regardless of the light source or the observer. It also says that mass and energy are always equal. The special theory of relativity is the foundation of modern physics.

- On March 1, 1909, Robert Peary (1856–1920) of the U.S. Navy set off for the North Pole with 23 men, 133 dogs, and 19 sleds. Peary was convinced that the North Pole was not part of Greenland, as popularly believed, but actually lay beyond that region. As they traveled north, the explorers lightened their load and reduced the number of men in their party. When Peary reached the North Pole on April 6, 1909, only five men remained with him. Upon returning to the United States, Peary was dumbfounded to learn that a man named Frederick Cook (1865–1940) was claiming to have reached the North Pole a full year before Peary's expedition. The American public was not sure who to believe until two Eskimos who had made the Arctic journey with Cook revealed that his photographic "evidence" had been faked. Peary truly was the first man to reach the North Pole.

For More Information

BOOKS AND PERIODICALS

Bankston, John. *Henry Ford and the Assembly Line.* Bear, DE: Mitchell Lane Publishers, 2004.

Coe, Brian. *Kodak Cameras: The First Hundred Years.* West Sussex, England: Hove Books, 2003.

Duncan, Sandy Frances. *Gold Rush Orphan.* Vancouver, BC, Canada: Ronsdale Press, 2004.

Means, James Howard. "Wheeling and Flying." *Aeronautical Annual* (1896).

Murphy, Claire Rudolf, and Jane G. Haigh. *Children of the Gold Rush.* Portland, OR: Alaska Northwest Books, 2001.

Murphy, Claire Rudolf, and Jane G. Haigh. *Gold Rush Dogs.* Anchorage: Alaska Northwest Books, 2001.

Murphy, Claire Rudolf, and Jane G. Haigh. *Gold Rush Women.* Anchorage: Alaska Northwest Books, 1997.

Stewart, Daniel Blair. *Tesla, the Modern Sorcerer.* Berkeley, CA: North Atlantic Books, 1999.

WEB SITES

"Alaska's Gold." *Alaska State Library.* http://www.library.state.ak.us/goldrush/ (accessed on June 8, 2006).

"As Precious as Gold." *National Postal Museum.* http://www.postalmuseum.si.edu/gold/asprecious.html (accessed on June 8, 2006).

Cyber Telephone Museum. http://www.museumphones.com/ (accessed on June 8, 2006).

"George Eastman—the Man." *Kodak.* http://www.kodak.com/US/en/corp/kodakHistory/eastmanTheMan.shtml (accessed on June 8, 2006).

"The Klondike Gold Rush." *University of Washington Libraries Digital Collections.* http://content.lib.washington.edu/goldrush/ (accessed on June 9, 2006).

"Klondike Gold Rush Yukon Territory 1897." *Adventure Learning Foundation.* http://www.questconnect.org/ak_klondike.htm (accessed on June 9, 2006).

"The Life of Henry Ford." *The Henry Ford.* http://www.hfmgv.org/exhibits/hf/default.asp#top (accessed on June 9, 2006).

"Literature of the Gold Rush." *National Postal Museum.* http://www.postalmuseum.si.edu/gold/literature.html (accessed on June 9, 2006).

PBS. "Robert Peary: To the Top of the World." *American Experience: Alone on the Ice.* http://www.pbs.org/wgbh/amex/ice/sfeature/peary.html (accessed on June 9, 2006).

PBS. *Tesla: Master of Lighting.* http://www.pbs.org/tesla/index.html (accessed on June 9, 2006).

RobertWService.com. http://www.robertwservice.com/ (accessed on June 9, 2006).

"The Wright Brothers: The Invention of the Aerial Age." *Smithsonian National Air & Space Museum.* http://www.nasm.si.edu/wrightbrothers/ (accessed on June 9, 2006).

Progressivism Reaches the White House

When the Spanish-American War (1898) (see Chapter 7) broke out in Cuba, thirty-nine-year-old Theodore Roosevelt (1858–1919) served as commander of the First U.S. Volunteer Cavalry, a unit better known as the Rough Riders. (The Spanish-American War occurred because Cuba wanted independence from Spanish rule; the United States fought on the side of Cuba and beat Spain within three months.) Roosevelt had left his job with the navy to join the cavalry, which included more than twelve hundred men of all backgrounds from New Mexico, Arizona, Oklahoma, and other western states.

Teddy Roosevelt and the Rough Riders

Roosevelt and Colonel Leonard Wood (1860–1927) trained their volunteers so well that the regiment, or unit, was allowed to engage in battle, something not all volunteer units experienced. They formed in Texas and shipped out to Cuba on June 14, 1898. Ironically, though they were called Rough Riders, they fought mainly on foot because there was no room for their horses on the ship to Cuba.

The Rough Riders landed in Cuba on June 22 and saw their first battle two days later. Their next assignment was to join trained military forces in the attack on the Spanish city of Santiago on July 1. Roosevelt's unit, along with regular regiments and the Buffalo Soldiers (African American infantrymen), captured Kettle Hill and moved on to San Juan Heights. With Buffalo Soldiers reaching the crest of the hill first, the Rough Riders joined in the battle, and the hill was captured. Santiago surrendered soon after, and the war was over in just three months. According to historian Virgil Harrington Jones, no American unit in the Spanish-American War suffered as many casualties (deaths) as the Rough Riders, which lost 37 percent of its men before leaving Cuba.

Although the Rough Riders are often given most of the credit for the capture of San Juan Heights, the Buffalo Soldiers played a key role in that

WORDS TO KNOW

electoral votes: The votes a presidential candidate receives for having won a majority of a state's popular vote (citizens' votes). The candidate who receives the most popular votes in a particular state wins all of that state's electoral votes. Each state receives two electoral votes for its two U.S. senators and a figure for the number of U.S. representatives it has (which is determined by a state's population). A candidate must win a majority of electoral votes (over 50 percent) in order to win the presidency.

imperialism: The practice of one country extending its control over the territory, political system, or economic system of another country.

Progressive Era: A period in American history (approximately the first twenty years of the twentieth century) marked by reform and the development of a national cultural identity.

Spanish-American War: A war fought in 1898 in Cuba. Cuba wanted independence from Spanish rule. The United States fought on the side of Cuba and beat Spain within three months.

trust: The concept of several companies banding together to form an organization that limits competition by controlling the production and distribution of a product or service.

---

battle. According to the General Joe Wheeler Foundation, Rough Rider Frank Knox (1874–1944) wrote of his impression: "In justice to the colored race, I must say that I never saw braver men anywhere! Some of those who rushed up the Hill will live in my memory forever."

Roosevelt returned to New York a war hero and used his popularity and status to get elected his state's governor in November 1898. He immediately set to work reforming the corrupt political system. In 1900, the Republicans chose Roosevelt as the running mate for incumbent (current) president William McKinley (1843–1901; served 1897–1901), who was running for his second term. (McKinley's first-term vice president, Garret A. Hobart, had died in November 1899.) As a campaigner, Roosevelt covered more than 21,000 miles (33,789 kilometers), and made hundreds of speeches in 567 cities and 24 states. McKinley, in contrast, gave speeches from the front porch of his home. Many historians believe Roosevelt's

popularity helped McKinley win the election (see Chapter 7). When McKinley died from an assassin's bullet on September 14, 1901, forty-two-year-old Roosevelt became the youngest president of the United States.

Roosevelt's first term in office

Roosevelt was an enthusiastic president whose friendly personality and unceasing activity made him one of the most popular presidents in American history. Roosevelt made it clear that he enjoyed being in the spotlight, and he was not afraid to speak his mind about any and all issues of the day. He was physically energetic in his speeches, often using broad gestures and waving his arms as he spoke. Roosevelt did not hesitate to share his moral judgments with anyone who would listen, and most of America loved him for it.

Roosevelt used the media and press to cultivate his popular position, and he had a flair for

Theodore Roosevelt (center front, standing to the left of the flag) and his Rough Riders on San Juan Hill in Cuba in 1898.
© BETTMANN/CORBIS.

the dramatic. His six children had complete run of the Executive Mansion, the presidential home Roosevelt renamed the White House. Stories of their antics appeared in newspapers on a regular basis. One particularly popular account told about a time when his young children led one of their many horses into the White House and gave it a ride in the elevator. Roosevelt's role as a loving father only increased his popularity, and the attention given to his family served to further endear the Roosevelts to the American public.

Reform president Although Roosevelt was forced rather abruptly into the presidency, he immediately took control. The president recognized the need for the kinds of reforms expressed in the writings of new journalists known as muckrakers (those who "rake" through "muck" are digging through dirt and filth). These writers exposed scandalous and unethical practices among established institutions in America. Some of the more famous muckrakers were Ida Tarbell (1857–1954), for her series on the Standard Oil Company; Upton Sinclair (1878–1968), for exposing the dangers and poor working conditions of the meatpacking industry in Chicago; and Lincoln Steffens (1866–1936), for his investigation of the scandals among city and state politicians. In fact, it was Roosevelt who gave these journalists their nickname in a 1906 speech. Though the president disliked the negative focus of muckraking, he believed in what the writers did because they focused on uncovering the truth.

Roosevelt believed that the government was responsible for promoting the common good of all citizens. He did not approve of the majority of economic power resting in the hands of a wealthy few. Roosevelt became known as a "trustbuster" because of his determination to break up trusts. (A trust was formed when several companies banded together to limit competition by controlling the production and distribution of a product or service.) Trusts were illegal under the 1890 Sherman Anti-Trust Act, and Roosevelt's administration began more than forty lawsuits against companies. The president was more in favor of regulating trusts than he was of dismantling them; he called the Sherman Anti-Trust act "foolish." Congress refused to enact his suggestions for federal licensing and regulation of interstate companies, which would have limited their power. The only choice Roosevelt had, then, was to enforce the Sherman Anti-Trust Act.

Roosevelt earned the somewhat misleading reputation as a trustbuster when, in 1902, he took action against both the Northern Securities Company (a railroad monopoly) and the beef trust. (In a monopoly, one company dominates a sector of business, leaving the consumer no choices and other businesses no possibility of success.) Northern Securities Company had

been established by some of the country's wealthiest businessmen: John D. Rockefeller (1839–1937), J. P. Morgan (1837–1913), James Hill (1838–1916), and Edward Harriman (1848–1909). Roosevelt ordered the Justice Department to file a suit to dissolve the company. Within a few months, the president filed suit against a Chicago meatpacking company called Swift & Company. America cheered as it watched the unethical companies struggle against the law. Roosevelt had made his point: Big business would have to deal with the federal government if it broke the law. For his hard-line stance on regulating big business—and on punishing it if the law was broken—Roosevelt became known as a "bully" activist.

The coal strike of 1902 In May 1902, coal miners in Pennsylvania went on strike (refused to work). They had tried for months to meet with management and mine owners to negotiate better pay, shorter hours, and safer working conditions. When negotiations failed, the workers refused to enter the mines.

In 1902, anthracite (hard) coal was used to fuel trains and heat houses and businesses. As spring passed into summer and then into fall, Americans became concerned that the continued strike would result in a coal shortage. Businesses would close and citizens would freeze. President Roosevelt also felt concerned, and in October he invited representatives from the miners and the coal operators to the White House. In doing so, he became the first president in history to mediate a labor strike. The meeting was called the Coal Strike Conference of 1902, and during the conference, Roosevelt expressed his concerns. The miners agreed to go back to work if they could get a small, immediate pay increase and a promise that negotiations would continue.

Theodore Roosevelt was a lover of the outdoors. This collaged photograph shows the politician superimposed on a moose.
© UNDERWOOD & UNDERWOOD/CORBIS.

The coal operators refused, despite the president's involvement.

When Roosevelt realized the strike would continue, he took direct action. He threatened to send military troops to take over operation of the mines. If this were to happen, miners and owners alike would lose money. Both sides entered into negotiations with a committee appointed by Roosevelt, and miners returned to work on October 23. They had received a 10 percent increase in wages as well as a guarantee of shorter work days.

Roosevelt's involvement in the mining dispute set a precedent (established example) of what could happen in future labor-management conflicts. The working class realized it had the support of an intelligent, influential president. Big business was all too aware that its authority was no longer limitless. Roosevelt called his program the "square deal," meaning both sides got fair treatment and consideration.

Hero of the conservation movement

Roosevelt was America's first environmentalist. Having spent his childhood sickly and often bedridden, he developed a special appreciation for the outdoors. An avid big game hunter,

Roosevelt went west in 1883. What he saw was not at all what he had imagined. The last of the big bison herds were gone, wiped out by careless hide hunters and disease. As years went by, Roosevelt became more alarmed over the state of the land and its wildlife.

Conservation became a personal interest. When Roosevelt became president, he used his power to establish 4 game preserves, 51 bird reserves, and 150 national forests. In 1902, Roosevelt signed the National Reclamation Act, which created the U.S. Reclamation Service (later renamed the U.S. Bureau of Reclamation). Reclamation is the process of altering or restoring a region or land to a healthy ecosystem. The Reclamation Act financed irrigation projects in western deserts, with a goal of making these regions inhabitable by humans. The Theodore Roosevelt Dam near Phoenix, Arizona, was one of the agency's first major projects. The dam formed Theodore Roosevelt Lake; both projects were completed in 1911.

Known by many as the Conservationist President, Roosevelt has a national park named after him in North Dakota. He is also represented in sculpture form on Mt. Rushmore in South Dakota, along with fellow presidents George Washington (1732–1799; served 1789–97), Thomas Jefferson (1743–1826; served 1801–9), and Abraham Lincoln (1809–1865; served 1861–65).

In 1903, Roosevelt passed a bill to establish the U.S. Department of Commerce and Labor. Later that year, he passed the Elkins Act, which prohibited railroad companies from giving rebates to those shippers who used their services most (see Chapter 2).

Big Stick diplomacy

Days before President McKinley was shot in 1901, Roosevelt spoke at the Minnesota State Fair. During his speech, he explained his stance on foreign policy by reciting an African proverb, "Speak softly and carry a big stick." By quoting this saying, Roosevelt expressed his belief that to be effective, one did not have to be the mightiest, but just needed the power to fight back if necessary. This philosophy became known as Big Stick diplomacy, and it was one the president embraced throughout his two terms in office.

Roosevelt proved the effectiveness of his philosophy in 1902. During that year, the Venezuelan government found itself heavily in debt to other countries. Germany, Italy, and Great Britain wanted to invade Venezuela to claim some of its territory as repayment. Roosevelt stepped in to help the countries reach an acceptable agreement, thereby avoiding war.

Election of 1904

Roosevelt knew he had come to the presidency by accident; no one had ever actually expected him to lead the country when McKinley was reelected in 1900. Armed with this knowledge, Roosevelt spent his first term strengthening his relationship with the public in both a personal and political way. When it was time to run for president on his own in 1904, Roosevelt had earned the trust of the Republican Party, including Southern African Americans. In 1901, he was the first president to invite an African American to the White House, when he had lunch with reformer Booker T. Washington (1856–1915).

The Republican Party nominated Roosevelt for president unanimously. Roosevelt was fairly certain he would win the presidency. The Republican Party (also known since 1880 as the Grand Old Party, or GOP) was the national force in politics. Roosevelt had made great efforts in

TR Firsts

Theodore Roosevelt was the first president to:

- own a car
- have a telephone in his home
- fly in an airplane
- invite an African American to the White House
- be submerged in a submarine
- travel outside the United States while in office
- win a Nobel Prize (he was also the first American to do so)

appealing to a greater ethnic base that included African Americans and immigrant populations. The Democratic Party continued to be split from within (see Chapter 7), which weakened whatever political power it had.

Although William Jennings Bryan (1860–1925) had been the Democratic candidate in the presidential elections in 1896 and 1900 (and would be again in 1908), Democrats did not nominate him for the 1904 race. Instead, they selected Alton B. Parker (1852–1926), chief judge of the New York Court of Appeals. Roosevelt and his running mate, U.S. senator Charles W. Fairbanks (1852–1918) of Indiana, did not travel extensively during the campaign. Roosevelt instead directed the campaign from the front porch of his home in Oyster Bay, New York. In addition, he turned to the some of the nation's wealthiest businessmen for funding. Edward Harriman, Henry Frick (1849–1919), and J. P. Morgan donated 70 percent of the more than $2 million raised by the Republican Party. These donations raised the ethical issue of campaign contributions by large corporations, a practice that logically gave one political party an advantage over the other (in this case, meaning the Republican Party over the Democratic Party). Within three years, Congress would prohibit contributions by national banks and corporations, but not by their officers as individuals.

Roosevelt beat Parker, 336 electoral votes to 140. Electoral votes are the votes a presidential candidate receives for having won a majority of a state's popular vote (citizens' votes). The candidate who receives the most popular votes in a particular state wins all of that state's electoral votes. Each state receives two electoral votes for its two U.S. senators and a figure for the number of U.S. representatives it has (which is determined by a state's population). A candidate must win a majority of electoral votes (over 50 percent) in order to win the presidency. Roosevelt also won the popular vote by a majority never seen in the country's history before—57.4 percent. Not only was Roosevelt the first man to be elected president on his own after serving out his deceased predecessor's term, he was viewed by many as the most popular president in history at that point. John Whiteclay Chambers II reported in his book *The Tyranny of Change* that upon learning he had won the election, Roosevelt told his wife he was "no longer a political accident."

Second term in the White House

Roosevelt became more aggressive in his domestic policy during his second term as president. Two major reforms were established, both in June 1906. On June 29, Roosevelt directed the passage of the Hepburn Act (named after U.S. representative William P. Hepburn [1833–1916] of Iowa, chairman of the Committee on Interstate and Foreign Commerce), which strengthened the Interstate Commerce Commission by adding two more members and allowing the committee to determine fair rates after complaints surfaced of a railroad shipper charging unfair rates. The Interstate Commerce Commission was established as a result of the Interstate Commerce Act, which had passed in 1887. The act demanded that all railroad shipping rates be fair and reasonable. The Commission's job was to enforce the new laws.

The other major reform applied to the food industry. One day after signing the Hepburn Act into law, Roosevelt passed the Pure Food and Drug Act. This act was designed to protect consumers from fraudulent food labeling and unsafe food. Although individual states had enacted food laws, they were difficult to enforce. Dr. Harvey Wiley (1844–1930), head of the Bureau of Chemistry in the U.S. Department of Agriculture, lobbied for stricter laws regarding food handling. Wiley enlisted the support of the more ethical food producers and drug manufacturers. Even so, his concerns were largely drowned out by the powerful Beef Trust (the five biggest meatpacking companies) as well as large pharmaceutical companies and small producers of patent medicines.

During the Spanish-American War, America experienced a beef scandal. Meat was being sent overseas to U.S. troops, and soon reports were printed claiming the beef was tainted with embalming fluid to preserve it. (Embalming fluid is what corpses are injected with to delay the decaying process.) Shortly after the war ended, muckraker Charles Edward Russell (1860–1941) wrote a serial documentary exposing the greed and corruption of the Beef Trust.

In 1906, journalist Upton Sinclair wrote the groundbreaking novel *The Jungle,* which detailed horrifying accounts of how meat was handled and processed in Chicago's meatpacking industry. With the public in an uproar over this health issue, Roosevelt signed the Pure Food and Drug Act as well as its accompanying Meat Inspection Act. The Meat Inspection Act required the U.S. Department of Agriculture to inspect all slaughtered animals to insure safety in the handling and processing of the meat. Lawbreakers could be jailed, fined, or both. These two food-related pieces of legislation were considered major efforts in progressive reform. Although the president did not introduce them, he is often given credit for doing so.

Panic of 1907 Throughout his second term, Roosevelt remained committed to ridding society of what he felt were "evil" trusts. He filed suits against DuPont, Standard Oil, American Tobacco, and New Haven Railroad. These lawsuits did nothing to improve the president's relations with the business community. The situation was only made worse with the Panic of 1907.

Several businesses and financial firms went bankrupt (declared themselves unable to pay their debts; often, this means the business closes) in the summer of 1907. In October of that year, the Knickerbocker Trust in New York and the Westinghouse Electric Company closed their doors to business, setting off what became known as the Panic of 1907. Stock market prices decreased, and people and businesses began pulling their money out of banks for fear they would lose it. Banks began closing rapidly.

In an attempt to restore order to the American economy, President Roosevelt called upon businessman J. P. Morgan for assistance. He had served in a similar role several years earlier, when President Grover Cleveland (1837–1908; served 1885–89 and 1893–97) was in office. Morgan was a financier, an investment banker who works on a grand scale with large amounts of money. Morgan called upon the best bankers and financial experts, and together the men gathered in Morgan's home. From there, they channeled money to the weaker businesses and institutions in an effort to keep them from going bankrupt. Economic conditions improved within weeks, and the crisis passed.

The Panic of 1907 led reformers from both political parties to call for change in the banking business and its procedures. Business leaders, however, blamed Roosevelt's reform legislation (such as his trust regulating), claiming it had upset the natural order of the economy. As a direct result of the panic, banking reforms and legislations were passed. The Federal Reserve System was established in 1913 and became the banking headquarters of the United States.

Foreign policy Winning the Spanish-American War made America a world power for the first time. The victory gave the United States the territories of Guam and Puerto Rico and allowed America to purchase the Philippine Islands. Taking over foreign countries and controlling their political and economic systems is known as imperialism, and Roosevelt was a firm believer in it. Many Americans disagreed. These anti-imperialists felt that imperialism was too costly and would eventually attract too many non-whites into the country.

The president preached his philosophy vigorously. "Far better is it to dare mighty things, to win glorious triumphs, even though checkered by failure, than to take rank with those poor spirits who neither enjoy nor suffer much because

they live in the grey twilight that knows neither victory nor defeat," he wrote in a collection of essays titled *The Strenuous Life* (1900).

Roosevelt dealt with foreign policy with the doctrine of "New Imperialism." Nations he personally believed were uncivilized would gain independence only once they conformed to the American model of government and democracy. The president believed in the superiority of his country's morals and history, and this belief justified America's involvement in countries with which it had little interaction. Under this direction, the United States became a sort of watchdog throughout the western half of the world. Under Roosevelt's leadership, America's empire grew to include the Philippines, Cuba, Haiti, the Dominican Republic, and Puerto Rico.

The Panama Canal

Perhaps the most famous of Roosevelt's foreign policy initiatives was the Panama Canal (a manmade waterway). For years, American naval leaders wanted to build a passage between the Atlantic and Pacific Oceans through Central America. Now that America owned territory that stretched into the Pacific, a canal took on even greater importance, as it would drastically reduce the amount of shipping and travel time.

Building of the canal across the Isthmus of Panama (then a territory of Colombia) had officially begun in 1878 by Ferdinand de Lesseps (1805–1894), the French engineer who had built the Suez Canal in Egypt. Construction came to a halt when laborers contracted tropical diseases and engineering problems arose. Even so, a French company retained rights to the project, so no one else could continue the construction. Roosevelt tried to buy those rights for $40 million. He also offered to pay $10 million for a

The Anti-Imperialist League

A bloody revolution took place in the Philippines soon after the Spanish-American War (see Chapter 7). The Philippine Insurrection occurred because Filipinos were not willing to accept America as either their landlords or their bosses. They did not want to be told how to run their country. They rebelled in what would be one of the bloodiest wars of the era. In reaction to the revolution, a small group of Americans formed the Anti-Imperialist League in 1899.

The Anti-Imperialist League was formed by men who were opposed to territorial expansion and the idea of colonialism in general. Under colonialism, a country is not permitted to make its own laws or run its own country. At the turn of the century, America was a major colonial power. The men who opposed imperialism were liberal (progressive), and many had ties to the antislavery movement.

Men such as writer Mark Twain (1835–1910) and millionaire industrialist Andrew Carnegie (1835–1919) joined the league, which is considered one of the first peace movements in history. Although the league began in Boston, it soon had a national membership of more than thirty thousand. Followers believed America could not possibly extend constitutional rights to citizens of other countries, nor could it absorb more ethnicities. It was already having difficulty dealing with the obvious racism against its African American citizens. To try to take on more at that point, they believed, would lead only to further injustice.

In 1900, the government threatened to imprison antiwar activists, which would include Anti-Imperialist League members. In addition, then-President William McKinley agreed to begin withdrawing troops from the Philippines. Those two events led to a decrease in the influence of the league. It was unable to save the Philippines from thirty years of colonial rule. By the time the war officially ended in 1902, more than two hundred thousand Filipino civilians (some historians estimate the figure as a half-million or higher) had lost their lives. Unofficially, the fighting continued well into the second decade of the twentieth century.

50-mile stretch across the isthmus, but Colombia refused. Roosevelt correctly predicted a revolution in Panama, and he sent in a naval ship and military troops to support Panama's government. When Roosevelt presented the rebels with the $10-million offer, they happily accepted, and America had total control of a 10-mile canal zone.

Thousands of workers began digging the canal. Many died of yellow fever, a disease carried by mosquitoes. Despite the disapproval of many Americans who felt Roosevelt acted in an unconstitutional manner, work continued. On August 15, 1914, the Panama Canal opened for business. In addition to building the canal, workers also constructed three railroads and a lake.

The project cost $400 million and was considered one of the world's greatest engineering projects. For ten years, thirty thousand workers, most from the West Indies, were paid 10 cents an hour for ten-hour shifts. By 1925, more than five thousand merchant ships had traveled the Panama Canal. The waterway shortened

Editorial cartoon showing Theodore Roosevelt carrying his "Big Stick" while traveling to Panama to orchestrate the building of the Panama Canal.
© BETTMANN/CORBIS.

the trip from San Francisco, California, to New York, New York, by nearly 8,000 miles (12,872 kilometers). Equally as important, the canal became a major military asset that made the United States the dominant power in Central America.

The Panama Canal remained an American asset until December 31, 1999, at which time it (and its surrounding land) was handed over to Panamanian authorities. During his presidency, Jimmy Carter (1924–; served 1977–81) signed a transfer agreement. During the twenty years between the signing of the agreement and the actual transfer, the Canal was run by a transitional committee, which was led by an American leader for the first decade and a Panamanian leader for the second. Along with the Canal, Carter offered Panama his apologies and acknowledged that although Roosevelt's vision was to be praised, the feelings of American colonialism in Panama created controversy. The agreement holds that the United States can interfere if the Canal loses its neutrality or threatens American interests in any way.

Russo-Japanese War

War erupted between Russia and Japan in 1904. Both countries had ideas for what they planned to do with Korea and Manchuria. At the time, China had control of a port in Manchuria that Russia wanted to take over. It convinced China to lease the port, which gave Russia occupation within southern Manchuria. Japan was angered over this move because Russia had forced Japan to give up its own right to be in Manchuria when Japan beat China in the Sino-Japanese War (1894–95). Then in 1896, Russia ended an alliance with China against Japan and won the rights to extend the Trans-Siberian Railroad across parts of China-controlled Manchuria. This gave Russia control of an important territory in Manchuria. Roosevelt had been expecting the conflict, and his sympathies lay with Japan. America had long wanted to put an end to Russia's plan of taking over Manchuria, and now that Japan was fighting the battle, America would not have to.

The war ended in 1905 with Japan defeating Russia's navy and overrunning Manchuria's neighbor, Korea. This defeat prohibited Russia from expanding its power in the Far East, while at the same time made Japan the first Asian power to defeat a European power. This victory suddenly made Japan a much stronger nation than it had been in the past, which concerned Roosevelt. To add further worry, Japan had already established an alliance (a partnership with another country or countries) with the powerful Great Britain in 1902. This alliance threatened the United States' desire to be the dominant superpower.

Roosevelt kept in mind the Open-Door policy the United States had with China. This policy stated that all trading nations of the world would have access to China's market. In order to keep the policy in action, he invited leaders from Japan and Russia to New Hampshire to work out a peace treaty. Japan, though victorious in its war against Russia, was in trouble financially, and both countries agreed to negotiate. Roosevelt would later be awarded the Nobel peace prize for his peacekeeping efforts. Although Roosevelt's mediation brought peace, the conference did not go quite as he had hoped. The president had to give Japan a similar position and influence in China that America demanded for itself in the Western Hemisphere. This was power he did not want to share.

In keeping with his belief that the world could be made up of great superpowers that maintained stability even as they competed, Roosevelt negotiated a secret deal with Japan in 1905 called the Taft-Katsura Agreement. This deal assured the United States that Japan had no interest in the Philippines, which had remained an important interest for America; in return, America pledged not to interfere in Japan's relations in Korea. Soon after, Korea became a Japanese protectorate (under the protection and partial control of a country).

Continued conservation reform

Roosevelt remained a dedicated environmentalist throughout his second term, and indeed, his life. By the time his presidency ended, he had placed under legal protection 230 million acres of land in the United States. He also established the U.S. Forest Service in 1905 and signed the 1906 American Antiquities Act, which allowed him to proclaim eighteen sites as national monuments. This designation gave the sites federal protection for the preservation of their natural value and importance.

A fellow conservationist named Gifford Pinchot (1865–1946; pronounced PIN-show;

see box) had been appointed chief of the Division of Forestry in 1898. Around the same time, Pinchot met and formed a friendship with Theodore Roosevelt. The men recognized in each other a common concern for and love of the land and all its resources. Both agreed that forest lands needed to be federally protected in order to keep them from being exploited (used to someone's advantage) by private interest groups. They also agreed that forests required ongoing management if they were to be sustained.

In 1905, the Division of Forestry was moved from the Department of the Interior to the Department of Agriculture and renamed the U.S. Forest Service, eventually to be known as the National Forest Service (NFS). Roosevelt appointed Pinchot the leader of the NFS, and within five years, America's forest land grew from 56 million acres to 172 million acres.

TR's positions on other issues

Roosevelt initiated many major progressive reforms while in the White House. Reform became such a big part of his reputation that the public credited him with reforms even when he did not initiate them. Controversy did not scare Roosevelt. He publicly spoke and wrote about hundreds of issues while in office, including birth control (immoral), morality, divorce (weakened the family bond), football, and even spelling (it should be made simpler.)

Roosevelt was not a champion of equality between men and women, though he did support women's suffrage (right to vote). He believed girls should be educated, becoming aware enough of world events to better the society in which they lived. He thought boys should be encouraged to use their fighting instincts to stand against injustice; cowards should be sternly punished.

On the issue of race, the president did not truly believe in equality among the races, nor did he believe African Americans could be integrated into American society. According to *AmericanPresident.org,* he agreed with the idea that they were little more than "burdens" on the white race. Whites, however, should deal with them and welcome them out of a sense of Christian duty. His racist attitudes were not limited to African Americans. He considered Asian Americans and Native Americans burdens as well.

Roosevelt's racism was evident in his everyday speech and behavior. A glaring example of it was his refusal to acknowledge the key role of the Buffalo Soldiers in the Battle of San Juan Heights. Not only did the Rough Riders leader not give the African American soldiers any credit in his written or oral accounts of the siege, they were not depicted in illustrations, paintings, or commemorations of that historical battle.

Election of 1908

During the 1904 election, Roosevelt had promised he would retire after his second term. He kept that promise and chose Secretary of War William Howard Taft (1857–1930) to be his successor. Taft was nominated by the Republican Party and ran against Democrat, and two-time presidential loser, William Jennings Bryan. Although Taft had been personally chosen by Roosevelt to succeed him, Bryan told the American public he would be the candidate more likely to uphold Roosevelt's policies. The public did not believe him, however, and Taft won the election by a landslide (321 of the electoral votes, 51.6

Gifford Pinchot: Controversial Conservationist

Conservationist Gifford Pinchot. LIBRARY OF CONGRESS.

Gifford Pinchot was born in 1865 to a wealthy Connecticut family. Because no colleges or universities at the time offered degrees in forestry, Pinchot studied in France. Upon his return, he immediately found work and was soon a government employee with the Division of Forestry.

Pinchot's proven wisdom and friendship with Theodore Roosevelt earned him a leadership role with the National Forest Service. In 1910, after five successful years, Pinchot was fired by

President William Howard Taft (Roosevelt's successor), who did not believe in government regulation of land. Pinchot's firing was directly related to a public controversy between himself and one of Taft's appointees.

The decision of Pinchot and Roosevelt to remove millions of acres of land from the public domain (ownership) infuriated many western senators and their voters, who wanted to use that land for mining, lumber, and grazing leases. Secretary of the Interior Richard A. Ballinger (1858–1922) sympathized with these men from the West, and returned a million acres of land to the public domain. An outraged Pinchot spoke against Ballinger in public meetings; he wrote magazine articles in which he attacked the secretary and accused him of corrupt political activity prior to his term in the Interior.

Taft's response was to fire Pinchot, a move that angered the public and only served to turn them against Taft. An investigation followed in which Ballinger was found not guilty of the charges against him.

In 1914, Pinchot ran unsuccessfully for the U.S. Senate. In 1922 and 1930, he was elected governor of Pennsylvania. When Roosevelt's fifth cousin, Franklin D. Roosevelt (1882–1945, served 1933–45), was elected president, Pinchot served as his advisor on conservation issues. The environmentalist died of leukemia (a blood disorder) in 1946 at the age of eighty-one.

percent of the popular vote). Taft became the twenty-seventh president of the United States, with former U.S. representative James S. Sherman (1855–1912) of New York as his vice president.

Taft takes office

Following in Roosevelt's footsteps as president of the United States was no easy task. America had grown accustomed to the "bully" activist president's loud and rowdy ways. Taft, in comparison,

Theodore Roosevelt (left) and his successor, William Howard Taft. © HULTON ARCHIVE/GETTY IMAGES.

was restrained and quiet. As a boy, he had been anxious, eager to please his parents, yet sure of their disapproval. His weight fluctuated a great deal throughout his lifetime, a physical symptom of his anxiety. He was 5 feet 11½ inches tall and weighed 320 pounds when he entered the White House. By the time he left, he had gained an additional 15 to 20 pounds.

When it became clear that Taft could not be favorably compared with Roosevelt, his public relations advisors took a different approach and turned the president's sluggishness into an asset by saying he never wanted to say anything negative about his opponents.

Reform legislation Taft was determined to continue Roosevelt's progressive program. But unlike his predecessor, Taft was not focused on pushing through legislation. He concentrated instead on administration. Regardless of his personal feelings about a particular law, Taft felt most comfortable in enforcing the law. This was where he was self-assured.

This does not mean reform legislation was ignored throughout Taft's presidency. One of the first reform acts was the reduction of tariffs. Tariffs were taxes imposed on products imported from other countries. High tariffs brought in extra money but also impeded global commerce because foreign manufacturers did not always want to pay the high tariffs.

One of the most important pieces of legislation passed during Taft's term was the Mann-Elkins Act of 1910. This law gave the Interstate Commerce Commission the authority to suspend railroad rate hikes and set rates. It also expanded their power beyond railroads to cover telephones, telegraphs, and radio.

Taft also boldly divided the Commerce and Labor Department into two separate departments. During his time in office, the president supported the statehood of New Mexico and Arizona. In 1913, Taft pushed the Sixteenth Amendment into law, meaning Americans paid income taxes for the first time. With much less enthusiasm, he supported the passage of the Seventeenth Amendment, which allowed senators to be directly elected by citizens of a state, rather than appointed by the state legislature.

Taft found himself in the midst of controversy when he decided the president should be the one to submit a government budget to Congress for approval. In the past, each agency of the federal government submitted its own budget. Congress refused to allow Taft that power, but in 1921, the Budget and Accounting Act was passed. Too late to affect the authority of Taft (who, by this time, had been out of office for eight years), the law gave all subsequent presidents expanded power in the control of the executive branch of the government.

More trust-busting Roosevelt may have been known as the trust-busting president, but more trust lawsuits were pursued during Taft's presidency. Two of the most famous cases, involving Standard Oil Company and American Tobacco Company, began under Roosevelt, but ended in victory under Taft. In all, nearly one hundred trust suits were completed under Taft. Although usually victorious in his trust-busting efforts, one such case—involving U.S. Steel—did not end in Taft's favor. The suit pitted Taft against his good friend Roosevelt, who had approved of the company's formation in 1901. The former president accused Taft of being unable to distinguish between "good" and "bad" trusts, and the men's friendship dissolved. The case remained without a verdict until 1920, at which time the federal Supreme Court ruled that U.S. Steel was not in violation of antitrust laws. The Court's decision came a year after Roosevelt's death and seven years after Taft left office.

Two big mistakes Taft made two irreversible errors while president. The first was his signing of the Payne-Aldrich Tariff. Sponsored by U.S. senator Nelson Aldrich (1841–1915) of Rhode Island and U.S. representative Sereno Payne (1843–1914) of New York, the bill called for only modest tariff reductions. This bill did not satisfy most Republicans, who were, as a group, in favor of more severe tariff reductions. Despite the fact that he had publicly threatened

to veto all bills that did not provide sufficient reductions, Taft called the Payne-Aldrich Tariff the best tariff bill ever passed by Congress. Progressives felt betrayed by this reversal of philosophy, and they did not forget their feelings when it came time to vote in the 1912 presidential election.

The second mistake was Taft's firing of Gifford Pinchot. This action seriously damaged the friendship between Roosevelt and Taft, and most of America sided with Roosevelt and Pinchot.

Relations abroad Roosevelt was committed to imperialism; Taft was equally enthusiastic about expanding foreign trade. He implemented a program called "dollar diplomacy" to encourage U.S. investments overseas. He encouraged American banks to rescue Honduras by sending along loans and grants. The president used military power to stabilize Nicaragua's U.S.-friendly government when rebels threatened to overthrow their leadership.

Despite Taft's efforts, foreign relations under his administration worsened. Trade with China decreased, and the "dollar diplomacy" program did little more than aggravate the feelings of resentment Central America had already had due to Roosevelt's imperialistic policy.

The decline in foreign affairs prompted a Pan-American (relating to North, South, and Central America) Conference. The purpose of the conference was to find a way to keep the United States from influencing and intervening in the affairs of South and Central America. Soon after, Taft ordered two thousand troops to the border of Mexico. They were ordered to intervene in a revolution taking place there so that U.S. investments would be protected.

When Congress refused to approve this move, Taft backed down and left the Mexico situation for the next president to handle. This surprise move earned him the nickname "Peaceful Bill."

Opinions about Taft

America had mixed feelings about its president. Though married with three children, he never quite fit the traditional role of president for several reasons.

His religion was a problem for many Americans. He was a Unitarian, which is a branch of Christianity that acknowledges God but rejects the divinity of Christ. In other words, Unitarians believe Heaven is open to people even if they have not accepted Jesus as their savior. At a time when religion was of great importance to the American public, many confused Unitarianism with atheism (disbelief in God). Taft also loved sports. He was the first president to play golf, a sport whose popularity surged as a result of Taft's interest. But his critics advised the president to spend less time on the golf course and more time in the White House.

Size was another issue that affected the image of the president. His largeness offended some; others were simply amused and could not take the man seriously. One of the most famous anecdotes about Taft involved the time he got stuck in the White House bathtub and had to be helped out by six of his staff. This prompted the building of a bigger tub. A new 7-foot, 41-inch tub was installed; it could hold four average-sized men.

Although the teasing and humorous remarks regarding Taft's weight were made gently throughout his first year in office, the tone of them became hostile and critical as his presidency wore on. In addition to the

President William Howard Taft stands on the golf course with a caddie in the background. Taft's size and his love of golf bothered many people, who felt that both hurt Taft's image as a president. © CORBIS.

issue with his size, Taft was known to embarrass his family and friends by falling asleep at concerts and even while presiding over his staff. Taft himself seemed to accept his size as well as his need for sleep after eating or physical exercise, but the American public had more trouble doing so. Modern medical experts generally agree that Taft most likely suffered

Taft in Hong Kong

Newspapers and magazines made light of William Howard Taft's enormous size, and the president himself was a good sport about his weight problem. At other times, his weight was a serious topic and one that required special consideration.

On his first visit to Hong Kong in 1907, Secretary of War Taft's sedan [portable] chair broke under his weight. At the time of collapse, local un-skilled laborers called coolies were transporting Taft and his chair. Prior to his second visit, officials in Hong Kong contracted with a local chair builder to fashion a chair that would hold up under Taft's weight. The paperwork was forwarded to Washington and released to news-papers in New York. As noted in Henry F. Pringle's 1939 book *The Life and Times of William Howard Taft: A Biography,* an excerpt of that contract read:

> I, the undersigned, Yu Wo of 15B Welling-ton Street agree to make a sedan chair for the American consul general.... This chair is to be used to carry the American giant, the Honorable William Howard Taft. Said Taft being one of the most conspicuous [obvious] ornaments of the American Wai Wu Pai [Imperial Cabinet], it would

obviously discredit this nation if the chair should disintegrate [fall apart].... To avert [avoid] international complications of this sort, I, Yu Wo, assert my skill as a chairmaker.

It shall be reinforced at all weak points.... The shafts shall be of double di-ameter. The body itself shall be of eventful width.... Red cloth shall adorn the seat of the chair and gleaming brass look defiantly out to a point that uncon-sciously, [people] shall say: "Certainly this nation of the open door that has so long befriended the Middle Kingdom is a great power."

The consul general may have the use of the chair October 11 and 12, 1907, after which the chair belongs to me, with the understanding that if ex-president Cleve-land, also reputed to be of heroic size, tours the world, the consul general shall direct his steps to my shop.... With such precautions do I safeguard the dignity of a friendly power and contribute an honest chairmaker's part in preserving the Peace of the East.

from what is known as obstructive sleep apnea, a condition worsened by obesity in which peo-ple stop breathing for brief periods throughout the night.

Women's issues

Women continued their struggle for suffrage throughout Taft's presidency. The fight brought to the public forefront the issue of female

identity. Prior to 1910, women who worked to-ward suffrage were part of the "women's move-ment." This term indicated their intention to push the limits of the role attributed to their gen-der. No longer content to remain in the home, women activists worked to be accepted as equal to men in social and political spheres. Their struggle was based on the idea that wom-en's superior morality would lift up society.

Around 1910, however, a new word was being used for the movement. "Feminism" and its supporters placed more emphasis on women's rights and seizing opportunities to live up to their potential in every way and less on duty and moral obligation.

Taft took no strong stance for or against suffrage and feminism during his tenure as president. His wife, Nellie Taft (1861–1943), was in favor of partial suffrage for women, though she smoked, drank liquor, and gambled without reservation at a time when "proper" women did not engage in what many viewed as immoral activity. Later, as chief justice of the United States, Taft handed down several rulings regarding women's rights that were progressive at the time.

The race issue

African Americans were the victims of great racial violence throughout the first two decades of the twentieth century. Between 1900 and 1914, white mobs lynched (hanged) more than one thousand African Americans. Lynching was meant to be a warning to other African Americans who might try to vote or otherwise assert their independence. Given this social atmosphere, it is not surprising that very few African Americans voted in the presidential elections of 1908 and 1912.

Many African Americans began migrating north at the turn of the century. They were met with segregated (separated) neighborhoods, job discrimination, and poor schooling, but at least they did not fear for their lives as they had in the South. (Despite the fact that slavery had been outlawed after the Civil War [1861–65], most Southerners held onto their deep-seated belief that African Americans were an inferior race.) As they gathered strength in urban ghettos (the poorest sections of the inner city), powerful African American leaders emerged. Men like W. E. B. Du Bois (1868–1963), who established the National Association for the Advancement of Colored People (NAACP) in 1914, and Booker T. Washington, who established the Tuskegee Institute, a school for African Americans, empowered their fellow African Americans with words of encouragement.

Leaving the White House

Taft was unable to live up to the Roosevelt legacy. His gentle personality, coupled with his lack of leadership, led to most of his difficulties as president. Rather than make sound decisions when called upon, he tended to consider every issue from all sides, a habit that led directly to indecisiveness. From the outset of his administration, Taft let others influence his leadership. For example, Congress made 847 amendments to the president's initial tariff reform package. Taft made no efforts to defend his reform proposal, and the result was a package of laws that meant nearly nothing.

Arthur Link, biographer of President Woodrow Wilson (1856–1924; served 1913–1921), considered Taft's administration a "disaster," and most historians agree. Taft lost the election of 1912 but went on to become chief justice for the U.S. Supreme Court in 1921. This appointment was Taft's lifelong dream, and a job for which he was much better suited. Taft retired in 1930 due to ill health. He died that same year due to complications from his weight.

The presidential election of 1912

Taft agreed to run for reelection in 1912, but not because he really wanted to remain in office.

Theodore Roosevelt, the man who nominated Taft for the presidency in 1908, had felt personally attacked and betrayed by several decisions Taft had made while president, including his dismissal of Gifford Pinchot and the lawsuit filed against U.S. Steel, a trust Roosevelt considered to be "good." By the time of the campaign, Roosevelt was convinced Taft would ruin the Republican Party. He was determined not to let that happen, and worked to replace him as the 1912 Republican candidate. Taft decided to run for a second term because he felt the need to defend himself against Roosevelt's many and public attacks on his judgment and ability.

The 1912 election was the first election in which presidential candidates would go through primaries. This meant the public would vote on who was to be the candidate for all political parties (in the past, candidates were nominated by party leaders). The early primary system was carried out at the state level, so not all states conducted primary elections. In fact, thirty-six states had no direct popular Republican primary. In these states, delegates were chosen by state conventions, and the delegates to the state conventions had most often been chosen in local conventions. This allowed for domination by professional politicians, men who did not necessarily represent the best interests of their state's citizens. As a result, many state delegates were competing for the same seats. In 1912, 254 delegate seats to the Republican convention were contested.

The Republican National Committee had the power to decide the delegate disputes. Most of the members of that committee were Taft supporters. As could have been predicted, Taft was awarded the majority of those 254 seats (235, compared to Roosevelt's 19). This unfair treatment split the Republican Party into two sides: those who supported Taft, and those who supported Roosevelt. When Roosevelt lost the primary election, he and his supporters broke away from the Republican Party and established the Progressive Party, commonly referred to as the Bull Moose Party. The resulting three-man election marked the first time an incumbent president ran for reelection against a former president as well as a future president.

The National Progressive Party The Progressive Party membership was well educated and respectable. It consisted of no professional politicians and a large number of professional and civic-minded women. As a result of this mix, it was the only major political party of the election to support women's rights. Aside from women's rights, the central idea of the party was to redistribute the nation's wealth so that more Americans could enjoy a better quality of life. Despite this concern for the nation's workforce, Progressives were not a labor party. They wanted to help, but not engage the participation of the workers themselves. Progressives were cultured, middle-class Americans, and that is how they intended the party to stay.

With the Republican Party now split in two, it was highly unlikely either Roosevelt or Taft would win the election. The winner of the election was New Jersey governor Woodrow Wilson, the first Democrat to serve in the White House in sixteen years. Wilson won 435 electoral votes, compared to Roosevelt's 88 and Taft's 8. Wilson claimed 41.9 percent of the popular vote, leaving 27.4 percent to Roosevelt and 23.1 percent to Taft; the remaining votes were divided between Socialist Eugene V. Debs (1855–1926) and Prohibition Party leader Eugene W. Chafin (1852–1920).

An editorial cartoon shows former president Theodore Roosevelt (left) and incumbent president William Howard Taft (Roosevelt's hand-picked successor four years earlier) both vying for the Republican nomination in 1912. Taft won the nomination and Roosevelt wound up running as the third-party Progressive Party candidate. Both lost to the Democratic candidate, New Jersey governor Woodrow Wilson. © THE GRANGER COLLECTION, NEW YORK.

Wilson's economic program was called "New Freedom," and it attacked Roosevelt for catering to the wealthy trusts. Wilson promised to reduce tariffs and increase opportunity for small businesses to compete in the marketplace. A progressive thinker, Wilson signed into law more reform legislation than Roosevelt and Taft combined. Unlike Roosevelt, who was constantly in motion and earned a reputation as a "bully" activist, Wilson was quiet and thoughtful, a man who gave great consideration to the issue at hand before deciding how to proceed. But once he decided, he moved with conviction.

A most important president

Historians generally agree that Wilson was one of the most important presidents in American

What Is Socialism?

For hundreds of years, America has operated in a capitalist society. Capitalism is an economic system in which production and distribution of goods are privately controlled. Its motivation is profit, or making more money than is spent on production.

Capitalism has always had its share of vocal opponents. Those opposed to this system dislike it for its uneven distribution of wealth: a small number of individuals control the largest percentage of wealth, leaving the rest to get by on comparatively little income. Opponents blame capitalism for the existence of poverty, and many advocate for a socialist economy.

In socialism, the public or government owns and controls the production and distribution of goods. In theory, a socialist economy would provide even distribution of wealth and eradicate poverty. Communism is a form of socialism.

In the Gilded Age and Progressive Era, socialism was held up as a means of dealing with the serious levels of intense poverty that suddenly seemed to spread throughout the nation as a result of rapid growth in industrialization. The socialist movement was closely related to the labor movement during that time, as it was the working class that suffered the most under capitalism.

Although socialist presidential candidates participated in many elections, the party had its best showing in the election of 1912, when its candidate, Eugene V. Debs, won 6 percent of the popular vote.

history not only for the reforms he passed, but for the way he dealt with the events of his time. Among the reforms passed during his two terms as president:

- Labor: Wilson passed the Keating-Owen Child Labor Act (1916), which limited the number of hours children could legally work and prohibited the interstate sale of goods produced by child labor. He supported the La Follette Seaman's bill (1915), which improved working conditions of sailors. He also signed into law the Adamson Act (1916), which limited interstate railroad workers to an eight-hour day. In addition, he passed legislation in support of labor unions.
- Suffrage: Wilson supported the Nineteenth Amendment, which was signed into law in 1921 and gave women the right to vote.

- Finance: Wilson passed the Federal Reserve Act in 1913, which provided for currency and banking reform. The Federal Reserve System is still in place in the twenty-first century.
- Trustbusting: Wilson passed the Federal Trade Commission Act as well as the Clayton Anti-Trust Act in 1914. Both laws strengthened the antitrust laws already in place and expanded the power of labor.

Wilson led America into World War I (1914–18), and his peace program, called "Fourteen Points," helped bring the war to a victorious end for America. Wilson's vision for the future, which was outlined in the Fourteen Points, imagined a world without imperialism or secret alliances. He wanted weaker countries to be heard alongside the stronger ones. The last of his

Fourteen Points was the formation of a League of Nations, an organization of representatives from all countries that would work to solve international disputes without war. Although the League was established in 1920, the U.S. Senate voted against joining. The majority of its members believed America was already involved in too many of Europe's disputes and conflicts, and many American citizens agreed. As a result, the United States never joined the League of Nations. As World War II began (1939–45), it became clear the League had failed to prevent war. It was eventually replaced by the United Nations. For his efforts toward international peace, Wilson earned the Nobel Peace Prize in 1920.

The shaping of America

The Progressive Era greatly influenced the shaping of modern America. It made clear not only the possibilities but also the limitations of reform and progress. That era saw America transform from an agricultural society into a consumer culture, where competition opened up a vast world of choice and directly connected materialism with success.

Perhaps what the Progressive Era proved once and for all is that history and progress are made through the efforts of all people, not just those in positions of power. Nowhere is this more evident than in the labor movement. This period in history forced people to accept the changes imposed upon them or summon their courage and fight for their values and goals. It was a time of greed and corruption, but also of great generosity and hope.

What lies ahead

America had survived World War I, and within two years, Prohibition (the outlawing of the

President Woodrow Wilson. LIBRARY OF CONGRESS.

sale and consumption of alcohol) would sweep the nation. It would be marked by a dramatic rise in organized criminal activity as well as a 24-percent increase in the number of homicides (murders) and burglaries between 1920 and 1921 alone. The number of federal convicts over the thirteen years that Prohibition was in effect increased 561 percent. Clearly, the law that aimed to reduce immoral and criminal behavior served only to increase it, as illegal drinking establishments called speakeasies dotted the urban landscape and bootlegging moonshine (illegally manufacturing alcohol) became a new career for thousands.

The 1920s would give America *Time Magazine* and *Reader's Digest*. Inventions would include bubble gum, the lie detector, and the first talking movie. Women would wear their hair and their dresses short, and dances like the tango and the Charleston would become the latest craze. The first winter Olympic games would be held, and Charles Lindbergh (1902–1974) would make the first successful Transatlantic flight.

America would once again find itself involved in political conflicts as it dealt with the rabid fear of communism in Russia, an American phenomenon known as the Red Scare (red is the color used to represent the Communist Party). The white supremacist terrorist group called the Ku Klux Klan would peak at five million members nationwide, and African Americans would be the targets of hate crimes at an intensity never before seen in the United States.

If the Progressive Era was one of hope, the Roaring Twenties was a decade of cultural and social decadence (decline in values) and political uncertainty.

For More Information

BOOKS

Benson, Michael. *William H. Taft (Presidential Leaders)*. Minneapolis: Lerner Publications, 2004.

Chambers, John Whiteclay II. *The Tyranny of Change: America in the Progressive Era, 1890–1920*. 2nd ed. New Brunswick, NJ: Rutgers University Press, 2000.

Dommermuth-Costa, Carol. *Woodrow Wilson (Presidential Leaders)*. Minneapolis: Lerner Publications, 2003.

Goldstein, Donald M., Katherine Dillon, J. Michael Wenger, and Robert J. Cressman. *Spanish-American War: The Story and Photographs*. Dulles, VA: Potomac Books, 2001.

Hays, Samuel P. *Conservation and the Gospel of Efficiency*. Cambridge: Harvard University Press, 1959. Reprint, Pittsburgh: University of Pittsburgh Press, 1999.

Ingram, Scott. *The Panama Canal (Building World Landmarks)*. San Diego: Blackbirch Press, 2003.

Kraft, Betsy Harvey. *Theodore Roosevelt: Champion of the American Spirit*. New York: Clarion Books, 2003.

Lansford, Tom, and Robert P. Watson, eds. *Theodore Roosevelt (Presidents & Their Decisions)*. San Diego: Greenhaven Press, 2003.

McPherson, Stephanie Sammartino. *Theodore Roosevelt (Presidential Leaders)*. Minneapolis: Lerner Publications, 2005.

Painter, Nell Irvin. *Standing at Armageddon: The United States, 1877–1919*. New York: W. W. Norton & Co., 1987.

Roosevelt, Theodore. *The Strenuous Life: Essays and Addresses*. New York: The Century Company, 1900.

Wiebe, Robert H. *The Search for Order, 1877–1920*. New York: Hill and Wang, 1967. Reprint, Westport, CT: Greenwood Press, 1980.

WEB SITES

"Gifford Pinchot." *Forest History Society*. http://www.lib.duke.edu/forest/Research/usfscoll/people/Pinchot/Pinchot.html (accessed on June 14, 2006).

"Life of Theodore Roosevelt." *Theodore Roosevelt Association*. http://www.theodoreroosevelt.org/life/lifeoftr.htm (accessed on June 14, 2006).

National Park Service. "Theodore Roosevelt." *Theodore Roosevelt National Park*. http://www.nps.gov/thro/tr_cons.htm (accessed on June 14, 2006).

PBS. "Woodrow Wilson." *American Experience*. http://www.pbs.org/wgbh/amex/wilson/ (accessed on June 14, 2006).

"Philippine Insurrection (1899–1902)." *Medal of Honor*. http://www.medalofhonor.com/Philippine-Insurrection.htm (accessed on June 14, 2006).

"Theodore Roosevelt (1901–1909)." *American President*. http://www.americanpresident.org/history/theodoreroosevelt/ (accessed on June 14, 2006).

"Theodore Roosevelt and Big Stick Diplomacy." *Mt. Holyoke*. http://www.mtholyoke.edu/~jlgarner/

classweb/worldpolitics/bigstick.html (accessed on June 14, 2006).

Tingle, Donald. "Spanish-American War Buffalo Soldiers." *Pond Spring—Home of General Joe Wheeler.* http://www.wheelerplantation.org/the.htm (accessed on June 14, 2006).

"William Howard Taft (1909–1913)." *American President.* http://www.americanpresident.org/history/williamhowardtaft/ (accessed on June 14, 2006).

"William Howard Taft." *The White House.* http://www.whitehouse.gov/history/presidents/wt27.html (accessed on June 14, 2006).

Where to Learn More

The following list focuses on works written for readers of middle school and high school age. Books aimed at adult readers have been included when they are especially important in providing information or analysis that would otherwise be unavailable.

Books

American Presidents in World History. Vol. 3. Westport, CT: Greenwood Press, 2003.

Bartoletti, Susan Campbell. *Kids on Strike!* Boston: Houghton Mifflin, 2003.

Brands, H. W. *The Reckless Decade: America in the 1890s.* New York: St. Martin's Press, 1995.

Brown, Joshua. *Beyond the Lines: Pictorial Reporting, Everyday Life, and the Crisis of Gilded-Age America.* Berkeley: University of California Press, 2002.

Calhoun, Charles W., ed. *The Gilded Age: Essays on the Origins of Modern America.* Wilmington, DE: Scholarly Resources, 1996.

Cashman, Sean Dennis. *America in the Gilded Age.* New York: New York University Press, 1993.

Chambers, John Whiteclay II. *The Tyranny of Change: America in the Progressive Era, 1890–1920.* 2nd ed. New Brunswick, NJ: Rutgers University Press, 2000.

Cherny, Robert W. *American Politics in the Gilded Age, 1868–1900.* Wheeling, IL: Harlan Davidson, 1997.

Cooper, John Milton, Jr. *Pivotal Decades: The United States, 1900–1920.* New York: W. W. Norton & Co., 1992.

Diner, Steven J. *A Very Different Age: Americans of the Progressive Era.* New York: Hill and Wang, 1998.

Edwards, Rebecca. *New Spirits: Americans in the Gilded Age, 1865–1905.* New York: Oxford University Press, 2005.

Espejo, Roman. *The Age of Reform and Industrialization, 1896–1920.* San Diego: Greenhaven Press, 2003.

Fink, Leon, ed. *Major Problems in the Gilded Age and Progressive Era: Documents and Essays.* New York: Houghton Mifflin, 2000.

Freedman, Russell. *Kids at Work: Lewis Hine and the Crusade Against Child Labor.* New York: Clarion Books, 1998.

Frost-Knappman, Elizabeth, and Kathryn Cullen-Dupont. *Women's Suffrage in America*. New York: Facts on File, 2004.

Furbee, Mary Rodd. *Outrageous Women of the American Frontier*. New York: Wiley, 2002.

Galbreath, Lester. *Campfire Tales: True Stories from the Western Frontier*. Albany, TX: Bright Sky Press, 2005.

Goldstein, Donald M., Katherine Dillon, J. Michael Wenger, and Robert J. Cressman. *Spanish-American War: The Story and Photographs*. Dulles, VA: Potomac Books, 2001.

Greenwood, Janette Thomas. *The Gilded Age: A History in Documents*. New York: Oxford University Press, 2000.

Hopkinson, Deborah. *Shutting Out the Sky: Life in the Tenements of New York, 1880–1915*. New York: Orchard Books, 2003.

Hughes, Pat. *The Breaker Boys*. New York: Farrar, Straus & Giroux, 2004.

Lynch, Denis Tilden. *"Boss" Tweed: The Story of a Grim Generation*. New York: Boni and Liveright, 1927. Reprint, New Brunswick, NJ: Transaction Publishers, 2002.

Marker, Sherry. *Plains Indian Wars*. New York: Facts on File, 2003.

McGerr, Michael. *A Fierce Discontent: The Rise and Fall of the Progressive Movement in America, 1870–1920*. New York: Free Press, 2003.

Murphy, Claire Rudolf, and Jane G. Haigh. *Children of the Gold Rush*. Portland, OR: Alaska Northwest Books, 2001.

Murphy, Claire Rudolf, and Jane G. Haigh. *Gold Rush Women*. Anchorage: Alaska Northwest Books, 1997.

Painter, Nell Irvin. *Standing at Armageddon: The United States, 1877–1919*. New York: W. W. Norton & Co., 1987.

Poliniak, Louis. *When Coal Was King*. Lancaster, PA: Applied Arts Publishers, 2004.

Riis, Jacob A. *How the Other Half Lives: Studies among the Tenements of New York*. New York: Charles Scribner's Sons, 1890. Reprint, New York: Barnes & Noble Books, 2004.

Roosevelt, Theodore. *The Strenuous Life: Essays and Addresses*. New York: The Century Company, 1900.

Sinclair, Upton. *The Jungle*. New York: Doubleday, 1906. Multiple reprints.

Smythe, Ted Curtis. *The Gilded Age Press, 1865–1900*. Westport, CT: Praeger, 2003.

Steeples, Douglas, and David O. Whitten. *Democracy in Desperation: The Depression of 1893*. Westport, CT: Greenwood Press, 1998.

Torr, James D., ed. *The American Frontier*. San Diego: Greenhaven Press, 2002.

Trachtenberg, Alan. *The Incorporation of America: Culture and Society in the Gilded Age*. New York: Hill and Wang, 1982.

Wiebe, Robert H. *The Search for Order, 1877–1920.* New York: Hill and Wang, 1967. Reprint, Westport, CT: Greenwood Press, 1980.

Web Sites

"Alaska's Gold." *Alaska State Library.* http://www.library.state.ak.us/goldrush/ (accessed on June 8, 2006).

"American Cultural History: 19th Century—1890–1899." *Kingwood College Library.* http://kclibrary.nhmccd.edu/19thcentury1890.htm (accessed on June 6, 2006).

"American Political Cartoons: An Introduction." *Truman State University.* http://www2.truman.edu/parker/research/cartoons.html (accessed on June 6, 2006).

AmericanPresident.org. http://www.americanpresident.org/ (accessed on September 12, 2006).

"Andrew Carnegie: The Gilded Age." *PBS.* http://www.pbs.org/wgbh/amex/carnegie/gildedage.html (accessed on April 3, 2006).

Blanke, David. "Consumer Culture During the Gilded Age and Progressive Era." *H-Net.* http://www.h-net.org/~shgape/bibs/consumer.html (accessed on June 30, 2006).

Byrne, Julie. "Roman Catholics and Immigration in Nineteenth-Century America." *National Humanities Center.* http://www.nhc.rtp.nc.us:8080/tserve/nineteen/nkeyinfo/nromcath.htm (accessed on April 7, 2006).

"Child Labor in America 1908–1912: Photographs of Lewis W. Hine." *The History Place.* http://www.historyplace.com/unitedstates/childlabor/ (accessed on May 17, 2006).

"Child Labor in U.S. History." *Child Labor Public Education Project.* http://www.continuetolearn.uiowa.edu/laborctr/child_labor/about/us_history.html (accessed on May 17, 2006).

Dalkey, Victoria. "Art: The 'American Renaissance.'" *Sacramento.com.* http://www.sacramento.com/portal/events/story/3848683p-4874088c.html (accessed on June 6, 2006).

Davis, Ronald L. F. "Creating Jim Crow: In-Depth Essay." *The History of Jim Crow.* http://www.jimcrowhistory.org/history/creating2.htm (accessed on April 28, 2006).

Dolkart, Andrew. "The Tenement House Act." *Lower East Side Tenement Museum.* http://www.tenement.org/features_dolkart.html (accessed on May 17, 2006).

Edwards, Rebecca. "The Depression of 1893." *1896: The Presidential Campaign: Cartoons & Commentary.* http://projects.vassar.edu/1896/depression.html (accessed on April 28, 2006).

"Freedom, a History of US." *PBS.* http://www.pbs.org/wnet/historyofus/web10/segment6_p.html (accessed April 28, 2006).

"From Haven to Home: A Century of Immigration, 1820–1924." *Library of Congress.* http://www.loc.gov/exhibits/haventohome/haven-century.html (accessed on April 17, 2006).

Gerckens, Laurence. "Ten Events That Shaped the 20th Century American City." *Planning Commissioners Journal: PlannersWeb.* http://www.plannersweb.com/intl/excerpts10events.pdf (accessed on May 17, 2006).

"Gilded Age and Progressive Era Resources." *H-SHGAPE.* http://www.h-net.msu.edu/~shgape/internet/index.html (accessed on September 8, 2006).

"The Gilded Age 1866–1901." *Carnegie Library of Pittsburgh.* http://www.carnegielibrary.org/subject/history/gilded.html (accessed on September 8, 2006).

"Immigration: The Living Mosaic of People, Culture, & Hope." *ThinkQuest.org.* http://library.thinkquest.org/20619/index.html (accessed on April 17, 2006).

"Learn About the Progressive Era." *Digital History.* http://www.digitalhistory.uh.edu/modules/progressivism/index.cfm (accessed on September 8, 2006).

Library of Congress. *America's Story from America's Library.* http://www.americaslibrary.gov/cgi-bin/page.cgi (accessed on September 12, 2006).

Library of Congress. "Progressive Era (1890–1913)." *America's Library.* http://www.americaslibrary.gov/cgi-bin/page.cgi/jb/progress (accessed on September 8, 2006).

Lower East Side Tenement Museum. http://www.tenement.org/index.htm (accessed on April 17, 2006).

Muncy, Robyn. "Women in the Progressive Era." *Places Where Women Made History.* http://www.cr.nps.gov/nr/travel/pwwmh/prog.htm (accessed on May 17, 2006).

"Nation Building: 1860–1900." *National Railroad Museum.* http://www.nationalrrmuseum.org/collections-exhibits/outline/nation-building.php (accessed on April 26, 2006).

"New Perspectives on The West: People." *PBS.* http://www.pbs.org/weta/thewest/people/ (accessed on April 26, 2006).

Norton, Henry Kittredge. "The Chinese." *The Virtual Museum of the City of San Francisco.* http://www.sfmuseum.org/hist6/chinhate.html (accessed on April 17, 2006).

Paul V. Galvin Library Digital History Collection, Illinois Institute of Technology. "The Book of the Fair, by Hubert Howe Bancroft." *World's Columbian Exposition of 1893.* http://columbus.iit.edu/bookfair/ch27.html (accessed on June 30, 2006).

"The Presidents of the United States." *The White House.* http://www.whitehouse.gov/history/presidents/ (accessed on March 16, 2006).

"Progressive Era Reform." *Oswego City School District: Regents Exam Prep Center.* http://regentsprep.org/Regents/ushisgov/themes/reform/progressive.htm (accessed on May 17, 2006).

"The Rise and Fall of Jim Crow." *PBS.* http://www.pbs.org/wnet/jimcrow/index.html (accessed on April 28, 2006).

Rutherford B. Hayes Presidential Center. http://www.rbhayes.org/hayes/ (accessed on March 16, 2006).

Strasser, Susan. "Consumer to Customer: The New Consumption in the Progressive Era." *Organization of American Historians.* http://www.oah.org/pubs/magazine/progressive/strasser.html (accessed on June 6, 2006).

Tarbell, Ida M. *The History of the Standard Oil Company.* http://www.history.rochester.edu/fuels/tarbell/main.htm (accessed on April 3, 2006).

"The Triangle Factory Fire." *Cornell University ILR School.* http://www.ilr.cornell.edu/trianglefire/ (accessed on May 17, 2006).

"Websites for the Gilded Age and Progressive Era." *San Francisco State University: College of Behavioral and Social Science.* http://bss.sfsu.edu/cherny/gapesites.htm (accessed on September 8, 2006).

Whitten, David O. "The Depression of 1893." *EH.Net Encyclopedia.* http://eh.net/encyclopedia/article/whitten.panic.1893 (accessed on April 28, 2006).

Index

Illustrations are marked by (ill.)

R